Famous Figures and Diagrams in Economics

Famous Figures and Diagrams in Economics

Edited by

Mark Blaug

Professor Emeritus, University of London and Professor Emeritus, University of Buckingham, UK

Peter Lloyd

Professor Emeritus, Department of Economics, University of Melbourne, Australia

Edward Elgar

Cheltenham, UK • Northampton, MA, USA

Published by
Edward Elgar Publishing Limited
The Lypiatts
15 Lansdown Road
Cheltenham
Glos GL50 2JA
UK

Edward Elgar Publishing, Inc.
William Pratt House
9 Dewey Court
Northampton
Massachusetts 01060
USA

A catalogue record for this book
is available from the British Library

Library of Congress Control Number: 2009941142

ISBN 978 1 84844 160 6 (cased)

Printed and bound by MPG Books Group, UK

Contents

Welfare economics

Special markets and topics

PART II GENERAL EQUILIBRIUM ANALYSIS

Basic tools of general equilibrium analysis

Open economies

PART III MACROECONOMICS

Macroeconomic analysis and stabilisation

Growth, income distribution and other topics

Figures

Contributors

Sowmiya Ashok, Micro Insurance Academy, Delhi, India.
Roger E. Backhouse, Department of Economics, University of Birmingham, UK.
William J. Baumol, Berkeley Center for Entrepreneurial Studies, New York University, USA.
Mark Blaug, Professor Emeritus, University of London and Professor Emeritus, University of Buckingham, UK.
Russell Boyer, University of Western Ontario, Canada
Lisa Cameron, Department of Economics, University of Melbourne, Australia.
John S. Chipman, Department of Economics, University of Minnesota, USA.
Avi J. Cohen, Department of Economics, York University, Canada.
J.S. Cramer, University of Amsterdam and Tinbergen Institute, Amsterdam, the Netherlands.
John Creedy, Department of Economics, University of Melbourne, Australia.
Alan V. Deardorff, Ford School of Public Policy, University of Michigan, USA.
Robert W. Dimand, Department of Economics, Brock University, Canada.
Avinash Dixit, Department of Economics, Princeton University, USA.
Robert Dixon, Department of Economics, University of Melbourne, Australia.
B. Curtis Eaton, Department of Economics, University of Calgary, Canada.
Jürgen Eichberger, Department of Economics, Heidelberg University, Germany.
Nisvan Erkal, Department of Economics, University of Melbourne, Australia.
Rolf Färe, Department of Economics, Oregon State University, USA.
Lata Gangadharan, Department of Economics, University of Melbourne, Australia.
Nicola Giocoli, Department of Economics, University of Pisa, Italy.
Yann Giraud, Department of Economics, Duke University, USA.

Shawna Grosskopf, Department of Economics, Oregon State University, USA.
Hans Haller, Department of Economics, Virginia Polytechnic Institute & State University, USA.
D. Wade Hands, Department of Economics, University of Puget Sound, USA.
Geoffrey C. Harcourt, Jesus College, Cambridge, UK.
Thomas M. Humphrey, Federal Reserve Bank of Richmond, USA.
Ronald W. Jones, Department of Economics, University of Rochester, USA.
Nanak Kakwani, University of New South Wales, Australia.
Murray Kemp, University of New South Wales, Australia.
John E. King, School of Economics and Finance, La Trobe University, Australia.
Anne O. Krueger, Department of International Economics, Johns Hopkins University, USA.
David Laidler, Department of Economics, University of Western Ontario, Canada.
Cassey Lee, School of Economics, University of Wollongong, Australia.
Richard G. Lipsey, Economics Department, Simon Fraser University, Canada.
Peter Lloyd, Department of Economics, University of Melbourne, Australia.
Fiona Maclachlan, Manhattan College, USA.
Roger Middleton, University of Bristol, UK.
Marc Nerlove, University of Maryland, USA.
Yew-Kwang Ng, Department of Economics, Monash University, Australia.
Arvind Panagariya, Department of Economics, Columbia University, USA.
Peter Rodenburg, Department of European Studies, University of Amsterdam, The Netherlands.
R. Rothschild, Lancaster University Management School, UK.
Michael Schneider, School of Economics and Finance, La Trobe University, Australia
He-ling Shi, Department of Economics, Monash University, Australia.
Andrew Skinner, Department of Economics, University of Glasgow, UK.
Barbara J. Spencer (née Swan), Sauder School of Business, University of British Columbia, Canada.
Henry Thompson, Department of Economics, Auburn University, USA.
John Whalley, Department of Economics, University of Western Ontario, Canada.

Ross Williams, Melbourne Institute, University of Melbourne, Australia.
Wai Chiu Woo, Department of Economics, The Chinese University of Hong Kong, Hong Kong.
Alan D. Woodland, School of Economics, The University of New South Wales, Australia
Warren Young, Department of Political Science, Bar-Ilan University.

Acknowledgements

This volume has drawn upon contributions from over fifty authors. First and foremost we would like to express our deep gratitude to these authors for responding so enthusiastically to our request for a contribution. Writing a short summary of one of the major figures or diagrams used regularly by economists is not a straightforward task, especially when all communication is electronic, but they all addressed it willingly and with great skill.

We are most grateful to others who assisted with the preparation of the manuscripts in various ways. The colleague of one of us at the University of Melbourne, Robert Dixon, helped us at short notice in converting some of the files sent to us into Word and in drawing some of the diagrams and giving other technical assistance. Without this assistance, the project would have languished. Puja Devi Slesha from the University of Melbourne also redrew some of the diagrams.

At Edward Elgar the project was supported wholeheartedly from the outset by Edward Elgar. We received prompt and courteous assistance from Alexandra O'Connell, Nep Elverd, Kate Pearce, Sylvia Potter and Margaret McCormack and other staff in sub-editing, preparing and handling the manuscript.

Every effort has been made to trace all the copyright holders but if any have been inadvertently overlooked the publishers will be pleased to make the necessary arrangements at the first opportunity.

Introduction

Mark Blaug and Peter Lloyd

1. THE BOOK PLAN

Economic theory is rich in figures and diagrams. This book was conceived in the belief that we do not know as much as we should about the role of these in the development of economic theory.

The book has two aims. One is to provide an account of the role of each of the chosen figures and diagrams in economic analysis. Figures are part of the basic toolbox of the modern economist. We have selected figures that have been prominent in the history of economic analysis and that are, with a few exceptions, still found in contemporary textbooks and research. Together the topics portrayed cover a large part of mainstream economic theory and analysis.

The second aim is to provide an account of their histories. Thus, it is partly an exercise in the history of economic thought. Klein (1995) has commented on the general use of geometry in economic theory. There are existing histories of some of the diagrams; for example, Humphrey (1992, 1993) has written essays on the history of the box diagram, the 'trade theorist's sacred diagram' (the subject of Chapter 42) and the Marshallian cross diagram (see Chapter 1). Others have commented upon the use of geometry by some economists – chiefly Alfred Marshall (see especially his biographers, Keynes, 1972 and Groenewegen, 1995) but also Lerner (Giraud, 2008) and Samuelson (Giraud, forthcoming) – or in some particular period (for example, Cook, 2005) or area of economics (for example, de Marchi, 2003).

Our selection of topics is of course a little arbitrary. Most suggested themselves as they are commonly regarded as essential knowledge. After an initial selection, we contacted potential authors. A number of them suggested other topics. We then had 'an embarrassment of riches', as one of our correspondents had predicted, and could accept only some of the suggestions.

All areas in the discipline of economics are covered but preference was given to figures that are widely used. The topics are divided into three areas: those dealing with a market for a single commodity, that is, partial equilibrium analysis, those dealing with multiple markets, that is, general equilibrium analysis, and those from macroeconomics. The selection includes some that arose from empirical research – such as the Phillips curve, the Kuznets curve, the Lorenz curve and the logistic growth curve. It does not cover time series graphics or devices to represent data such as pie diagrams and bar charts.[1] Consequently we do not include the justly celebrated work of Playfield, *The Commercial and Political Atlas*, published in 1786.

Within these three areas, the topics have been put in groups that seem useful in terms of a commonality or overlap between the topics. Thus, in the first group of single market analyses, we distinguish between 'basic tools of demand and supply curve analysis', topics used in welfare economics, and those which arose in the study of particular markets such as the backward-bending supply curve in labour markets, the cobweb diagram in agricultural markets and the Markowitz diagram in asset markets.

In a similar way, general equilibrium diagrams are grouped into 'basic tools of general equilibrium analysis' and the extension of general equilibrium analysis to open economies, that is, the standard theory of international trade in goods. Open economy general equilibrium economics has been a particularly fertile area for the generation of figures.

Macroeconomic figures are grouped into two categories, tools of 'macroeconomic analysis and stabilisation' and 'growth, income distribution and other topics'. The former include the Keynesian income determination diagram, the IS-LM diagram and its extension to open economies, the Fleming-Mundell diagram, the aggregate demand-aggregate supply diagram, the Phillips curve and the UV or Beveridge curve and the demand for money. All of these are fundamental to the way macroeconomists approach questions relating to the time path of macroeconomies.

For each topic we asked an expert who has written about it in the past to prepare an entry. We sought a diversity of authors to try and bring out all aspects of graphical analysis. They include leading theorists, leading historians of economic thought and some younger economists. They did bring a diversity of approaches. Some are more formal than others. Some devote more space to tracing the origin of figures and controversies surrounding them. Some reproduce the original figure in their area and some do not. Some trace later developments of the original concept or curve and applications to areas that were not contemplated by the originators. This diversity enriches our appreciation of the development of graphical methods in economics and their contribution to economic theory.

2. MATHEMATICAL AND METHODOLOGICAL ISSUES

Mathematical Issues

The frequent use of geometry in economics is not surprising. Most of the figures and diagrams are figures in coordinate geometry. Figures are representations of one or more functional relationships in Euclidean 2 space. Functions of one variable, which lend themselves to portrayal by graphs in two-dimensional space, appear regularly in all areas of economic theory. A few of our entries are not figures in coordinate geometry terms. This applies to the diagrams relating to circular flows and to some of the diagrams in location theory and graph theory.

More than ten of the figures in the book are single curves – the Engel curve, Phillips curve and so on. Curves come in many shapes. Variously the curves hinge on some feature such as a minimum (the U-shaped average cost curve) or a maximum (the Laffer curve or the inverted U-shaped Kuznets curves), a point of inflection (the logistic curve), a change in sign of the slope (the backward-bending labour supply curve) or a kink (the kinked demand curve).

Many figures have two curves: a demand and a supply curve, two reaction curves and so on. The point of intersection of these curves provides the solution to the model. In some of these, the curves are representations of a system of several equations that can be reduced to two equations (as in the IS-LM curves). Some diagrams are a set of many curves, for example, an isoquant or indifference map.

Economists have shown great ingenuity in devising figures and diagrams. In addition to graphs or figures containing interactions between two or more curves, they have produced boxes and more complex figures with multiple quadrants (see Chapter 43, on the four-quadrant diagram showing general equilibrium in the two-sector Heckscher-Ohlin model). The Edgeworth box (and the variants used in examining the production allocation, the Stolper-Samuelson box and the box of the integrated world equilibrium diagram) keep track of relationships between 12 variables, as Humphrey (1996) noted. Curves have been manipulated in many ways. Shifts of curves illustrate comparative static propositions. There are figures showing dynamic relationships, for example, stability analysis and the cobweb diagram.

Some figures have been borrowed from mathematics or physics. An example of the former is the unit simplex and an example of the latter is the phase diagram used in the analysis of stability of equilibria (see Chapter 2 by Blaug on stability of equilibrium).

Conventions in economic theory figures

Generally economists have followed the standard conventions of coordinate geometry but there are instances when they have constructed their figures differently.

Almost invariably economists draw the horizontal and vertical axes to the right and upwards from the origin respectively, using only the non-negative orthant of Euclidean space. This is because the quantities of goods produced and consumed are necessarily positive and, with few exceptions, prices are defined as positive (that is, zero or strictly positive). Consequently, graphs with prices and quantities on the axes are in the first quadrant of Euclidean space. One exception to this general rule is diagrams relating to excess demand (or supply), as in offer curve analysis in international trade.

There is one peculiarity in the use of geometry by economists by comparison with pure mathematics and some other disciplines. Universally today economists draw demand and supply curves with the dependent variable, the quantity demanded or supplied, on the horizontal axis, whereas in mathematics it is conventionally on the vertical axis. Cournot (1838) drew demand and supply curves with the dependent variables on the vertical axis. Dupuit and Jenkin after him used this convention too. However, the German economists Rau and Mangoldt and later the English economist Alfred Marshall, whose *Principles of Economics* was published in 1890, drew them the other way. (For the history of these curves, see Chapter 1 in this volume). Although it is not widely remembered today, Marshall (1920, pp. 83 n.1 and 286 n.2) interprets his demand and supply curve with price as the dependent variable. His terms 'demand price' and 'supply price' indicate the prices at which consumers will demand and producers will supply the quantities specified.[2] However, in his discussion of the elasticity of demand and at other times he switches to price as the independent variable. Later generations of English-speaking economists have followed Marshall's axis convention but treated price as the independent variable. There is another example in economics of this odd practice. In his presentation of the Laffer curve, in which tax revenue is plotted as a function of the tax rate, Laffer puts the dependent variable, tax revenue, on the horizontal axis.

Many economists use graphs of functions in a rather casual way in that they draw curves over an unspecified domain of the independent variable. In the case of a demand or supply curve, for example, the curves often do not extend to zero price and they stop at some arbitrary point. We do not then know the quantity demanded or supplied if the price is zero or if it goes to infinity, or even if it can go to infinity. Marshall, for example, in the diagram which puts together the demand and supply curves (Marshall,

1920, Figure 19) does not extend his demand and supply curves to a zero price. At the other end of the curve, we normally take it that the price is unbounded upwards. However, there are instances where the independent variable is bounded upwards.

It is notable that figures and diagrams in economic theory make only occasional use of geometric theorems and propositions relating to shapes such as triangles or rectangles and hyperboles. They are chiefly concerned with laying out relationships among variables.

Methodological Issues

Figures and diagrams have been used in economic theory in several ways. They have been used as a device to discover economic results; theorems or properties of models; or comparative static propositions and dynamic propositions. They have been used to prove some results. And they have been used as an expository device.

It is not easy to uncover the role of figures and diagrams in the discovery of results. Discovery could have been made through a figure or diagram, or algebra or logic or sheer intuition. No doubt figures have on occasion been the way in which an economist or economists first perceived some result. Two examples where figures seem to have provided the vehicle of discovery are the Engel curve and the Lorenz curve. Both are examples of curves which were fitted to data. Where the curve or curves are functions derived from economic models, however, the discoverer(s) rarely tell us how the result was first conceived or understood. One clear example of discovery by the use of geometry is Scitovsky curves, for there is no mathematics other than geometry in his paper. Another example where the diagram seems to have been the vehicle of discovery is Marshallian stability analysis. In some other cases, algebra is evidently the vehicle of discovery. Two examples are Slutsky derivation of the income and substitution effect[3] and Nash equilibrium. In these cases, the diagram came after the discovery of the result.

In his early work on international trade, written in 1879, Marshall (1930) used what he described as the 'method of diagrams':

> It happens with a few unimportant exceptions all the results which have been obtained by the application of mathematical methods to pure economic theory can be obtained independently by the method of diagrams. Diagrams represent simultaneously to the eye the chief forces which are at work, laid out, as it were, in a map; and thereby suggest results to which attention has not been directed by the use of methods of mathematical analysis. The method of diagrams can be freely used by every one who is capable of exact reasoning, even though he has no knowledge of mathematics.

Thus Marshall advocated the use of diagrams as a method of investigation or exploration.

The use of figures and diagrams as a vehicle of proof has a chequered history. Mathematicians have always warned of the danger of proving propositions by geometry. Although an advocate and frequent user of figures, Marshall (1920, p.129 n.2) warns of this danger: 'It is to be remembered that graphical illustrations are not proofs. They are merely pictures corresponding very roughly to the main conditions of certain problems.' The reason is that one cannot draw a curve without its having a particular shape which gives it particular properties. In proving a proposition, one needs to make sure there is nothing about the shape of the curve or curves, the properties, which is critical to the proposition. There is another way of expressing this problem. Any curve can be represented by a function. But this function has a particular form. Hence, one needs to make sure that the proposition holds for all acceptable functions, not merely the one which represents the arbitrary curve drawn.

One example will suffice, the Law of Diminishing Returns. This can be stated in terms of either marginal or average returns, and the returns can diminish everywhere or eventually. The requirements for it to hold in any of these forms are stringent and there are many false proofs of versions of the Law supposedly holding under certain conditions. There was a long string of articles in the *American Economic Review* from 1963 to 1970 devoted to proofs of the Law. One statement of the Law, the textbook by Stonier and Hague (1957, p.229) – which was widely used in the UK and elsewhere at that time – contended that the Law of (everywhere) Diminishing (marginal) Returns holds if the production function is linearly homogeneous. The proof is geometric. But it is false. They had drawn their isoquants as strictly concave from above (that is, the production function is strictly quasiconcave) and with positive marginal products, without realising that linear homogeneity plus these assumptions suffice but linear homogeneity alone does not. (For an extensive discussion of alternative necessary and sufficient conditions, see Eichhorn, 1978, Chapters 4 and 10 and references therein).

This salutary example raises the rather deep issue of exactly what has been proven by graphical analysis. There is no simple answer since what is proven by geometry varies from author to author.

Even when geometry is used as the only form of mathematics, the proof of any theorem or proposition or assertion may use a combination of verbal logic and geometry. Historians of mathematical thought have examined the logical processes of Ancient Greek mathematics, which is the origin of geometry (see Knorr, 1987 and Netz and Noel, 2007, Chapter 4). The Ancient Greek mathematicians did not use any equations. They used a combination of verbal logic and geometry and they used their geometry in a subtle way. Their diagrams are schematic, representing the qualitative features of an object, and form part of a proof. Twentieth century economists like Lerner and Scitovsky used geometry in much the same way.

For other economists, geometry is a supplement to a proof using algebra or calculus. Cournot uses geometry in this way. The analysis in his text uses algebra and calculus only.

The use of geometry as a device for discovery and proof has declined in recent decades. This is due mainly to changes in the nature of economic models. They have become more complex in terms of the number of variables and relations. Growing complexity has clearly played a role in all three areas of economic theory examined here. In macroeconomic theory, for example, the growing complexity of analysis of aggregate demand in the form of more explanatory variables of consumption and investment behaviour and the introduction of aggregate supply forced macroeconomists to expound their models in terms of systems of equations rather than figures.

One aspect of complexity is especially important in this context, namely, the dimensions of a model. In general equilibrium theory, one can state these dimensions in terms of the number of goods and factors and sometimes of agents (as in models of a continuum of agents) and, in models of international trade, of countries. The geometry of Edgeworth and Pareto was appropriate to a version of the model in which there were only two consumers consuming only two goods, though Edgeworth used this geometry cleverly to explore the situation with more than two consumers (see Creedy's entry, 'The role of numbers in competition', Chapter 32). The same is true of the geometry of the staple Heckscher-Ohlin model with only two goods, two factors and two countries as pursued by Lerner and Stolper-Samuelson and others. However, from about 1950 to 1980, the thrust of developments in the theory of international trade was to extend the dimensions of the model from 2x2x2 (two goods, two factors and two countries), or 'twoness' as it was called, to any number of goods and factors and countries. This required the development of new tools of duality theory. Modern textbooks of international trade theory use geometry strictly as a low-dimensional illustration, not as a device for discovery or proof. Similarly, from the late 19th century, there was a drive to develop utility maximisation models of household demand with $n>2$ goods. Two-dimensional geometry could handle only two goods and here it again became increasingly a low-dimensional illustration of the more general theory, as in, for example, the discussion of income and substitution effects in Hicks and Allen 1934.[4]

After Cournot's work began to be read more widely there was a debate about the relative merits of geometry and algebra. This debate resurfaced after the publication of Samuelson's *Foundations* in 1947, which was another major advance in the application of mathematics to economic theory. Some reviewers accepted geometry but questioned the use of algebra. In reply, Samuelson (1952, p. 59) insisted 'Geometry is a branch of mathematics. . .'.

The comparison of algebra and geometry as alternative mathematical approaches can be clarified best by considering closely the relationships between a graph (or curve) and the equation of a function. The equation of a function that represents a graph is unique but the graph that represents a function is not, unless the function has a specific form with no parameters.[5] A non-specific function $y = f(x)$ may have some minimal restrictions imposed on it. If it is a demand function, for example, it may be restricted to being continuous and downward sloping. One can draw an infinity of graphs with these restrictions. It is not necessary that a graph is less precise than a function. For every graph and its representing function, one can be equally precise about the properties of both. However, it is usual to indicate the domain of the function and restrictions which apply, whereas, as noted above, economists using graphs are often vague about both. Thus algebra has advantages of being more general and more precise.[6]

On the other hand, in his review of Samuelson's *Foundations*, Boulding (1948) argued that geometry was more suited to dealing with functions 'in the large'. This can be a real advantage when curves have complex shapes or there are several curves. It may be the reason for the popularity of some graphs as expository devices (see below).

It is in the third role, as an expository device, that diagrams or figures have excelled and continue to excel. Textbooks in microeconomic theory, macroeconomic theory or other areas of economic theory all continue to use figures freely. They are used as illustrations of models. But they are much more than illustrations. In many areas of economic theory, the way in which economists understand economic concepts and propositions is through figures and diagrams. What teacher of economic theory has not seen the dawn of understanding come over students when, failing to understand an exposition of some complex model in algebra or calculus, they are presented with a simple illustration? This is the power of figures, an expression in economics of the old dictum that 'one picture is worth a thousand words' (or should we say a dozen equations?)

The big advantage of a diagram, from the point of view of information conveyed, is that it brings together and juxtaposes information contained in two or more curves that cannot be easily comprehended in equations or words.[7] One can comprehend relationships among a number of variables (as in the box diagrams) or the effects of shifting curves or multiple equilibria more readily than in the corresponding algebra. This advantage has been increased by modern technologies. Textbooks today use multi-coloured diagrams to great effect and the delivery of diagrams in class-room from computer-based programs allow overlays and other graphical techniques that aid the exposition of complex ideas.

3. HISTORICAL ISSUES

Confusion and Controversies

Some of the historical accounts show that the origin of the figures involved is unclear. One surprising example is the isoquant. Despite the fundamental importance of isoquants to production theory and the thousands of economists who have used them, it is not certain who first drew an isoquant.

In some cases, the diagram which is used by contemporary economists is not the diagram first used in the development of the analysis. It emerged from earlier diagrams as a result of debate and clarification. Four examples in this book are the backward-bending labour supply curve (see King's entry, Chapter 20), Edgeworth's consumption box (see Creedy's entry, Chapter 31), the elasticity of substitution (see Dixon's entry, Chapter 4) and the four-quadrant diagram in international economics (see Panagariya's entry, Chapter 43). Similarly, in some cases, the names have changed over time.

In other cases, there are controversies about the nature or meaning of diagrams. In our selection, there is a much greater prevalence of controversy reported for our selection of macroeconomic figures compared to those of microeconomics or general equilibrium. In most of the entries in the Macroeconomics section, the authors document controversies relating to who did what and what they meant. By comparison, the disputes or controversies that have arisen in microeconomics and general equilibrium are less common and, with a few exceptions, less heated. One of the exceptions is the vigorous controversy surrounding the idea of a homogeneous function as a representation of a constant returns to scale technology, which was quite radical when first suggested in the late 19th century[8] (see Stigler, 1941, chapter 12).

What is it about the early diagrams in macroeconomics that made their interpretation so debatable and the debate so heated? One aspect is the complexity of the models in terms of the number of variables. There are alternative ways of representing these relationships graphically (as in the controversies surrounding the IS-LM and the IS-LM-BP curves). A related factor may be the mixture of graphical, verbal and algebraic analysis that characterises these models. Yet, in microeconomics this is often true too but it did not generally give rise to prolonged debate. There are secondary controversies concerning the interpretation of variables (for example, desired versus realised outputs and expenditures) and the adjustment from one equilibrium to another. The pervasive factor is the absence of a clear microeconomic foundation for the behaviour of consumers and investors. For some of the functions, there are multiple theories, for example, those relating to the determination of the interest rate and the many specifications of the consumption function. The description of relationships was often imprecise. This gave rise to arguments about the sign and magnitude of slopes of curves and their linearity or nonlinearity. On this score, see Richard Lipsey on aggregate demand aggregate supply analysis (Chapter 49), Warren Young on the IS-LM curve (Chapter 47) and Warren Young and Russell Boyer on the Fleming-Mundell extension (Chapter 48).

The First Figures and Diagrams in Economics

The early writings in economics were verbal, with the occasional use of numerical examples. Adam Smith's *Wealth of Nations*, published in 1776, does not contain a single figure. Nor do any of the editions of David Ricardo's *Principles of Political Economy and Taxation* published in 1817, 1819 and 1821, nor those of the editions of John Stuart Mill's *Principles of Political Economy* published between 1848 and 1871.

The first figure or diagram to appear in economics is the zigzag diagram of flows of income and expenditure in a rural economy produced by Quesnay in 1758. This is perhaps the most famous figure or diagram in economics, but there is still disagreement about its interpretation (see Chapter 29, on circular flow diagrams, by Backhouse and Giraud).

It is not certain when the first graph or figure appeared in economics. Theocharis (1983) traces a few examples of graphs in the 18th and early part of the 19th centuries, a time when economics was not yet a separate discipline. Daniel Bernouilli, writing in Latin in 1738, graphed utility as a logarithmic function of wealth (Bernouilli, 1738, reproduced in Baumol and Goldfeld, 1968). His now celebrated paper was finally published in English in *Econometrica* in 1954. His concave function is that of a risk-adverse individual in modern terms.

The French physiocrat, Pierre du Pont de Nemours, drew a diagram of 'the level of natural prices as they would have been in the absence of excise and as they would be after the suppression'. His curve follows a geometric progression. In fact, his curve has the same form as the total product curve when the Law of Diminishing Returns is a decreasing geometric series.

This simple approximation was used by von Thünen and many other agricultural economists and scientists. The continuous function which passes through these points is the Mitscherlich-Spillman function (see Lloyd, 1969).

The Italian Guiglielmo Silio, following the analysis of smuggling by his fellow Milanese Cesare Beccaria, in 1792 plotted a graph of the quantity of goods smuggled as a function of the total duty paid. This curve is a hyperbola though the axes are not displayed in the conventional vertical and horizontal locations (see Theocharis, 1983, p. 24).

The Frenchman Comte Germain Garnier drew a curious diagram in 1796, using a 'pyramid' rather than Cartesian axes. Garnier's pyramid is in reality an isosceles triangle in which the vertical distance is the price of a good. The horizontal width at a point of the Garnier pyramid represents either the number of people willing to buy the good or the share of wealth which each individual is willing to use for the purchase of the good. The first interpretation implies a very particular demand curve in which the number of buyers is a declining function of price. Translated into coordinate geometry, it is in fact a straight line.[9]

In 1830, the Englishman T. Perronet Thompson, when discussing a desirable scale of income taxation, plotted the tax payment as a proportion of income as a continuous function of income which approaches a maximum proportion asymptotically. The equation of the curve is $y=(x-a)/x$ (Theocharis, 1983, p. 123). In his figure Thompson shifts the origin to $(a,0)$ so that his curve passes through the origin.

These five are isolated cases in that each deals with a different problem that arose in public discussion of the time. The graphs are used as illustrations and all are graphs of simple specific functions that were known at the time. Only Bernouilli's curve follows modern conventions with respect to axes and the origin. Their occurrence in economic literature broadly parallels the increasing use of coordinate geometry in the physical sciences in the 18th and 19th centuries after the great work of Descartes, *Geometria*, published in 1637 (see Klein, 1995).

The introduction of graphical methods of analysing economic problems is due to the Frenchman Antoine-Augustin Cournot in *Recherches sur les Principes Mathématiques de la Theorie des Richesse (Researches into the Mathematical Principles of the Theory of Wealth)* published in 1838. He made enormous advances. Cournot used functions with no specific form.[10] He was the first economist to do so extensively.[11] He did this both in his treatment of demand and supply and in his analyses of monopoly and duopoly. He wrote the demand function as $D=\mathrm{f}(p)$, argued that it has the restrictions of being continuous and downward sloping and graphed it. He had an unspecified total revenue function, $pF(p)$. He also used the inverse demand function, in his analysis of duopoly and competition, which he wrote as p=f(D). On the supply side, he had a total cost and marginal cost function and the supply function, Ω(p), which he argued is upward sloping and which he graphed. Humphrey (1992, p. 4) states that 'Cournot . . . was the first to draw market demand and supply curves'. In his analysis of production, he introduced unspecified demand and net profit functions.[12] In his classic analysis of duopoly, he introduced unspecified reaction functions. These advances are colossal, but he was after all a mathematician who wrote a treatise on functions and infinitesimal calculus. There are a total of 10 diagrams in his book, all of which appear as a loose leaf section at the end. They show the demand curve, equilibrium in the case of duopoly, the 'Marshallian' scissors diagram and the incidence of a commodity tax.

We can also state that Cournot was the first economist to produce a figure in which curves intersect to determine a solution. He brought the downward-sloping demand and upward-sloping supply functions together in a single diagram for the first time to yield the market clearing price. Unfortunately, Cournot's work received little attention for several decades.

After 1850, the use of figures in economic theory spread steadily as all forms of mathematical analysis became more common in economic works. Figures play an important part in the work of English economists such as Jevons (who was one of the first English economists to discover the works of Cournot but only after he had done his major work) and Edgeworth. Jenkin used demand and supply curves in the way they are used today to examine market equilibria.

Marshall was a strong advocate of the use of diagrams. He cited the presentations of demand and supply curves by Cournot and Jenkin. He introduced possibilities of multiple and of unstable equilibria in his figures. In Marshall's *Principles*, algebra is relegated to the Mathematical Appendix and diagrams are the main form of mathematics, though all of these too are relegated to footnotes. This relegation reflects Marshall's strong views on the limitation of mathematics in economic theory (see Groenewegen, 1995, pp. 412–3). In the eighth edition, published in 1920, there are 41 numbered figures plus four more in the Mathematical Appendix.

In his biographical essay on Marshall, Keynes (1972, pp. 185–86) credits him with being the 'founder of modern diagrammatical economics':

> Marshall's mathematical and diagrammatical exercises in Economic Theory were of such a character in their grasp, comprehensiveness, and scientific accuracy, and went far beyond the 'bright ideas' of his predecessors, that we may justly claim him as the founder of modern diagrammatical economics.

As noted above, this credit should go to Cournot. He matched Marshall in every one of these respects and, moreover, he had no precedents at all to follow.

Marshall's *Principles* certainly did have a profound influence on the development of economic theory in the English-speaking world. One aspect of this influence is that later economists took many of the graphs and figures used thereafter in economic theory from his work, including downward-sloping demand curves and upward-sloping supply curves, the elasticity of demand, the marginal product function, the central 'Marshallian' cross diagram, derived demand, the incidence of a tax or bounty, the diagram of rent determination and the diagram showing consumers' and producers' surplus. In *The Pure Theory of International Trade*, published in 1879, he introduced offer curves, though he called them 'international trade' curves.

The Chronology of our Figures and Diagrams

Appendix 0.1 contains a chronology of the figures and diagrams covered in this book. They are presented in the same order as in the book. Further detail of discovery can be found in the individual entries.

In some cases, one or more authors presented a new concept in algebra and a later author or authors presented it in terms of geometry. An initial algebraic statement in such cases is indicated by square brackets. In other cases, the listing is debatable as there is no clear single discoverer or discoverers. For some, there are antecedents which have not been listed because the form of the antecedent diagrams differed from that of the diagram used today; for example, a number of writers had presented the essential ideal of the Laffer Curve for various kinds of taxes.

Despite the complexity and uncertainty with respect to the origin of some curves and diagrams, the general pattern of the evolution of these figures is clear. The first figures arose in microeconomic theory, apart from Quesnay's circular flow diagram in 1758. The very first diagram in microeconomics listed in the table is that of von Thünen's location theory in 1826. Cournot's figures analysing market behaviour and the logistic growth curve of Verhulst both appeared in 1838. Thereafter there was a steady stream of new figures and diagrams in microeconomic theory. Figures illustrating aspects of general equilibrium in closed or open economy began to appear from the 1880s, after Walras had developed the theory. In macroeconomic theory, surprisingly, diagrams did not appear until after the publication of Keynes's *General Theory*, apart from Marshall's curve relating to the demand for money.

The modal decade in terms of the number of figures that first appeared is the 1930s by a large margin (most of these are by British or British-trained authors, reflecting the influence of Marshall). Figures continued to appear regularly for the first time in the 1940s and 1950s and with decreasing frequency in the subsequent decades. The last diagram we have listed is that in graph theory in 1996 by Economides.

Another result from this chronology is that two kinds of multiple discoveries can be observed. These are multiples discoveries of a curve or diagram, and multiple discoveries of different curves or diagrams by one economist.

Multiple Discoveries and Eponomy

Eponomy

Eponomy is 'the practice of affixing the name of the scientist to all or part of what he has found, as with the Copernican system, Hookes' law, Planck's constant, or Halley's comet' (Merton, 1973, p. 299). This practice is common to all sciences. The naming is done by someone after the event, often a long time after, as a form of public recognition of the contribution.

Segara and Braun (2004) have produced a dictionary of eponyms in economics, that is laws, theorems, functions, equations and other entities named after their discoverer or discoverers, or at least a person or persons credited with their discovery. There are over 300 in their list. This includes the great majority of those named in our collection (starting with the Marshallian cross diagram, the Engel curve and so on) though there are some omissions – the Lerner diagram, Beveridge curve and Fisher's diagram – all of which are surprising.

The eminent sociologist of science, Robert Merton (1973, p. 356), has examined the application of eponomy to scientific discoveries. He advanced the hypothesis that 'all scientific discoveries are in principle multiples, including those that on the surface appear to be singletons', meaning that they were 'in the air' and not the product of unique genius.

In the literature on the history of economic thought, multiple discoveries have been noted many times. In discussing one such example, the origin of the marginal revenue curve, Andrew Skinner cites Joan Robinson's vivid metaphor: 'There are many occasions when several explorers are surprised, on meeting each other at the pole' (Joan Robinson, 1933, pp. vi–vii). George Stigler (1980), the eminent historian of economic thought, gives several examples of multiple discoveries in economics. These include three in our set: the Slutsky equation, the kinked oligopoly demand curve and monopolistic and imperfect competition (though in this instance, there are important differences between the models of Edward Chamberlin and

Joan Robinson). Several more of our authors found that more than one person independently discovered or invented the graph or diagram they report, for example, the utility possibility curves.

Stephen Stigler, statistician and son of George Stigler, modified the Merton thesis. He advanced Stigler's Law of Eponomy: 'No scientific discovery is named after its original discoverer' (Stigler, 1980, p. 147). The person named is someone who made the discovery after an earlier discoverer, sometimes when the earlier work was known to the person named. In a few cases the named discoverer did not even make the discovery. A well-known example of this in economics is Giffen's paradox and a lesser known example is the Beveridge curve. A more famous example is Pythagoras's Theorem.[13]

Stigler's Law, which he asserts holds with the same generality as other laws in sciences, certainly holds for at least three of the curves or diagrams named in this collection. It holds for the Marshallian cross diagram. In his entry on this diagram in Chapter 1, Humphrey examines in detail five other economists who used this diagram before Marshall. Marshall himself acknowledges the work of four of these, Cournot, Dupuit, Mangoldt and Jenkin. It holds for the Edgeworth box too; the four-sided box first appeared in Pareto's 1960 *Manual*. It also holds for the Stolper-Samuelson box. This box was presented by Lerner in 1933. However, there is no suggestion that Stolper and Samuelson knew of the earlier discovery: Lerner's piece was presented as a seminar paper at the London School of Economics in 1933 but was not published until 1952, after the article by Stolper and Samuelson. Stigler's Law also holds for the Laffer curve. There are several antecedents of this curve. In this instance, as noted by Roger Middleton, Laffer (2004) admitted these antecedents and claimed only to be a populariser.

On the other hand, there are more instances in this collection of eponymous namings which, contrary to Stigler's Law, are to the original discoverer. The first of these is the Engel curve. The next, in time sequence, are Edgeworth's indifference curve, the Lerner diagram, and Nash equilibrium. No one, to our knowledge, has provided evidence of a Stiglerian predecessor in these instances.

In some cases too, the multiple diagrams are slightly different but closely related diagrams; examples of this are Marshallian and Walrasian stability analyses, the two variants of monopolistic competition, the various classifications of technical change and various rent-seeking diagrams. In the case of circular flow diagrams, these have arisen in quite different contexts – general equilibrium and macroeconomic models of an economy – and therefore look different, but the essential idea of diagrams showing two-way flows is the same.

Economists who made multiple discoveries

The second kind of multiple discoveries occurs when one economist makes multiple discoveries. In this volume, several economists are credited with discoveries of multiple figures, in some cases along with but independently of other discoverers. For example, Cournot is credited, before several other independent discoverers, with demand and supply curves, the 'Marshallian' cross diagram and 'Cournot' duopoly. Marshall is credited with the stability diagram, the phase diagram, the monopoly diagram and the demand for money diagram. Edgeworth is credited with the indifference curve, the Edgeworth box and the first presentation of u-shaped average cost curves (see Chapter 8). Hicks is credited with discovering the elasticity of substitution, the income and substitution effect diagram (jointly with Allen), the IS-LM diagram and the 'Hicksian' form of technological change. Joan Robinson is credited with the elasticity of substitution, the diagrams of discriminating monopoly and imperfect competition, and the backward-bending labour supply curve. Samuelson is credited jointly with Stolper with the production box, the utility possibility curve, the factor price frontier and the Keynesian cross diagram. Solow is credited with the Solow classification of technical change, the Solow model and one of the diagrams showing the non-neutrality of money (jointly with McDonald). Leontief and Kuznets are credited with two discoveries, though the Kuznets environmental curve is named after him because of its similarity to the Kuznets curve describing the relationship between the level of per capita income and income inequality. These multiple discoveries are one aspect of the creativity of great economists.

The star performer in our collection, in this respect, is Abba Lerner. He is credited with the Lerner diagram and the box construction for the analysis of the production side of an economy, and is recognised (in Chapter 3 by Lloyd and Blaug) as one of the first economists to draw an isoquant. He was the originator of the Lerner degree of monopoly in Lerner (1934) and its diagram. Lerner is now recognised as one of the most prolific and productive users of geometry in the history of economic analysis (see Giraud, 2008).

4. FINAL REMARKS

This review of the mathematical, methodological and historical aspects of the use of figures and diagrams shows that they have played a central role in the development of economic theory. First, they have been a major vehicle of discovery of economic concepts and propositions, although the process of discovery in some cases was confused. Second, they have excelled as an expository device. There are some people whose visual sense is stronger than their sense of prose or their sense of numbers. For others, complex relationships can be comprehended more clearly in terms of figures. If you are one of these, this is a book for you. It teaches economics by looking at curves and shapes.

NOTES

1. Maas and Morgan (2002) give an interesting history of graphs of time series in 19th century Britain. The use of graphs was contentious in the beginning of the history of statistics and econometrics.
2. In the Mathematical Appendix to the *Principles*, Marshall writes the (market) demand and the supply function in the inverse price form. Gordon (1982) traces Marshall's ambivalence with respect to the choice of axes and attributes his preference for the inverse form to his treatment of consumers' surplus. Here price is the maximum price consumers are willing to pay for a given quantity.
3. Hicks and Allen seem to have come to the geometry first. In presenting the diagram, they say 'Here we may conveniently begin with a geometrical treatment, concentrating on the case where income is spent on two goods only – the case most amenable to the geometrical method' (Hicks and Allen, 1934, p. 65). They derive a different form of the Slutsky equation. The terms 'income effect' and 'substitution effect' are not used until Hicks's *Value and Capital,* published in 1938, where the treatment is again geometrical.
4. Earlier Edgeworth had made the same point: 'The mathematical version of the theory consists either of Geometry or Algebra. Geometry is directly applicable to the simplest possible cases. If more than two commodities are considered, solid geometry must be called in. The dimensions of space are not adequate to represent the case of more than three variables' (Edgeworth, 1894, p. 424).
5. For example, $y = \log x$. For a straight line, $y = a+bx$, there is a multiple infinity of lines as the parameters a and b may vary from $-\infty$ to $+\infty$. Once the values of a and b are specified, there is a unique graph.
6. Boulding (1948) also argued that geometry was a more convenient way of dealing with discontinuities. This is arguable and, in any case, discontinuities do not figure frequently in economic theory (one exception is the kinked demand curve).
7. Larkin and Simon (1987) compare the computational efficiency of diagrams and equivalent words arranged in sentences, using information theory. They argue that diagrams can be superior to words because they group information together, use the location of information and support perceptual inferences. They do not compare diagrams and equivalent equations.
8. Edgeworth made the celebrated jibe: 'Justice is a perfect cube, said the ancient sage: and rational conduct is a homogeneous function, adds the modern savant' (quoted in Stigler, 1941, p. 342). This comment was made by one of the most skilful geometricians in the history of economic analysis and the best mathematical economist of his time.
9. Let x denote the number of buyers, p the price, b the base of the triangle and a its height. Then $x = b-(b/a)p$, with $p \geq 0$ and $x \geq 0$.
10. In the Preface, he wrote, 'I propose to show that the solution of the general questions which arise from the theory of wealth, depends essentially not on elementary algebra, but on that branch of analysis which comprises arbitrary functions, which are merely restricted to satisfying certain conditions'.
11. Baumol and Goldfield (1968, p.14) comment that 'As far as we know, it was not until (almost exactly) 100 years after the publication of Bernouilli's essay that functions of

unspecified form were first introduced into economics (by Cournot)'. Certainly, the five curves in the text above that were presented before Cournot are all graphs of specific functions. However, this distinction should go to the German Georg von Buquoy. In 1815 he used non-specific revenue and cost functions and used the equality of marginal revenue and marginal cost to determine the optimal level of ploughing a field. (Theocharis, 1983, p. 111).

12. Baumol and Goldfeld (1968, pp. 162–63) praise a number of features of his careful mathematical analysis of monopoly.
13. On the basis of recent scholarship, Stigler (1980, p. 148) claims that 'the Pythagorean Theorem, was known before Pythagoras, was first proved after Pythagoras, and in fact Pythagoras himself may have been unaware of the geometrical significance of the theorem!'

REFERENCES

Baumol, William J. and Stephen M. Goldfield (eds) (1968), *Precursors in Mathematical Economics: An Anthology*, London: The London School of Economics and Political Science.

Boulding, Kenneth (1948), 'Samuelson's *Foundations*: the role of mathematics in economics', *Journal of Political Economy*, 56, 187–99.

Cook, Simon (2005), 'Late Victorian visual reasoning and Alfred Marshall's economic science', *British Journal for the History of Science*, 38, 179–95.

Cournot, Antoine-Augustin (1838/1927), *Researches into the Mathematical Principles of the Theory of Wealth*, translated by N. T. Bacon, New York: Macmillan.

De Marchi, Neil B. (2003), 'Visualizing the gains from trade, mid-1870s to 1962', *Journal of the History of Economic Thought*, 10, 551–72.

Edgeworth, Francis Y. (1894), 'Theory of international values', *Economic Journal*, 4, 424–43.

Eichhorn, Wolfgang (1978), *Functional Equations in Economics*, Reading, MA: Addison-Wesley Publishing Co.

Giraud, Yann (2008), 'Abba Lerner and the peculiar place of diagrammatic analysis in 1930s British economics', paper presented at the *HES Annual Meeting*, Toronto, 27–30 June.

Giraud, Yann B. (2010), 'The changing place of visual representation in economics: Paul Samuelson between principle and strategy', *Journal of the History of Economic Thought*, 32 (2), pp. 175–97.

Gordon, Scott (1982), 'Why did Marshall transpose the axes?', *Eastern Economic Journal*, 8, 31–45.

Groenewegen, Peter (1995), *A Soaring Eagle: Alfred Marshall 1842–1924*, Cheltenham: Edward Elgar.

Hicks, John R. and R. G. D. Allen (1934), 'A reconsideration of the theory of value, *Economica*, N.S. 1, Parts 1–2, 52–76 and 196–219.

Humphrey, Thomas M. (1992), 'Marshallian cross diagrams and their uses before Alfred Marshall: the origins of supply and demand geometry', *Federal Reserve Bank of Richmond Economic Review*, 78, 3–23.

Humphrey, Thomas M. (1993), *Money, Banking and Inflation: Essays in the History of Monetary Thought*, Cheltenham: Edward Elgar.

Humphrey, Thomas M. (1996), 'The early history of the box diagram', *Federal Reserve Bank of Richmond Economic Quarterly*, 82, 37–75.

Keynes, John Maynard (1972), *Essays in Biography*, vol. X, The Collected Writings of John Maynard Keynes, London: Macmillan St Martin's Press, published for the Royal Economic Society.
Klein, Judy (1995), 'The method of diagrams and the black arts of inductive economics', in Ingrid H. Rima (ed.), *Measurement, Quantification and Economic Analysis*, London and New York: Routledge.
Knorr, W. R. (1987), *The Ancient Tradition of Geometric Problems*, New York: Croom Holm.
Laffer, Arthur B. (2004), 'The Laffer curve: past, present and future', *Backgrounder*, 1765, 1 June www.heritage.org/research/taxes/upload/64214_1.pdf, accessed 7 December 2010.
Larkin, Jill H. and Herbert A. Simon (1987), 'Why a diagram is (sometimes) worth ten thousand words', *Cognitive Science*, 11, 65–99.
Lerner, Abba P. (1934), 'The concept of monopoly and the measurement of monopoly power', *Review of Economic Studies*, 1, 157–75.
Lerner, Abba P. (1952), 'Factor prices and international trade', *Economica*, 19, 1–15.
Lloyd, Peter J. (1969), 'Elementary geometric/arithmetic series and early production theory', *Journal of Political Economy*, 77, 21–34.
Maas, Harro and Mary Morgan (2002), 'Timing history: The introduction of graphical analysis in 19th century British economics', *Revue d'Histoire des Sciences Humaines*, 7, 97–127.
Marshall, Alfred (1920), *Principles of Economics*, eighth edition, reprinted in 1956, London: Macmillan and Co. Ltd.
Marshall, Alfred (1930), *Pure Theory of Foreign Trade: The Pure Theory of Domestic Values*, Reprints of Scarce Tracts in Economics and Political Science No. 1, London: London School of Economics.
Merton, Robert (1973), *The Sociology of Science: Theoretical and Empirical Investigations*, Chicago, IL: University of Chicago Press.
Netz, Reviel and William Noel (2007), *The Archimedes Codex*, London: Phoenix.
Robinson, Joan (1933), *The Economics of Imperfect Competition*, London: St Martin's Press.
Samuelson, Paul A. (1952), 'Economic theory and mathematics: an appraisal', *American Economic Review*, 42, 56–66.
Segara, Julia and Carlos Rodríguez Braun (2004), *An Eponymous Dictionary of Economics: A Guide to Laws and Theorems Named after Economists*, Cheltenham: Edward Elgar.
Stigler, George J. (1941), *Production and Distribution Theories: The Formative Period*, New York: Macmillan.
Stigler, George J. (1980), 'Merton on multiples, denied and affirmed', *Transactions of the New York Academy of Sciences*, new series, 39, 143–6.
Stigler, Stephen (1980), 'Stigler's law of eponomy', *Transactions of the New York Academy of Sciences*, new series, 39, 147–57.
Stonier, A. W. and D. C. Hague (1957), *A Textbook of Economic Theory*, London: Longmans.
Theocharis, Reghinos D. (1983), *Early Developments in Mathematical Economics*, second edition, London: Macmillan.

APPENDIX 0.1 A CHRONOLOGY OF CURVES AND DIAGRAMS

Curve/diagram	Discoverer(s)	Date
Microeconomics		
'Marshallian' cross	Cournot	1838
	Rau	1841
	Dupuit	1844
	Mangoldt	1863
	Jenkin	1870
Stability of equilibrium	Walras	1874
	Marshall	1879
Indifference curves	Edgeworth	1881
Isoquants	Bowley	1924
Elasticity of substitution	Hicks	1932
	Robinson	1933
Income and substitution effects	[Slutsky]	1915
	Hicks and Allen	1934
Engel curves	Engel	1857
Homogeneous functions	[Wicksteed]	1894
	[Flux]	1894
Homothetic functions	Shephard	1970
Long-run and short-run curves	Edgeworth	1913
Product exhaustion	[Wicksteed]	1894
	[Flux]	1894
Classifications of technical change	Hicks	1932
	Harrod	1937
	Solow	1963
Nash equilibrium	Nash	1951
Consumer surplus	Dupuit	1844
	Jenkin	1872
	Marshall	1890
Harberger triangles	Dupuit	1844
	Jenkin	1872
	Harberger	1964
Scitovsky curves	Scitovsky	1941

Table (continued)

Curve/diagram	Discoverer(s)	Date
Taxation of external costs	[Pigou]	1912
Monopoly	[Cournot]	1838
	Auspitz and Lieben	1880
	Marshall	1890
Discriminating monopoly	Robinson	1933
Duopoly	[Cournot]	1838
Monopolistic competition	Chamberlin	1933
	Robinson	1933
Kinked demand curves	Sweezy	1939
	Hall and Hitch	1939
Backward-bending labour supply curves	Robbins	1929
	Phelps Brown	1936
	Robinson	1937
Location theory	von Thünen	1826
	Launhardt	1885
	Lösch	1940
Hotelling's model	Hotelling	1929
The cobweb diagram	Ezekiel	1938
The Markowitz diagram	Markowitz	1952
Rent seeking diagrams	[Tullock]	1967
	Krueger	1974
	[Posner]	1975
Logistic growth curve	Verhulst	1838
	Pearl and Reed	1920
Graph theory	Economides	1996
General equilibrium analysis		
Circular flow diagrams	Quesnay	1758
	Knight	1932
	Samuelson	1948
The unit simplex	[Arrow and Debreu]	1954
Exchange of consumption box diagram	Edgeworth	1881
The role of numbers in competition	Edgeworth	1881

Table (continued)

Curve/diagram	Discoverer(s)	Date
Production possibilities frontier	Haberler Viner Leontief	1930 1931 1937
Utility possibility frontier	Allais Samuelson	1943 1947
Factor price frontier	Samuelson	1957
Pareto efficiency	Pareto	1906
Phase diagram	Marshall	1879
Theory of the second best and third best	Lipsey and Lancaster McManus	1956 1959
Offer curves	Marshall	1879
Stolper-Samuelson box	Lerner Stolper and Samuelson	1933 1941
Lerner diagram	Lerner	1933
Trade theory diagram	Leontief	1933
Four-quadrant diagram of the Heckscher-Ohlin model	Johnson	1957
Integrated world equilibrium	Dixit and Norman	1980
Optimum tariff	Edgeworth Bickerdike	1894 1906
Macroeconomics		
Keynesian income determination diagram	Samuelson	1948
Fleming-Mundell diagram	[Fleming] Mundell	1962 1963
Aggregate demand aggregate supply diagram	Dillard Patinkin	1948 1956
Phillips curve	Phillips	1948
UV or Beveridge curve	Dow and Dicks-Mireaux	1958

Table (continued)

Curve/diagram	Discoverer(s)	Date
Demand for money curve	Marshall	1871
	Keynes	1936
Non-neutrality of money	Keynes	1936
	Ng	1980
	Taylor	1980
	McDonald and Solow	1981
Laffer curve	Laffer	1981
Intertemporal utility maximisation	Fisher	1907
Solow-Swan model	Solow	1956
	Swan	1956
Lorenz curve	Lorenz	1905
Kuznets curve – income inequality	Kuznets	1955
Kuznets curve – environment	Grossman and Krueger	1991

Note: Square brackets indicate that the original presentation was algebraic.

PART I

Single market analysis (partial equilibrium)

Basic tools of demand and supply curve analysis

1. Marshallian cross diagrams

Thomas M. Humphrey

The most frequently used geometric tool of microeconomic analysis is the familiar partial equilibrium demand-and-supply curve diagram of the textbooks. Generations of students and their teachers have employed its intersecting curves (1) to depict the equilibrium or market clearing price and quantity of any particular good or factor input, and (2) to explain how (Walrasian) price or (Marshallian) quantity adjustments ensure this equilibrium, the first by eliminating excess supply and demand, the second by eradicating gaps between supply price and demand price.

The diagram achieves much with little. It illustrates how parametric shifts in its two curves caused by changes in tastes, incomes, technology, factor prices and prices of related goods operate to alter a good's equilibrium price and quantity. It shows how the shifting and incidence of a per-unit tax or tariff on buyers and sellers depends upon elasticities of demand and supply. It depicts how price ceilings and price floors generate shortages and surpluses respectively. With it one can compare the allocative effects of competitive versus monopoly pricing and indicate the welfare costs of market imperfections. For all its simplicity, it is a powerful and flexible tool.

Economists typically associate the diagram with Alfred Marshall, the English neoclassical economist who was its most influential nineteenth century expositor. So strong is this association that the diagram has been christened the Marshallian cross, or Marshallian scissors after Marshall's analogy comparing the price-determining properties of a brace of demand and supply curves with the cutting properties of the blades of a pair of scissors (Figure 1.1). Such labeling unfortunately is a bit misleading. For Marshall fathered neither the diagram, nor its applications, nor the techniques and concepts he employed in its analysis. Their sources are to be found elsewhere.

The French philosopher, mathematician and economist Antoine-Augustin Cournot was the first to publish a market demand and supply curve diagram for a particular good, albeit with price measured on the horizontal axis and quantity on the vertical, the reverse of the Marshallian

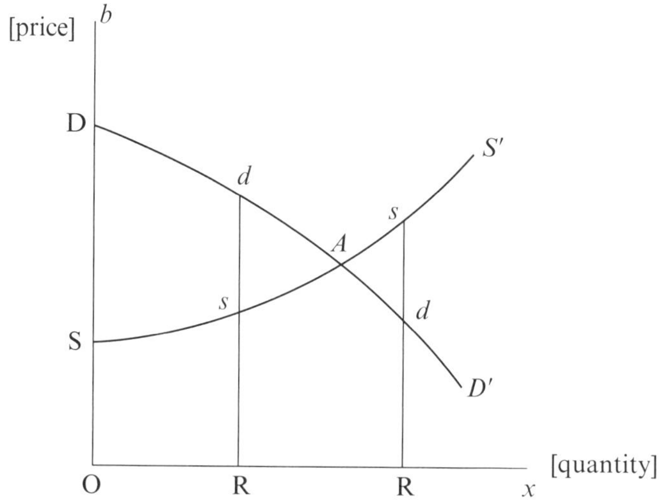

Source: Marshall, *The Pure Theory of Foreign Trade*, p.16, fig. 22a, http://socserv2.mcmaster.ca/~econ/ugcm/3113/marshall/foreigntrade.pdf

Figure 1.1 Marshall's diagram

convention. In his 1838 *Researches into the Mathematical Principles of the Theory of Wealth*, Cournot presents an industry demand curve as an empirical sales schedule in which sales, or quantity demanded, varies inversely with price. Then, formulating an expression equivalent to Marshall's measure of price elasticity of demand, he identifies the unit elastic, or revenue maximizing, price-quantity combination on the curve (Figure 1.2).

Next he introduces into his diagram an industry supply curve, derived by summing over constituent firms' rising marginal cost schedules, and specifies the equilibrium, or market clearing point of intersection of the two curves. Last, he uses his curves to analyze the shifting and incidence of a per-unit tax levied on a particular good. He has the tax shifting the supply curve horizontally in his diagram (vertically in the conventional one) by the amount of the tax. With his negatively sloped demand curve, however, he shows that the equilibrium price increase is always less than the amount of the tax, such that shifting is incomplete and the incidence falls on sellers and buyers alike (Figure 1.3, with axes reversed to conform to the conventional Marshallian case). Noting that the extent of shifting depends upon the demand curve's slope, Cournot points out that if the curve were horizontal the tax would not increase price at all and the seller

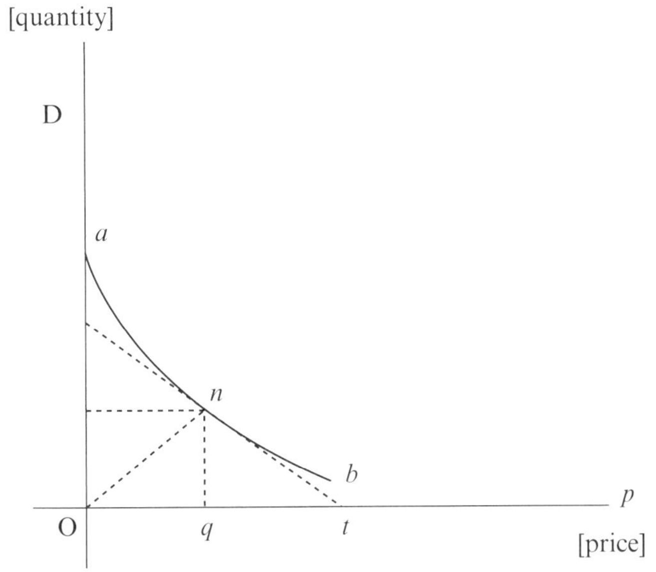

Source: Cournot, *Researches into the Mathematical Principles of the Theory of Wealth*, Fig. 1 in the packet of diagrams accompanying the book

Figure 1.2 Cournot's demand curve

would absorb the levy. Cournot was thus the first to show that given a conventionally shaped supply curve, the portion of an excise tax shifted to buyers in the form of higher prices varies inversely with elasticity of demand, being nil at infinite and complete at zero values of that parameter. Cournot, not Marshall, invented geometrical tax-incidence analysis.

Cournot failed to investigate stability of equilibrium with his demand and supply curve diagram (although he did so in his famous reaction-function model of duopoly). The German economist Karl Heinrich Rau corrected this oversight (albeit with no knowledge of Cournot's work) in the fourth or 1841 edition of his textbook *Grundsätze der Volkswirthschaftslehre* (Hennings, 1979). In so doing, he became the first to employ a Marshallian cross diagram to investigate the stability of market-clearing equilibrium and to indicate the forces that restore that equilibrium once it is disturbed. From his diagram, he deduced that a below-equilibrium price would produce an excess demand. Suppliers would take advantage of the resulting shortage of the good to raise the price until the shortage disappeared and equilibrium was restored.

Neither Cournot nor Rau derived welfare propositions from their

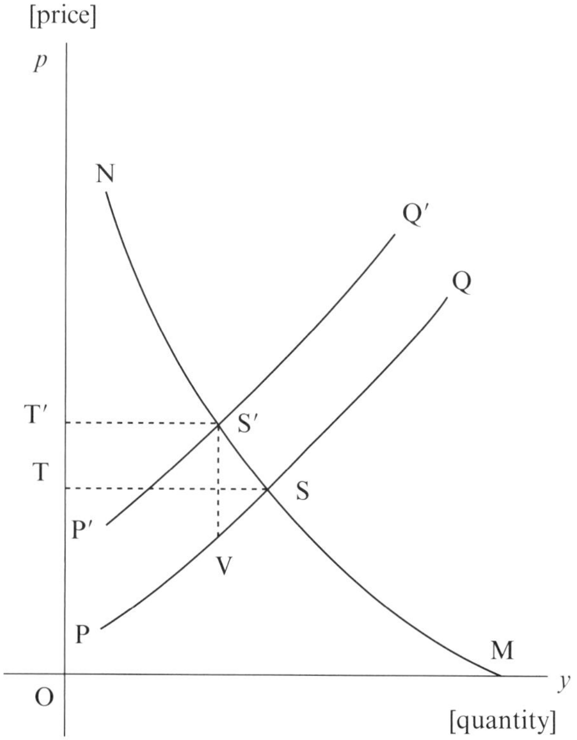

Source: Cournot, *Researches into the Mathematical Principles of the Theory of Wealth*, Fig. 6 with axes reversed, in packet of diagrams accompanying the book

Figure 1.3 Cournot's scissors diagram and tax incidence analysis

diagrams. Because they treated demand curves as empirical sales schedules instead of replicas of underlying marginal utility functions, they said nothing about the welfare implications of competitive versus monopoly pricing, public utility rate setting, discriminatory pricing or commodity taxation. The French civil engineer and economist Jules Dupuit was not so restricted (Ekelund and Hébert, 1999). Explicitly identifying demand curves with marginal utility schedules, he became, in his 1844 essay 'On the Measurement of the Utility of Public Works' and his 1849 piece 'On Tolls and Transport Charges', the first to derive welfare theorems from Marshallian diagrams. True, he drew no supply curves. But he made path-breaking use of the demand curve to invent geometrical prototypes of such Marshallian constructs as total utility, consumer surplus and deadweight loss triangles, not to mention Laffer curve relationships between tax rates and revenues. It was Dupuit, not Marshall, who first identified total utility with the area under the demand curve from zero to the quantity consumed. And it was he who first partitioned this area into a price-times-quantity rectangle showing buyer expenditure or seller receipts, and a consumers' surplus triangle showing the excess of what consumers would pay for the good rather than do without over what they actually do pay. He extended this consumer-rent notion – that buyers get more utility than they pay for when they purchase at a single market price – to the evaluation of public works, arguing that the potential benefits of such works are not properly measured by their costs but by the area under the demand curve. Finally, it was Dupuit who conceived of deadweight loss triangles as the waste of total utility, due to monopoly pricing or government taxation, over and above that part of total utility appropriated by the monopolist or the government itself.

Dupuit drew the demand curve as downward sloping and convex: downward sloping because each extra unit of the good, due to diminishing marginal utility, yields less additional satisfaction and so commands a lower price; convex because each price fall activates the demands of a new group of buyers larger and poorer than the groups before. The new demands, added to those already existing at higher prices and also responding to lower prices, gives the curve its convex shape.

From this demand curve Dupuit derived three key propositions regarding the welfare effects of commodity taxes. First, an excise tax results in a loss of consumers' surplus in excess of the yield of the tax. This deadweight loss measures the tax-induced distortion of relative prices and consumption patterns away from the optimum. Second, the deadweight loss is proportional to the square of the tax, which implies that the government can minimize the welfare burden of a given tax bill by imposing a low tax rate on many different goods rather than a high rate on a few. For the deadweight loss, which shrinks as the square of the rate, approaches zero as the tax becomes perfectly general, or widely diffused, and its rate correspondingly small. Third, the yield of a tax is no measure of its true welfare cost. For the same yield can be obtained by two different rates entailing greatly different deadweight losses. For example, zero and prohibitive tax rates both yield zero revenue. But the zero rate produces no deadweight loss whereas the prohibitive rate produces a loss equal to the entire area under the demand curve.

Finally, Dupuit, anticipating the work of Marshall's students A.C. Pigou and Joan Robinson in the 1920s and 1930s, demonstrated diagrammatically that price discrimination – charging separate consumers different prices for the same good – could, by yielding larger revenues than a single price, lead a monopolist to produce more than he otherwise would, thereby enhancing welfare. Were the monopolist able to practice perfect discrimination and charge a separate maximum price for each unit sold so as to extract all consumers' surplus for himself, output would reach its competitive, or most efficient level. Overall, Dupuit established that discriminatory pricing could induce monopolists to serve markets that, because of high entry and production costs, would be unprofitable at a single price.

Following Dupuit, but with no knowledge of his work, was the German economist Hans von Mangoldt (Hennings, 1980) who reintroduced supply curves into the diagrams that he presented in great profusion in his 1863 *Outline of Political Economy*. Like his predecessors, Mangoldt identified the market-clearing equilibrium price-and-quantity point of intersection of the curves, and, like Rau, whose work he knew, described how the market's response to excess demand or supply restores price to equilibrium following temporary deviations from it. His enumeration of the determinants of the shapes and shifts of demand curves could have been lifted from today's textbooks, as could his treatment of possible exceptions to the law of downward-sloping demand. He was the first to show how constant, increasing and decreasing costs of production affect the shape of the supply curve, causing it to be flat, rising and falling, respectively. And, pioneering the partial equilibrium, comparative statics analytical technique usually attributed to Marshall, he showed not only how shifts in demand and supply curves alter equilibrium price and quantity, but also how the new equilibrium is attained through a precise sequential adjustment path. He also described how multiple equilibria (in which the curves intersect more than once) could occur in unusual cases in which both curves slope in the same direction, and how unique (single) equilibrium results when they slope in opposite directions. Finally, in a treatment that was not superseded until Marshall's *Principles*, Mangoldt applied his diagrammatic apparatus to analyze price determination when goods are jointly demanded and supplied in fixed proportions and when they appear in composite demand and supply. Small wonder that F.Y. Edgeworth (1894) called him 'one of the independent discoverers of the mathematical theory of Demand and Supply'.

Last but not least among pre-Marshall inventors of cross diagrams was English electrical engineer and inventor Fleeming Jenkin, who, in three important papers published in 1868–1872, introduced demand and supply curves – indeed the entire technique of diagrammatic analysis – into the English economic literature (Brownlie and Lloyd Prichard, 1963). It was Jenkin, not Marshall, who first conceived of the market period (in which stocks of goods are fixed and cost of production plays no role in price determination) and the long run (when output and quantities of factor inputs can vary). Jenkin emphasized the volatility of market-period prices stemming from the mercurial nature of demand and supply. Market-period demand curves, he argued, shift with every whim, desire, expectation and event, real or imagined. Supply curves, consisting of the (variable) fraction of fixed stocks of goods offered for immediate sale rather than held for future sale, shift with changes in sellers' expectations. Changing expectations of higher or lower future prices shift demand curves to the right or left, and supply curves oppositely to the left or right, resulting in exaggerated swings in market-period equilibrium prices. By contrast, such volatility is absent in the long run. Like Marshall and Mangoldt (whose work he did not know), Jenkin held that, depending upon whether factor inputs were in limited or unlimited supply, long-run cost of production would be increasing or constant, giving rise to steeply upward sloping or flat long-period supply curves, respectively. In the latter case he noted that cost determines price and demand determines output.

In what was the first application of cross diagrams to the analysis of the labor market, Jenkin showed how trade unions, via their influence on the labor supply curve, can raise wage rates and lower employment in both the market period and the long run. And Jenkin, with no knowledge of the similar findings of Cournot and Dupuit, used his scissors diagrams to show how the slopes of demand and supply curves determine the shifting and incidence of taxes, and how a tax reduces consumers' and producers' surpluses by more than it yields the government in revenue such that deadweight losses occur. Jenkin also demonstrated that these excess burden triangles increase in size with tax rates, dwarfing tax-yield rectangles at very high rates. Here was reason enough, he thought, to keep rates low.

Taken together, the foregoing examples, drawn from an early microeconomics literature featuring occasional demand and supply geometry, contradict the notion that Marshall was the father of the diagram that bears his name. Instead, they indicate that:

1. The diagram did not originate with Marshall. Five economists – Cournot, Rau, Dupuit, Mangoldt and Jenkin – employed it in print before Marshall published it in his *Pure Theory of Domestic Values* (1879) and later in his *Principles of Economics* (1890). And the first four did so before Marshall began his career as an economist.
2. Of the diagram's five originators, all but Mangoldt, who knew of Rau's contribution, were ignorant of the work of the others. The diagram was a multiple independent discovery.
3. Besides conceiving the diagram, its originators supplied all its components and pioneered most of its applications. Cournot contributed the original curves. Rau and Mangoldt provided the stability analysis.

Mangoldt furnished the comparative statics exercises which Jenkin applied to the analysis of price determination in the market period and long run, respectively. The tax incidence analysis stems from Cournot, Dupuit and Jenkin. The consumers' surplus and deadweight loss triangles are Dupuit's and Jenkin's. Jenkin devised the geometric measure of producers' surplus. Mangoldt applied the diagram to the problem of the pricing of joint and composite goods. Jenkin extended it to the labor market to explain the determination of wage rates and employment. Cournot formulated the elasticity concept and Dupuit analyzed price discrimination. There is little in Marshall's, or today's economists' use of the diagram that was not anticipated by his predecessors.

4. The diagram therefore illustrates Stephen Stigler's Law of Eponymy, according to which no scientific discovery is named for its original discoverer. The Marshallian cross diagram bears Marshall's name because he gave it its most complete, systematic and persuasive statement, not because he was the first to invent it. His version was definitive, not pathbreaking. For this he received, and deserved, credit.
5. Later economists and textbook writers could have obtained their demand-and-supply analysis from Marshall's predecessors as well as from his *Principles of Economics*. Had they done so, today's microeconomics textbooks would be little changed. Given the existence of a well-formulated geometry of supply and demand before Marshall, it follows that his contribution was a sufficient but hardly a necessary condition for the diagram's subsequent dissemination. Had he never published, later economists probably would have discovered the work of his predecessors or invented the diagram themselves.

REFERENCES

Brownlie, A.D. and Lloyd Prichard, M.F. 1963. Professor Fleeming Jenkin, 1833–1885, pioneer in engineering and political economy. *Oxford Economic Papers*, NS 15: 204–16.

Cournot, A.A. 1838. *Researches into the Mathematical Principles of the Theory of Wealth*. Trans. N.T. Bacon, New York: Macmillan, 1929; reprinted edn, New York: Augustus Kelley. 1971.

Edgeworth, F.Y. 1894. The pure theory of international values. *Economic Journal*, 4; reprinted in his *Papers Relating to Political Economy*, Vol. 2, London: Macmillan, 1925, p. 53.

Ekelund, R.B., Jr. and Hebert, R.F. 1999. *Secret Origins of Modern Microeconomics: Dupuit and the Engineers*. Chicago, IL: University of Chicago Press.

Hennings, K. 1979. *Karl Heinrich Rau and the Graphic Representation of Supply and Demand*. Diskussionspapier Serie C, No. 35. Hannover: Fachbereich Wirtschaftswissenschaften, Universität Hannover.

Hennings, K. 1980. The transition from classical to neoclassical economic theory: Hans von Mangoldt. *Kyklos*, 33: 658–81.
Humphrey, T.M. 1992. Marshallian cross diagrams and their uses before Alfred Marshall: the origins of supply and demand geometry. *Federal Reserve Bank of Richmond Economic Review*, 78 (2): 3–23.
Niehans, J. 1990. *A History of Economic Theory*. Baltimore, MD: The Johns Hopkins University Press.

2. The stability of equilibrium

Mark Blaug

By stability, economists basically mean the question of whether the relevant variables in some economic model converge to an equilibrium value over time. Much of economic theory depends on the comparative statics of equilibrium positions and comparing equilibria makes sense only if the underlying system is stable. Consider, for example, an elementary demand and supply model. How are we to explain the change in the price of strawberries that occurs every winter when the temperature plummets? The answer, based on the familiar cross diagram of Figure 2.1, is that the price will increase because the cold weather decreases the quantity supplied of strawberries (shifts the supply curve to the left).

This comparative statics explanation depends on the stability of the underlying equilibrium. For instance, consider the case depicted in Figure 2.3. In this case, the equilibrium price is p^* but the market is unstable: for any price above p^*, there is positive excess demand or a shortage, and thus competition on the demand side will bid the price up, away from p^*1. Similarly, for prices below p^*, competition on the supply side will cause the price to fall, again moving away from p^*. For a market like the one shown in Figure 2.3, a reduction in supply will cause the price to fall, not rise, and thus the lower equilibrium price will never be reached after the change in supply. If the supply is reduced in such a market, there will be excess demand at the old equilibrium price p^* and so the price will rise, moving continuously away from p^*. For such an unstable market, comparative statics is an inappropriate mode of analysis, even though there is a unique equilibrium both before and after the change.

Since we are concerned with stability, we want to find out whether the price will converge to p^* from any initial price. The economic argument for convergence is that competitive forces will move the price towards its equilibrium value. Positive excess demand or a shortage will cause the price to rise, while excess supply or a surplus will cause the price to fall. For the case depicted in Figure 2.4, such competitive forces will cause the price to converge to p^* as indicated by the arrows along the price axis.

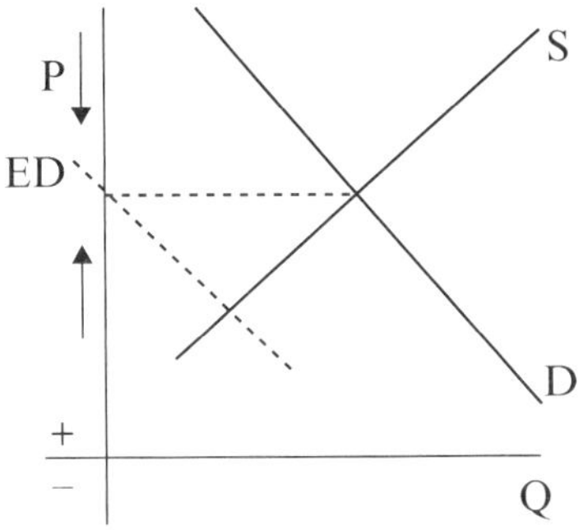

Figure 2.1 *Walras*

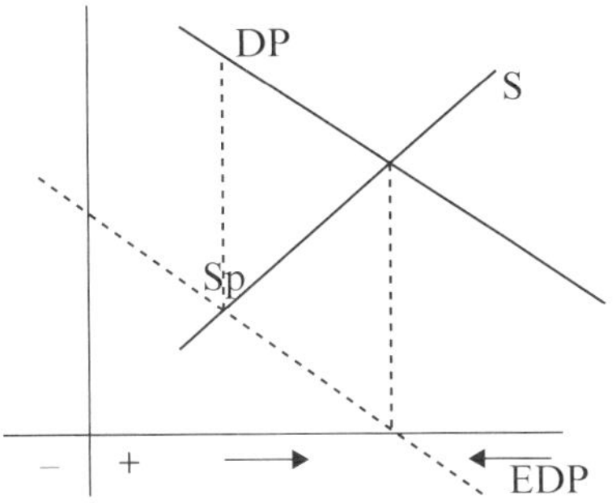

Figure 2.2 *Marshall*

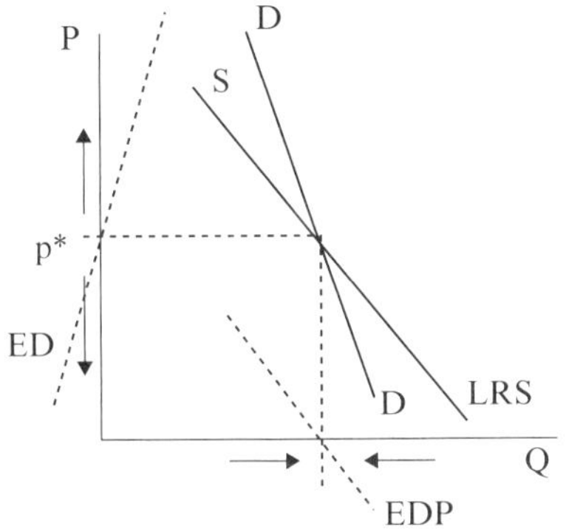

Figure 2.3 *Marshall stable*
Walras unstable

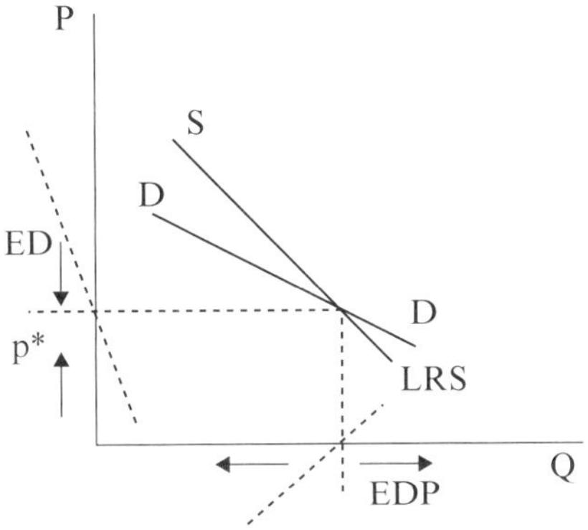

Figure 2.4 *Marshall unstable*
Walras stable

When the price converges to the equilibrium price from every disequilibrium position as in Figure 2.4, we say the equilibrium is stable. But this is not guaranteed under any and all circumstances. Figures 2.3 and 2.4 tell us that the stability of the market is related to the shapes of the supply and demand functions. In Figure 2.3, the adjustment mechanism is unstable: prices will move away from equilibrium for any initial p not equal to p^* as indicated by the arrows along the price axis.

A close examination of Figures 2.3 and 2.4 suggests that the equilibrium is stable whenever the demand curve is less steeply inclined than the supply curve, which is to say that the excess demand function is negatively inclined. If this condition holds, positive excess demand will force prices upward towards p^*, and negative excess demand will force prices downward towards p^*.

All this is about stability of equilibrium in a single market and even so, we have glossed over the possibility that such a market does not necessarily adjust out of equilibrium by altering prices but perhaps by altering quantities. This was in fact the subject of a dispute between Walras and Marshall. The now standard Walrasian approach, which we presented above, treats demand and supply curves as end points of horizontal lines corresponding to the quantity demanded or supplied at a given price. But Marshall typically viewed the schedules as end points of a set of vertical lines, each corresponding to the price at which a given quantity is produced or consumed. Marshall should have called his schedules 'bid curves' and 'sales curves', not demand and supply curves, since they depict the highest price an individual is willing to pay or the lowest price a supplier is willing to accept for a certain amount of a commodity. On Walras's criterion, an equilibrium price is stable, as we have seen, if the excess demand (*ED*) curve is negatively inclined as in Figure 2.4 and unstable if *ED* is positively inclined as in Figure 2.3; on Marshall's criterion, an equilibrium quantity is stable if the excess demand price (*EDP*) curve is negatively inclined as in Figure 2.3 and it is unstable if *EDP* is positively inclined as in Figure 2.4. To dramatize this contrast, we draw the *ED* function in the negative quadrant of the price-quantity axis to the left of the price axis and likewise we draw the *EDP* function below the quantity axis.

But so what? Surely, in any normal market with negatively inclined demand curves and positively inclined supply curves, we shall get the same price-quantity answers on either criterion? Indeed, we shall, but it is perfectly possible to encounter markets in which the two criteria lead to opposite results, that is, stability in the sense of Walras but instability in the sense of Marshall, and the converse, and hence the labels attached to Figures 2.3 and 2.4.

Both Walras and Marshall recognized that there are two possible types of disequilibrium adjustment in a competitive market and that they may contradict each other, but each illustrated his own adjustment process diagrammatically and left the other to a verbal description. Marshall had in mind the case of a long-run forward-falling supply curve exhibiting external economies, and that can produce either of the two diagrams in Figures 2.3 and 2.4; in any case, in the context of the long-run theory of production, it seems perfectly reasonable to think of sellers adjusting output in response to a change in demand. Walras, on the other hand, was thinking of a backward-rising supply curve (really an 'offer curve') in a market period when stocks of goods are given, and that too can produce either of the two diagrams; again, in this context, it is perfectly reasonable to assume that buyers adjust prices in response to changes in demand.

Neither Walras nor Marshall recognized why their approaches led to directly opposite results and neither realized that the question whether buyers and sellers in disequilibrium adjust output or adjust prices cannot be decided by a priori reasoning. In the short run, when output can be varied from existing plant and equipment, the output-adjusting model is just as plausible as the price-adjuster model, even though the latter is generally the only one mentioned in textbooks. Only empirical investigation can reveal just how buyers and sellers actually behave when the price departs from its equilibrium value.

Having said that, we must point out that the argument does not in any way depend on the somewhat perverse case of negatively sloped long-run or backward-bending short-run supply curves. There is absolutely nothing to exclude quantity-adjusting competitive behavior in markets with normal demand and supply functions, such that prices never converge on equilibrium or at any rate too slowly to be taken into account by buyers and sellers; as Hicks used to say, it is simply the case that there are 'fixprice' markets and there are 'flexprice' markets, the former typified by labor markets and goods markets for specialized producer goods and the latter by most commodity and financial markets.

There is of course no reason why the two adjustment processes cannot take place simultaneously as expressed by simultaneous differential equations, and several authors have written down models that involve such simultaneous adjustments. But there is no escaping the point that the two types of reactions involve different behavioral responses and these cannot be deduced from abstract principles of rational conduct.

Even so, we are still not done with the question of stability. Everything we have said so far deals with comparative statics and in effect says that any market with what engineers call 'negative feedback' is stable because it is automatically self-adjusting. But to really know if a market is stable we need to know the market's dynamic adjustment properties and we cannot know these without empirical work specifying a lag structure that governs the adjustment process. That 'negative feedback' is a necessary but not a sufficient condition for stability is known to every engineer who has designed an automatic control system for such things as steering a ship or regulating heating: correction of error is necessary but such things as long response lags or too rapid corrections can destabilize the system. M. Ezekiel was one of the first to point this problem out to economists with his famous cobweb model of the corn hog cycle (1938).

REFERENCES

De Vroey, M. 2006. 'Marshall versus Walras', *The Elgar Companion to Marshall*, eds. T. Raffaeli, M. Becattinini and M. Dardi. Cheltenham: Edward Elgar: 237–48.

Ezekiel, M. 1938. The Cobweb Theorem, *Quarterly Journal of Economics*, 53, 255–80.

Leijonhufvud, A. 2006. 'Market Adjustment Processes', *The Elgar Companion to Marshall*, eds. T. Raffaeli, M. Becattinini and M. Dardi. Cheltenham: Edward Elgar: 226–36.

Marshall, A. 1920. *Principles of Economics: An Introductory Volume*, 8th edition, London: Macmillan.

Takayama, A. 1985. *Mathematical Economics*, 2nd ed. Cambridge: Cambridge University Press, Chapter 3: 295–302, 313–20, 331–39.

Walras, L. 1956. *Elements of Pure Economics*, translated by W. Jaffe. Homewood, IL: Richard D. Irwin, Translator Notes: 107–14, 502–5.

Williams, P.L. 1987. *The Emergence of the Theory of the Firm*. London: Macmillan.

3. Indifference curves and isoquants

Mark Blaug and Peter Lloyd

1. INDIFFERENCE CURVES

Indifference curves and their use for the analysis of consumer behaviour were invented by Francis Ysidro Edgeworth in his *Mathematical Psychics*, published in 1881. After Edgeworth, Pareto in his *Manual of Political Economy* (1927/1972) made use of indifference curves to illuminate utility theory and preference relations between commodity bundles, without however acknowledging Edgeworth. Despite their use by Johnson (1913) and Slutsky (1915), indifference curves did not catch on until Bowley's *Mathematical Groundwork* (1924) popularized them.

The indifference curve is a graph in the goods space that shows different combinations of quantities of two goods between which the consumer is indifferent, that is, the consumer would not prefer one combination over another. A set of indifference curves is called an indifference map, that is, a representation of preference patterns of individual consumers. This is the basis of the economic theory of consumer demand. Indifference curves are also used widely in general equilibrium theory, as in the concept of Pareto efficiency (see Chapter 31, 34 and 36, on the Edgeworth Box diagram, the utility possibility frontier and Pareto efficiency). Fisher (1907) was the first to combine indifference curves and a production transformation curve to illustrate an individual's optimum investment decision (see Chapter 55, on intertemporal utility maximization – the Fisher diagram).

Indifference curves are typically defined only in the positive quadrant of commodity space. The preferences of the consumer or household are assumed to depend only on its own consumption of the two goods. Each indifference curve is commonly assumed to have certain basic properties: it is negatively sloped, strictly convex and continuous. The indifference map is usually assumed to be everywhere dense (that is, through every point in the space there passes an indifference curve), and no two indifference curves intersect. Indifference curves may or may not intersect the axes or they may approach one or both axes asymptotically. Three indifference curves from an indifference map with these properties are depicted in Figure 3.1.

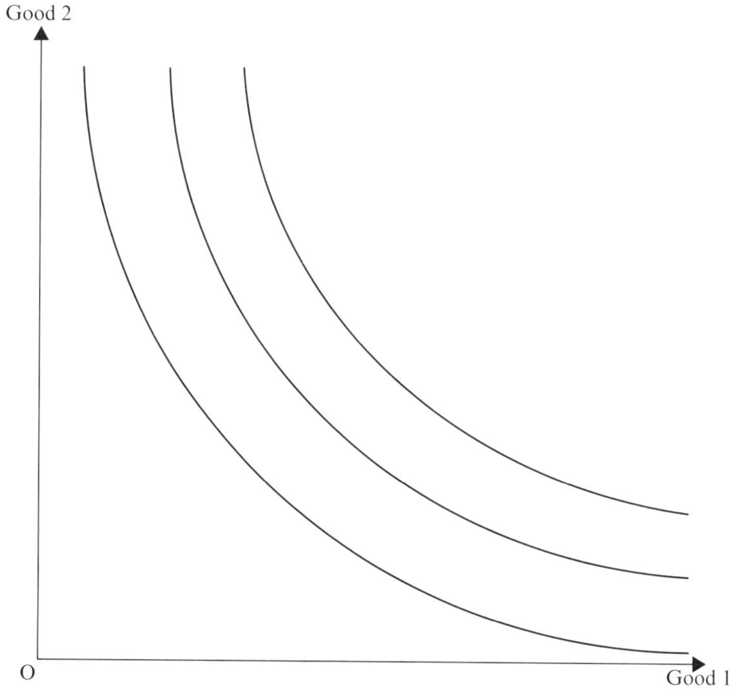

Figure 3.1 An indifference map

The slope of an indifference curve (in absolute value), which is called the marginal rate of substitution (MRS), shows the rate at which the consumer is willing to give up one good in exchange for more of the other good. For most goods, the MRS is not constant, so their indifference curves are curved and convex to the origin. This is called the Principle of the Diminishing Marginal Rate of Substitution. As a limiting case, if two goods are perfect substitutes, the indifference curves will have constant slope and the MRS will likewise be constant. At the other limit, if two goods are perfect complements, the indifference curves will be L-shaped. In fact, these two are limit cases of the constant elasticity (CES) utility function (see Chapter 4, on the elasticity of substitution in production and utility theory).

Graphical analysis of consumer choice proceeds by combining the indifference map with the constraint of the household's fixed budget or 'income'. This constraint is shown graphically by a budget line. Ordinary demand curves are derived by varying the household's income and the prices of the two goods. When the price of one good changes, the change in the household demand for a good can be decomposed graphically into an income and a substitution effect (see Chapter 5).

Modern textbooks usually begin with the utility function as the representation of the household's preferences. For two goods and one household, the utility function is $U = f(x_1, x_2)$ where x_i is the quantity demanded of good $i = 1, 2$. The indifference curves are now the level surfaces of this function, each defined for a given level of utility: $f(x_1, x_2) = u$. It is usually assumed that the function is continuous and strictly quasi-concave. Hence the indifference map is everywhere dense and the indifference curves are strictly convex. At any point on an indifference curve, assuming U is differentiable,

$$dU = \partial U/\partial x_1 dx_1 + \partial U/\partial x_2 dx_2 = 0$$

Hence, the marginal rate of substitution is

$$dx_2/dx_1 = -(\partial U/\partial x_2)/(\partial U/\partial x_1)$$

that is, the negative of the ratio of marginal utilities. The consumer maximizes utility subject to the budget constraint

$$p_1 x_1 + p_2 x_2 = const.$$

where p_1 and p_2 are the prices of goods 1 and 2. Under the usual assumptions, utility maximization yields well-defined ordinary demand functions.

A utility function $f(x_1, x_2)$ is an ordinal function, that is, its only purpose is to order two or more bundles of the goods. One may take an increasing transformation of the utility function without changing any consumer behaviour. All such a transformation does is to change the utility numbers attached to each indifference curve. The indifference map itself is completely unchanged and in particular the marginal rate of substitution at any point in goods space is unchanged. This illuminates the meaning of 'utility'.

The utility function approach has several additional advantages. The theory can be extended immediately to consumer choice over more than two goods. Restricting the analysis to two goods, as one must do graphically, is a severe limitation. More generally, n is any fixed number of goods and the utility function is $U = f(x_1, \ldots, x_n)$. It is usually assumed that the n-dimensional function has the same properties as we give it in the case of n=2. Another advantage is the use of duality relations. In consumer theory, duality theory states that, under certain regularity conditions, the (direct) utility function and the expenditure function are duals, that is, each is an equally good representation of the consumer's preferences. Alternatively one may regard the direct utility function and another function, such as the indirect utility function, as duals. Duality theory is a very expeditious way of deriving properties of demand functions and other related functions; for example the Slutsky decomposition of a change in demand into the income and substitution effects.

After the articulation of utility maximization theory, there was one development to the way economists think of indifference maps. This was the restatement of preference relations in terms of preference orderings, as in Debreu (1950). Here the primitive objects over which the consumer has a preference relation are a pair of bundles of goods and axioms are stated for the preference ordering over all possible pairs of bundles of goods. Indifference between two bundles means that one bundle, say x^1, is not preferred to another bundle, say x^2, and x^2 is not preferred to x^1. From a complete preference ordering one obtains the utility function of the consumer and from this in turn one derives the indifference map.

2. ISOQUANTS

In the theory of production and producer behaviour, isoquants play a role that parallels that of indifference curves in consumer theory, but there are some key differences. Historically, the production function – which is the analogue of the utility function in production theory – was developed first and the isoquant was presented later as the level surface of a production function. The concept of the production function was clearly articulated by the German economist von Thünen before 1850 and developed further by neoclassical economists in the late 19th century. In early production theory, there are invariably one output and two inputs. For example, $Y = g(K, L)$ where Y is the output and K and L are the level of the inputs of capital and labour. An isoquant is given by the equation $g(K, L) = y$.

The concept of the isoquant as a level surface was surprisingly slow to emerge. The first appearance of isoquants seems to be in Bowley (1924) and in Lerner (1933)[1] and Tarshis (1934), where they are unnamed or called fixed product curves or isoquants. Frisch used isoquants and coined the term in 1926 but his work was written in Norwegian and was not known to the English-speaking world until it was translated 40 years later (Frisch, 1965). Once introduced, however, the isoquant became standard very quickly, for example, Allen (1938) (where it is called the constant product curve) and Carlson (1939) (where it is called the isoquant).

Isoquants illustrate the trade-off between two inputs in producing a certain output of some good. An isoquant shows that a producer (or firm) has the ability to substitute between the two inputs in order to produce any level of output. The isoquant shows all combinations of the two inputs that yield the same output. Along the isoquant, the proportions of the inputs vary.

An isoquant map is usually given all of the properties that were listed above for an indifference map. Consequently Figure 3.1 provides an illustration of a typical graph of isoquants. One merely reinterprets the quantities on the axes as the quantities of the two inputs, say labour and capital, and the quantity of the level surface as a particular level of output. To a greater extent than in utility theory, it is common to impose other restrictions on the production function and isoquants. In particular, the restriction of homogeneity of the first degree, or constant returns to scale, is frequently imposed. As another example, it is common to impose the restrictions that the marginal products of both inputs are positive[2] and diminish as the output increases. Such restrictions of course affect the shape of the isoquant map. The restriction of positive marginal products ensures that the isoquants are everywhere negatively sloped. The restriction of homogeneity implies that the isoquant map is a radial blow up of any one isoquant (see Chapter 7, on homogeneous and homothetic production and utility functions).

If two inputs are perfect substitutes, the resulting isoquant map is a set of parallel lines. If there is zero substitutability between them, the isoquant map takes a set of L-shaped curves. Again these cases turn out to be limit cases of the CES production function (see Chapter 4, on the elasticity of substitution in production and utility theory).

However, unlike the utility function, the production function is a cardinal function. Consequently, the isoquants, which are the level surfaces, cannot be subject to an increasing transformation. Given a technology, any combination of inputs yields a particular output.

As in utility theory, one can consider the problem of maximizing output for a given expenditure on inputs. However, in production theory, it is more interesting and usual to consider the problem of minimizing the cost of producing a chosen level of output, given input prices. The solution to this problem gives us the cost function: this is $C(w, r, Y)$ where w and r are the prices of the two inputs.

The later history of the production function follows quite closely that of the utility function. Production processes were generalized to processes with more than two inputs. Duality theory was used to show that, under certain regularity conditions, the cost function is the dual of the production function. Set theory and axioms can be used as the primitive concepts of production processes.

These developments that occurred after the early statements of consumer theory in terms of indifference curves and producer theory in terms of isoquants give economists a deeper understanding of consumer and producer theory. But they do not in any way change the geometry of indifference maps and utility maximization or the geometry of isoquants and cost minimization. The graphs of indifference curves and isoquants and budget lines continue to be the way we approach the theory of demand and supply. They remain a fundamental expository tool of economics.

NOTES

1. Although this article was not published until 1952, it is accepted as having been presented to a seminar at the London School of Economics in December 1933 by Lerner, who was a part-time student who had barely completed a first degree. In the present context, it is important as being the second article in which Lerner presents isoquants. In this case he refers to them specifically as 'isoquants'.

   In the more general context of the development of figures in the history of economic thought, this article is truly remarkable as it presents isoquants for the family of functions which are homogeneous of degree 1, and it presents the first diagram of the production box and, finally, introduces the extension of the isoquant to show the general equilibrium of factor prices with two goods, both using the same two factors in fixed supply, that has become know as the Lerner Diagram (see Chapter 41).
2. Many of the early expositions of production functions had isoquant maps with regions where the isoquants had a positive slope due to the negative marginal product of one input; see, for example, Cassels (1936) and Allen (1938, chapter 11.8). These were called the 'uneconomic' regions. The graph of the marginal product function with a rising and a falling section is usually credited to Frank Knight's *Risk, Uncertainty and Profit*, but it goes back further; see Marshall (1920), Figure 14.

REFERENCES

Allen, R.G.D. (1938), *Mathematical Analysis for Economists*, New York: St Martins Press.
Bowley, A.L. (1924), *The Mathematical Groundwork of Economics: An Introductory Treatise*, Oxford: Clarendon Press.
Carlson, S. (1939), *A Study on the Pure Theory of Production*, Reprint, New York: Augustus M. Kelley.
Cassels, J.M. (1936), 'On the Law of Variable Proportions', in *Explorations in Economics: Notes and Essays Contributed in Honor of F. W. Taussig*, New York and London: McGraw-Hill.
Debreu, G. (1950), *Theory of Value: An Axiomatic Analysis of Economic Equilibrium*, New Haven, CT, and London: Yale University Press.
Edgeworth, F.Y. (1881), *Mathematical Psychics: An Essay on the Application of Mathematics to the Moral Sciences*, London: C. Kegan Paul.
Fisher, I. (1907), *The Rate of Interest*, New York: Macmillan.

Frisch, R. (1965), *Theory of Production*, translated from the ninth edition by R.L. Chrisophersen, Chicago: Rand McNally & Company.
Johnson, W.E. (1913), 'The Pure Theory of Utility Curves', *Economic Journal*, 23, 483–513.
Knight, F. (1921), *Risk, Uncertainty and Profit*, Boston MA: Houghton Mifflin.
Lerner, A.P. (1933), 'The Diagrammatical Representation of Elasticity of Substitution', *Review of Economic Studies*, 1, 147–8.
Marshall, Alfred (1920), *Principles of Economics*, eighth edition, London: Macmillan and Co. Ltd.
Pareto, V. (1927/1972). *Manual of Political Economy*, translated from the French edition of 1927 by A.S. Schwier, London: Macmillan Press.
Slutsky, E. (1915), 'On the Theory of the Budget of the Consumer', *Giornale degli Economisti*, 51, 1–26. English translation in G. Stigler and K. Boulding (eds), *Readings in Price Theory*, Homewood, IL: Irwin.
Tarshis, L. (1934), 'Notes on the Elasticity of Substitution', *Review of Economic Studies*, 1, 146–7.

4. The elasticity of substitution

Robert Dixon

The elasticity of substitution was discovered independently of each other by John Hicks (1932) and Joan Robinson (1933). Both authors were discussing the ease with which one factor of production may be substituted for another.

Robinson presented two definitions. One was expressed in terms of input prices:

> The degree to which substitution of factors is possible can best be measured by considering the change in the ratio of the factors which occurs when the relative prices alter . . . It appears appropriate to call the proportionate change in the ratio of the quantities of factors employed divided by the proportionate change in the ratio of their prices to which it is due, the elasticity of substitution (1933, p. 256).

The second definition was expressed in terms of marginal products and was described as being 'equivalent but more fundamental' than the first. This definition is 'the proportionate change in the ratio of the amounts of the factors divided by the proportionate change in the ratio of their marginal physical productivities' (p. 330 n2).

Figure 4.1 illustrates the relationship between relative factor prices and relative factor use (this is the basis for Robinson's first definition). The convex line I–I is an isoquant showing the rate at which K and L may be substituted for each other holding output constant. The lines C^1–C^1 and C^2–C^2 are iso-cost or budget lines showing combinations of K and L that can be purchased with a fixed budget, given the prices of the two factors. The slope of the budget line reflects relative factor prices. The relative price of labour is higher in the case of line C^2–C^2 than for C^1–C^1. Given relative factor prices represented by C^1–C^1, profits will be maximised if the producer operates at point A, where the line C^1–C^1 is tangential to the isoquant. The capital–labour ratio which would be observed for this set of relative factor prices is given by the slope of the line commencing at the origin and passing through point A. If the relative price of labour were to be higher, such that the relevant budget line is that given by C^2–C^2, profits will be maximised if the producer operates at point B, where the

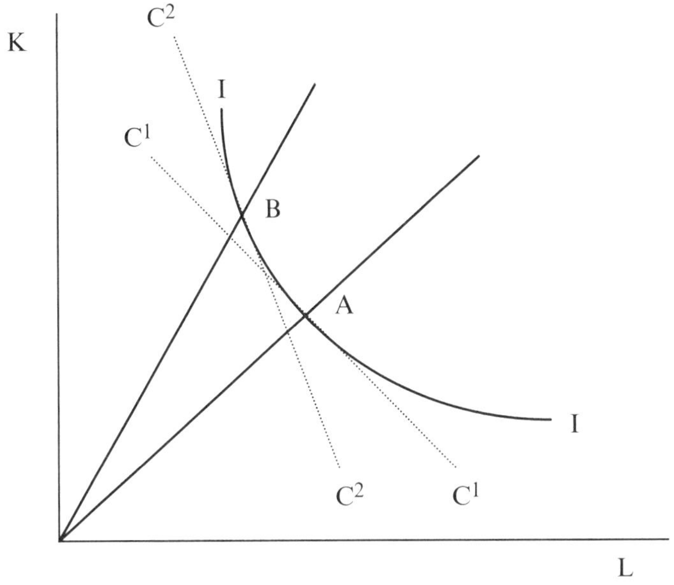

Figure 4.1 The tangency points for a given isoquant and two budget lines

line C^2–C^2 is tangential to the isoquant. The capital–labour ratio which would be observed for this set of relative factor prices is given by the slope of the line commencing at the origin and passing through point B. Clearly the difference in relative factor prices is associated with a difference in the capital–labour ratio. For a given difference in relative factor prices, it is the curvature of the isoquant which determines the difference in the capital–labour ratio which would result. The flatter the isoquant, the greater will be the difference in the capital–labour ratio.

Hicks described the elasticity of substitution as:

> a measure of the ease with which the varying factor can be substituted for others. If the same quantity of the factor is required to give a unit of the product, in any circumstances whatever, then its elasticity of substitution is zero. If all the factors employed are for practical purposes identical, so that the varying factor can be substituted for any co-operating factor without any trouble at all, then the elasticity of substitution is infinite (1932, p. 117).

In an appendix to the book, he presented a mathematical exposition for the case of two factors of production (1932, p. 245). Letting $x = f(a, b)$ be a production function where a and b are the amounts of the factors employed and assuming constant returns to scale, the elasticity of substitution may then be defined as

$$\sigma = [(\partial x/\partial a)(\partial x/\partial b)]/[x(\partial^2 x/(\partial a\partial b))].$$

This definition holds only for production functions which are homogeneous of degree one. Hicks was later to write that Robinson's 'definition is superior to mine, for . . . it is capable of being expressed verbally in terms of familiar notions, which mine, unfortunately, does not appear to be' (Hicks, 1933, p. 78).

A clear mathematical exposition of the concept as a measure of the curvature of an isoquant and its relationship to the marginal rate of substitution of one factor for another was provided by Allen (1938, p. 341) – see also Hicks (1963, pp. 373–384) and Samuelson (1968). Key features were present from the very beginning: the elasticity is independent of the units in which inputs and output are measured, it is positive and varies from zero to infinity (for the two factor case). It is also symmetrical with respect to the two factors, this being consistent with a production function in which 'every element that is technologically variable can be changed at will, without any loss of time, and without any expense' (Schumpeter, 1954, p. 1031).

The publication of the books by Hicks and Robinson (and especially the former) led immediately to a flurry of notes and articles in the *Review of Economic Studies* and in the *Economic Journal*. Inter alia, these contributions explored the relationship between the Hicks and Robinson definitions and also the relationship between the concept of diminishing returns and the elasticity of substitution. The contributions by Kahn and Lerner were pivotal. Kahn (1933) demonstrated that Hicks's and Robinson's definitions were identical (at least in the case of two inputs and with perfect competition in all markets) while Lerner (1933, 1934) showed that the elasticity of substitution was a measure of the curvature of an isoquant or 'equal product curve'.

Both articles played an important role in influencing the development of Hicks's ideas. In Hicks (1936), referring to Lerner's (1933) paper, he writes:

> Under perfect competition and constant returns to scale each factor is thus paid according to its marginal product. But the marginal products depend only upon the ratios in which the factors are used. The relative values of the factors therefore depend only upon the ratios in which the factors are used. . . . In the case where there are only two factors we can draw a curve,[1] measuring along one axis the ratio of the quantities of the factors used (A/B), along the other the ratio of the values per unit of the factors (p_a/p_b). . . . The elasticity of this curve we call the *elasticity of substitution* (1936, p. 2f)

and he presents a diagram (Figure 4.2) based on one constructed by Lerner (1933, p. 71):

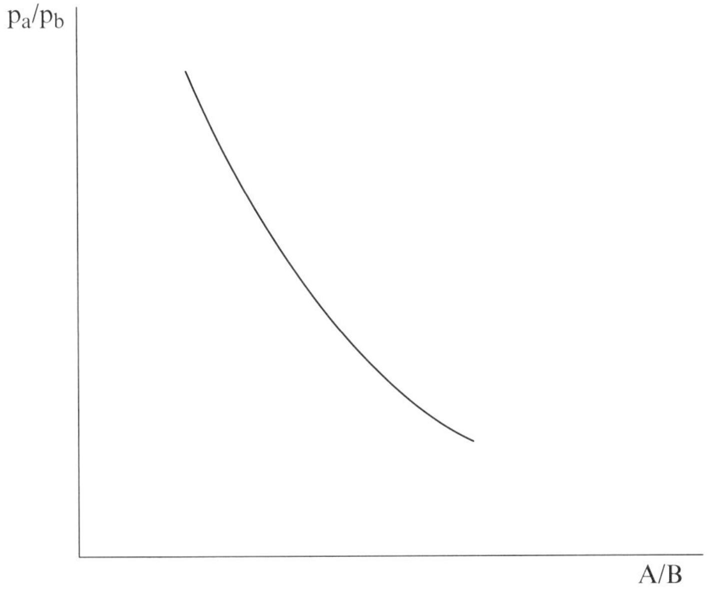

Source: Hicks (1936, p. 3)

Figure 4.2 Lerner-Hicks diagram relating relative factor prices to relative factor intensities

Hicks points out that:

> If the elasticity of substitution is greater than unity, an increase in the employment of A relative to that of B will increase the area under the curve. But this area measures $p_a/p_b \times A/B = p_aA/p_bB$ which is the ratio in which the total product is divided between the factors. A's relative share will thus be increased by a relative increase in its employment if the elasticity of substitution is greater than unity (1936, p. 3).

A similar diagram to this - sometimes with factor price ratios and factor intensities both expressed in logarithms - is common in the literature on international trade (see for example Samuelson, 1948, and Arrow et al., 1961) and on technological change (see for example Brown, 1966).

The elasticity of substitution is a point elasticity; it holds at one point on one isoquant. In general, it can therefore vary along and across isoquants. The restriction of constant returns to scale is important in this context because it imposes the restriction that the elasticity of substitution is constant along a ray from the origin.

The elasticity of substitution may also be constant along an isoquant. Once the concept of an elasticity of substitution in production had been enunciated by Hicks and Robinson, it was natural to consider its relationship to the Cobb-Douglas production function. Machlup (1935, p. 205) pointed out in relation to 'Professor Douglas' production function' that if the relative share of labour was constant then this 'implies an elasticity of substitution of unity'. Allen, in his magisterial 1938 book, showed that 'in the particular case where the production function is $x = Aa^{\alpha}b^{1-\alpha}$, . . . $\sigma = 1$ at all points' (1938, p. 343).

It was then only a matter of time before production functions were developed which allowed the elasticity of substitution to be constant everywhere in the input space but to depart from unity. An important development was the invention of the Constant Elasticity of Substitution (CES) production function, which would appear to have been discovered and formalised independently by Arrow et al.(1961), Brown and De Cani (1963a and b) and Kendrick and Sato (1963). Assuming constant returns to scale, the CES function takes the form

$$Y_t = \gamma_t[\delta K_t^{-\rho} + (1 - \delta)L_t^{-\rho}]^{(-1/\rho)}$$

where γ is the 'efficiency' parameter ($\gamma > 0$), δ is the 'distribution' or 'factor-intensity' parameter ($0 < \delta < 1$) and ρ is the substitution parameter ($\rho \geq -1$). It is this last parameter which determines the magnitude of the elasticity of substitution σ, which is equal to $1/(1 + \rho)$. If $\rho \rightarrow 0$, the CES function has an elasticity of substitution of unity, the Cobb-Douglas case. In general, in a CES function the (constant) elasticity of substitution may take any value between zero and infinity. At the limits, as $\rho \rightarrow +\infty$, the elasticity of substitution is zero and the isoquants are L-shaped, and as $\rho = 1$ the elasticity of substitution is infinite and the isoquants are linear.

Lerner's demonstration that the elasticity of substitution could be regarded as a measure of the curvature of an isoquant led Hicks to observe that the concept could be applied in consumer theory to the curvature of an indifference curve. He went on to show how the decomposition of the price effect into an income and a substitution effect could be expressed in terms of familiar elasticity concepts. This gave rise to Hicks's 'fundamental formula', which, for the case of two goods, linked the (own) price elasticity of demand for good X to the income elasticity of demand for X, the elasticity of substitution and the proportion of income spent on good X. Hicks and Allen (1934a, p. 66f) describe it this way:

> with two commodities:
> Price-elasticity of demand for X

$= k_x \times$ income elasticity of demand for X
$+ (1 - k_x) \times$ elasticity of substitution between X and Y
(where k_x is the proportion of income spent upon X).

This decomposition was applied to the case of three goods in Hicks and Allen (1934b, pp. 199–202).

In 1936 Bergson (Burk), building on the ideas of Hicks and Allen, presented the first formulation of the Constant Elasticity of Substitution utility function. His derivation precedes the derivation in production theory but he did not recognise his function as a CES function. Instead, it is presented as the function which has the two properties of 'expenditure proportionality' (homotheticity) and additivity.

The CES function can be generalised to a space with n factors (or consumer goods). However, as noted by Fuss and McFadden (1978, p. 241) with regard to the production function, there is no unique natural generalisation of the two-factor version: it all depends on what is held constant. One generalisation is the 'direct' partial elasticity of substitution between any two of many inputs along an isoquant. This is a generalisation of the 'fundamental' form given by Joan Robinson. Another generalisation is the Allen-Uzawa elasticity of substitution (Allen, 1938, pp. 503–9). Uzawa (1962) transformed the determinantal expression given by Allen into a simple expression in terms of the unit cost function and its derivatives for the case of a linearly homogeneous function. This form is a generalisation of the algebraic form given by Hicks. There is a function in which the direct partial elasticities of substitution are held constant for all pairs of inputs (McFadden, 1963) and another in which the Allen-Uzawa elasticities of substitution are constant (and equal) (Uzawa, 1962). Yet another generalised function is the two-stage CES function put forward by Sato (1967). This is a CES function with arguments (inputs) that are themselves CES functions. It is widely used as a device to aggregate inputs into composite inputs, such as 'capital' and 'labour'. A production function which allows the elasticity of substitution to vary with the level of output and the level of inputs is the Transcendental Logarithmic (Translog) Production Function, introduced by Christensen, Jorgenson and Lau (1973). Kmenta's linear approximation to the CES (1967) can be seen as a special case of the Translog Production Function.

Parallel with these developments, we have seen the introduction of utility functions of the CES and other forms with their associated elasticities of substitution. We have also seen the concept of the elasticity of substitution applied in the context of choice between different varieties of a product (see Spence, 1976, and Dixit and Stiglitz, 1977, whose models have become central to the modern theories of monopolistic competition and economic growth), including the choice between products differentiated by place of origin (see Armington, 1969, whose model has become an important component of computable general equilibrium models of trade).

NOTE

1. At this point Hicks inserts a footnote which reads 'First suggested by Mr. Lerner (Review of Economic Studies, Vol. 1, p. 71)'.

REFERENCES

Allen, R. G. D. (1938), *Mathematical Analysis for Economists*, London: Macmillan.
Armington, P. S. (1969), 'A Theory of Demand for Products Distinguished by Place of Production', *IMF Staff Papers*, Vol. 16, No. 1, pp. 159–176.
Arrow, K., Chenery, H., Minhas, B. and Solow, R. (1961), 'Capital-Labor Substitution and Economic Efficiency', *Review of Economics and Statistics*, Vol. 43, No. 3 (Aug.), pp. 225–250.
Brown, M. (1966), *On the Theory and Measurement of Technological Change*, Cambridge: Cambridge University Press.
Brown, M. and J. de Cani (1963a), 'Technological Change and the Distribution of Income', *International Economic Review*, Vol. 4, No. 3 (Sep.), pp. 289–309.
Brown, M. and J. de Cani (1963b), 'A Measure of Technological Employment', *Review of Economics and Statistics*, Vol. 45, No. 4 (Nov.), pp. 386–394.
Burk (Bergson), A. (1936), 'Real Income, Expenditure Proportionality, and Frisch's "New Methods of Measuring Marginal Utility"', *Review of Economic Studies*, Vol. 4, No. 1 (Oct.), pp. 33–52.
Christensen, L., D. Jorgenson and L. Lau (1973), 'Transcendental Logarithmic Production Frontiers', *Review of Economics and Statistics*, Vol. 55, No. 1 (Feb.), pp. 28–45.
Dixit, A. K. and J. E. Stiglitz (1977), 'Monopolistic Competition and Optimum Product Diversity', *American Economic Review*, Vol. 67, No. 3 (June), pp. 297–308.
Fuss, M. and D. McFadden (eds) (1978), *Production Economics: A Dual Approach to Theory and Applications*, Amsterdam: North-Holland Publishing Company.
Hicks, J. R. (1932), *The Theory of Wages*, London: Macmillan.
Hicks, J. R. (1933), 'Notes on Elasticity of Substitution IV: A Note on Mr. Kahn's Paper', *Review of Economic Studies*, Vol. 1, No. 1 (Oct.), pp. 78–80.
Hicks, J. R. (1936), 'Distribution and Economic Progress: A Revised Version', *Review of Economic Studies*, Vol. 4, No. 1 (Oct.), pp. 1–12.
Hicks, J. R. (1963), *The Theory of Wages*, Second Edition, London: Macmillan.
Hicks, J. R. (1981), *Wealth and Welfare: Collected Essays on Economic Theory, Vol. 1*, Oxford: Blackwell.
Hicks, J. R. and R. G. D. Allen (1934a), 'A Reconsideration of the Theory of Value, Part I', *Economica*, New Series, Vol. 1, No. 1 (Feb.), pp. 52–76.

Hicks, J. R. and R. G. D. Allen (1934b), 'A Reconsideration of the Theory of Value, Part II: A Mathematical Theory of Individual Demand Functions', *Economica*, New Series, Vol. 1, No. 2 (May), pp. 196–219.

Kahn, R. F. (1933), 'Notes on Elasticity of Substitution III: The Elasticity of Substitution and the Relative Share of a Factor', *Review of Economic Studies*, Vol. 1, No. 1 (Oct.), pp. 72–78.

Kendrick, J. and R. Sato (1963), 'Factor Prices, Productivity, and Economic Growth', *American Economic Review*, Vol. 53, No. 5 (Dec.), pp. 974–1003.

Kmenta, J. (1967), 'On Estimation of the CES Production Function', *International Economic Review*, Vol. 8, No. 2 (June), pp. 180–189.

Lerner, A. P. (1933), 'Notes on Elasticity of Substitution: The Diagrammatical Representation', *Review of Economic Studies*, Vol. 1, No. 1 (Oct.), pp. 68–71.

Lerner, A. P. (1934), 'Notes on Elasticity of Substitution II', *Review of Economic Studies*, Vol. 1, No. 2 (Feb.), pp. 147–148.

Machlup, F. (1935), 'The Commonsense of the Elasticity of Substitution', *Review of Economic Studies*, Vol. 2, No. 3 (June), pp. 202–213.

McFadden, D. (1963), 'Constant Elasticity of Substitution Production Functions', *Review of Economic Studies*, Vol. 30, No. 2 (June), pp. 73–83.

Robinson, J. (1933), *The Economics of Imperfect Competition*, London: Macmillan.

Samuelson, P. (1948), 'International Trade and the Equalisation of Factor Prices', *Economic Journal*, Vol. 58, No. 230 (June), pp. 163–184.

Samuelson, P. (1968), 'Two Generalisations of the Elasticity of Substitution' in J. N. Wolfe (ed.), *Value, Capital and Growth: Papers in Honour of Sir John Hicks*, Edinburgh: Edinburgh University Press, pp. 467–480.

Sato, K. (1967), 'A Two-Level Constant-Elasticity-of-Substitution Production Function', *Review of Economic Studies*, Vol. 34, No. 2 (Apr.), pp. 201–218.

Schumpeter, J. A. (1954), *History of Economic Analysis*, London: George Allen and Unwin.

Spence, M. (1976), 'Product Selection, Fixed Costs, and Monopolistic Competition', *Review of Economic Studies*, Vol. 43, No. 2 (June), pp. 217–235.

Uzawa, H. (1962), 'Production Functions with Constant Elasticities of Substitution', *Review of Economic Studies*, Vol. 29, No. 4 (Oct.), pp. 291–299.

5. Substitution and income effects

Hans Haller

Changes in market conditions or taxes may affect a consumer's budget constraint. The consumer's response to a change of the budget constraint is of theoretical and practical relevance. But in general, it proves difficult if not impossible to determine how the consumer's demand is affected by a new budget situation. With n goods, a consumption bundle is represented by an n-dimensional vector of the form $x = (x_1, \ldots, x_n)$ and a price system assumes the form $p = (p_1, \ldots, p_n)$. Moreover, a number $m > 0$ stands for the consumer's nominal income or wealth. Attention will be confined to price–income pairs (p, m) that give rise to a unique bundle $x = f(p, m)$ demanded under the corresponding budget constraint. Then the comparative statics question of how the consumer responds to a change of the budget constraint can be formulated as follows: Suppose an original budget situation (A) given by the price–income pair (p,m) and demand $x^A = f(p, m)$ and a new budget situation (C) given by the price–income pair (p', m') and demand $x^C = f(p', m')$ What is the total effect $TE = x^C - x^A$?

The answer is easy if the numerical values of $x^A = f(p, m)$ and $x^C = f(p', m')$ are explicitly given and easily computed. A greater challenge occurs if the numerical values are unknown or hard to obtain. Then little can be said about the total effect TE without further restrictions on the individual's consumption choice problem. In the sequel, as in standard demand theory, it will be assumed that the consumer is utility or, more generally, preference maximizing under the budget constraint; that indifference curves are well behaved; and that utility functions and demand functions are sufficiently smooth whenever warranted by a derivation or illustration.

Slutsky (1915), translated as Slutsky 1952, and independently Hicks and Allen (1934) proposed to decompose the total effect into a substitution effect SE and an income effect IE. Both Slutsky (1915) and Mosak (1942) introduce a hypothetical budget situation (B) given by a price-income pair (p', m') that reflects an income-compensated price change. Let $x^B = f(p', m')$ be the demand at the hypothetical budget situation. Then the substitution effect is defined as $SE = x^B - x^A$ and the income effect is defined as $IE = x^C - x^B$. The decomposition $TE = SE + IE$ results. This single identity for consumption bundles can be rewritten as n identities $TE_i = SE_i + IE_i$, one for each good or component $i = 1, \ldots, n$.

From now on, the focus lies on the case $n = 2$ and the decomposition $TE_1 = SE_1 + IE_1$ for the first good. Both Slutsky (1915) and Mosak (1942) consider the special case of a change in the price of a single good and the effect of that change on the demand for that good. Without restriction, consider the case $p'_1 < p_1$, $p'_2 = p_2$, $m' = m$, that is, starting from the original budget situation (A), a fall of the price of the first good results in the new budget situation (C). If one wants to know how the demand for good 1 is affected by that change, the decomposition $TE_1 = SE_1 + IE_1$ may provide the answer. Under many circumstances, both SE_1 and IE_1 are positive for the change at hand, and, consequently, TE_1 is positive as well.

Slutsky (1915) and Mosak (1942) differ in the compensation that leads to the hypothetical income m^* in situation (B). Mosak suggests that after the price adjustment from p_1 to p'_1, the consumer should be compensated in such a way that the new optimum x^B lies on the old indifference curve, labeled I I in Figure 5.1. The particular compensation is nowadays referred to as Hicks compensation and the decomposition as Hicks decomposition. A figure similar to Figure 5.1 is already contained in Mosak (1942, Fig. 2).

Slutsky (1915) suggests that after the price adjustment from p_1 to p'_1, the

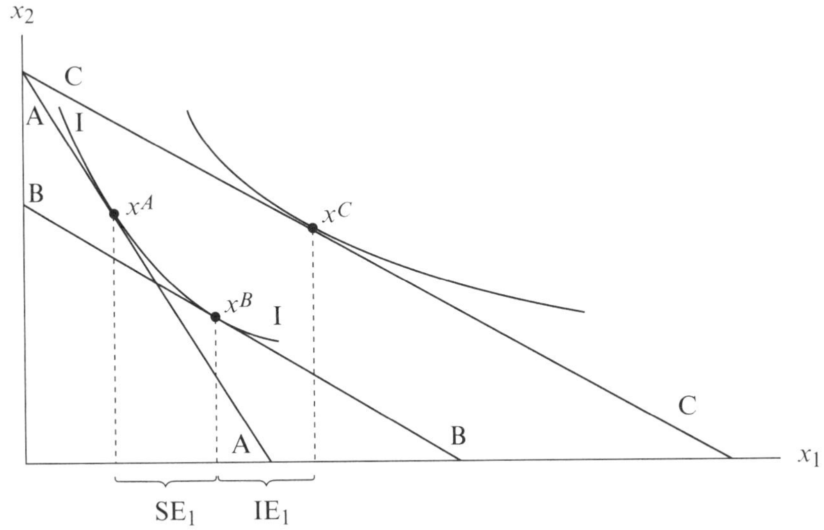

Figure 5.1 Hicks decomposition

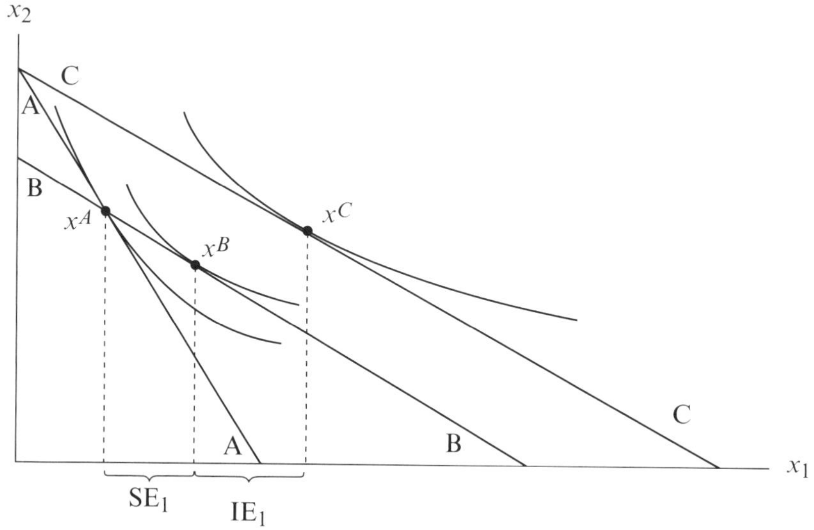

Figure 5.2 Slutsky decomposition

consumer should be compensated in such a way that the old optimum x^A remains affordable, that is, x^A lies on the hypothetical budget line labeled B B in Figure 5.2. The particular compensation is nowadays referred to as Slutsky compensation and the decomposition as Slutsky decomposition. Slutsky (1915) does not contain a figure depicting the Slutsky decomposition. To my knowledge, Schultz (1935) is the first publication with a figure similar to Figure 5.2 that illustrates the Slutsky decomposition. In Schultz (1935, Fig. 1), the price of the second good is falling, *ceteris paribus*.

With sufficiently smooth utility and demand functions, the infinitesimal counterpart and direct consequence of the Hicks decomposition is the Slutsky equation. It assumes the form

$$\frac{\partial f_1}{\partial p_1} = \frac{\partial h_1}{\partial p_1} - f_1 \cdot \frac{\partial f_1}{\partial m}$$

where f_1 is the (Marshallian) demand function for good 1 and h_1 is the Hicksian demand function for good 1, given the utility level at the status quo $x^A = f(p, m)$. In fact, equations of the form

$$\frac{\partial f_i}{\partial p_j} = \frac{\partial h_i}{\partial p_j} - f_j \cdot \frac{\partial f_i}{\partial m}$$

for arbitrary goods i and j had already been derived by Slutsky (1915). Modern textbook derivations of the Slutsky equation(s) – see for example Varian (1992, p. 120) or Mas-Colell, Whinston and Green (1995, p. 71) – follow Cook (1972) and use duality theory. Solving these equations for the Hicksian substitution terms $\partial h_i/\partial p_j$ yields the entries of the Slutsky matrix.

Slutsky himself did not work with the Hicks decomposition, but rather with the Slutsky decomposition. Nevertheless, he arrived at the Slutsky equation(s). As modern textbook authors, for instance Varian (1992) and Mas-Colell, Whinston, and Green (1995), point out, one could replace the Hicksian demand functions by Slutsky compensated demand functions and would obtain identical equations. Hence at the status quo x^A where the partial derivatives are taken, both types of compensated demand functions have the same gradients. Mosak (1942) provides a proof thereof which he attributes to A. Wald.

A different decomposition was pioneered by Hicks and Allen (1934), who consider an income effect followed by a substitution effect. They introduce a hypothetical budget situation (B) given by a price–income pair (p, m^*) such that $x^B = f(p, m^*)$, the demand at the hypothetical budget situation, lies on the same indifference curve as x^C. Then the income effect is $IE = x^B - x^A$ and the substitution effect is $SE = x^C - x^B$. A corresponding figure can be found in Hicks and Allen (1934, p. 66), Hicks (1939, Fig. 8), and Mosak (1942, Fig. 1). The decomposition à la Hicks and Allen gives rise to the Slutsky equation as well. But Hicks and Allen do not formulate the Slutsky equation in differential form, by way of partial derivatives. Instead, they find an equivalent identity in terms of elasticities. The income differential $EV = m^* - m$ in the Hicks-Allen decomposition is known as the equivalent variation, while the income differential $CV = m' - m^*$ in the Hicks decomposition is known as the compensating variation. Both serve as measures of consumer welfare change.

Prior to 1934, very few authors seem to have been aware of the existence of Slutsky's seminal paper and none comprehended its significance. The precedence and importance of Slutsky's (1915) contribution was recognized in the English language literature soon after the 1934 articles by Hicks and Allen. Schultz (1935) asserts: 'For an individual consumer, however, the interrelations of demand, income, and price are essentially at hand in the writings of Vilfredo Pareto, Eugen Slutsky, and J. R. Hicks and R. G. D. Allen; and some of these relations also hold for aggregate market phenomena.' He stresses the advances made by Slutsky beyond the achievements of Pareto. Allen (1936, p. 433) summarizes Slutsky's analysis and compares it with that of Hicks and Allen. He objects that Slutky's analysis is confined to the 'integrability case', that is the case where a utility representation of consumer preferences exists. To the interested reader, I highly recommend Chipman and Lenfant (2002) for an account of the rediscovery of Slutsky (1915) and the ensuing controversy. Hicks (1939, p. 19) acknowledges: 'The theory to be set out in this chapter and the two following is essentially Slutsky's'. He reports on the Hicks-Allen decomposition in the main text and elaborates on the Slutsky decomposition in the appendix, without any cross-reference or direct comparison of the two approaches.

The decomposition of the total effect of a change in budget parameters into a substitution effect and an income effect is not restricted to the case depicted in Figures 5.1 and 5.2: two goods, well-behaved indifference curves, the response of the demand for one of the goods to a change of its own price. First of all, similar figures can still be drawn, if indifference curves have kinks but no flat pieces, and conceivably, x^B lies on the boundary of the consumption set. This is obvious for the Slutsky decomposition. It becomes obvious for the Hicks decomposition from the observation that x^B is the solution of the cost minimization problem:

$$\text{Min } p \cdot x \text{ subject to } x \text{ at least as good as } x^A.$$

Secondly, the basic concepts carry over to more than two goods, whereas the illustration via diagrams is lost. Thirdly, the concepts also apply and prove useful when more than one of the budget parameters $p_1, \ldots, p_n; m$ changes. For instance, when one proceeds from partial equilibrium to general equilibrium, the consumer's income is price dependent: $m = p \cdot \omega$ where ω is the consumer's endowment bundle. Then typically, a price change implies a change in income as well. Finally, the concepts also apply if only income changes. But then the decomposition is trivial: $SE = 0$ and $TE = IE$.

REFERENCES

Allen, R.G.D. 1936. 'Professor Slutsky's Theory of Consumers' Choice'. *Review of Economic Studies*, 3, 120–129.

Chipman, J.S. and J.-S. Lenfant. 2002. 'Slutsky's 1915 Article: How it Came to be Found and Interpreted'. *History of Political Economy*, 34, 554–597.

Cook, P.J. 1972. 'A "One Line" Proof of the Slutsky Equation'. *American Economic Review*, 62, 139.

Hicks, J.R. 1939. *Value and Capital*. Oxford: Clarendon Press.

Hicks, J.R. and R.G.D. Allen. 1934. 'A Reconsideration of the Theory of Value'. Parts 1–2. *Economica*, N.S. 1, 52–76, 196–219.

Mas-Colell, A., M.D. Whinston and J.R. Green. 1995. *Microeconomic Theory*. New York: Oxford University Press.

Mosak, J.L. 1942. 'On the Interpretation of the Fundamental Equation of Value Theory'. In Lange, O., F. McIntyre and T.O. Yntema, eds. *Studies in Mathematical Economics and Econometrics: In Memory of Henry Schultz*. Chicago, IL: University of Chicago Press. 69–74.

Schultz, H. 1935. 'Interrelations of Demand, Price, and Income'. *Journal of Political Economy*, 43, 433–81.

Slutsky, E. 1915. 'Sulla teoria del bilancio del consumatore'. *Giornali degli Economisti e Rivista di Statistica*, series 3, 51, 1–26.

Slutsky, E. 1952. 'On the Theory of the Budget of the Consumer'. Translated by Olga Ragusa. In Stigler, G.J. and K.E. Boulding, eds. *Readings in Price Theory*. Homewood, IL: Irwin. 27–56. 1953 British Edition, London: George Allen and Unwin.

Varian, H.R. 1992. *Microeconomic Analysis*. 3rd ed. New York: W.W. Norton and Company.

6. Engel curves

Ross Williams

Engel curves are the diagrammatic representation of how expenditure on a commodity (or quantity consumed) varies with income or total expenditure. The name derives from the nineteenth century work of the German statistician Ernst Engel. Using survey data from working-class Belgian households, Engel (1857) observed a number of regularities between expenditure on different commodities and income or total expenditure. In particular he observed that while expenditure on food increased with total household expenditure it fell as a share of total expenditure. This empirical regulatory has been observed for households in many countries and over time at the national level and has become known as Engel's Law. The early estimates of Engel curves from budget studies are surveyed in Stigler (1954) and Houthakker (1957).

It is usual to use total expenditure rather than income as a measure of resources in estimating Engel curves, although total expenditure is often loosely referred to as 'income', paralleling the treatment used in standard consumer demand analysis. Total expenditure is more stable than income and can be interpreted as encompassing aspects of permanent income. As a practical matter, household budget studies frequently do not record income, or if they do, the estimates of income often suffer from significant measurement bias.

The dependent variable in an Engel curve can be expressed in either quantity or expenditure terms. If consumers all face the same set of prices, which is the usual assumption in cross-section studies, the two curves have identical shapes. In practice, the data usually relate to expenditures, so it is convenient to use this form. The equation to the Engel curve can thus be written in general terms as

$$v_i = f(y) \quad i = 1, 2, \ldots\ldots n \text{ goods} \qquad (6.1)$$

where v_i is expenditure on good i and y is 'income'. The budget share for commodity i is given by $w_i = v_i/y$. If the income elasticity of demand, η_i, is one, the budget share w_i is a constant and the Engel curve is a

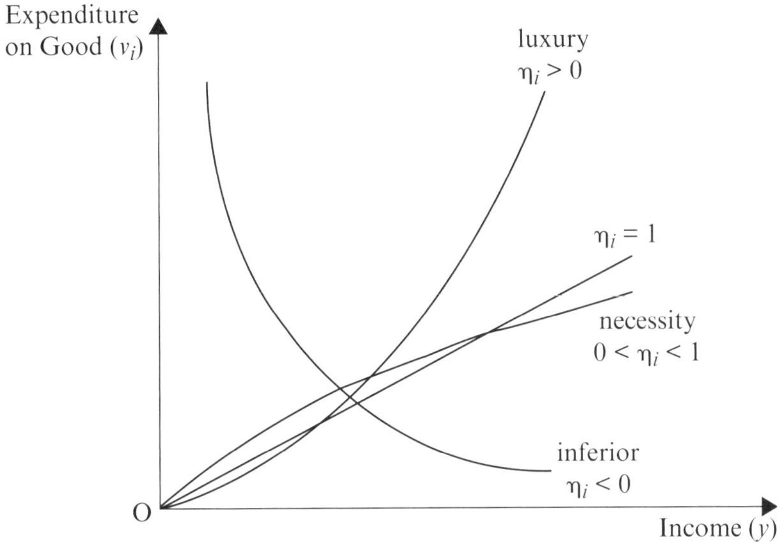

Note: η_i = income elasticity

Figure 6.1 *Engel curves*

straight line through the origin. If the good is a 'luxury', then the Engel curve increases at an increasing rate and the budget share is increasing. If the good is a necessity, then the curve increases at a decreasing rate and the budget share is decreasing. For inferior goods, expenditure falls as income increases. Figure 6.1 provides a schematic representation of these cases. However, the income elasticity of demand for a commodity may itself vary with income, in which case the Engel curve will exhibit different geometric properties at different income levels. In practice, this is most likely to be the case, at least for disaggregated levels of commodities.

From the 1930s, the preferred shape of Engel curves was influenced by the formal introduction of income into demand theory by Hicks and Allen. Allen and Bowley (1935) assumed that marginal utilities were linear in commodities to derive and estimate linear Engel curves (constant marginal propensities to consume) from British household expenditure surveys. While linear curves may be valid over some income ranges, they have the undesirable property that all income elasticities converge to unity as income increases. Prais and Houthakker (1955) used a range of functional forms in order to find those of best fit, including the double logarithmic form, in which the coefficient on income provides a direct measure of the income elasticity of demand (see Figure 6.1).

It is desirable, at least when using broad commodity classes such as food, clothing, housing and so on that exhaust total expenditure, that the Engel curve estimates satisfy a number of global properties, such as predicted budget shares lying between zero and one, and summing to one (the adding-up property). The double logarithmic form, for example, does not satisfy the adding up property (unless all income elasticities are unity).

For most goods, there is a tendency for income elasticities of demand to eventually fall as income increases. The semi-logarithmic model in which expenditures are expressed as a function of the logarithm of income has this feature, but it does not satisfy the adding-up property. An alternative semi-logarithmic equation, suggested by Working (1943), in which budget shares are the dependant variable, does satisfy the adding-up criteria:

$$w_i = a_i + b_i \log y \tag{6.2}$$

where the income elasticities of demand, η_i, are given by

$$\eta_i = 1 + (b_i/w_i) \tag{6.3}$$

Adding up requires that the coefficients satisfy $\Sigma a_i = 1$ and $\Sigma b_i = 0$. If the n equations (one for each commodity) are estimated by ordinary least squares, the estimates of the coefficients will automatically satisfy the adding-up constraints. The Working equation is also consistent with the Almost Ideal Demand System of Deaton and Muellbauer (1980).

It is apparent from equation (6.2) that if, for a given commodity, b_i is greater than zero, its share of the budget is increasing with income and the good is a luxury; if b_i is less than zero, then the good is a necessity since as income rises the budget share falls. From equation (6.3) it is clear that if b_i is negative and w_i falls below the absolute value of b_i, the good becomes an inferior one. The various cases are illustrated in Figure 6.2.

There is less need for Engel curves to satisfy the postulates of demand theory when modelling expenditure on a narrowly defined good, for example, chocolate or shoes. In these cases, a flexible functional form can be used which allows the relationship between expenditure on a good and income to vary in a more complex way with income. More recently, the desire for greater flexibility has been met through semi-parametric and non-parametric estimation.

In order to estimate Engel curves in the usual case where only expenditure data are available, it is necessary to assume that all households face the same prices. How realistic is this assumption? There are two issues.

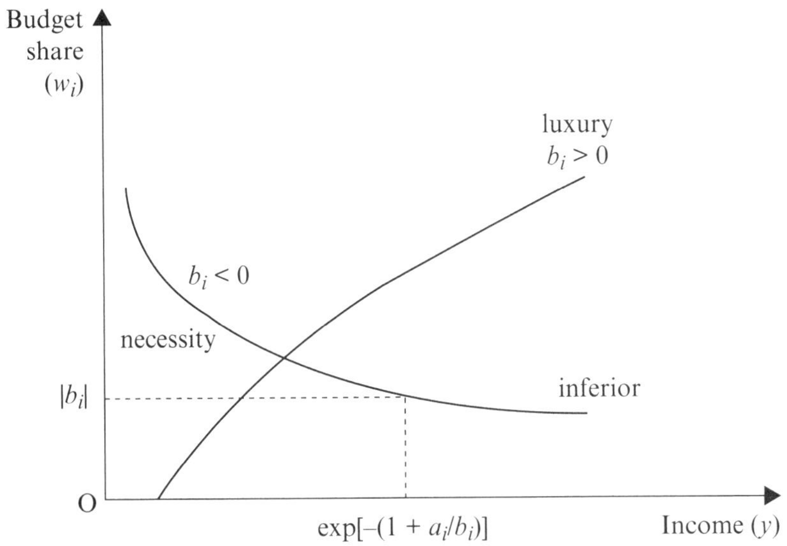

Note: $w_i = a_i + b_i \log y$

Figure 6.2 Working-Engel curves

First, there may be quality differences between goods recorded under a single heading. Prais and Houthakker (1955) assumed that price differences reflected quality and estimated quality elasticities for various types of food, where both expenditure and quantity data were available. Second, even for homogeneous goods, prices may differ according to factors such as household income and location; estimation of Engel curves for relatively homogeneous groups of households will limit any biases. Engel himself looked at expenditure patterns for three different socio-economic groups. Price data are required in estimating Engel curves from time series or panel data.

Family size and composition affect expenditure patterns. Engel curves can be drawn for different family types. The simplest approach in estimation is to express expenditures and income in per capita terms, but this ignores economies of scale in consumption which differ across commodities. Alternative ways of incorporating family effects into Engel curves through additional explanatory variables are given in Pollack and Wales (1981) and Deaton (1997, chapter 4). Such models have been used to estimate 'equivalence scales' for different household members and different commodities, but Pollack and Wales (1979) have shown that identification problems arise here.

Empirical estimates of Engel curves have been used in a number of policy areas, including economic development (notably by Colin Clark and Simon Kuznets), taxation policy, measures of poverty, and computable general equilibrium modelling.

REFERENCES

Allen, R.G.D. and Bowley, A.L. (1935), *Family expenditure*, P.S. King and Son, London.
Deaton, Angus (1997), *The analysis of household surveys: a microeconometric approach*, World Bank, Johns Hopkins Press, Baltimore, Maryland.
Deaton, Angus and Muellbauer, John (1980), *Economics and consumer behavior*, Cambridge University Press, Cambridge.
Engel, Ernst (1857), 'Die Productions- und Consumptionsverhältnisse des Königreichs Sachsen', *Zeitschrift des Statistischen Bureaus des Königlich Sächsischen Ministerium des Inneren*, Nos. 8 and 9. Reprinted as an appendix in Engel, E. (1895) *Die Lebenskosten belgischer Arbeiter-Familien*, C. Heinrich, Dresden, and in *Bulletin of the International Statistical Institute* (1895), 9, 1–124.
Houthakker, H.S. (1957), 'An international comparison of household expenditure patterns commemorating the centennial of Engel's Law', *Econometrica*, 25, 532–51.
Pollack, R. and Wales, T.J. (1979), 'Welfare comparisons and equivalence scales', *American Economic Review*, 69, 216–21.
Pollack, R. and Wales, T.J. (1981), 'Demographic variables in demand analysis', *Econometrica*, 49, 1533–51.
Prais, S.J. and Houthakker, H.S. (1955), *The analysis of family budgets*, Cambridge University Press, Cambridge (Second impression, abridged, 1971).
Stigler, George J. (1954), 'The early history of empirical studies of consumer behavior', *Journal of Political Economy*, LXII, 95–113.
Working, H. (1943), 'Statistical laws of family expenditure', *Journal of the American Statistical Association*, 38, 43–56.

7. Homothetic production and utility functions

Rolf Färe and Shawna Grosskopf

Let us begin by quoting Professor Dale W. Jorgenson, from the Forward to the 1981 reprint of Shephard's *Cost and Production Functions*, first published in 1953:

> Shephard developed the notion of a homothetic production function and employed the idea in function and formulating the concept of homothetic separability. The critical importance of homothetic separability to duality in the theory of aggregation and index numbers was fully appreciated by Shephard.

Although Shephard developed the notion of homotheticity and homothetic separability in 1953, it was not until his 1970 book *Theory of Cost and Production Functions* that we can find a figure illustrating homotheticity. This figure illustrates that a 'homothetic production function (structure) may be obtained from that for unit output rate by radial expansion' (Shephard, 1970, p. 34). This type of expansion is equivalent to stating that the production function has linear expansion paths.

We note that the figure may not be as famous as the concept itself. To introduce it, we need some formalities. Using Shephard's notation, inputs are denoted by $x \in \Re_+^N$, the scalar output by $u \in \Re_+$. The production function $\Phi(x)$ denotes the maximal feasible output that inputs x can produce. A production structure is said to be homothetic if we can write $F(\Phi(x))$, where $\Phi(x)$ is homogeneous of degree +1 ($\Phi(\lambda x) = \lambda\Phi(x), \lambda > 0$) and F is a monotone transformation of Φ. Denote the level set for output level u (where $F^{-1}(u) = f(u)$) by

$$L_\Phi(f(u)) = \{x: \Phi(x) \geq f(u)\}, \tag{7.1}$$

then Shephard's illustration (1970, p. 34) of homotheticity is given in Figure 7.1. This figure illustrates that for a homothetic production structure, the isoquant for $u = u$ is a radial expansion of $u = 1$. Notice that the kinks in these piecewise linear isoquants are indeed radial expansions/contractions of each other.

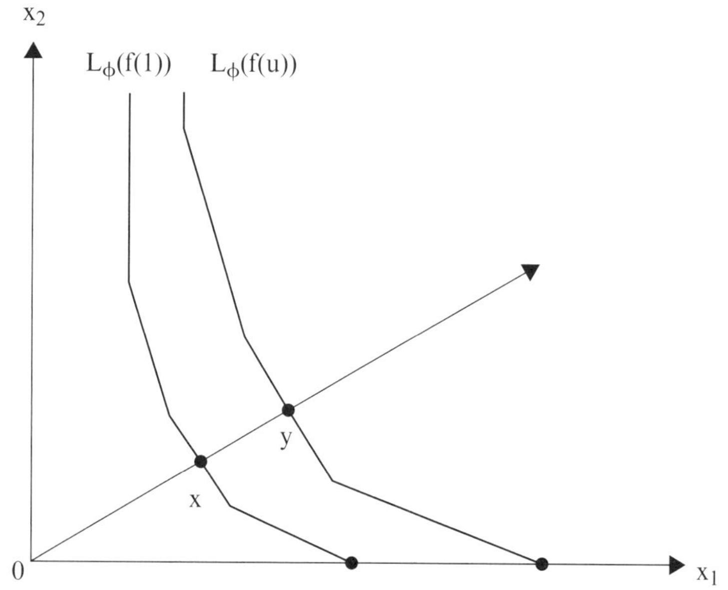

Source: © Princeton University Press.

Figure 7.1 Isoquant map under homotheticity

Returning to Professor Jorgenson's quote, we follow up on the role of homothetic separability and duality. Let $p \in \Re^N_+$ be a vector of input prices and define the cost function as

$$Q(u, p) = \min_x \{px: \Phi(x) \geq u\}. \quad (7.2)$$

If the production function is homothetic, the cost function takes the form

$$Q(u, p) = f(u) P(p), \quad (7.3)$$

where again $f(u) = F^{-1}(u)$ (the inverse exists due to the monotonicity of F). Thus the resulting cost function is separable in output quantity and input prices. This is an important and useful property of a homothetic production function. Unfortunately the equivalence between linear expansion paths and separability does not hold for a multi-output technology. Rather, a generalization dubbed ray-homotheticity is introduced to model linear expansion paths – see Färe and Shephard (1977).

Turning to utility functions, recall that they are unique up to a monotone transformation, thus under homotheticity these functions are homogeneous of degree +1. Such functions are known to have linear Engel curves, the analog of the linear expansion paths on the production side.

Returning to production theory, when homogeneity is combined with differentiability the following useful relation is obtained

$$\Phi(x) = \sum_{n=1}^{N} \frac{\partial \Phi}{\partial x_n} x_n. \tag{7.4}$$

When (4) holds, then the production function $\Phi(x)$ is homogeneous of degree +1; thus (4) characterizes homogeneity.

Homogeneity of the production function yields important distributional results. Let r be the price of the (scalar) output, then $r\Phi(x)$ is the value of production, or revenue. If the inputs (factors of production) are compensated by the value of their marginal productivity, $r(\partial\Phi(x)/\partial x_n)$, then (7.4) yields the well-known 'marginal productivity theory of distribution' Stigler (1941, p. 320), that is,

$$r\Phi(x) = \sum_{n=1}^{N} r \frac{\partial \Phi}{\partial x_n} x_n \tag{7.5}$$

In this case the value of production – revenue – just equals the sum of the payments to the factors – cost. Thus profit, which is revenue minus cost, is zero. Stigler (1941) provides a complete discussion of marginal productivity theory and distribution (see also Chapter 9, on the product exhaustion theorem).

From (7.3) with $F(.)$ being the identity function, it follows that the technology which is homogeneous of degree +1 equals

$$Q(u, p) = uP(p). \tag{7.6}$$

Thus it has constant marginal productivity

$$\partial Q(u, p)/\partial u = P(p). \tag{7.7}$$

Moreover since the homogeneous technology is a subtechnology of the homothetic technology, it has linear expansion paths, which in calculus terms means that the marginal rate of substitution is constant along rays from the origin.

Next, define the graph of the technology as

$$GR = \{(x, y): \Phi(x) \geq y\}, \tag{7.8}$$

then GR is a cone, that is,

$$\lambda GR = GR, \lambda > 0 \tag{7.9}$$

if and only if the production function $\Phi(x)$ is homogeneous of degree +1. In economic terms, this technology satisfies constant returns to scale.

Generalizations of the cone (CRS) technology are the super- and sub-homogeneous technologies, namely

$$\lambda GR \subseteq GR, \lambda \geq 1, \tag{7.10}$$

and

$$\lambda GR \subseteq GR, 0 \leq \lambda \leq 1, \tag{7.11}$$

respectively. The former represents non-decreasing returns to scale, which has proved to be important to international trade, and the latter is non-increasing returns to scale.

REFERENCES

Färe, Rolf and Ronald W. Shephard (1977), 'Ray-homothetic Production Functions', *Econometrica*, 45, 133–146.

Shephard, Ronald. W. (1953), *Cost and Production Functions*, Princeton, NJ: Princeton University Press.

Shephard, Ronald. W. (1970), *Theory of Cost and Production Functions*, Princeton, NJ: Princeton University Press.

Stigler, George, J. (1941), *Production and Distribution Theories*, New York: Macmillan.

8. Long-run and short-run cost curves

Fiona Maclachlan

Cost curves form a staple part of the curriculum of undergraduate microeconomics. Their presentation across textbooks is fairly uniform and has not varied much over the years since Marshallian partial equilibrium analysis was first codified in a set of diagrams. The uniformity and stability of the presentation of the curves belies their controversial beginnings in the 1920s and 1930s, as economists struggled to contain Marshall's realistic descriptive insights and biological analogies into a logically coherent static equilibrium model. In the battle that played out between descriptive realism and neat formalisms, the latter won out for center stage in textbook studies of cost.

Cost curves are drawn with the quantity of a specific product along the horizontal axis and money cost on the vertical. For an analysis of perfect competition, the assumption is that each firm faces identical input prices and choices of technology. Under this assumption, the curves can be interpreted to correspond either to the industry as a whole, or to a representative firm. They can represent the total cost of the quantity, the average (per unit) cost, or the marginal cost. For the short run, total and average costs can be broken down into the portion reflecting the amount spent on factors of production whose quantities can be varied, and the portion reflecting the sunk costs of the fixed factors of production. Further, one can consider long-run cost curves drawn under the assumption that the quantities of all factors can be varied. Drawn together in one diagram, cost curves can appear daunting to students of economics, and even their teachers can have difficulty disentangling them in a comprehensible way. Evidence of the difficulty can be seen in three pedagogical articles on cost curves that have appeared in the *Journal of Economic Education* in recent years (Sexton, Graves and Lee, 1993; Boyd and Boyd, 1994; Silberberg, 1999).

The typical textbook presentation starts with the short run and shows the average cost curves (total, fixed and variable) along with the marginal cost. The curves are presented in Figure 8.1. The short-run cost curves are normally based on a production function with one variable factor of

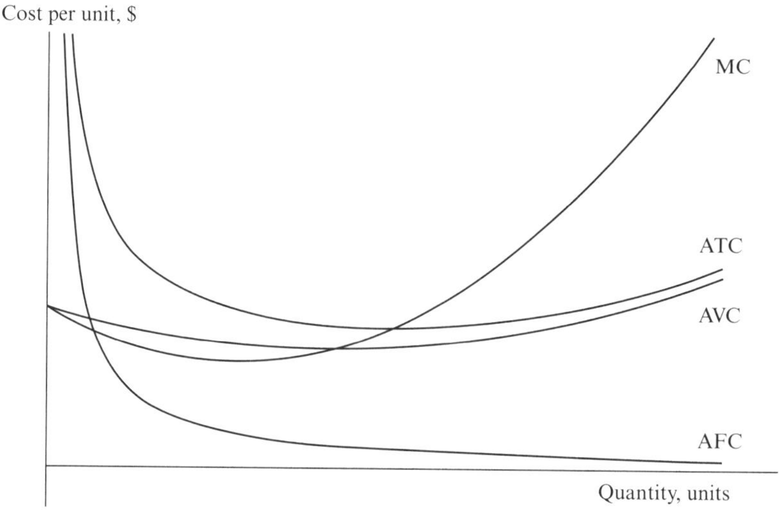

Note: Marginal cost (MC), average total cost (ATC), average variable cost (AVC) and average fixed cost (AFC).

Figure 8.1 Short-run unit cost curves

production that displays first increasing and then decreasing marginal productivity. Increasing marginal productivity is associated with the negatively sloped portion of the marginal cost curve, while decreasing marginal productivity is associated with the positively sloped portion. The average fixed cost (AFC) curve is the cost of the fixed factor of production divided by the quantity of units of the output, while the average variable cost (AVC) curve cost traces out the per unit cost of the variable factor of production. The U-shaped average total cost (ATC) curve is derived by adding the average fixed and variable costs. The marginal cost (MC) intersects both the AVC and ATC curves at their minimum points. Declining average total costs are explained as the result of spreading the fixed costs over greater quantities and, at low quantities, also the result of the increasing marginal productivity. Increasing average costs occur when the effect of declining marginal productivity overwhelms the effect of spreading the fixed costs.

The long-run cost curves, usually presented in a separate diagram, are also expressed most commonly in their average, or per unit form, represented here in Figure 8.2. The long-run average cost (LRAC) curve is shown to be an envelope of the short-run average cost (SRAC) curves, lying everywhere below or tangent to the short-run curves. The firm is

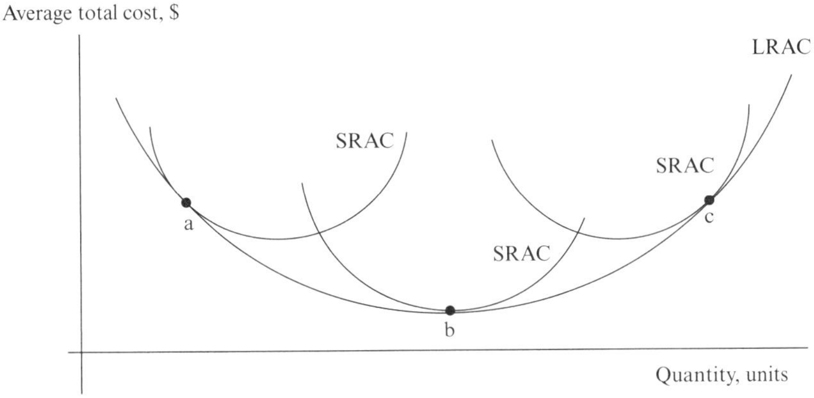

Note: The long-run average cost (LRAC) curve is an envelope curve of the short-run average cost (SRAC) curves. Increasing, constant and decreasing returns to scale are exhibited at points a, b and c respectively.

Figure 8.2 Long-run and short-run average cost curves

constrained in the short run in selecting the optimal mix of factors of production and so will never be able to find a cheaper mix than can be found in the long run when there are no constraints. If there is a discrete number of plant sizes available, the LRAC will be the scalloped curve obtained by joining those parts of the SRAC curves that represent the lowest cost of production for a given quantity.

In the case of constant returns to scale, the most common assumption for production functions, the LRAC curve is horizontal. If it is the case that a larger scale of production is obtained through increasing the number of identical plants, then the long-run cost curve approaches a horizontal line as the number of plants increases (Joseph 1933); that is, the production function will exhibit 'asymptotic-first-degree-homogeneity' (Samuelson 1967, p. 131). Long-run average cost curves that are everywhere decreasing will arise in industries with a large fixed cost and constant variable costs. Traditionally, decreasing long-run cost curves have been associated with natural monopolies. More generally, the LRAC curve can be drawn as a U-shape displaying increasing returns at lower levels of output and decreasing returns at higher levels.

The long-run marginal cost curve is usually omitted in introductory treatments. If it is included, it is drawn so that it lies above the short-run marginal cost curve to the left of their intersection point, and below to the right. Understanding the relationship between the short-run and long-run marginal cost curves can be challenging, and may require conjuring up additional diagrams. Sexton, Graves and Lee (1993) couch their explanation using isocosts and isoquants, whereas Boyd and Boyd (1994) show how the relationship can be explained using the total cost curves.

Keppler and Lallement (2006) trace the cost curve construction back to Enrico Barone's 1908 *Principi di economia politica*. Barone presents a diagram that contains a total cost curve with costs increasing at a decreasing and then increasing rate – equivalent to the textbook U-shaped average cost curve. He represents the marginal cost of a particular quantity as the slope of a tangent to the cost curve at that quantity, and the average cost of a particular quantity as the slope of a ray from the origin to the relevant point of the cost curve. Total revenue is represented on the diagram as a line with the slope equivalent to the price. The construction allows him to identify the profit maximizing quantity as that for which the price equals marginal cost, and the zero profit long-run equilibrium quantity as that for which price equals both marginal cost and average total cost.

The first U-shaped cost curve, in which cost is expressed in per unit terms, was uncovered by Keppler and Lallement (2006) and appears in an article by Edgeworth (1913) on railway rates. Since the discussion was of a monopoly firm, the relationship between price, marginal cost and average cost found in Barone's 1908 work is not brought out. Piero Sraffa presented the first per unit cost curve construction of a firm in perfect competition bearing a close resemblance to contemporary textbook treatments; the paper was published in 1925 in an Italian language journal (reproduced in Keppler and Lallement, 2006). Upon reading the article in Italian, Edgeworth commissioned Sraffa to write a similar piece for the *Economic Journal*, which appeared in 1926 but did not contain the diagram. A virtually identical diagram, however, appears in a related article by Pigou (1928). It is reasonable to suspect that Pigou derived it from Sraffa's 1925 paper.

Roy Harrod (1931) and Jacob Viner (1931) contemporaneously published articles containing diagrams showing the relationship between the LRAC curve and a set of SRAC curves. In his now legendary 1931 *Zeitschrift für Nationalökonomie* article, Viner had instructed his draughtsman, the mathematician Y. K. Wong, to draw the long-run average total cost curve so that it would run tangent to the bottoms of the short-run U-shaped curves, be downward sloping, and nowhere lie above the short-run curves. Wong insisted that it was impossible to satisfy all three requirements and produced a diagram with the long-run curve lying, in one portion, above the short-run curve.

In a footnote, Viner (1931, p. 36n) admits that the diagram was in error in placing the long-run curve above the short-run, but confesses that he did not understand Wong's mathematical reason for it being impossible to draw the long-run curve so that it was never above the short-run curves while running along the bottoms of the short-run curves: 'I could not persuade him to disregard his scruples as a craftsman and to follow my instructions, absurd though they might be'. Harrod (1959, p. 262) recounts the experience, when working on his 1931 paper at Oxford, of wandering outside with his curves on Tom Quad in Christ Church in quest of a scientific colleague who could tell him the proper name for the long-run curve. His quest was successful and allowed him in the 1930s, unlike Viner, to properly describe the LRAC curve as an envelope.

In *Foundations of Economic Analysis*, Paul Samuelson (1947) provides a proof of what he calls the Wong-Viner envelope theorem showing the proper relationship between constrained and unconstrained functions. Samuelson, who had been a student in Viner's class in 1935, recalls how after admitting his error in class, Viner had told him privately after the bell had rung, that he still thought it possible to draw a downward sloping LRAC curve that would smoothly join the bottoms of a set of SRAC curves. In the same reminiscence, Samuelson (1972, p. 9) reports that Schumpeter, as well, continued to be confused about the matter: 'He always insisted somewhere in the third dimension of the parametrized surface of U-shaped cost curves, the envelope did go through Viner's bottom points'. Silberberg (1999), noting the opacity of Samuelson's proof in the *Foundations*, provides a clarifying explanation using the total cost curve diagram.

The confusion leading to the error may be related to the result from the theory of the competitive firm that firms will produce at the minimum point on the average total cost curve after entry and exit has driven economic profit to zero. If the price of the product (P) is such that the marginal cost (MC) for the representative firm intersects the horizontal price line above the minimum point on the SRAC curve, the firm will be earning economic profits and there will be entry and expansion. As more firms enter, and as existing firms expand production, supply of the product will increase and the price will fall. Long-run equilibrium is reached when P = MC = SRAC. If the price intersects the marginal cost below the minimum point on the SRAC, the opposite process of exit and contraction will reduce supply and increase the price, and a new long-run equilibrium will be established, with the representative firm producing at the minimum point of the SRAC curve.

At first sight, it seems reasonable to suppose that the points on the LRAC curve will coincide with the minimum points on the SRAC curves, since they are the long-run equilibrium points. The confusion is due to the conflation of two separate notions of the long run. In Marshall's theory of the firm in perfect competition, the long run, or long period as he termed it, is the hypothetical state that is achieved after economic profits have been driven to zero. The LRAC curve, on the other hand, is tracing out the unit costs of different levels of output under the assumption that all factors of production can be optimally adjusted. It does not refer to the long-run equilibrium of the firm and might be better labeled the *unconstrained* average total cost curve. It may be a recognition of the conflation of the two notions of the long run that lead Schumpeter to believe that if an additional dimension was added, the LRAC curve would run through the minimum points. In any event, the confusion surrounding the curves seems to bear out well Marshall's (1920, p. 461) warning about the limitations of the 'statical theory of equilibrium' in analyzing the progress of industries through time: 'limitations . . . so constantly overlooked, especially by those who approach it from an abstract point of view, that there is a danger of throwing it into definite form at all'.

REFERENCES

Barzne, E. (1908), *Principi di economica politica*, Rome: Tipeqinfin Nazionale di G. Bertero.

Boyd, L. A. and D. W. Boyd (1994), 'The Short- and Long-Run Marginal Cost Curve: An Alternative Explanation', *Journal of Economic Education*, **25** (3), 261–265.

Edgeworth, F. Y. (1913), 'Contributions to the Theory of Railway Rates: IV', *Economic Journal*, **23** (90), 206–226.

Harrod, R. (1931), 'The Law of Decreasing Cost', *Economic Journal*, **41** (164), 566–576.

Harrod, R. (1959), 'Review of *The Long and the Short*', *Economica*, New Series, **26** (103), 260–262.

Joseph, M. F. W. (1933), 'A Discontinuous Cost Curve and the Tendency to Increasing Returns', *Economic Journal*, **43** (171), 390–398.

Keppler, J. H. and J. Lallement (2006), 'The Origins of the U-Shaped Average Cost Curve: Understanding the Complexities of the Modern Theory', *History of Political Economy*, **38** (4), 733–774.

Marshall, A. (1920), *Principles of Economics*, 9th ed., New York: Macmillan.

Pigou, A. C. (1928), 'An Analysis of Supply', *Economic Journal*, **38** (150), 238–257.

Samuelson, P. A. (1947), *Foundations of Economic Analysis*, Cambridge, MA: Harvard University Press.

Samuelson, P. A. (1967), 'The Monopolistic Competition Revolution', in *Monopolistic Competition Theory: Studies in Impact: Essays in Honor of Edward H. Chamberlin*, edited by R. E. Kuenne, New York: Wiley.

Samuelson, P. A. (1972), 'Jacob Viner, 1892–1970', *Journal of Political Economy*, **80** (1), 5–11.

Sexton, R. L., P. E. Graves and D. R. Lee (1993), 'The Short- and Long-Run

Marginal Cost Curve: A Pedagogical Note', *Journal of Economic Education*, **24** (1), 34–37.
Silberberg, E. (1999), 'The Viner-Wong Envelope Theorem', *Journal of Economic Education*, **30** (1), 75–79.
Viner, J. (1931), 'Cost Curves and Supply Curves', *Zeitschrift für Nationalökonomie*, **3**, 23–46.

9. The product exhaustion theorem

Cassey Lee

There are many mathematical theorems that are associated with Leonhard Euler (1707–1783), one of the greatest mathematicians. One in particular found its way into economics, namely Euler's work on homogeneous function of the first degree, which was applied in the theory of factor pricing and income distribution. In the 1880s, following Ricardo's theory of rent, Clark (1889, 1891, 1899, 1901), P. Wicksteed and Wicksell argued that any variable factor input is paid its marginal product (Blaug 1997). This led to the formulation of the 'Product Exhaustion Theorem' which states that the total product is exhausted if each factor input is paid its marginal product. Wicksteed (1894) provided an early mathematical expression of the theorem but did not relate it to Euler's work (Stigler 1941, fn.1, p.326). It was A.W. Flux (1894) who pointed out the theorem's association with Euler's work. Aside from the importance of the theorem to factor pricing, it is also widely used as a basis for a marginal productivity theory of income distribution.

The simplest way to illustrate the theorem is by using a two-factor model. At the core of the theorem is an assumption that factor inputs such as labor (L) and capital (K) are each paid a price (P_L and P_K, respectively) that is equal to the value of its marginal product (MP_L and MP_K, respectively).

If we assume that the total revenue ($P_Q \cdot Q$) collected from the sale of a product is equal to the total cost of production, we have:

$$P_Q \cdot Q = P_L L + P_K K = \frac{\partial Q}{\partial L} \cdot P_Q L + \frac{\partial Q}{\partial K} \cdot P_Q K \tag{9.1}$$

or

$$Q = \frac{\partial Q}{\partial L} \cdot L + \frac{\partial Q}{\partial K} \cdot K. \tag{9.2}$$

The above equations summarize the essence of the Product Exhaustion Theorem, which states that the total output is exhausted by the sum of

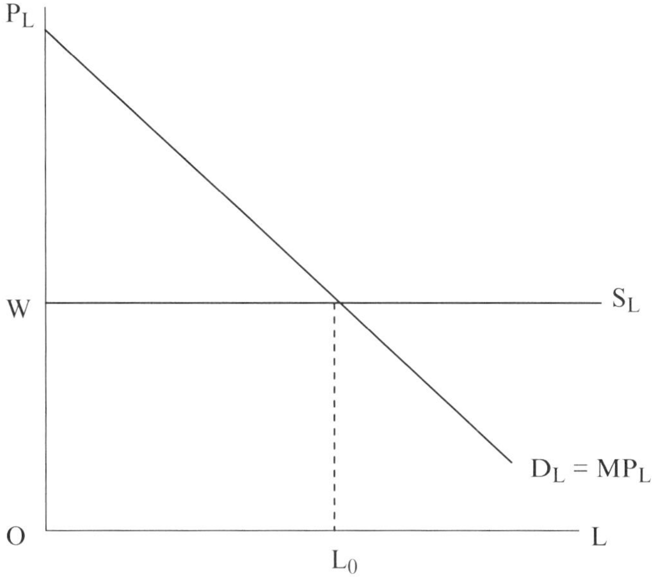

Figure 9.1 Labor demand and supply

factor input incomes if each factor input is paid its marginal product. In terms of income distribution, each factor input's share in the total product is represented by the partial derivative of the product with respect to the factor input.

In terms of graphical representation, the theorem is associated with two important graphical representations. The first is associated with the determination of factor input prices. This is presented in Figure 9.1, where both the demand for labor (represented by MP_L) and supply of labor (SL) jointly determine the factor input price (W or wage).

The second graph provides a depiction of the relevance of the Product Exhaustion Theorem to income distribution. In Figure 9.2, the earlier diagram (Figure 9.1) is extended by including the average product of labor (AP_L). Total product is represented by OL_0BC. The total wage paid to labor is given by the rectangle OL_0AW. If we assume that the other factor input is capital, the rectangle WABC is the total factor payment to capital. This is a relatively simple diagram that conveys how total product in an economy would be distributed between capital and labor.

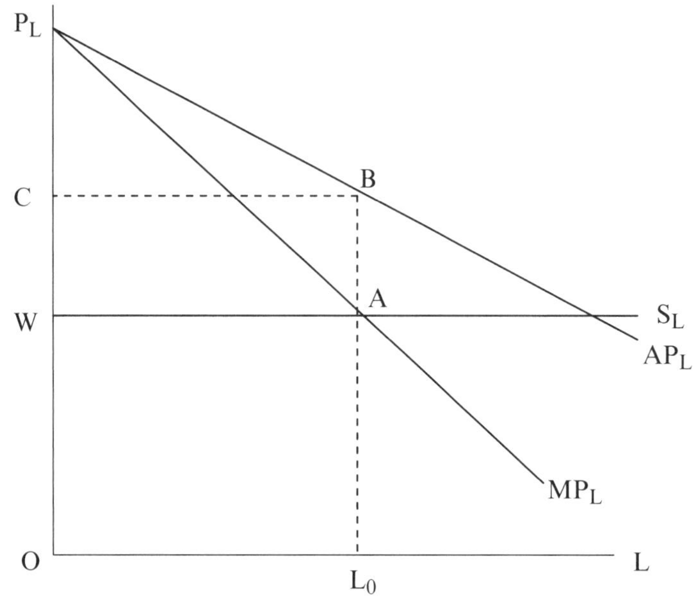

Source: Adapted from Fonseca (n.d.)

Figure 9.2 Income distribution

REFERENCES

M. Blaug. (1997) *Economic Theory in Retrospect*. Fifth edition, Cambridge: Cambridge University Press.

J.B. Clark (1889) 'Possibility of a Scientific Law of Wages', *Publications of the American Economic Association*, Vol. 4 (1), pp. 39–63.

J.B. Clark (1891) 'Distribution as Determined by a Law of Rent', *Quarterly Journal of Economics*, Vol. 5, pp. 289–318.

J.B. Clark (1899) *The Distribution of Wealth: A theory of wages, interest and profits*. 1927 edition, New York: Macmillan.

J.B. Clark (1901) 'Wages and Interest as Determined by Marginal Productivity', *Journal of Political Economy*, Vol. 10, pp. 105–109.

A.W. Flux (1894) 'Review of Wicksteed's Essay', *Economic Journal*, Vol. 4, pp. 305–8.

G.L. Fonseca (n.d.) *The Neoclassiscal Theory of Distribution*, http://cepa.newschool.edu/het/essays/margrev/distrib.htm, accessed 8 January 2010.

G. Stigler (1941), *Production and Distribution Theories*. London: Macmillan.

P.H. Wicksteed (1894) *Essay on the Co-ordination of the Laws of Distribution*. 1932 edition, Reprint No. 12. London: London School of Economics.

10. Classification of technical change

Robert Dixon

Technical change can be thought of as a situation where the same output can be produced with less of one or more of the inputs or, what amounts to the same thing, where more output can be produced from the same inputs. Since 'technical progress shifts the entire production function, an index-number type problem arises in deciding which point on the old production function to compare with which point on the new one' (Hahn and Matthews, 1964, p. 825). This problem has led to the formulation of a number of alternative classifications of technical change.

In his study of wages and the functional distribution of income, Hicks (1932, pp. 121–127) followed Pigou (see for example 1932, p. 674f) in making a distinction between labour saving, capital saving and neutral inventions. Hicks writes:

> If we concentrate on two groups of factors, labour and capital, and suppose them to exhaust the list, then we can classify inventions according as their initial effects are to increase, leave unchanged or diminish the ratio of the marginal product of capital to that of labour. We may call these inventions 'labour saving', 'neutral' and 'capital saving' respectively. Labour saving inventions increase the marginal product of capital more than they increase the marginal product of labour; capital saving inventions increase the marginal product of labour more than they increase the marginal product of capital; neutral inventions increase both in the same proportion (Hicks, 1932, p. 121f).

Clearly these definitions are meant to be read for given factor supplies and/or a given capital–labour ratio.

Hicks's definitions are sometimes illustrated with reference to an isoquant map (see Figure 10.1). The convex lines are representative isoquants with I^0 indicating the location of an isoquant before the technical change and $I^1 - I^3$ indicating the combinations of capital and labour which produce the same level of output after the change. The straight line running out from the origin shows the initial capital–labour ratio. The two parallel dotted lines show the ratio of the marginal products (if we have perfect competition in output and factor markets this will be the same as the relative factor price ratio) which applied in the initial

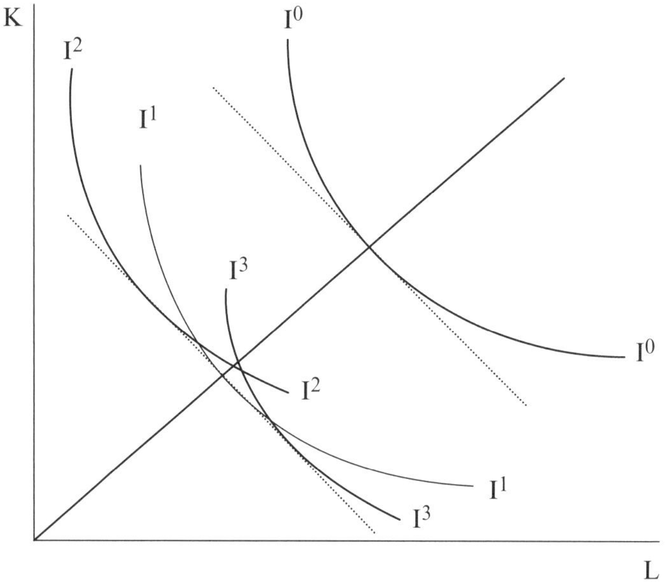

Figure 10.1 Hicks's classification of technical change

state before the change took place. If, for the same capital–labour ratio, the shift in the isoquant is such that the ratio of the marginal products (the relative factor price ratio) is unchanged, then the technical change is Hicks neutral. This is depicted by the case where the technical change has shifted the isoquant to I^1 (at the same capital–labour ratio the slope of the isoquant I^1 is the same as I^0). If, for the same capital–labour ratio, the shift in the isoquant is such that the marginal product of labour has fallen relative to the marginal product of capital, then the technical change is Hicks labour saving. This is depicted by the case where the isoquant has shifted to I^2 (at the same capital–labour ratio the slope of the isoquant I^2 is shallower than I^1). If, for the same capital–labour ratio, the shift in the isoquant is such that marginal product of labour has risen relative to the marginal product of capital, then the technical change is Hicks capital saving. This is depicted by the case where the isoquant has shifted to I^3 (at the same capital–labour ratio the slope of the isoquant I^3 is steeper than I^1).

There is an alternative method of depicting technical change which has become quite common – due especially to the popularity of the Solow-Swan growth model – and that is a diagram which shows the relationship between output per worker (on the vertical axis) and capital per worker

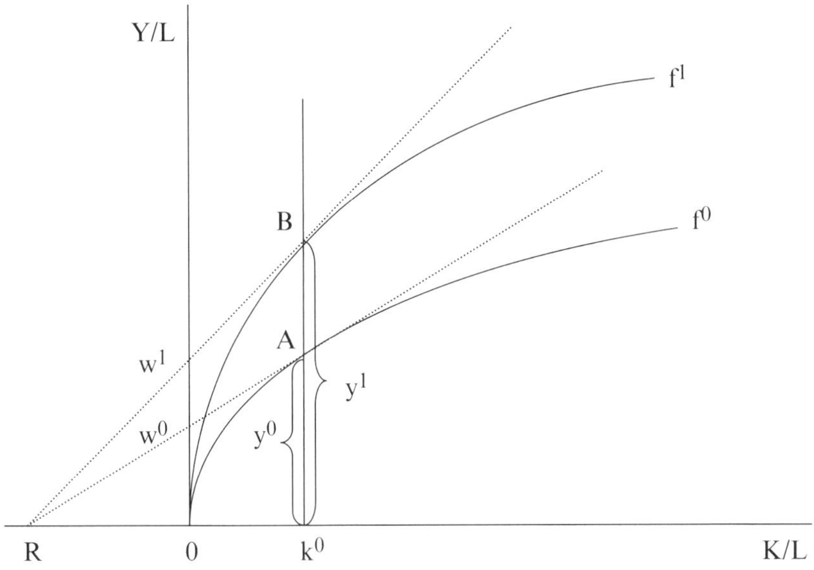

Figure 10.2 Hicks-neutral technical change

(on the horizontal axis) under the assumption of constant returns to scale (see Figure 10.2).

The lines f^0 and f^1 in Figure 10.2 represent the (per-worker) production function $y = Y/L = f(K/L)$ before and after the technical change. The distances $0w^0$ and y^0 are the real wage and the average product of labour respectively when the capital–labour ratio is that given by k^0 for the initial level of technology (f^0). The slope of the line beginning at R and which is tangential to the function f^0 at A is the marginal product of capital associated with k^0 – call this r^0. If perfect competition prevails in all markets and producers are maximising profits then r^0 will also be the rental per unit of capital and $0w^0$ will be the marginal product of labour. Since (the slope) r^0 is also equal to the distance $0w^0$ divided by the distance 0R, it follows that 0R is the wage–rental ratio consistent with the initial level of technology when the capital–labour ratio is that given by k^0. If perfect competition prevails in all markets, then this (0R) will also be the ratio of the marginal products, that is, $(\partial Y/\partial L)/(\partial Y/\partial K)$. Imagine now that technology changes in such a way that Y/L rises for every level of K/L. This is shown by an upwards shift in the (per-worker) production function from f^0 to f^1. Notice that with an unchanged capital–labour ratio (k^0) the level of output per worker has risen from y^0 to y^1, the real wage (marginal product of labour) has risen from $0w^0$ to $0w^1$ and the marginal product of capital (the capital rental, call this r^1) – given by the slope of the line beginning at R and which is tangential to the function f^1 at B – has also risen. However since the distance 0R has remained unchanged, the wage–rental ratio and thus the ratio of the marginal products has remained the same, and so the technical change in this case is Hicks neutral.

While Hicks's definitions are appropriate to a short-run situation with given supplies of inputs (and/or a given capital–labour ratio), Harrod (1937, 1948) proposed an alternative classification, one more suited to studying 'the long-run effects of technological progress when input supplies are able to adjust to economic conditions' (Ferguson, 1969, p. 217). In the context of modelling equilibrium growth, Harrod defined 'a neutral advance as one which, at a constant rate of interest, does not disturb the capital coefficient [i.e. the capital–output ratio]' (Harrod, 1948, p. 23). Thus, for a given rate of interest, 'a neutral stream of inventions [is] one which shall require a rate of increase of capital equal to the rate of increase of income engendered by it. If the stream of inventions requires capital to increase at a greater rate, then it is labour-saving or capital-requiring; and conversely' (ibid., p. 26f).

It is common to depict Harrod-neutral technical change using a (per-worker) production function (see Figure 10.3). Again, the lines f^0 and f^1 in the figure represent the production function $y = Y/L = f(K/L)$ before and after the technical change. The vertical line at k^0 indicates the initial capital–labour ratio. The distances $0w^0$ and y^0 are the real wage and the average product of labour for the initial level of technology when the capital–labour ratio is that given by k^0. The slope of the line beginning at real wage w^0 and which is tangential to the function f^0 at A is the marginal product of capital. If perfect competition prevails in all markets, then the marginal product of capital will be equal to the interest rate. Imagine now that technology changes in such a way that Y/L rises for every level of K/L. This is shown by an upwards shift in the production function from f^0 to f^1. Notice that with an unchanged capital–labour ratio (k^0) the level of output per worker has risen from y^0 to y^1, the real wage (marginal product of labour) has risen from $0w^0$ to $0w^1$ and the marginal product of capital – given by the slope of a (an imaginary) line beginning at w^1 and which is tangential to the function f^1 at B – has also risen. In other words at point B relative factor prices have changed in such a way that firms will have an incentive to raise the capital–labour ratio (the rise in the average product of labour will itself, as explained by Solow and Swan, have led to a rise in savings and net investment per worker) and so the economy will move along the new production function (f^1) to point C where, due to the presence of diminishing returns, the marginal product of capital is again equal to the rate of interest (the two dotted lines have the same slope). Although

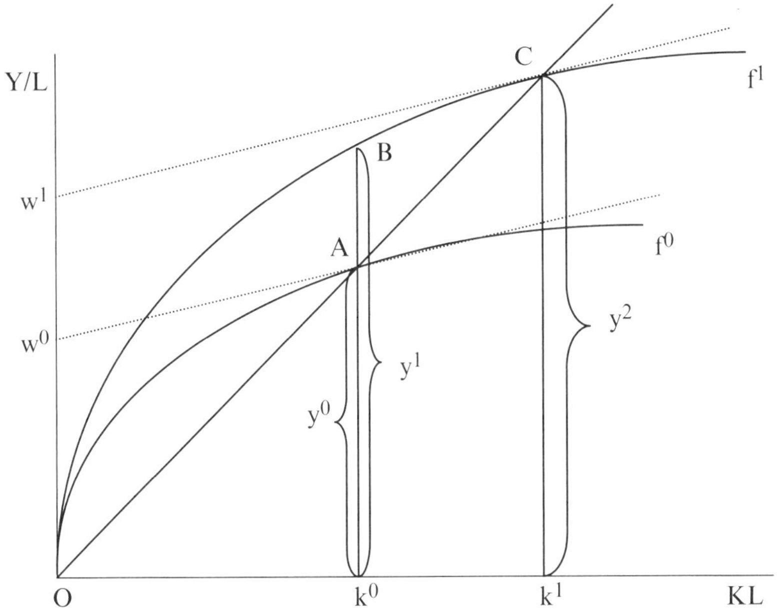

Figure 10.3 Harrod-neutral technical change

the level of output per worker has risen from y^1 to y^2, the ratio of output to capital, that is, $(Y/L)/(K/L)$ – which is given by the solid line starting at 0 and running through C – is the same as it was at point A. In other words, if we compare A with C, the conditions for Harrod neutrality are satisfied as both the interest rate and the capital–output ratio are the same at C as they were at A.

Robinson (1938) showed that Hicks and Harrod neutrality can co-exist if the production function has an elasticity of substitution of unity. She also demonstrated that Harrod-neutral technical change is purely labour-augmenting and that 'a neutral invention in Mr Harrod's sense has the same effect as an increase in the supply of labour . . . and is seen to be equivalent to an all-round increase in the efficiency of labour' (Robinson, 1938, p. 140). A mathematical proof was provided by Uzawa (1961).

A third type of neutrality was introduced by Solow (1960, 1963). This is where technical change (which is entirely embodied in new capital goods) at the rate λ per period 'is "purely capital augmenting" in the sense that after an improvement has occurred one unit of capital (measured in replacement cost) and x units of labour can produce precisely what $1/(1 + \lambda)$ units of capital and x units of labour could produce before the change' (Solow, 1963, p. 59).

A useful way to compare the different definitions is to use an explicit production function with only two inputs, labour (L) and capital (K) and with all the usual properties and to assume also that technical change can be regarded as a function of time (Allen, 1967, Ch 13, has an excellent discussion). Hicks-neutral technical change then is where the production function can be written in a form where technical change is equally capital- and labour-augmenting:

$$Y(t) = F[a(t)K(t), a(t)L(t)] = a(t)F[K(t), L(t)].$$

Harrod-neutral technical change is where the production function can be written in labour-augmenting form $Y(t) = F[K(t), a(t)L(t)]$, while Solow-neutral technical change is where the production function can be written in capital-augmenting form, $Y(t) = F[a(t)K(t), L(t)]$.

REFERENCES

Allen, R. G. D. (1967), *Macro-Economic Theory*, London: Macmillan.
Ferguson, C. E. (1969), *The Neoclassical Theory of Production and Distribution*, Cambridge: Cambridge University Press.
Hahn, F. H. and R. C. O. Matthews (1964), 'The Theory of Economic Growth: A Survey', *Economic Journal*, Vol. 74, No. 296 (Dec.), pp. 779–902.
Harrod, R. F. (1937), 'Review of Essays in the Theory of Employment by Joan Robinson', *Economic Journal*, Vol. 47, No. 186 (June), pp. 326–330.
Harrod, R. F. (1948), *Towards a Dynamic Economics: Some Recent Developments of Economic Theory and their Application to Policy*, London: Macmillan.
Hicks, J. R. (1932), *The Theory of Wages*, London: Macmillan.
Pigou, A. C. (1932), *The Economics of Welfare*, Fourth edition, London: Macmillan.
Robinson, J. (1938), 'The Classification of Inventions', *Review of Economic Studies*, Vol. 5, No. 2 (Feb.), pp. 139–142.
Solow, R. M. (1960), 'Investment and Technical Progress', in K. J. Arrow, S. Karlin and P. Suppes (eds), *Mathematical Methods in the Social Sciences*, Stanford: Stanford University Press, pp. 89–104.
Solow, R. M. (1963), *Capital Theory and the Rate of Return*, Amsterdam: North Holland.
Uzawa, H. (1961), 'Neutral Inventions and the Stability of Growth Equilibrium', *Review of Economic Studies*, Vol. 28, No. 2 (Feb.), pp. 117–124.

11. Nash equilibrium

Jürgen Eichberger

Nash equilibrium[1] is arguably the most important equilibrium concept in economics. Debreu (1952) shows that even the traditional notion of a demand and supply equilibrium is a special case of a Nash equilibrium if one introduces a player who adjusts prices. Most important, however, is the application of this equilibrium concept in the context of strategic interactions, as one can find them in oligopoly theory, industrial organization models, in models with externalities or public goods, or in modern industrial-organization-based international economics. We will focus here on the case of strategic interaction between two players. All concepts introduced here can and have been extended to many-player situations. There are innumerable text books on Game Theory, as the theory of strategic interactions is usually called; for a very informal introduction one can recommend Binmore (2007), for an excellent more advanced treatment we recommend Osborne and Rubinstein (1994).

Strategic interaction between two players, say Player A and Player B, can be described by the strategy sets of these players, S_A and S_B, and their payoff functions $p_A(s_A, s_B)$ and $p_B(s_A, s_B)$, which indicate the individual evaluation of the outcome arising from the strategic interaction by the two strategies s_A and s_B. A pair of strategies (s_A, s_B), a so-called strategy combination, describes an interactive situation where Player A chooses strategy s_A from the set of strategies S_A and Player B chooses s_B from the strategies in S_B. If each player has only a small and finite number of strategies, then one can represent the game in a matrix. Some very famous games take this special form, for example, the Prisoners' Dilemma or Matching Pennies, or coordination games like the Stag-Hunt Game (Figure 11.1).

The entries in the matrix cells are the payoffs for Players A and B in a situation where the strategy combination defining the cell is played. For example, in the Prisoners' Dilemma, both players have the choice between the strategies 'Confess' and 'Not confess'. At a strategy combination (C, N) where Player A confesses and Player B does not confess, Player A will have a payoff of 3 while Player B will obtain −1. The stories of these games and an extensive discussion can be found in Osborne and Rubinstein

Player A \ Player B	*N*	*C*
N	1,1	–1,3
C	3, –1	0,0

Prisoners' Dilemma

Player A \ Player B	*H*	*T*
H	1,–1	–1, 1
T	–1, 1	1, –1

Matching Pennies

Player A \ Player B	*h*	*l*
h	2, 2	0, 0
l	0, 0	1, 1

Stag Hunt

Figure 11.1 Three matrix games

(1994, pp. 14–17). There are many economic applications where there are too many strategies for each player for the situation to be represented by a matrix.

A Nash equilibrium is a strategy combination (s_A^*, s_B^*) where no player can increase her payoff by choosing another strategy available in her strategy set. Formally, (s_A^*, s_B^*) is a *Nash equilibrium* if:

$$p_A(s_A^*, s_B^*) \geq p_A(s_A, s_B^*) \text{ for all } s_A \text{ in } S_A$$

$$p_B(s_A^*, s_B^*) \geq p_B(s_A^*, s_B) \text{ for all } s_B \text{ in } S_B$$

holds. A Nash equilibrium represents a situation (strategy combination) where no player can win by unilaterally deviating to another strategy. Note that this equilibrium notion contains no information about how such a situation may arise. In particular, there is generally no dynamic process described which would lead to such an equilibrium (compare Chapter 2, on stability of equilibrium). In economic applications, the interpretations of a Nash equilibrium situation reach from the notion of a 'rational expectations equilibrium' to that of a 'self-enforcing agreement'; one can easily check that, in the Prisoners' Dilemma, the strategy combination (*C*, *C*) is a Nash equilibrium, that there is no Nash equilibrium in the Matching Pennies game, and that both (*h*, *h*) and (*l*, *l*) are Nash equilibria in the Stag Hunt.

BEST-REPLY CURVES

The analysis of a two-player interaction can often be conducted in a diagram where the best reply of each player to the other player's strategies is depicted, $R_A(s_B)$ or $R_B(s_A)$ respectively. Note that there may be more than one best-reply strategy to a strategy of the opponent.

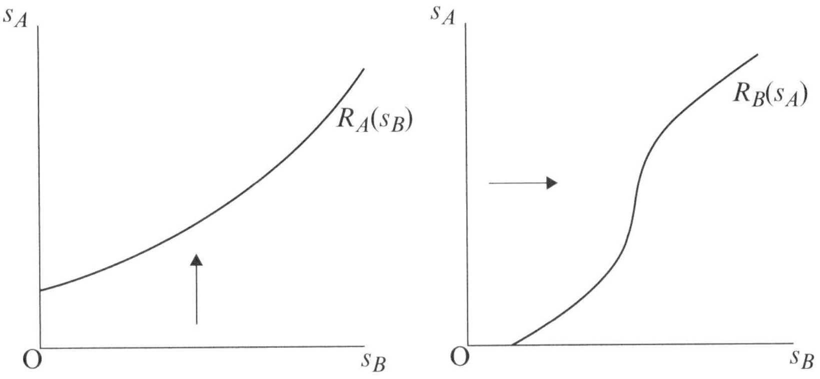

Figure 11.2 Best reply

The curve in the left diagram of Figure 11.2 shows the best-reply strategies of Player A, $R_A(s_B)$, to the different strategies of Player B, s_B, and the curve in the right-hand diagram of this Figure indicates the best replies of Player B, $R_B(s_A)$, to all possible strategies of Player A, s_A. Notice that the best-reply curve of Player A must be read from the abscissa as indicated by the upward arrow, while the best-reply curve of Player B must be read from the ordinate, as the right-pointing arrow indicates. In these diagrams, the best-reply curves are upward sloping. In general, depending on the game one considers, the best-reply curves may be upward sloping, downward sloping or non-monotonic. For example in the quantity duopoly of Cournot, the best-reply functions will be downward sloping, while they will be upward sloping in a price duopoly with heterogeneous products (see Chapter 17, on duopoly reaction curves). Combining the two diagrams of Figure 11.2 will demonstrate whether the best-reply curves of the two players will intersect once, several times or not at all.

Figure 11.3 illustrates the case of a unique Nash equilibrium (s_A^*, s_B^*). Deviations from a best-reply curve for a given strategy of the opponent will make the player worse off. Clearly, in a Nash equilibrium, such a profitable deviation is impossible in this case. The figure is the prototype of a diagram showing a Nash equilibrium of a two-player game. Notice that we have treated the strategies s_A and s_B as continuous variables. In many economic applications, strategies are prices or quantities which can be treated in this way. For games with a finite number of strategies, such as the matrix games shown before, the best-reply curves consist of a few isolated points. Hence, one cannot count on finding a non-empty intersection. Nash equilibrium may not exist in pure strategies, as in the case of Matching Pennies.

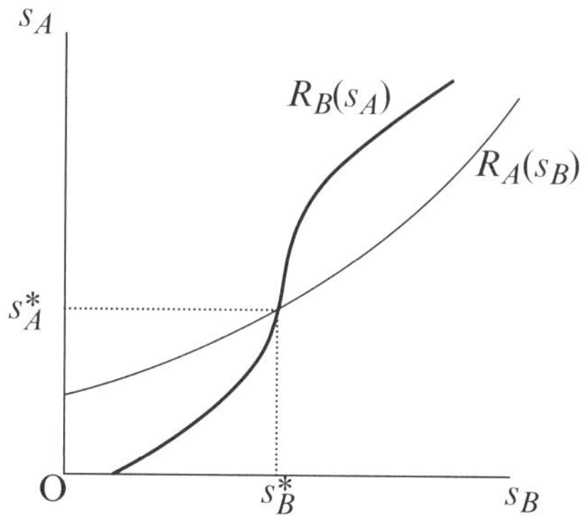

Figure 11.3 Nash equilibrium

MIXED STRATEGIES

For any strategic interaction, one can consider the possibility that players enlarge their strategy sets by playing their strategies according to a random device of their choice. For example, a player with two pure strategies could consider flipping a coin and playing one or the other strategy according to the outcome of the coin toss. Or, a player may roll a die and choose one strategy if the die shows one or two spots and the other strategy otherwise. In the first case she would randomize with the probability distribution $(\frac{1}{2}, \frac{1}{2})$, in the second case with probability distribution $(\frac{1}{3}, \frac{2}{3})$. In principle, any probability distribution $(q, 1 - q)$ could be chosen. If Player A chose her first pure strategy s_A^1 with probability q_A and Player B her first pure strategy s_B^1 with probability q_B, the expected payoff of the players, $P_A(q_A, q_B)$ and $P_B(q_A, q_B)$ respectively, would be

$$\begin{aligned} P_A(q_A, q_B) :=& q_A \cdot q_B \cdot p_A(s_A^1, s_B^1) + q_A \cdot (1 - q_B) \cdot p_A(s_A^1, s_B^2) \\ &+ (1 - q_A) \cdot q_B \cdot p_A(s_A^2, s_B^1) + (1 - q_A) \cdot (1 - q_B) \cdot p_A(s_A^2, s_B^2), \\ P_B(q_A, q_B) :=& q_A \cdot q_B \cdot p_B(s_A^1, s_B^1) + q_A \cdot (1 - q_B) \cdot p_B(s_A^1, s_B^2) \\ &+ (1 - q_A) \cdot q_B \cdot p_B(s_A^2, s_B^1) + (1 - q_A) \cdot (1 - q_B) \cdot p_B(s_A^2, s_B^2), \end{aligned}$$

where the strategy sets for the mixed strategies q_A and q_B now equal the unit interval. Notice that the mixed strategies are now continuous variables even if the pure strategies are finite. Figure 11.4 now shows the best-reply curves in the mixed strategies for the two players of Matching Pennies. In the left diagram of this figure, the best-reply curve of Player A is shown. If Player B plays her first strategy H with low probability $q_B < \frac{1}{2}$, then Player

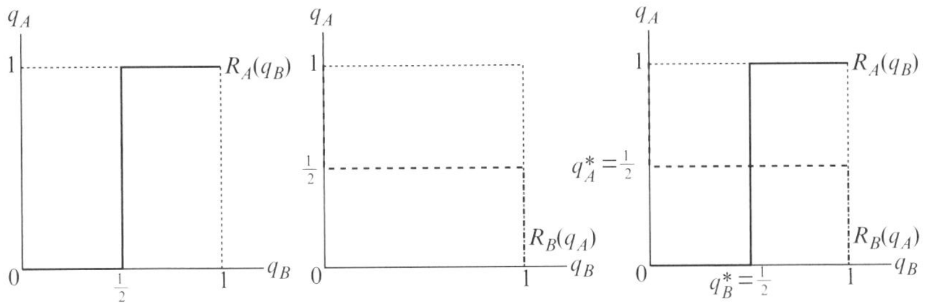

Figure 11.4 Nash equilibrium in mixed strategies

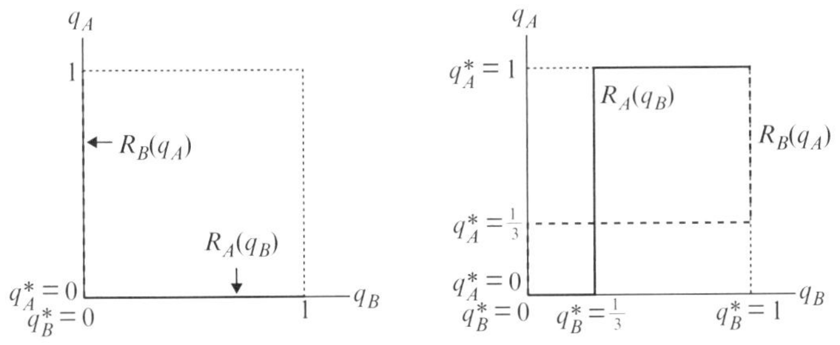

Figure 11.5 Prisoners' Dilemma and Stag Hunt

A, who wins if (H, H) occurs, should play her strategy H with the lowest probability possible, $q_A = 0$. In contrast, for $q_B > \frac{1}{2}$, Player A should play H with the highest possible probability, $q_A = 1$. Notice, that for $q_B = \frac{1}{2}$, Player A has a constant expected payoff $P_A(q_A \frac{1}{2}) = 0$. Hence, she is indifferent between all her mixed strategies and all are equally optimal.

The middle diagram of Figure 11.4 shows the best reply of Player B in mixed strategies and the right-hand diagram combines the best replies of the two players. The Nash equilibrium in mixed strategies for Matching Pennies is the intersection of these two curves at $(q_A^*, q_B^*) = (\frac{1}{2}, \frac{1}{2})$. Obviously, in this Nash equilibrium in mixed strategies, both players are indifferent about their mixed strategy choice. However, if either of them deviated from their equilibrium strategy, for example, if, Player A deviated from $q_A^* = \frac{1}{2}$, then the other Player would have an incentive to deviate as well.

We conclude this chapter with the diagrams showing the Nash equilibria of the Prisoners' Dilemma and the Stag Hunt (Figure 11.5).

NOTE

1. John F. Nash, Jr, introduced the concept of an 'equilibrium point' for general non-cooperative n-person games as a generalisation of the concept of a 'solution' in two-player zero-sum games. The formal proof of existence of an equilibrium was published in Nash (1950). The equilibrium concept was introduced in Nash (1951).

REFERENCES

Binmore, K. (2007). *Game Theory: A Very Short Introduction.* Oxford: Oxford University Press.

Debreu, G. (1952). 'A social equilibrium existence theory'. *Proceedings of the National Academy of Sciences of the U.S.A.* 38, 886–893. (Reprinted as Chapter 10 in Debreu, G. (1983), *Mathematical Economics.* Cambridge: Cambridge University Press).

Nash, J.F. (1950). 'Equilibrium Points in N-Person Games'. *Proceedings of the National Academy of Sciences* 36, 48–49.

Nash, J.F. (1951). 'Non-cooperative Games'. *Annals of Mathematics* 54, 289–295.

Osborne, M. and Rubinstein, A. (1994). *A Course in Game Theory.* Cambridge, MA: MIT Press.

Welfare economics

12. Consumer surplus

Yew-Kwang Ng

While consumer surplus has been regarded as superfluous or of debatable theoretical foundation, its use in cost-benefit analyses and policy discussion has been widespread.

1. THE ORIGIN OF THE CONCEPT: DUPUIT AND MARSHALL

The concept of consumer surplus was first formulated by the French engineer Dupuit (1844). Marshall (1890/1920) was first in introducing the concept to the English-speaking world, but was said to be less than generous in admitting Dupuit's priority (Pfouts, 1953, p. 316). See Hines (1999) on the history and controversies of consumer surplus and the associated Harberger triangle (on which see Chapter 13, which also discusses some issues on the use of consumer surplus areas for welfare measurement).

Marshall defined consumer surplus as 'the excess of the price which he would be willing to pay rather than go without the thing, over that which he actually does pay' (Marshall, 1890/1920, p. 124). According to this definition, the surplus is the difference of an all-or-none comparison, that is, between (i) not being allowed to buy any quantity of the good, and (ii) buying the chosen quantity of the good at the prevailing price. As a measure of this, Marshall used the triangular area under the demand curve and above the rectangle representing the actual money expenditure of the consumer. As shown in Figure 12.1, this is measured by the curvilinear (if the demand curve is not a straight line) ΔIPA where OP is the price of the good. As pointed out by Hicks (1940, p. 109), this Marshallian measure is not a definition but a theorem, true under certain assumptions. In his mathematical appendix, Marshall did remark on the assumption of a constant marginal utility of money (MUM). He justified this assumption on the grounds that the expenditure on one particular commodity is usually small relative to total income. Any change in the MUM is neglected as of the second order of smallness. It is not the constancy in MUM as money income changes but the constancy in MUM

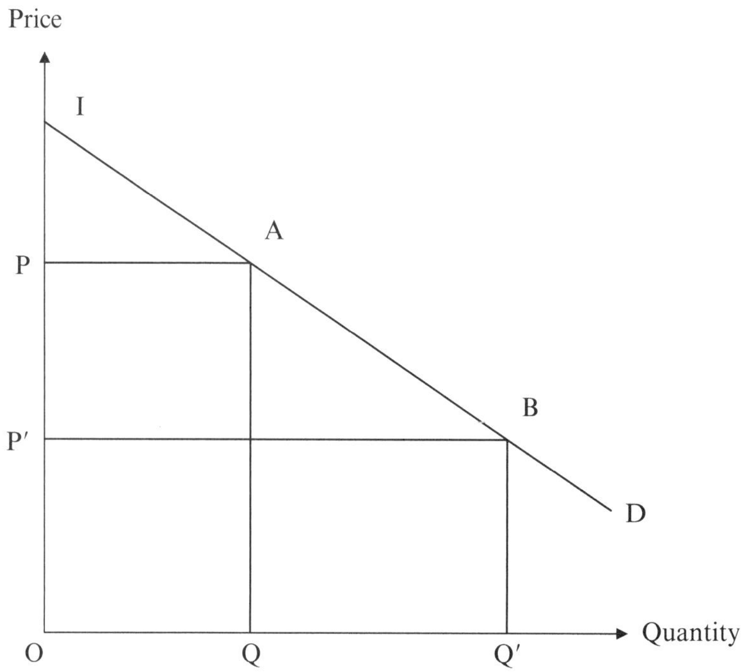

Figure 12.1 The Marshallian measure of consumer surplus

as prices change that is relevant (Samuelson 1942). Despite the probably sharply diminishing MUM as money or wealth increases, MUM may stay approximately constant for a particular price change.

When the price of the good falls from P to P′, other things being equal, the amount of consumer surplus so measured by the Marshallian triangle increases by the amount PP′BA.

2. HICKS'S FOUR MEASURES

Associated with the attempt to rid economic analysis of the cardinal measures of utility, Hicks (1941) introduced the concept of compensating variation (discussed below). With further clarification by Henderson (1941), four measures of surplus (or changes thereof) were distinguished (Hicks, 1943):

1. Compensating variation (CV) of a change in prices (or other variables, if we are not confined to changes in prices) is the amount of

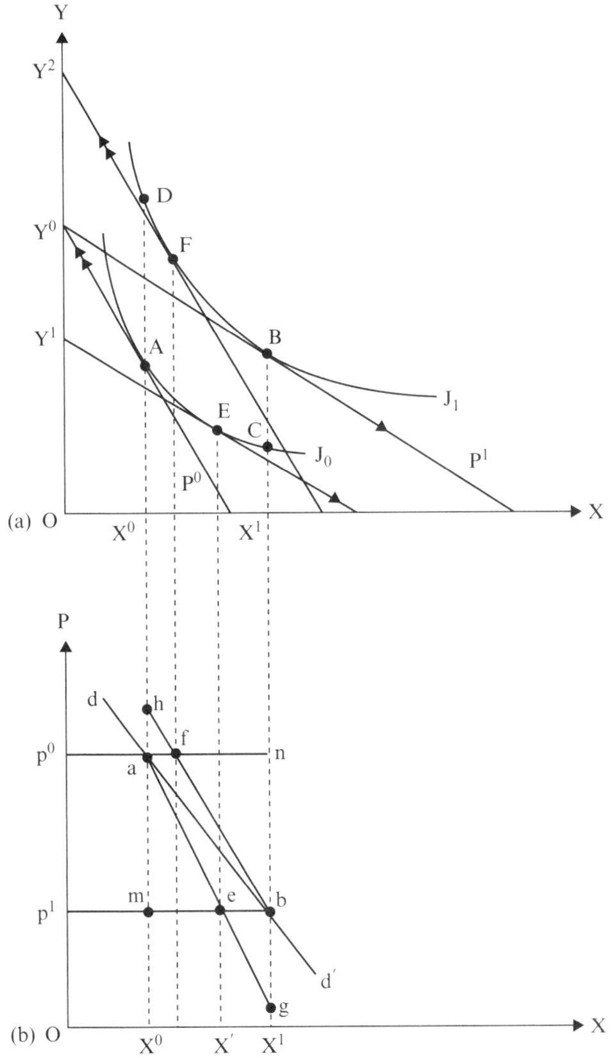

Figure 12.2 Hicks's four measures

compensation (usually in monetary terms or the composite good Y in Figure 12.2) that can be taken from an individual while leaving him just as well off as before the change.

2. Compensating surplus (CS) is the amount of compensation that can be taken from the individual while leaving him just as well off as before the change, if he were constrained to buy at the new

price the quantity of the commodity he would buy in the absence of compensation.

3. Equivalent variation (EV) is the amount of compensation that has to be given to the individual, in the absence of the change, to make him as well off as he would be with the change.
4. Equivalent surplus (ES) is the amount of compensation that has to be given to the individual, in the absence of the change, to make him as well off as he would be with the change, if he were constrained to buy at the old price the quantity of the commodity he would buy in the absence of compensation.

Consider Figure 12.2, where the axes measure the amount of the good X and (composite) good Y consumed by the consumer. As the price of X falls from p^0 to p^1, the consumer moves from point A on the indifference curve J_0 to point B on J_1. It can be seen that, for this price fall, the four measures (all positive) are: CV = Y^oY^1, CS = BC, EV = Y^0Y^2, ES = AD.

In Figure 12.2b, an ordinary demand curve dd′ is derived from the indifference map in Figure 12.2a. When the price falls from p^0 to p^1, the consumer increases her purchase from X^0 (or p^0a) to X^1 (p^1b). If the consumer has to pay the CV of Y^0Y^1, she will end up at E instead of at B. Hence, the curve aeg is the compensated (or Hicksian) demand curve from the point a (and refers to the indifference curve J_0). (If the good were inferior, aeg would lie to the right of dd′.) Similarly bfh is the compensated demand curve as the consumer is kept at the indifference curve J_1. It can then be seen that, while in Figure 12.2a, consumer surplus is measured as distances, in Figure 12.2b it is measured as areas, as follows: CV = p^0p^1ea; CS = p^0p^1ea – egb; EV = p^0p^1 bf; ES = p^0p^1 bf + afh.

When the price is p^0, a marginal decrease in price benefits the consumer by p^0a. As price falls continuously from p^0 to p^1, the total amount of money that can be taken from him while leaving him just as well off without the fall (that is, on indifference curve J_0) is thus the area p^0p^1ea, remembering that, as compensation is extracted from the consumer, he is traveling along the compensated demand curve aeg, not the ordinary one dd′. To see that the area p^0p^1ea measures the CV associated with the price fall p^0 to p^1, note that, for a marginal price fall, the consumer is made better off by the amount of the good consumed, that is, by p^0a at p^0. (Intuitively, how much you benefit from a marginal fall in the price of X depends on how much you consume X. Formally, from Roy's equality, misnamed identity, $-\partial u/\partial p_i$ divided by the marginal utility of money equals x_i.) Hence for the whole series of marginal price falls from p^0 to p^1, CV is measured by p^0p^1ea.

For CS, since the consumer is constrained to purchase the quantity

X^1 while he in fact prefers to purchase X', he will be made worse off if we extract p^0p^1ea from him. Hence, CS is measured by p^0p^1ea − egb; this little triangle being the loss he suffers by having to stick to the constrained quantity. This is so since he has to pay the unit price p^1 while his marginal valuation for the units between X' and X^1 is indicated by the height of the compensated demand curve eg. For ES, he is also made worse off by the constraint. But here, it is the amount we have to pay him and so ES exceeds EV by the little triangle afh.

The Marshallian measure is the area p^0p^1ba, which falls somewhere in between the four measures. If the income effect is negligible, the consumer demand is not affected by the payment of compensation. Then the compensated demand curve coincides with the ordinary demand curve and all the five measures are equal.

The measurement discussed refers to a single individual with a change in the price of only one good. With multiple price changes, we have the problem of path dependency (Hotelling 1938) where the amount of surplus measured depends on the path or order of the goods; when aggregated over different individuals, we have the Boadway (1974) paradox where a positive surplus does not ensure that the gainers could compensate the losers. See Ng (2004, Ch.4) for a discussion of such issues as well as the usefulness of different measures, the implication of diamond effects for surplus measurement, and his proposal to use 'marginal dollar equivalence' where CV and EV differ by a large amount for huge changes.

3. THE APPROXIMATE NATURE OF SURPLUS MEASUREMENT

The welfare of an individual is a subjective state of mind. Hence, any non-approximate measurement has to reflect this subjective character. However, it is convenient (in economic calculation, almost essential) to have some objective measures such as a monetary measure. Nevertheless, since the relation between units of any external yardstick of welfare such as money and internal unit of welfare (however defined) is in general not a constant, such objective measures can be, by their very nature, no more than an approximate measure of welfare, even abstracting from the problem of inaccuracies in practical data collection. If we recognize that the surplus measurement and in fact any other objective measurement of welfare must be regarded as approximate only, then all the problems of path dependency, inconsistencies and so on, shrink into insignificance unless the discrepancies involved are substantial.

To illustrate the approximate nature of any surplus measurement,

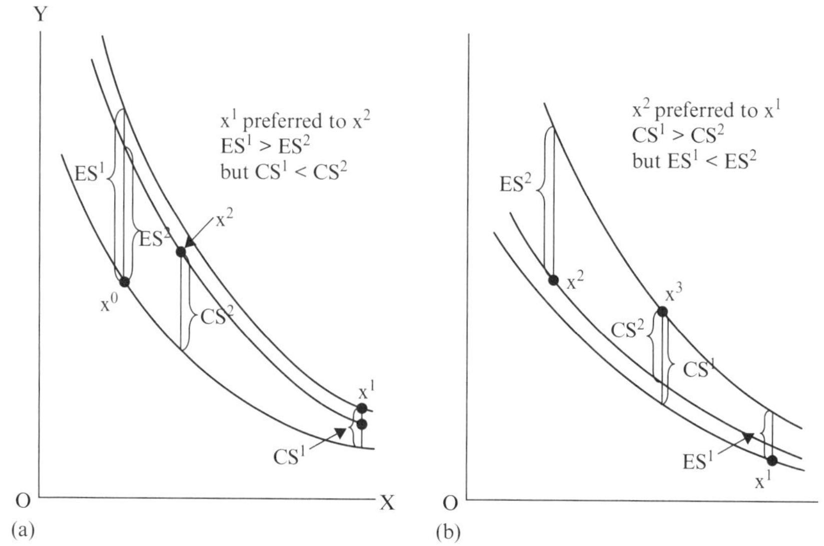

Figure 12.3 The equivalence measures are not superior to the compensating measures

consider the argument by Hause (1975, pp. 1150–1) that the EV and ES measures have the following advantage over the CV and CS measures (see also for a demonstration McKenzie 1983 that the equivalent measures are perfect measures of welfare changes). Based on Ng 2004, we see that starting from a given initial point x° (say a bundle of goods consumed), the consumer moves to a new point x^1 due to a certain change (in prices, quotas and so on). Starting from the same initial point x°, he moves to x^2 with another change. An ideal measure of welfare change ΔW should possess the following property: $\Delta W(x^0 \rightarrow x^1) > \Delta W(x^0 \rightarrow x^2)$ if and only if x^1 is preferred to x^2. It can be seen that the EV and ES measures possess this property while the CV and CS measures do not, in general. (Readers may attempt to show this as an exercise before consulting Figure 12.3a, where this point is shown for the surplus measures. The point can also be similarly shown with respect to the variation measures, using price lines.)

The reason is that the equivalent measures use the initial point as the welfare reference point while the compensating measures use the end point. In the above comparison, the initial point is fixed but the end points are not. This explains why EV and ES satisfy the required property while CV and CS do not. But this looks at only one side of the coin. For any given end point x^e, the ideal measure of welfare change for different points x^1, x^2, taken as the original point, should possess the following property:

$\Delta W(x^1 \rightarrow x^e) > \Delta W(x^2 \rightarrow x^e)$ if and only if x^2 is preferred to x^1. It can then be seen that CV and CS possess this property but EV and ES do not (see Figure 12.3b). Hence neither pair can be regarded as superior to the other. Both measures may be acceptable as approximate measures for changes whose effects are thinly spread. The prevalent acceptance of the equivalent measures as perfect cannot be justified.

REFERENCES

Arrow, Kenneth J. and Scitovsky, Tibor (eds) (1969). *Readings in Welfare Economics*, London: Allen and Unwin.

Boadway, Robin W. (1974). 'The welfare foundations of cost-benefit analysis', *Economic Journal*, 84:926–39.

Dupuit, Jules (1944), 'De la mesure de l'utilité des travausx publics', *Annales des Ponts et Chaussées*, translated by R. H. Barback (1952) in *International Economic Papers*, 2:83–110. Reprinted in Arrow and Scitovsky (1969).

Hause, John C. 1975. 'The theory of welfare cost measurement', *Journal of Political Economy*, 83:1145–82.

Henderson, A. (1941), 'Consumer's surplus and the compensating variation', *Review of Economic Studies*, 8:117–21.

Hicks, John R. (1940), 'The valuation of social income', *Economica*, 7:105–24.

Hicks, John R. (1941), 'The rehabilitation of consumers' surplus', *Review of Economic Studies*, 8:108–16.

Hicks, John R. (1943), 'The four consumers' surplus', *Review of Economic Studies*, 11:31–41.

Hines, James R., Jr (1999). 'Three sides of Harberger triangles', *Journal of Economic Perspectives*, 13(2):167–88.

Hotelling, Harold (1938), 'The general welfare in relation to problems of taxation and of railway and utility rates', *Econometrica*, 6:242–69. Reprinted in Arrow & Scitovsky (1969).

Marshall, Alfred (1890/1920). *Principles of Economics*, London: Macmillan.

McKenzie, George W. (1983). *Measuring Economic Welfare: New Methods*, Cambridge: Cambridge University Press.

Ng, Yew-Kwang (2004), *Welfare Economics: Toward a Complete Analysis*, London: Macmillan.

Pfouts, R. W. (1953), 'A critique of some recent contributions to the theory of consumers' surplus', *Southern Economic Journal*, 19:315–33.

Samuelson, Paul A. (1942), 'Constancy of the marginal utility of income', in *Studies in Mathematical Economics and Econometrics in Memory of Henry Schultz*, eds O. Lange, F. McIntyre and T. O. Yntema, Chicago, IL: Chicago University Press.

13. The Harberger triangle

Yew-Kwang Ng

Harberger triangles are areas of net losses in consumer surplus (on which see Chapter 12) and producer surplus used to measure the deadweight losses or welfare costs of such distortions as monopolies, price controls and taxes. Though the concept has a much longer history well before Harberger's papers (1964a, 1964b), 'Welfare triangles are "Harberger triangles" because Harberger's papers measured them, did so in a consistent manner, and assisted and encouraged a host of others to do likewise' (Hines 1999, p.185, which provides an excellent review of the history and issues involved with the triangle and on which parts of the following discussion are based).

The textbook illustration of the triangle is shown in Figure 13.1.[1] The initial equilibrium price P and quantity Q of a good is determined by the demand curve and supply curve S at the point A. The imposition of a per unit tax equal to the distance BD shifts the supply curve from S to S', the quantity traded from Q to Q', the price to the consumers/demanders to P_c and the net-of-tax price to the producers/suppliers to P_p. The tax revenue raised is measured by the area P_cBDP_p, being the per unit tax BD times the post-tax transaction OQ'. However, the loss in consumer surplus is measured by P_cBAP, and the loss in producer surplus is measured by PADP_p. The combined losses exceed the tax revenue by the Harberger triangle BAD. (The choice of the three alphabets is intentional to emphasize that the triangle is a deadweight loss, hence bad.) Thus, it is concluded that, even ignoring administrative, compliance and policing costs, a tax typically imposes burdens on the economy in excess of the tax revenue collected by the Harberger triangle or the excess burden of taxation. For taxes on incomes, the excess burden is related to the disincentive effects (a form of substitution). It may be noted that the size of this triangle or welfare costs increases with the square of the size of the distortion. This property is unchanged in many applications and generalizations, for example, the Anderson-Neary concept of a trade restrictiveness index. However, some qualifications to the deadweight loss nature of the triangle and its measurement may be added.

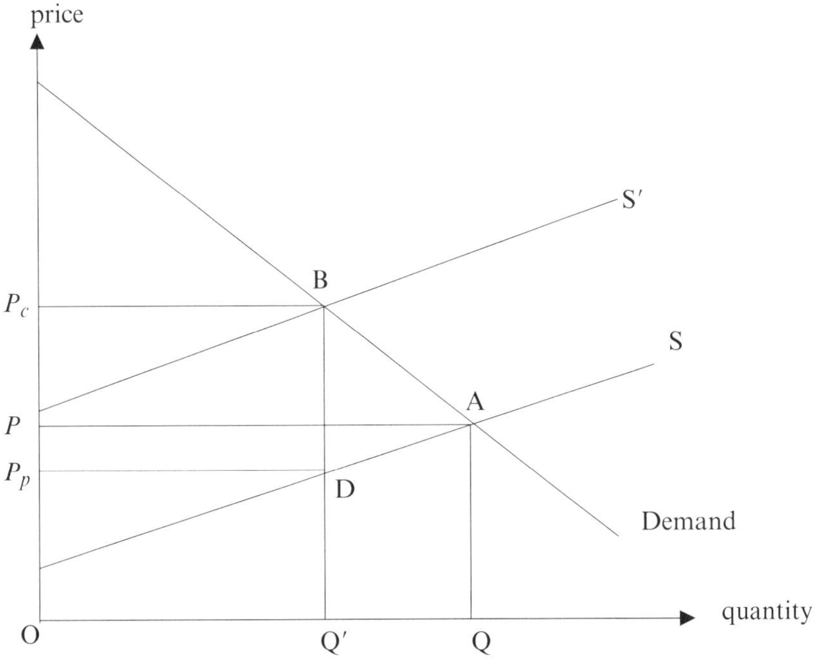

Figure 13.1 The Harberger triangle

First, the original equilibrium A is assumed to be efficient. If the production and/or consumption of the good imposes significant external costs like pollution, the original equilibrium A is likely to be inefficient to begin with. A tax on this good or the pollution may then increase efficiency and impose a negative excess burden; see Chapter 15, on the taxation of external costs.

Second, even if taxation does impose excess burdens, it does not follow that there should be no taxation or less taxation. Tax revenues may be needed to finance essential legal, social and economic infrastructures, including law and order, defense, research, transportation and communications that are public goods. In other words, the large consumer surpluses created in the provision of these public goods financed by tax revenues may offset the excess burdens of taxation many times over. In fact, if we combine the spending side with the taxation and revenue side, the excess burden or disincentives may disappear or even become negative.

A simple example may help. If we only consider the taxation side, it may be the case that the incentive to earn incomes is higher if one can keep all the extra \$1000 earned, instead of having to pay 20 per cent in income tax and keeping only $800. However, with no taxes, there is no public spending in providing for police protection. The extra $1000 earned may easily be stolen, perhaps even with one's life lost in the incident. If we combine taxation with the spending side, it becomes quite possible that one may have higher incentives to earn the $800 with police protection, than to earn the unprotected $1000.

Based on looking only at the taxation side, economists traditionally believe that public projects have to pass a more stringent cost-benefit test than private projects. As public projects have to be financed by taxation, their benefit-to-cost ratios have to be larger than say 1.3 (instead of just one) for them to be efficient, with the 30 per cent being the average estimate of the excess marginal cost of public funding. Looking at the two sides of taxation and spending together, Kaplow (1996) and Ng (2000) favor the use of a benefit-to-cost ratio of just one (or even lower for Ng as he considers some wider factors like the relative competition in private consumption that is mutually offsetting at the social level and the ineffectiveness of private consumption in increasing happiness in advanced countries).

Third, the textbook illustration of the Harberger triangle uses the Marshallian demand curve (holding the prices of other goods and consumer incomes unchanged). If compensated demand curves are drawn from the original point A or from the final point B to get the compensated variation or equivalent variation measures (on which see Chapter 12, on consumer surplus) of the deadweight losses, the amount involved will differ from the Marshallian measure illustrated in Figure 13.1 by the presence of income effects. If the good in question accounts only for a small fraction of total consumption, these differences are small. Harberger's empirical estimation of the deadweight losses is based on demand curves with tax revenue returned to consumers in lump sums. Though consumers still lose by the excess burden of taxation, they do not lose the tax revenues, making the income effects much smaller, and hence the question of which demand curves (Marshallian or compensated) to use becomes less of a problem. Thus, Rosen (1978) finds that the Harberger triangles estimated in this way track the compensated measures quite closely, though examples where they may differ significantly cannot be ruled out (Hausman 1981).

Fourth, the principle that the deadweight loss involved may be measured by the Harberger triangle illustrated in Figure 13.1 is based on ignoring some possible general-equilibrium or second-best considerations (on which see Chapter 38, on second and third-best theories) or on the assumption that all other sectors in the economy except the good under discussion have no distortions. For example, if the taxation of good X causes an increase in demand for good Y, which is already taxed, the higher demand for good Y generates marginal benefits in excess of the marginal costs (due to the pre-existing tax on Y). This offsets the excess burden on good X. Even if the interaction effects (such as the one between X and Y just mentioned) are small, the offsetting effects may be large if the pre-existing distortions are significant, as the relevant effects are rectangles, not triangles. Such complications have been taken account of in Harberger's discussion and estimation. Before Harberger, among other contributors, Boiteux (1951) generalized measures of deadweight loss to situations in which some initial prices may be distorted and Meade (1955) analyzed the welfare consequences of interactions between multiple distortions with respect to tariffs and other trade restrictions, before the formalization of the general theory of the second best by Lipsey and Lancaster (1956).

Fifth, just like the measures of consumer surplus, the Harberger triangle measures welfare losses in pure monetary values unweighted by income distributional considerations. In other words, a dollar is counted as a dollar whether of the rich or the poor. Harberger (1971) provides an influential case in favour of this efficiency-only approach in applied welfare economics. Ng (1979, 1984) justifies this proposition by showing that, for any alternative using some purely equality-oriented distributional weights or some other non-efficiency principles on specific issues, there exists a Pareto-superior alternative without using such weights or principles but with the general tax/transfer system possibly made more progressive.

Sixth, according to Harberger's estimates, while various types of resource misallocation amount to a total welfare loss equivalent to a large 15 per cent of Chilean GNP (Harberger 1959), the welfare costs of monopolistic behaviour in the U.S. industry amount to only 0.1 per cent of GNP. While still sizable in absolute terms, this relatively small figure led to a number of different estimates. In particular, the estimate by Cowling and Mueller (1978) produced a figure well in excess of 10 per cent. The huge difference is due to accounting for the waste from rent-seeking activities, which was first analyzed by Tullock (1967). If some factors (for example, exclusive rights, tariff protection) create monopolistic power that gives rise to excess profits, people will invest resources to try to gain such exclusive positions. With free entry into such competition, the whole of the monopolistic profits may be dissipated into deadweight losses.

As illustrated in Figure 13.2, in comparison to the competitive or social optimal output Q at the intersection of the demand curve and the marginal cost (MC) curve at A, the monopolistic restriction of output to Q' (where the MC and the marginal revenue MR curves intersect) involves a deadweight loss measured by the Harberger triangle BAD, somewhat similar to the case of taxation discussed above. Assuming no fixed costs, the amount of monopolistic profits is measured by the area PBDC. With full rent

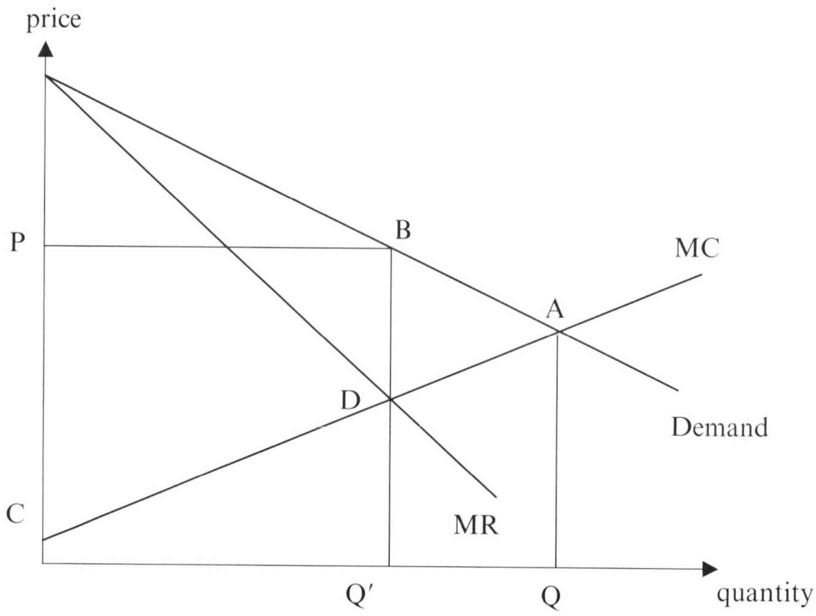

Figure 13.2 The Tullock trapezoid

dissipation, this probably much larger area (the Tullock trapezoid) also measures the cost of monopoly rent dissipation.

NOTE

1. On the contrast of the supply-demand curve illustration of excess burden in terms of the Harberger triangle with the indifference curve illustration, see Liu and Rettenmaier (2005).

REFERENCES

Anderson, J.E. and J.P. Neary (2005), *Measuring the Restrictiveness of International Trade Policy* (Cambridge, MA: MIT Press).
Boiteux, Marcel (1951). 'Le "revenue distribuable' et les pertes économiques"', *Econometrica*, 19 (2): 112–33.
Cowling, Keith, and Dennis C. Mueller (1978). 'The social costs of monopoly power', *Economic Journal*, 88: 727–48.
Harberger, Arnold C. (1959). 'Using the resources at hand more effectively', *American Economic Review*, 49 (2): 134–46.

Harberger, Arnold C. (1964a). 'The measurement of waste', *American Economic Review*, 54 (3): 58–76.
Harberger, Arnold C. (1964b). 'Taxation, resource allocation, and welfare', in John F. Due ed., *The Role of Direct and Indirect Taxes in the Federal Revenue System* (Princeton, NJ: Princeton University Press, 25–70.
Harberger, Arnold C. (1971). 'Three basic postulates for applied welfare economics', *Journal of Economic Literature*, 9 (3): 785–97.
Hausman, Jerry A. (1981). 'Exact consumer's surplus and deadweight loss', *American Economic Review,* 71 (4): 662–76.
Hines, James R., Jr (1999). 'Three sides of Harberger triangles', *Journal of Economic Perspectives*, 13 (2): 167–88.
Kaplow, Louis (1996). 'The optimal supply of public goods and the distortionary cost of taxation', *National Tax Journal*, 49 (4): 513–33.
Lipsey, R.G. (1997). *The Selected Essays of Richard Lipsey: Volume I: Microeconomics, Growth and Political Economy* (Cheltenham: Edward Elgar).
Lipsey, R.G., and Lancaster, K. (1956). 'The general theory of second best', *The Review of Economic Studies*, 24: 11–32. Reprinted with errors corrected in Lipsey (1997).
Liu, Liqun and Rettenmaier, Andrew J. (2005). 'A graphical exposition of the link between two representations of the excess burden of taxation', *Journal of Economic Education*, 36 (4): 369–78.
Meade, James E. (1955). *The Theory of International Economic Policy*, *Vol. 2: Trade and Welfare*, Mathematical Supplement (London: Oxford University Press).
Ng, Yew-Kwang (1979). *Welfare Economics: Introduction and Development of Basic Concepts* (London: Macmillan).
Ng, Yew-Kwang (1984). 'Quasi-Pareto social improvements', *American Economic Review*, 74 (5): 1033–50.
Ng, Yew-Kwang (2000). 'The optimal size of public spending and the distortionary costs of taxation', *National Tax Journal*, 52 (2): 253–72.
Rosen, Harvey S. (1978). 'The measurement of excess burden with explicit utility functions', *Journal of Political Economy*, 86 (2), part 2: S121–S135.
Tullock, Gordon (1967). 'The welfare costs of tariffs, monopolies, and theft', *Western Economic Journal*, 5 (3): 224–32.

14. Community indifference curves and the Scitovsky 'paradox'

Richard G. Lipsey

The Scitovsky 'paradox' was discovered early in the development of the 'New Welfare Economics' that began in the late 1930s.[1] (For an excellent treatment of the evolution of welfare economics from its earliest days to the mid-1960s see Mishan (1967).) This new approach replaced the cardinal utility functions that were the basis of Pigovian welfare economics with ordinal welfare functions that made interpersonal comparisons of utility impossible and that came into British economics from the great Italian economist Vilfredo Pareto. When the full set of new welfare economics' efficiency conditions were fulfilled, the result was a Pareto optimum in which it was impossible to raise one person's welfare without simultaneously lowering at least one other person's. A Pareto improvement was then defined as a change in which at least one person's welfare was raised while no other person's welfare was lowered, and it was accepted that such a change would raise the community's overall welfare.[2] A change that produced winners and losers would be a Pareto improvement if the gainers fully compensated the losers.

To make their efficiency analysis applicable to those common cases in which losers were not fully compensated, a social gain was defined to occur if the gainers could, but not necessarily did, fully compensate the losers. This was the so-called hypothetical compensation test, (hereafter called the 'h-c test'). Nicholas Kaldor (1939: 550) argued that economists could give policy advice based on whether or not a change satisfied the h-c test, but whether the losers 'should in fact be given compensation or not, is a political question on which the economist, *qua* economist, could hardly pronounce an opinion'. John Hicks (1939: 711) put it this way: 'The main practical advantage of our line of approach is that it fixes attention upon the question of compensation. . .. [T]he reforms we have studied are marked out by the characteristic that they will allow of compensation to balance . . . [any] loss, and they will still show a net advantage . . .. I do not [however] contend that there is any ground for saying that compensation ought always to be given'.

Two years later, Tibor Scitovsky (1941) showed that the use of the h-c test could lead to a contradiction in that a move from Situation I to Situation II and a return move from II to I could both pass the test. This so-called 'Scitovsky's paradox' – a term that he did not apply to his result – was much misunderstood at the time, and is still widely misunderstood today. Far from being a paradox in the formal sense of the word, it reveals an important potential social conflict. To understand the Scitovsky case, we need to develop one of the major tools of the New Welfare Economics, community indifference curves.

COMMUNITY INDIFFERENCE CURVES

The construction of these curves can be illustrated geometrically for a two-person community following Figure 14.1, which comes from Mishan (1952: 315).[3] He takes individual *A*'s indifference map for two goods (not labelled on his axes) with origin A_o and superimposes individual *B*'s map with origin B_o. Now assume a distribution of welfare that puts the two

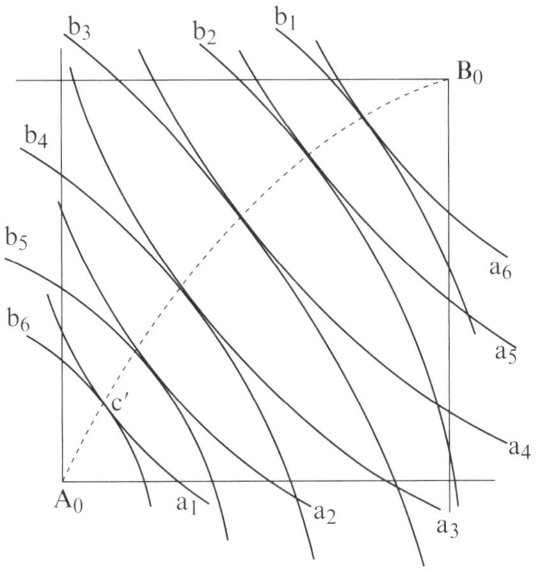

Source: Mishan (1952: 315).

Figure 14.1 Construction of community indifference curves through a given point (B_o)

individuals on some given indifference curves, say b_6 and a_1. If they are on the contract curve, they are at *c'* facing a common relative price given by the slope of their curves at that point. Holding each individual's welfare constant while altering the goods available to the community, can be shown by sliding the map centred at B_0 around the fixed map centred at A_0, keeping the b_6 and a_1 curves tangent to each other and letting the origin B_0 trace out the locus of a community indifference curve. It has the property that each of the community's individuals remains on his or her given indifference curve while the common price they all face is altered.

Now start at another distribution of welfare on the contract line, say that shown by the curves b_3 and a_4. Since the contract line is non-linear, the common slope of the two individual indifference curves will be different from what it was at *c'*. It follows that the slope of the community indifference curve at point B_0 in community consumption space will be different from what it was when the distribution of welfare was at *c'*. Only if the two individuals have unit income and price elasticities, so that the contract line is the diagonal of the box, implying that relative prices are independent of the distribution of welfare, will there be a unique community curve through each point in community space. Otherwise, there will be a pencil of curves through each point, each curve relating to a different distribution of the two goods between the two individuals and hence a different common slope of their individual indifference curves.

All that the existence of a pencil of curves through any one community consumption point implies is that each distribution of a given community consumption bundle will require a different relative price if the market is to clear. This will always be true except when all price and income elasticities are unitary so that the distribution of income does not affect market demands.

The Scitovsky 'paradox' arises directly from this property of community curves. To see it best, we need one more construction. Mishan (1952: 317) draws what he calls comparable community curves which make up a consistent community indifference curve map. Start from some point in community consumption space and alter the consumption bundle so that there are more of both goods (or more of one good and no less of the other). This moves the consumption point upwards and to the right. Since there is now more of both goods, both consumers can be made better off. Select one such point on the new contract line and construct a new community indifference curve based on that distribution of welfare. Repeating the process with ever larger totals of both goods produces a map of non-crossing curves with the property that every individual is better off on any higher curve compared with any lower curve. It is clear that there will be many such maps, depending on the initial distribution of welfare and on how we distribute each new higher bundle of goods, allowing only that no one is made worse off.

THE 'PARADOX'

Now consider a situation in which the two-person community contemplates a change in policy that moves it between total consumption bundles indicated by b_I and b_{II} in Figure 14.2. The solid community curve through b_I is based on the distribution of welfare ruling at situation *I* while the solid curve through b_{II} is based on the distribution ruling at *II*. (For the moment, ignore the broken line curves.) Part (i) shows the case where

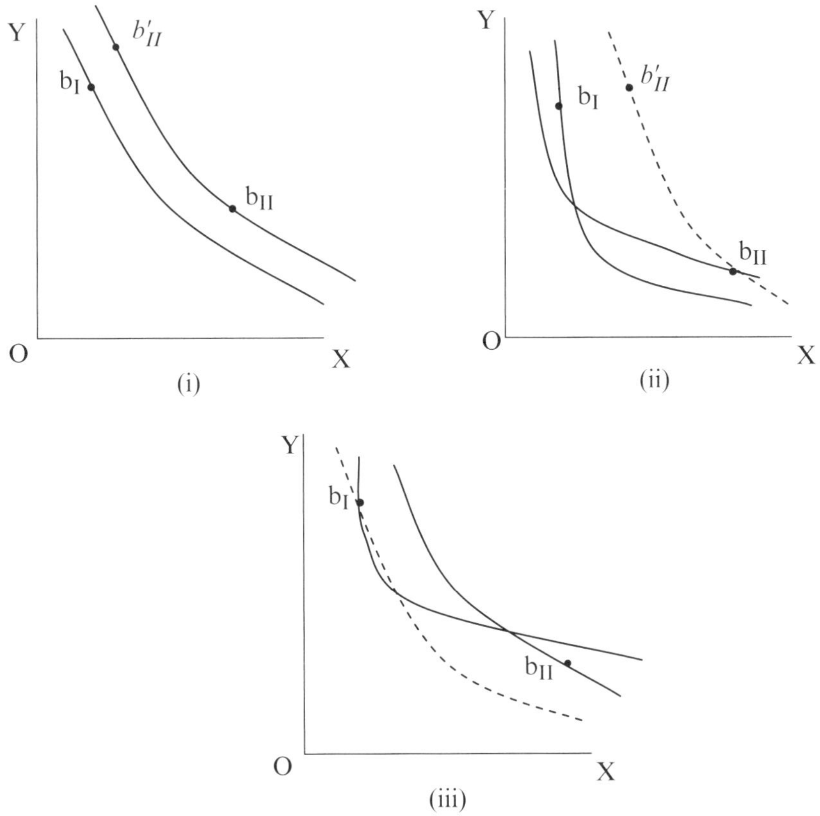

Figure 14.2 Compensation tests with crossing and non-crossing community indifference curves

the h-c test produces unambiguous results. Because the curve through b_{II} is everywhere higher than the curve through b_I, it follows that everyone can be made better off on *II* than on *I*. Now let the community be already in situation *II* and consider a move to *I*. The h-c test cannot then be passed. Since the community is indifferent between all points on I_{II}, some of which have more of both goods than b_I, the move from b_{II} to b_I must fail the h-c test. Otherwise everyone could be made as well off at b_I, where there is less of both goods, than at b_{II}'. So the h-c test works in both cases: if the community is at situation *I*, it will move to *II*, and if it is at *II*, it will not move to *I*.

In contrast, cases (ii) and (iii) in Figure 14.2 reveal contradictions in the h-c test. In (ii), each point lies above the curve through the other point based on the distribution of welfare ruling at that point. Here the gainers can compensate the losers if the change from *I* to *II* is made. But if we are at *II* with its distribution of welfare, the gainers could compensate the losers if a move were made to *I*. Viewed from the point of view of either position, the other looks better on the h-c test. If that test were used exclusively, the community would perpetually oscillate between the two positions. In case (iii), each point lies below the curve through the other point based on the distribution ruling at that point. Now if the community is at either situation *I* or *II* and considers a move to the other situation, the gainers are unable to compensate the losers in either case. Viewed from either position, the other looks worse on the h-c test. If that test were used exclusively, the community would stay in either position if it were put there initially.

To deal with this case, Scitovsky proposed a two-way h-c test: A move from situation I to situation II is to be regarded as a social gain only if (1) the gainers could compensate the losers if the change were made and (2) the gainers could not compensate the losers if the reverse move from II back to I were made.

The cases illustrated in parts (ii) and (iii) of Figure 14.2 rise because compensation is not paid. In part (ii), if the move from *I* to *II* were made and compensation were paid, the dashed curve through b_{II}, based on the new post-compensation distribution of welfare, would, being a comparable curve to that through b_I, lie everywhere above the curve through b_I. Thus, once there, the community would stay put in the face of future h-c tests. But if the community started at *II* with its original distribution of welfare, then moved to *I* with compensation being paid, the curve through b_I (not shown in the figure) would then lie everywhere above the curve through b_{II} and the community would stay at *I* if further h-c tests were applied. So if compensation were paid, the community would move from whichever situation it started in to the other situation and then stay put. In the case in part (iii), the community stays in whichever position it is placed since the potential gainers cannot compensate the potential losers for either move. In both cases, there is no way that the compensation and/or bribery tests can be used consistently to order these two situations.

Scitovsky's test is stated above in its two-way compensation form: that the single h-c test is passed for a move from one situation to the other but fails for the reverse move. The case in part (i) then passes the two-way test while part (ii) fails because both moves pass the one-way test while part (iii) fails because neither passes the one-way test. An equivalent but more dramatic form of this test was often stated in the literature as the compensation-bribery test: it must be possible for the potential gainers to compensate the potential losers if the move from I to II is made, while it must be impossible for the potential losers to bribe the potential gainers not to make the move. Stated this way, case (i) passes but case (ii) fails for both moves because gainers can compensate the losers if the move is made while the losers can bribe the gainers not to make the move. Case (iii) fails because in both moves the potential gainers cannot compensate the potential losers if the change is made, nor can the potential losers bribe the potential gainers to accept the status quo.

The interpretation of Scitovksy's result has been the subject of much debate and has caused not a little confusion. For example, one of the most prolific and insightful writers on welfare economics at the time, E. J. Mishan (1957: 331, n.1) stated that our situation (ii) should not be interpreted as one in which the potential losers can bribe the potential gainers to oppose the change from *I* to *II*. For this, he says, implies:

> (i) that individual *J* can bribe individual *K* to make the change to *II* while at the same time, (ii) individual K can successfully bribe individual *J* to oppose the change. Or, in other words, everybody could be made better off (i) by moving to *II* and (ii) by staying at *I*. These are logically contradictory propositions. Stated correctly, the apparent contradiction should read: (i) individual *J* could bribe individual *K* to make the change from *I* to *II* but (ii) *having made the change to II*, and no compensation having being paid, individual *K* could bribe individual *J* to return to *I*.

Mishan's statement of Scitovsky's two-way h-c test is correct, but his interpretation of the twofold, bribery-compensation test is wrong. His mistake is in assuming that under bribery everyone is made better off by staying at *I*. All that successful bribery means is that the potential loser loses less by paying the bribe than he would lose if he allowed the change to take place with no compensation being paid. It is correct that if the change were made and compensation paid, everyone would be better off. But if the change is not made and bribery is paid, everyone is not better off; the potential loser is just not as badly off as he would be if the change were made.

Also, there is an identity relation between compensation and bribery tests that seems to have escaped Mishan. The gainers in the move from situation *I* to *II* are the same individuals as the losers in the move from *II* back to *I*. So the statement that the gainers in the move from *I* to *II* can compensate the losers (*A*'s gain in the *I* to *II* move is larger than the *B*'s loss) is the same thing as that the losers from the move from *II* to *I* can bribe the gainers not to make the move (*A*'s potential loss in the *II* to *I* move exceeds *B*'s potential gain). More generally, the statement that the potential gainers in the move from situation *I* to situation *II* can/cannot compensate the potential losers is identical to the statement that the potential losers in the move from *II* to *I* can/cannot bribe the potential gainers to maintain the status quo.

If we apply this to the three cases in Figure 14.2, we obtain the following. In case (i), according to the two way h-c test in the move from *I* to *II*, the gainers can compensate the losers but in the move from *II* to *I* they cannot. This is the same thing as saying for the compensation-bribery test that in the *I*–*II* move, the gainers can compensate the losers but the losers cannot bribe the gainers, while in the *II*–*I* move the gainers cannot compensate the losers and the losers can bribe the gainers. In case (ii) the two-way h-c test shows that the gainers can compensate the losers in both moves, which is the same thing as saying that the losers can bribe the gainers not to make either move. So for either move, the potential gainers can compensate the potential losers while the potential losers can bribe the potential gainers to maintain the status quo. In case (iii), the gainers cannot compensate the losers in either move, which is the same thing as saying that the losers cannot bribe the gainers to stay put. We conclude that the Scitovsky two-way h-c test is identical to the twofold compensation-bribery test.

As long as compensation is not paid, these two cases present genuine social conflicts, but of a different sort. In case (ii), distant pastures always look greener. Potential gainers can argue that there is social gain because gainers could compensate the losers. Potential losers can argue that if they paid bribes to maintain the status quo, they would be better off and the potential gainers no worse off than if the change were made, so there is social gain in maintaining the status quo. In contrast, under case (iii), the gainers will want the change but cannot show that everyone could be made better off by it, while the potential losers will want to maintain the status quo but cannot show that they could pay enough to bring the potential gainers on side. There is a genuine social conflict that cannot be removed as long as no judgments are made about the ordering of the distributions of welfare under the two situations.

Subsequently, Gorman (1955) showed that the Scitovsky two-way test was not transitive. Following it in a four-situation comparison could lead to: *I p II, II p III, III p IV,* and *IV p I* (where *p* stands for preferred to). That shows that the Scitovsky two-way test is not a satisfactory method for ordering more than two alternative situations. But the Scitovsky case still reveals a genuine conflict in the existence of a situation in which potential gainers desire a change but cannot compensate the potential losers while the potential losers desire to maintain the status quo but cannot bribe the potential gainers to accept this.

JUDGMENTS ABOUT THE DISTRIBUTION OF WELFARE

Scitovsky's demonstration of the failure of the one-way h-c test showed conclusively that the efficient allocation of resources cannot be separated from the distribution of welfare (except in the case of universal unit-elastic price and income demands). What is a Pareto efficient allocation for one distribution will not be for another. He argued that the h-c test was 'asymmetrical in attributing undue importance to the particular distribution of welfare obtaining before the contemplated change. In the absence of a governmental policy [favouring the status quo distribution of welfare over others] there can be no justification in attaching greater importance to the welfare distribution as it was before than as it is after the change' (1941, p. 88). His two-way test used the distribution of welfare ruling in situations I and II symmetrically. He went on to argue that these were the only two distributions of welfare that needed to be considered, those ruling before and after the change.

I. M. D. Little (1957: 101 ff) presented an ingenious analysis showing that if judgments could be made about the preference ordering of different distributions of welfare, the conflicts shown in both parts (ii) and (iii) of Figure 14.2 could be removed. (The argument is Little's but the graphical presentation is from Mishan (1957: 51).) Assume that the distribution of welfare ruling in situation II is judged superior to that in situation I. Now in part (ii) draw the dashed community curve through b_{II} that is consistent with the curve through b_I. It follows that to move from b_I to any point on this new curve is an increase in welfare since everyone is better off on it than on the curve through b_I. Now locate the community at the point b_{II} on this new curve and then redistribute welfare to recreate the solid curve through b_{II}. Since this is a move to a preferred welfare distribution, it produces further gain. It follows that the move from b_I to b_{II} brings gain. Similarly, in part (iii), draw the dashed curve through b_I consistent with the curve through b_{II}. A redistribution of the bundle at b_I that altered the community indifference curve from the solid to the dashed curve represents a gain since it establishes a distribution that is superior to the original distribution of the b_I bundle. Next, a movement from any point on the dashed curve to b_{II} makes everyone better off. It follows that the move from b_I to b_{II} is a gain. Of course, if we reverse the judgment and prefer the distribution of welfare at b_I, then b_I will be preferred to b_{II} in both cases (ii) and (iii).

Subsequent authors argued that the only neutral criterion was to show that some situation was superior to another for all conceivable welfare distributions (see for example, Samuelson, 1956). Mishan (1957) demonstrated that there was then still validity in the lower level optimum conditions. First, for any given community production bundle, everyone is made better off by moving them from a position off the contract curve to one on it. Second, there is value in fulfilling the production efficiency conditions because more of everything can be produced by moving from a position where they are not fulfilled to one where they are. He went on to show, however, that there is nothing to chose between any one of the possible top level optima in which a community indifference curve is tangent to a production possibility curve. For any two distributions of welfare, there are two different tangency points between the relevant community indifference curve and the transformation curve. The convexity of the latter curve implies that the two community curves must intersect as in part (iii) of Figure 14.2. Thus there is an intractable social conflict between any two top-layer optima based on different distributions of income. The potential gainers in a move from either position to the other are always unable to compensate the potential losers, while the potential losers are always unable to bribe the potential gainers to accept the status quo.

ALTERNATIVES

Samuelson (1956) rejected the tool of community indifference curves because they do not allow a unique welfare ordering to be assigned to any pair of consumption bundles. He proposed replacing them with his social indifference curves, which would produce a unique ordering through lump sum transfers of income that actually made everyone better off whenever there was a potential gain. But as Mishan (1957: 330) comments:

> Now one can always 'fix' a community indifference map, making the welfare of the community depend only on the quantities of the goods involved, by using some method such as lump sum transfers in order to maintain constant the initial distribution of welfare. This is in essence what Samuelson's 'social indifference curves' amount to. Such a construction, however, is rather a vehicle for by-passing the crucial problem posed by the interdependence of prices and

> distribution than a device for its investigation. . . . if the community indifference curves have to be constructed with due regard to this interdependence constraint it is not a defect in them but a virtue. Properly understood it makes explicit a relationship which we overlook to our cost.

Indeed Mishan was being prophetic since most of the complications briefly studied in this essay are now ignored by each of the two main measures currently in use. The first is the simple Harberger test of maximizing consumer surplus. This test suppresses the possible conflicts just analysed by reducing everything to a single monetary expression implicitly based on a potential one-way h-c test and paying no attention to the effect of policy changes on the distribution of income. The second is the use of a social welfare function that requires an explicit evaluation of interpersonal comparisons. The literature on optimal taxes, as well as the Stern Report[4] on the environment, rely on one form or another of such a function. It would appear from these developments that the revealed preference of many economists is to prefer conclusive results that suppress inconvenient truths over inconclusive results that take account of these truths – an attitude as old as the practice of ancient medicine.

ACKNOWLEDGEMENTS

I am indebted to Robin Boadway for helpful comments and suggestions.

NOTES

1. Although known to modern economists as Tibor Scitovsky, when he wrote his famous article on the 'paradox' he signed it Scitovszky. Sometime after that, the 'z' was dropped.
2. Although generally used in almost all welfare analysis, past and present, this is not an obviously acceptable assumption since it takes no account of tastes with respect to the distribution of income. It implies, for example, that there is an obvious social gain if incomes double for society's richest ten persons and remain unchanged for the rest, thus greatly increasing income inequality.
3. This figure is similar to Figure 1 in Scitovsky (1941: 80) except that Mishan's contract line makes the issues clearer.
4. www.hm-treasury.gov.UK/sternreview_index.htm, accessed 20 January 2010.

REFERENCES

Gorman, W. M. (1955), 'The Intransitivity of Certain Criteria Used in Welfare Economics', *Oxford Economic Papers*, **7** (1), 25–35.

Hicks, John R. (1939), 'The Foundations of Welfare Economics', *The Economic Journal*, **49**, 696–712.
Kaldor, Nicholas (1939), 'Welfare Propositions of Economic and Interpersonal Comparisons of Utility', *The Economic Journal*, **49** (195), 549–552.
Little, I. M. D. (1957), *A Critique of Welfare Economics*, Oxford: Oxford University Press, 2nd Edition.
Mishan, E. J. (1952), 'The Principles of Compensation Reconsidered', *The Journal of Political Economy*, **60** (4), 312–322.
Mishan, E. J. (1957), 'A Re-Appraisal of the Principles of Resource Allocation', *Economica*, **24** (96), 324–342.
Mishan, E. J. (1967), *Welfare Economics: Five Introductory Essays*, New York: Random House.
Samuelson, Paul A. (1956), 'Social Indifference Curves', *The Quarterly Journal of Economics*, **70** (1), 1–22.
Scitovsky, Tibor (1941), 'A Note on Welfare Propositions in Economics', *The Review of Economic Studies*, **9** (1), 77–88.

15. The taxation of external costs

Yew-Kwang Ng

1. THE TEXTBOOK DIAGRAM

External effects are prevalent, especial in their negative forms like environmental disruption. The idea of taxing goods producing important external costs may be traced at least to Pigou (1912/1932). The simple diagram of Figure 15.1 illustrating the efficiency gain is available in most first or second-year principles of microeconomics textbooks. The horizontal and vertical axes represent respectively the quantity and price of a good. In the absence of a tax on this good, the market equilibrium is at the point A where the market supply curve S and demand curve D intersect. Assuming perfect competition, the supply curve reflects the private marginal costs (MC) of producing the good, that is, MC to the producers.

If the production or consumption of the good involves important external costs such as pollution, the additional costs of pollution are largely external to the producers. Adding these external MC to the private MC of production results in the social MC being reflected by the curve S'. If a Pigovian tax in accordance to the external MC is imposed on the production of the good, the market supply curve shifts from S to S', reflecting the social MC (private MC plus external MC). From the social point of view, the efficient amount of output is at the intersection of the demand curve (reflecting social marginal benefits, assuming no other factors causing inefficiency) with the social MC curve S' at the point B, with output level Q_2. The excess amount of output from Q_2 to Q_1 involves an efficiency loss measured by the triangle ABC. (On the measurement of welfare gains and losses, see Chapter 12, on consumer surplus.) The Pigovian tax that shifts the supply curve from S to S' and output from Q_1 to Q_2 thus involves an efficiency gain for this triangle, in comparison to the untaxed equilibrium point at A. This is in contrast to an efficiency loss or excess burden (distortionary cost) of the triangle BAD if the tax is imposed in the absence of the external cost (see Chapter 13, on the Harberger triangle). In fact, in a realistic system with pre-existing distortive taxes for revenue raising, the taxation of external costs will raise double dividends by reducing the need

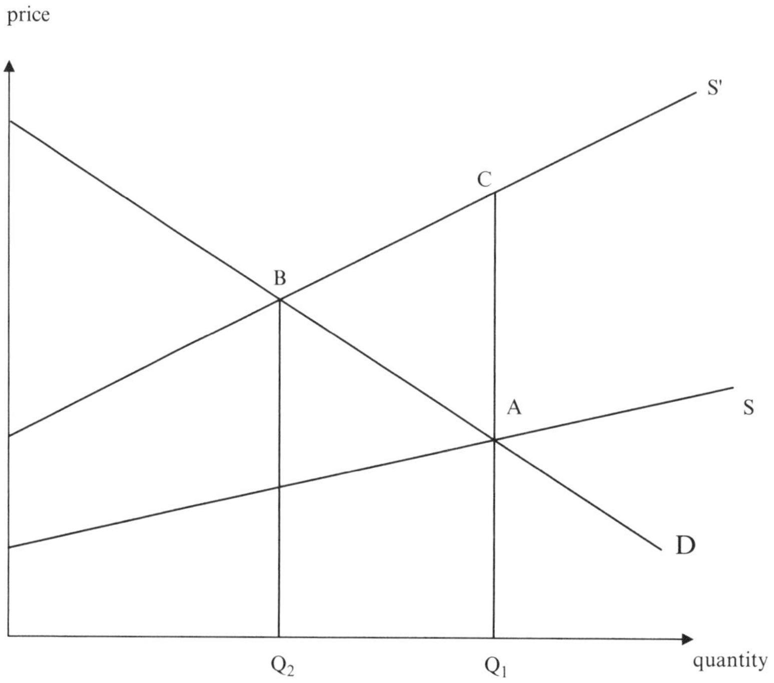

Figure 15.1 The textbox diagram

for distortive taxes (see Schob 2005 for a survey on double dividends and Etheridge and Leicester 2007 on more issues of environmental taxation).

2. THE BUCHANAN/STUBBLEBINE DIAGRAM

The simple analysis above is based on the assumption that the amount of the external effect is related only to the amount of the good under consideration. This hides the important point that, for any given amount of the good produced and/or consumed, different methods of production and/or consumption may involve different levels of pollution. To overcome this deficiency in the above simple diagram, Figure 15.2 focuses on the amount of pollution or whatever variable that directly causes the external costs. The horizontal axis measures the value of x, an activity (such as pollution) undertaken by a party A. Up to a point, A derives positive benefits from undertaking the activity. His net marginal valuation curve is given by MV^A. Maximizing his own profit/utility, he undertakes x till the point

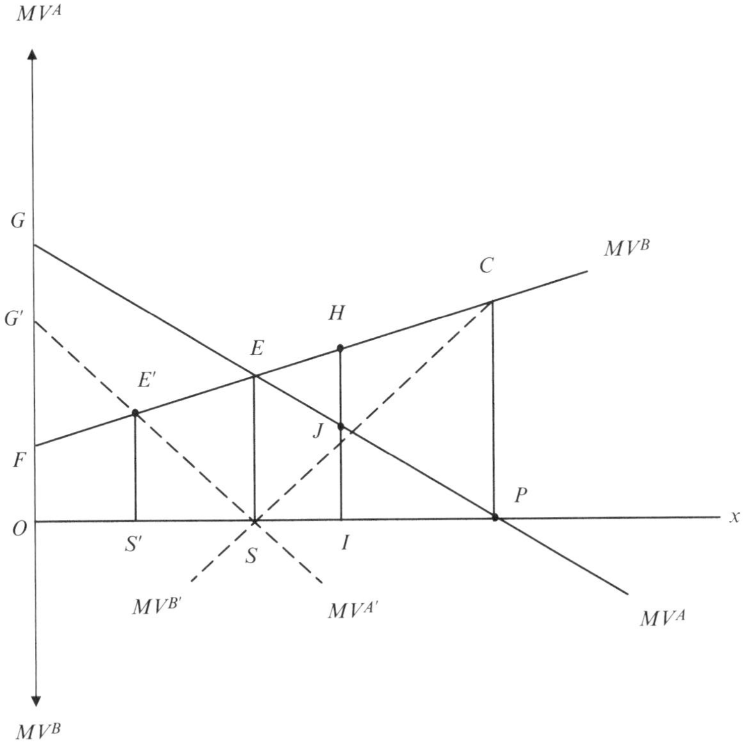

Note: x represents A's activity that generates external costs

Source: Adapted from Buchanan and Stubblebine 1962

Figure 15.2 The Buchanan/Stubblebine diagram

P, his private optimum. This private or market equilibrium point will be efficient if the activity causes no external effects. If *x* is an external cost like pollution, it causes damages to another party *B*. While *A*'s marginal valuation (MV) is measured upward from the origin, *B*'s marginal valuation is measured *downward* from the origin. Thus, the fact that the activity is harmful to *B* is reflected by the position of MV^B being above the horizontal axis.

In comparison to the socially optimal point S (determined by the intersection of the two MV curves at E), the private equilibrium point P involves an efficiency loss measured by triangle *EPC*. A Pigovian tax on A in accordance with the marginal damages of *x* imposed on *B* (measured by the curve MV^B, for example, the marginal tax rate on the first unit of

x is given by $OF = GG'$) shifts the net MV curve of A from MV^A to $MV^{A'}$, and the equilibrium level of x from P to S, obtaining an efficiency gain (or eliminating the efficiency loss) measured by triangle EPC. (While the Pigovian tax is shown here in its ideal form with tax rates variable in accordance to the marginal damages, it may also be in the simpler form of a constant rate equaling ES. This simpler form does not affect its static optimality but may not provide the perfect amount of incentives regarding the use of preventive technology.)

While the Pigovian tax on external costs in accordance with the marginal damages inflicted is conceptually unassailable, the practical estimation of the amount concerned may be difficult, especially for the most important external costs, like environmental disruption, which typically involves the far future. However, Ng (2004) shows that it is desirable to charge disruption (at least) at the marginal cost of abatement (which is easier to estimate than the marginal damage of disruption) and such a charge will normally yield total revenue in excess of the amount of abatement spending.

3. COASE'S CRITIQUE AND THE IGNORED ASYMMETRY

However, Coase (1960) attacks the Pigovian tax as looking at only one side of the problem by concentrating only on the restriction of A's activity that harms B. But this restriction harms A. The problem is to avoid the more serious harm. Coase believes that a change of approach is necessary.

As Coase dispenses with not only maths but also graphical analysis, he compares the two extreme points of all (point P) or nothing (the origin with no pollution at all). He correctly shows that which one is more efficient depends on the case or the parametric values assumed. In terms of Figure 15.2, it depends on whether triangle GFE is larger or smaller than triangle EPC. Either case is possible and no general conclusion could be made.

The argument of Coase ignores an important asymmetry (as pointed out in Ng 2007) due to his all-or-nothing comparison. At the market equilibrium, a marginal reduction of the activity level decreases *A's* net valuation by an infinitesimal amount but increases B's by a significant amount (PC). It is this asymmetry that makes the Pigovian tax on an external cost, provided that it is not excessive and ignoring administrative costs, always efficiency improving, despite the two-sided nature of the problem correctly pointed out by Coase.

4. THE BEAUTY OF BILATERAL TAXATION

In a system of bilateral taxation to tackle the problem of external cost (bilateral subsidy or tax for external benefit), not only should *A* be taxed (subsidized) according to the damage (benefit) imposed on *B*, but *B* should also be taxed in accordance with the cost sustained by *A* in having to reduce (increase) the level of *x* from his private optimal point. In fact, it was Coase who was probably the first to mention such a bilateral tax. 'If the factory owner is made to pay a tax equal to the damage caused, it would clearly be desirable to institute a double tax system and to make residents of the district pay an amount equal to the additional cost incurred by the factory owner (or the consumers of his products) in order to avoid the damage' (1960, p. 41). In fact, this largely ignored proposal is, in my view, a much more important contribution than the Coase theorem that has attracted overwhelming attention. However, Coase (1988, p.181) himself does not see his mention of the bilateral tax as a proposal as he is skeptical of the desirability of any taxation solution.

Buchanan and Stubblebine (1962, p. 383) proposed a similar bilateral tax on an external cost. Their reason for doing so is different. After the imposition of the unilateral Pigovian tax on *A*, *A*'s marginal valuation curve is shifted to $MV^{A'}$, which passes through the social optimal point *S* (see Figure 15.2). However, $MV^{A'}$ intersects MV^{B} at *E'*, corresponding to a non-optimal point *S'*. Given the unilateral tax, Buchanan and Stubblebine are afraid that *A* and *B* have incentives to negotiate to move from *S* to *S'*, as they can gain the area *E'SE*. This is an inefficient move as the reduction in government tax revenue of *E'S'SE* has not been taken into account. They thus propose the bilateral tax on *B*, shifting the marginal valuation curve from MV^{B} downward to $MV^{B'}$. (This is so since the tax is positively correlated with the reduction in *x* from the point *P* and hence is negatively correlated with *x*.) The bilateral tax thus ensures that the new marginal valuation curves of both parties intersect at the social optimal point *S*, hence giving them no incentive to negotiate a movement elsewhere.

The proposed bilateral taxation may be unnecessary for the purpose of avoiding a further movement away from optimality. If negotiation between the parties concerned is feasible, no tax at all is necessary. If negotiation to move from *P* to *S* is not feasible such that the Pigovian tax is needed, negotiation to move from *S* to *S′* is even less likely to be feasible. However, the bilateral tax may serve two different purposes. The first is Coase's point of encouraging *B* to use other methods of reducing the damage if efficient. With just the unilateral tax on *A*, *B* does not take into account the gain to *A* if *B* undertakes some damage-reduction measure which also increases *A*'s optimal level of *x* through a reduced tax schedule.

The bilateral tax gives both parties the right incentives with respect to both the optimal level of *x* and whatever other arrangements that may affect the damage. This point is particularly important in a growing economy with new technologies becoming available from time to time. For example, if it is less costly to install double glaze windows to reduce the costs of noise, it may be more efficient for *B* to do that than for *A* to avoid or reduce the noise. With the bilateral tax, *B* has the appropriate incentives to do this.

Secondly, and to my knowledge unnoted by other commentators (except for Ng 1979, ch.7), bilateral taxation is very useful in preventing the exaggeration of the damage. In the real world, the government has no perfect knowledge of the *MV* curves. To estimate the appropriate amount of tax on *A*, the government has to rely to some extent on the report of *B* on the amount of the damage. Under a unilateral tax system, *B* clearly has the incentive to exaggerate the amount of damage sustained so as to increase the amount of the tax on *A* and hence reduce the level of *x* further below the social optimal point *S*. Under the bilateral tax system, *B* does not have such incentives. Making the tax on *A* exceed the true damage reduces the equilibrium *x* below *S*. But *B* only benefits from the reduction of *x* in accordance to the true marginal damage (negative marginal value) function MV^B but has to pay a tax in accordance to MV^A. Thus, *B* clearly loses from the reduction of *x* below *S* (or *E*) where the two *MV* curves intersect. It can also be seen that *B* has no incentive to understate her damage either. So she will report truthfully under the bilateral tax system. Does *A* have the same incentives to report his *MV* curve truthfully? Yes. Over- or under-reporting by *A* does not affect *A* directly, but undertaking the level of *x* consistent with either under- or over-reporting is detrimental to *A* himself, as may be seen from Figure 15.2. For example, if he overstates his MV from *PE* to *PH* (not drawn) and, consistent with this report, undertakes the level of *x* at *I*, he has to pay *ESIH* in extra tax but gains only the area *ESIJ*, thus losing *EJH*.

Unfortunately, if *B* consists of a large number of heterogeneous parties, the problem becomes more complicated, as discussed in Ng (1979, 2007), who also argues in favor of amenity rights over pollution rights, despite the Coase theorem.

REFERENCES

Buchanan, James M. and Stubblebine, W. C. (1962). 'Externality', *Economica*, 29:371–84.

Coase, R. H. (1960). 'The problem of social cost', *Journal of Law and Economics*, 3:1–44.

Coase, R. H. (1988). *The Firm, the Market, and the Law*, Chicago, IL: University of Chicago Press.
Etheridge, Ben and Leicester, Andrew (2007). *Environmental Taxation*, London: Institute for Fiscal Studies.
Ng, Yew-Kwang (1979). *Welfare Economics: Introduction and Development of Basic Concepts*, London: Macmillan.
Ng, Yew-Kwang (2004). 'Optimal environmental charges/taxes: Easy to estimate and surplus-yielding', *Environmental and Resource Economics*, 28(4):395–408.
Ng, Yew-Kwang (2007). 'Eternal Coase and external costs: A case for bilateral taxation and amenity rights', *European Journal of Political Economy*, 23:641–59.
Pigou, Arthur C. (1912/1932), *Wealth and Welfare*. Later editions (1920, 1924, 1929, 1932) entitled *The Economics of Welfare*, London: Macmillan.
Schob, Ronnie (2005). *The Double-Dividend Hypothesis of Environmental Taxes: A Survey*, New Horizons in Environmental Economics series, Cheltenham, UK and Northampton, MA: Edward Elgar.

16. Monopoly and price discrimination

William J. Baumol

Formal study of the theory of monopoly, as well as that of price discrimination, goes back to Cournot (1838, 1927), with a good deal contributed to the analysis of the latter by Dupuit. But the use of diagrams for the purpose apparently first occurred much later, in Marshall's Principles (1920) and in the work of Auspitz and Lieben (1880) in the case of the determination of the output and prices that one can expect to be adopted by a monopolistic seller of a commodity.

Early discussions of price discrimination without graphs also occur in Cournot and, more extensively, in Dupuit (1853), as well as in work by a number of engineers, including Charles Ellet, an American, and Dyonysius Lardner, British (see Ekelund and Hébert, 1999, Chapter 8). Later contributions early in the twentieth century were made by Hadley (1885), Edgeworth (1910, 1925), and Pigou (1912), among others. What appears to be the first use of graphics in the analysis of discriminating monopoly, however, occurs only in the work of Joan Robinson[1] (1933). In two of these cases (Auspitz and Lieben, and Robinson), there is no substantive change between the initial diagrams and those used in textbooks today.

GRAPHIC ANALYSIS OF MONOPOLY BEHAVIOR

Marshall, and Auspitz and Lieben, both avoid explicit use of the concept of marginal revenue, though the concept does appear without the modern nomenclature in Cournot, in the form of the first derivative of total revenue, as deduced from the demand function. The term 'marginal revenue' first appears in the 1920s in the writing of Jacob Viner, among others. In Cournot's work, and in a number of the writings that followed, the substance of the firm's calculation of the output of one of its products that yields the maximum possible profit contribution is a matter of the most elementary differential calculus. All that is required is adoption of the definition of total profit $[T\pi(y)]$ as total revenue $[TR(y)]$ minus total cost $[TC(y)]$, where y represents the firm's output of the commodity. Then, obviously, if we are dealing with an interior maximum, y^*, the profit maximizing quantity of output must satisfy

$$\frac{d[TR(y) - TC(y)]}{dy} = 0$$

or,

$$\frac{dTR}{dy} = \frac{dTC}{dy}.$$

Calling dTR/dy 'marginal revenue' and dTC/dy 'marginal cost' brings us in substance fully abreast of the writings of the 1930s and the discussion in modern elementary textbooks. The only absent element for a modern textbook discussion, aside from the terms, was an explicit explanation of the shapes of the pertinent *MR* and *MC* curves.[2] Auspitz and Lieben (1880) are the earliest writers of whom I am aware, in whose writings the $MC=MR$ maximization requirement appears. Figure 16.1 is a simplified version of their graph, using the original notation. There, *TR* is the total revenue curve, *TC* is the total cost curve, and *MR* and *MC* (printed in red in the original) are the marginal revenue and marginal cost curves, respectively. The equilibrium output is Y_0, at which the two marginal curves intersect. It is also clear that at this output the slopes of the total cost and total revenues are equal, which is hardly surprising since marginal revenue is the slope of the total revenue curve, and marginal cost is the slope of the total cost curve. But this elementary observation does have its use in exposition, for, since total profit is equal to $TR - TC$, it is evident that if the former is rising more quickly than the latter, an increase in output must add to profit, while profit must be raised by a diminution of output, if the slope of *TC* is greater than that of *TR*.

ON THE GRAPHICS OF PRICE DISCRIMINATION

So far, we have considered only the case where the monopolist charges the same price to all customers, whom it is equally expensive to serve. But the reality is that such uniform pricing is the exceptional case. In reality, almost every major consumer product is sold with discounts to students, senior citizens or other strategically selected groups because, as we will see, properly selected discriminatory prices (prices that differ from customer to customer when the cost of serving them is the same) will almost always yield higher profits than any uniform price, all other things being equal.

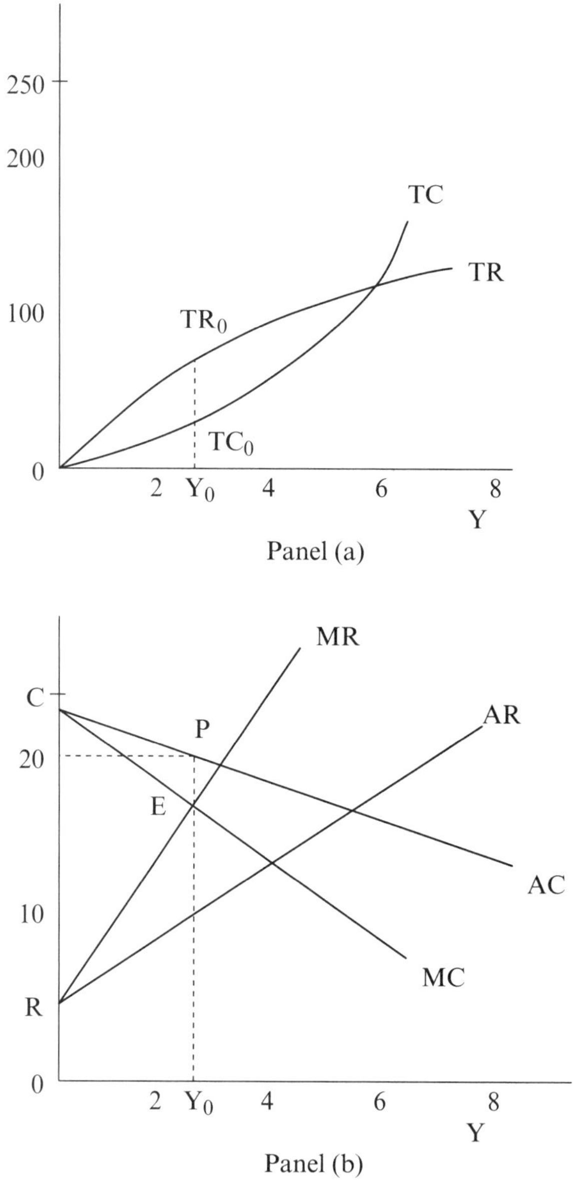

Figure 16.1 The Auspitz and Lieben constructs

This is well known, but what is not generally recognized is that the connection of such discriminatory pricing with monopoly power is questionable at best, though this was already recognized by Walras (1926, 1954).

But before turning to such matters, let us first consider the graph that is now generally utilized to determine the set of discriminatory prices that maximize the seller's profits, given the state of the production process and conditions in the pertinent markets. A number of noted economists, among them Dupuit, Walras, Edgeworth and Pigou, had contributed valuable insights into the theory of price discrimination and, as in the case of uniform monopoly price, had correctly described the profit-maximizing equilibrium without use of the graph that is now employed in the textbooks for the purpose. But it was Joan Robinson, in her classic contribution of 1933, who seems first to have provided that graph.

THE JOAN ROBINSON GRAPH OF DISCRIMINATION

As already noted, in the Robinson graph there is also a minor deviation from the currently common representation. Today the common graphic approach employs a three-graph approach. The first two represent the pair of markets in which different prices for the same commodity may be charged. The third graph is a horizontal summation of the quantities sold in the two individual markets. This facilitates easy drawing of the relevant curves of marginal cost and marginal revenue and, as will be recapitulated, facilitates the process of deriving the desired conclusions. Robinson, in contrast, superimposes the three graphs and, thereby, combines them in a single diagram. This leads to the requirement that her graph be printed in two colors, thereby increasing both the difficulty of comprehension, as well as the cost of publication. This problem is currently dealt with by breaking the Robinson graph into three interrelated graphs. Today, the determination of the profit-maximizing discriminatory prices in two markets with equal costs but different prices is explained with the aid of the three graphs that follow (Figure 16.2).

The construction assumes for simplicity that the firm deals with two separate customer groups, A and B, that cannot trade with one another and whose demand curves differ (in their elasticities) so that the customers do not react identically in response to a high price. If the cost of providing a unit of product to any member of either group is the same, then profit maximization is easily shown to require that the price to Group A and the price to Group B are such that they yield the same marginal revenue, so that the *MR* from each customer group is equal to the uniform *MC* of the product, that is:

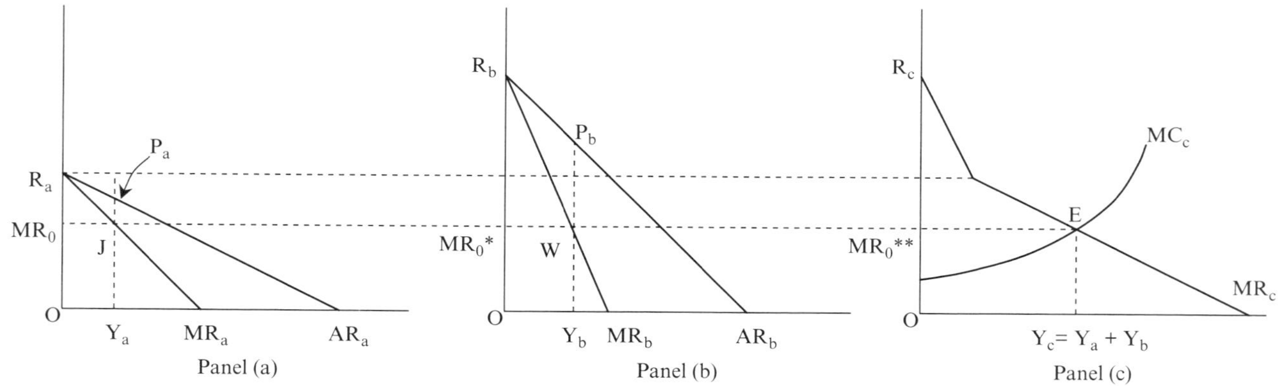

Figure 16.2 Joan Robinson's construction updated

The marginal revenue from a sale to a Group A customer must be the same as that from a sale to a Group B customer: $MR_a = MR_b$.

The reasoning is straightforward. Suppose that the sale of an additional widget to a Group A customer brings in MR_a = \$28 in revenue, whereas the corresponding sale to a Group B customer adds only MR_b = \$12. Such an arrangement cannot possibly be a profit-maximizing solution. By switching one unit of its shipments from its B customers and sending that unit instead to an A customer, at the same cost of production and delivery, the firm gives up \$12 in revenue to gain \$28 – a net gain of \$16 from the same total quantity of sales. Because a similar argument holds for any other pair of marginal revenues that are unequal, profit maximizing clearly requires that the marginal revenue from each group of customers be equal.

The equal marginal revenue rule enables us to determine the profit-maximizing prices and sales volumes for two such groups of customers diagrammatically. The first two panels of Figure 16.2 show the demand curves and corresponding marginal revenue curves for customer groups A and B. Suppose that the firm is selling the quantity Y_a to Group A customers at price P_a. How much must the firm then sell to Group B customers, and at what price, in order to maximize profits? Our rule gives the answer. The marginal revenue from selling to Group A is $Y_a J$ – as we see from point *J* directly above Y_a on the *MR* curve in Panel (a). The rule tells us that the firm must charge a price to Group B customers that induces them to buy the quantity that yields the same marginal revenue, *J*. We find this quantity by drawing a horizontal line MR_oE through point *J* from Panel (a) to Panel (b). The marginal revenues of the two customer groups will clearly be equal where MR_oE cuts the Group B marginal revenue curve – at point *W*. The profit-maximizing sales volume to Group B will be Y_b, directly below point *W*. And at sales volume Y_b, the market B price is clearly given by the corresponding point on the market B demand curve, price P_b directly above Y_b.

That is not quite the end of the story – we have not yet said anything about costs, and we know that profit maximization must take account of both costs and revenues. We can deal with the cost issue quite easily, if the marginal cost of the product is the same whether supplied to an A customer or a B customer. Even under price discrimination, we still have the fundamental $MR = MC$ rule for profit maximization in each market segment. The extended profit-maximization rule under price discrimination with uniform costs then must be: $MR_a = MR_b = MC$. We observe also that if the demand curves of the two sets of customers are not identical, discriminatory prices will always yield profits greater than uniform prices because, according to the usual elasticity formula, *MR* in the two markets cannot be equal, and profits can be increased by moving to (discriminatory) prices and sales quantities that satisfy the preceding formula for profit-maximizing discriminatory prices.

SOME FURTHER OBSERVATIONS ON PRICE DISCRIMINATION AND ITS EQUILIBRIUM

From its beginnings, a number of writers on the subject have interpreted the adoption of discriminatory prices by a firm as decisive evidence of the possession of monopoly power by that enterprise. This was already implied in Dupuit's discussion, though he tells us, 'there is almost no industry where this phenomenon is not present' (1852–53, 2:342). But as early as the work of Walras (1926, 1954, pp. 443–4), he also tells us, '[c]learly, even under free competition, an entrepreneur may profit by price discrimination'. He does follow Dupuit in pointing out that this is sometimes achieved by deliberate reduction by the firm in the quality of a portion of one of its products, so that it can be sold at a lower price without eliminating the sales of the superior products. He cites theater seats, the cheaper of which may not only be less well located, but also less comfortable. Joan Robinson also has it right when she observes, '[u]nder conditions of perfect competition price discrimination could not exist even if the market could be easily divided into separate parts. . ..but if there is some degree of market imperfection there can be some degree of discrimination' (pp. 179–80).

It may be noted, however, as the current author has recently argued, that full freedom of entry (a high degree of contestability) can force a firm to adopt a set of discriminatory prices that is apt to be unique and yields zero profit (see Baumol and Swanson, 2003).[3]

The intuitive explanation of the result is straightforward. Assume that the markets at issue satisfy the requirements for adoption of discriminatory pricing, notably that customers of the lower priced products cannot or cannot easily resell them to high price customers, and that the elasticities of demand of the two customer sets differ. Then discriminatory prices will yield profits higher than uniform prices can provide. But with free entry, the rate of profits will be driven to the level that prevails in competitive markets, that is, maximum economic profits must be zero. It follows that, with any uniform prices, economic profits must be negative, and the result that one must have price discrimination to break even follows.

Not merely a bit of abstract theorizing, this has significant implications for anti-trust litigation. For, if only a monopolist is in a position to adopt discriminatory prices, then the adoption of such prices by a defendant firm must constitute proof positive of its possession of monopoly power. But if this can occur in highly (but imperfectly) competitive markets as well, then its presence is not conclusive evidence either way of the truth of an allegation of monopoly power.

This analysis also permits a formal examination of pricing and profits in Schumpeter's model, in which successful inventors initially face little competition for their new product and, as such, can initially impose a high price for it. But as imitators appear, the price is driven downward, and with sufficient competitive pressure, they can expect to just barely recoup their R&D and other innovation costs, using prices that are discriminatory – not among customers, but among the dates at which the sales take place. The pertinent graphs and mathematics are precisely the same as they are for the standard case of inter-customer discrimination.[4]

NOTES

1. Mrs. Robinson (p. 182n) credits T.O. Yntema (1928) with previous use of the graph, but only for the derivation of a special proposition that is not discussed here.
2. Since this was missing from Marshall's discussions, he was unable to use the intersection of the *MR* and *MC* curves as their solution. Marshall did not use the concepts total and marginal revenue or total and marginal cost. Instead, he employed an average cost curve, $AC = TC(y)/y$, and a corresponding average revenue curve, $AR = TR/y$, which were more familiar at that time, though they were clumsier tools for the purpose. He then depicted the total profit curve, $yAR - yAC$, and added in a set of iso-profit curves, $y(AR-AC)=k$, for different values of k. The point on the total profit curve that reached the highest iso-profit curve gave the most profitable output level. This way of describing the issue is evidently clumsier than the $MR = MC$ approach, but there is no difference in substance.
3. It can also be shown that the discriminatory pricing equilibrium, if it is unique, must also satisfy the conditions of second-best optimality provided by Frank Ramsey.
4. Walras (1926, 1954) provides an example of such inter-temporal price discrimination in publishing, with customers who are anxious to read a new book being charged a higher price after it has just appeared.

REFERENCES

Auspitz, R. and R. Lieben (1880), *Untersuchungen über die Theorie des Preises*, Leipzig: Duncker and Humblot.

Baumol, W.J. (2010), *The Microtheory of Innovative Entrepreneurship*, Princeton, NJ: Princeton University Press.

Baumol, W.J. and D.G. Swanson (2003), 'The New Economy and Ubiquitous Competitive Price Discrimination: Identifying Defensible Criteria of Market Power', *Antitrust Law Journal*, Vol. 70, Issue 3, pp. 661–685.

Cournot, A.A. (1838, 1927), *Mathematical Principles of Economics*, translated by Nathaniel Bacon, with notes by Irving Fisher, New York: Macmillan.

Dupuit, Jules (1852–53), 'Péage', in *Dictionnaire de l'économie politique*, ed. Charles Coquelin, Vol. 2, Paris: Guillaumin, pp. 339–344.
Dupuit, Jules (1853, 1933) *De l' utilité et de sa mesure,* ed. Marie de Bernardi, Turin: La Riforma Sociale.
Edgeworth, F.Y. (1910, 1925), *Application of Probabilities to Economics, II: Discrimination of Prices*, Papers relating to Political Economy, London: Macmillan, pp. 404–428.
Ekelund, R.B. and R.F. Hébert (1999), *Secret Origins of Modern Microeconomics: Dupuit and the Engineers*, Chicago, IL: University of Chicago Press.
Hadley, A.T. (1885), *Railroad Transportation: Its History and Its Laws*, New York: G. P. Putnam's Sons.
Marshall, Alfred (1920), *The Principles of Economics*, London: Macmillan.
Pigou, A.C. (1912), *Wealth and Welfare*, London: Macmillan.
Robinson, Joan (1933, second edition 1969), *The Economics of Imperfect Competition*, London: Macmillan.
Walras, Léon (1926, 1954), *Elements of Pure Economics*, translated by William Jaffé, Homewood, IL: Richard D. Irwin.
Yntema, T.O. (1928), 'The Influence of Dumping on Monopoly Prices', *Journal of Political Economy*, Vol. 36, pp. 686–695.

17. Duopoly reaction curves

Nicola Giocoli

BASIC CONCEPTS

A reaction curve (RC), also called reaction function or best-reply function, is the locus of optimal, that is, profit-maximizing, actions $R_i(a_j)$ that a firm i may undertake for any given action a_j chosen by a rival firm j. The RC diagram is the standard tool for the graphical analysis of duopoly. In the diagram, the market equilibrium is at the intersection of the RCs, one for each firm. The commonest case of a RC diagram is that of the Cournot duopoly model.

Consider two firms 1 and 2 producing a homogeneous product with output levels q_1 and q_2 and aggregate output $Q = q_1 + q_2$. Provided invertibility conditions are met, the inverse demand function gives the market price associated with aggregate output $p(Q) = p(q_1 + q_2)$. Assume each firm has a cost function $c_i(q_i)$, $i = 1, 2$, and take the strategic variable for both firms to be the output level, so that firm 1's maximization problem is: $\max_{q_1} \pi_1(q_1, q_2) = p(Q)q_1 - c_1(q_1)$. Given that firm 1's profit also depends on firm's 2 output, firm 1's optimal choice must also take into account firm 2's choice. A similar problem can be formulated for firm 2.

Following the so-called Cournot assumption, we model each firm as taking as given the rival's quantity. The first order condition (FOC) for each firm is therefore:

$$\frac{\partial \pi_i(q_1, q_2)}{\partial q_i} = p(Q) + p'(Q)q_i - c_i'(q_i) = 0, i = 1, 2$$

Firm 1's FOC determines the optimal, that is, profit-maximizing, output choice by firm 1 as a function of either its belief about firm 2's expected output choice or its observation of firm 2's actual choice (see below for an explanation of these two possible interpretations). As in Cournot (1971 [1838], Fig. 2), we depict the pair of FOCs with the RC diagram, where the RC of firm 1 (RC_1) is implicitly defined by the FOC $\partial\pi_1(R_1(q_2), q_2)/\partial q_1 = 0$, and that of firm 2 ($RC_2$) by $\partial\pi_2(R_2(q_1), q_1)/\partial q_2 = 0$. The name reaction curve captures the idea that a firm will optimally modify its choice

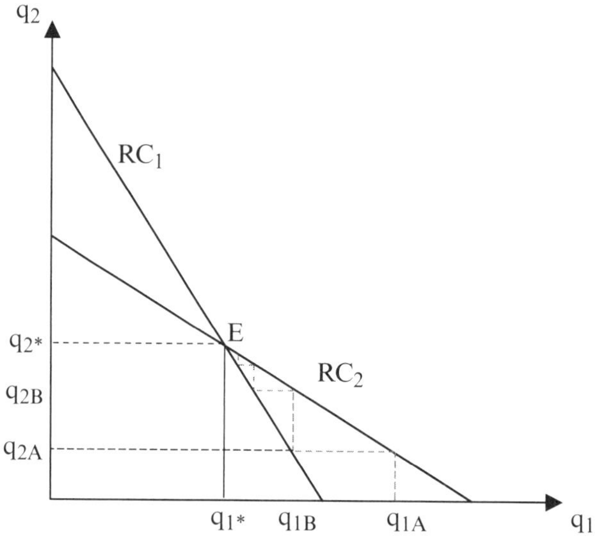

Figure 17.1 Reaction curves – linear demand case with constant and identical costs

following the change in its belief about (or its observation of) the rival's choice. The slope of each RC indicates the size of a firm's optimal reaction to such a change. For example, the slope of RC_1 is:

$$R_1'(q_2) = -\frac{\dfrac{\partial^2 \pi_1}{\partial q_1 \partial q_2}}{\dfrac{\partial^2 \pi_1}{\partial q_1^2}},$$

and similarly for $R_2'(q_1)$.

The Figure 17.1 is based on the simplifying assumption of linear demand and constant and identical marginal cost (see Fulton 1997 and Martin 2002 for a step-by-step derivation of the diagram). In such a case, the RCs are straight lines with negative slope. The equilibrium pair (q_1^*, q_2^*) lies at the intersection of the RCs.

TWO INTERPRETATIONS

In the belief-based version of the model, two conditions need to be satisfied for the firms' choices to constitute an equilibrium (Kreps 1990). First, no firm, on the basis of its own beliefs, must wish to modify its own choice. Second, the firms' equilibrium actions must be consistent with the beliefs upon which they act. Hence, a Cournot equilibrium in a basic duopoly model is given by the output pair (q_1^*, q_2^*) such that: i) each firm is choosing its profit maximizing output given the beliefs about the other firm's choice, and, ii) each firm's beliefs are correct at equilibrium. The similarity with the game-theoretic notion of Nash equilibrium, and with the static fixed point concept underlying it, is well known. Yet the association with non-cooperative game theory came only with Shubik (1959).

Before the belief-based version, the interpretation of the Cournot model was based on a dynamic analysis of actual firms' choices. This involved a sequential adjustment process undertaken by two firms which ignored the fact that their own choices could influence the rival's behavior. The outcome of the process – the equilibrium position – was viewed as the end state of a trial-and-error sequence of actual output choices along the RCs. An instance of such a sequence is shown in Figure 17.1. Assume firm 2 observes output q_{1A} chosen by firm 1. Its profit-maximizing reaction to the rival's choice may be read on RC_2 and amounts to producing q_{2A}. Then firm 1 in its turn optimally reacts to 2's choice by modifying its production to q_{1B}, and so on. The process actually converges to equilibrium (more on this convergence below), that is, to the pair (q_1^*, q_2^*), such that neither firm has any further incentive to modify its own choice.

The dynamic reading of the Cournot model is highly questionable because it requires the two firms to adopt a myopic, almost irrational behavior. As William Fellner put it, at equilibrium the duopolists turn out to be 'right for the wrong reasons' (1949, p.58). Each firm is in fact assumed to go on making its output choice by always taking as given the rival's quantity – this despite the evidence clearly showing that the rival is actually reacting to one's own choice. Indeed, the only consequence of the rival's reaction is taken to be the modification of the quantity that each firm still takes as given in its own RC. Though not 100 per cent faithful to Cournot's own words, the interpretation of RCs as the illustration of a myopic sequence of actual actions and reactions was dominant in the first half of the 20th century, starting at least from Fisher (1898). Cournot actually assumed that duopolists only looked at the direct influence of each other's output choices, while disregarding the indirect ones – the reactions – because that would demand too much from their reasoning power, see Giocoli 2003.

However it would be a mistake dating the belief-based version of the Cournot model to the game-theoretic turn of industrial economics because this version also has a long history. As early as 1924, Arthur Bowley argued that in order to solve the FOCs of a standard duopoly problem 'we should need to know $[q_2]$ as a function of $[q_1]$, and this depends on what each producer thinks the other is likely to do' (Bowley 1924, 38). A new notion, the conjectural variation $v_{ij} = \partial q_i/\partial q_j$, $i = 1, 2$, was introduced, to represent firm *i*'s arbitrary conjecture about how its rival *j* would respond to a (small) variation of *i*'s output. The conjectural variation then entered both FOCs to highlight the fact that the solution of the duopoly model should depend upon the exact value of each firm's conjecture over the rival's reaction. The Cournot model became just a special case – that with $v_{12} = v_{21} = 0$, to indicate that each firm believed the rival would not react to its own choice – but an infinite array of v_{ij} values were equally possible. A stream of literature elaborated Bowley's intuition, to emphasize the intrinsic indeterminacy of duopolistic interaction.

Despite their early formulation, a clear distinction between the two approaches has only been achieved in the 1970s. Here the contribution of game theory has been really decisive (see for example, Friedman 1977). In the conjectural approach, the RCs are viewed as purely mental tools to be used in the reasoning process that underlies the solution of any static game where both firms simultaneously make their choices. A belief-based RC is thus a decision rule giving the firm's optimal choice as a function of the conjectured action of the rival. This is the only interpretation of RCs which makes economic sense in a simultaneous game, where no room exists for interpreting RCs in terms of the firms' actual choices since, by definition, each firm selects its action before observing the rival's one and thus has no chance at all to react. In such a game, each RC indicates what a firm would do if it happened to know of a change in the rival's action, which of course it does not because no RC point outside the Nash equilibrium can ever be observed. Therefore, if we stick to the actual-choice interpretation of Cournot competition even in a simultaneous set-up, we must admit that the construction of the RC diagram is a mere technical device, only used for expositional purposes. On the contrary, actual-choice RCs have a real economic content in the dynamic set-up typical of sequential games. The RC may now be read as a function determining a firm's (myopic) reaction in a given period in terms of the other firm's action during the preceding period; moreover, each firm may well exploit the rival's RC to calculate how a change in its behavior may affect the rival's (myopic) choice.

EXTENSIONS

The simple, textbook version of the RC diagram enjoys some useful properties. Assuming quantity competition, a linear inverse demand and constant marginal costs, the RCs are straight lines with constant negative

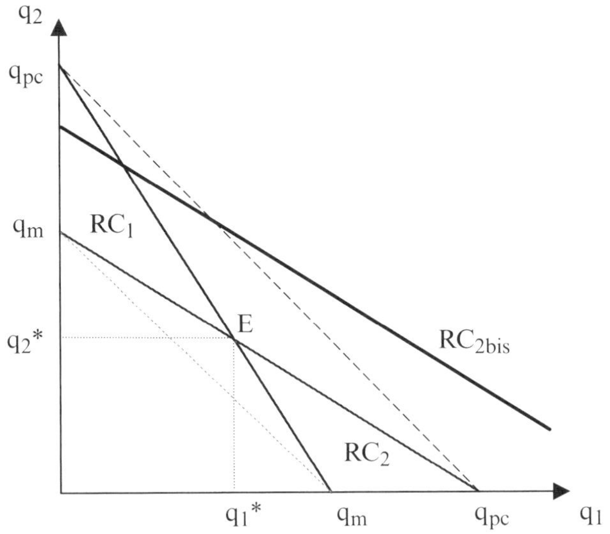

Figure 17.2 Reaction curves – stability analysis and comparison of market performances

slopes and intercepts with the axis equal to, respectively, the perfectly competitive and the monopoly quantities (see Figure 17.2).

Consider RC_1 and adopt the actual-choice interpretation. RC_1's intercept with the X axis identifies the optimal choice when $q_2 = 0$, that is, when firm 1's residual demand (the demand left after firm 2 has chosen its output level) coincides with market demand. But when firm 1 faces the whole demand curve, its optimal choice is to produce the monopoly quantity q_m. Conversely, RC_1's intercept with the Y axis captures the situation when firm 2's output choice has been such that firm 1's optimal reaction is to produce nothing. Thus, firm 2 must have chosen an output level capable of inducing the rival to abstain from production (the so-called limit quantity). This may only happen when q_2 is so large as to push the market price down to equal the common average and marginal cost, that is, when firm 2 offers the perfectly competitive quantity q_{pc} (because in such a case any positive output by firm 1 would push the price further down, below cost). A similar argument explains the intercepts of RC_2.

Given that q_{pc} is larger than q_m, it follows that whenever q_1 is measured on the X axis, RC_1 always crosses RC_2 from above. This, in turn, warrants the stability of Cournot equilibrium as implemented through the above-mentioned trial-and-error process. Remarkably, Cournot himself acknowledged that, though stability might not be warranted in general, it was actually implied by the relative size of RCs' intercepts (1971, 81–2). In a more general setting, the equilibrium may either be non-existent or multiple (see Martin 2002). A non-existence result may emerge when RCs are discontinuous (as in Amoroso's counterexample (1921) or because firms' profit functions are not concave due to the 'excessive' convexity of demand). Multiplicity may ensue when the slope of the RCs (say, of $R_1'(q_2)$) is larger than 1 in absolute value. Both cases are obviously excluded in the standard, linear version of the model.

Figure 17.2 also shows a simple graphical technique for comparing the market performance of a Cournot equilibrium with that of the two extreme cases, monopoly and perfect competition. Given the RCs' intercepts with the axes, we may draw a dashed line representing the (q_1, q_2) pairs that jointly give the perfectly competitive output q_{pc} and a dotted line for the pairs giving the joint monopoly output q_m. The two lines allow an immediate understanding of the intermediate nature of the Cournot equilibrium pair (q_1^*, q_2^*): total output $q_d = q_1^* + q_2^*$ is lower than q_{pc} and larger than q_m. It follows that the price level and the firms' profits are also intermediate between those in the two extreme cases.

The standard RC diagram may also encompass the case of a difference in the firms' efficiency. The thick line in Figure 17.2 is RC_{2bis}, that is, firm 2's RC when it enjoys a cost advantage over firm 1. RC_{2bis} is higher because firm 2 optimally produces more than before for any quantity offered by firm 1. Hence, also q_2^* will be larger (and q_1^* smaller) than in the traditional Cournot equilibrium.

Finally, take the most general form of the slope of the RC, namely, $R'_1(a_2) = -(\partial^2\pi_1/\partial a_1\partial a_2)/(\partial^2\pi_1/\partial a_1^2)$, where a_i is a generic strategic variable, or action. Given that the second order condition for the maximum profit requires $\partial^2\pi_1/\partial a_1^2 < 0$, it turns out that the sign of $R'_1(a_2)$ depends on that of the cross partial derivative of firm 1's profit function, that is, on how π_1 varies as an effect of a change in the rival's action. RC_1 is negatively sloped when, as in the Cournot model, the cross partial $\partial^2\pi_1/\partial a_1\partial a_2$ is negative and positively sloped when it is positive. In the former case, firms' actions are said to be strategic substitutes (for example, quantities), in the latter, strategic complements (for example, prices; see Bulow *et al.* 1985).

The RC diagram for the case of strategic complements is therefore as in Figure 17.3, which represents two firms competing in prices and producing a homogeneous product (so-called 'pure Bertand' case). The equilibrium price pair is (p_{pc}, p_{pc}), where p_{pc} is the perfectly competitive price, namely a price equal to marginal cost c. In the case of partial product differentiation, both RCs would shift upward and the equilibrium pair (p_1^*, p_2^*) would lie somewhere between the competitive and the monopoly price pairs. If the differentiation is complete, the RCs become orthogonal to the axes, with

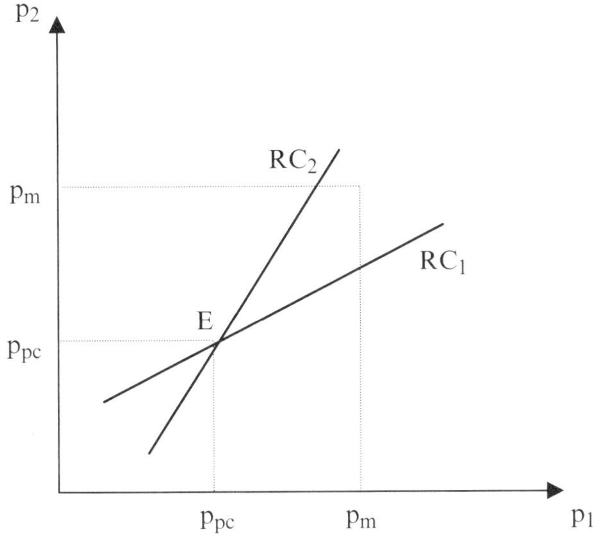

Figure 17.3 *Reaction curves – strategic complements*

intercepts at the monopoly price p_m, to suggest the independence of each firm's price decision from the rival's choice.

REFERENCES

Amoroso L. 1921, *Lezioni di Economia Matematica*, Bologna: Zanichelli.

Bowley A.L. 1924, *The Mathematical Groundwork of Economics*, Oxford: Oxford University Press.

Bulow J., Geanakoplos J. and Klemperer P.D. 1985, 'Multimarket oligopoly: strategic substitutes and complements', *Journal of Political Economy*, 93 (3), 488–511.

Cournot A.A. 1971 [1838], *Researches into the Mathematical Principles of the Theory of Wealth*, New York: Augustus M. Kelley Publishers.

Fellner W. 1949, *Competition Among the Few*, New York: A.A. Knopf.

Fisher I. 1898, 'Cournot and mathematical economics', *Quarterly Journal of Economics*, 12, 119–138.

Friedman J. 1977, 'Cournot, Bowley, Stackelberg and Fellner, and the evolution of the reaction function', in: Balassa B. and Nelson R. (eds), *Economic Progress, Private Values and Public Policy: Essays in Honor of William Fellner*, Amsterdam: North-Holland, 139–160.

Fulton M. 1997, 'A graphical analysis of the Cournot-Nash and Stackelberg models', *Journal of Economic Education*, 28 (1), 48–57.

Giocoli N. 2003, 'Conjecturizing Cournot: the conjectural variations approach to duopoly theory', *History of Political Economy*, 35 (2), 175–204.

Kreps D. 1990, *A Course in Microeconomic Theory*, Hemel Hempstead: Harvester-Wheatsheaf.

Martin S. 2002, *Advanced Industrial Economics Second Edition*, Oxford: Blackwell.

Shubik M. 1959, *Strategy and Market Structure: Competition, Oligopoly and the Theory of Games*, New York: John Wiley and Sons.

18. Monopolistic competition

Andrew Skinner

INTRODUCTION

Monopolistic competition was part of the intellectual debate of the time. Even if we leave Joan Robinson aside, the debate was an old one. Pigou, as Chamberlin points out, had already used the term. Marshall himself was aware of pricing policy in the light of 'sources of possible competition', noting that even where 'large and strong' the monopolist will not make full use of his power 'but will adjust his prices to obtaining a firm hold on the market before he can be caught by competitive supply' (1920, pp. 396–97). The reference to competitive supply is interesting, believing as Marshall did that:

> Though monopoly and free competition are ideally wide apart; yet in practice they shade into one another by imperceptible degrees; that there is an element of monopoly in nearly all-competitive business; and that nearly all monopolies that are of any practical importance in the present age, hold much of their power by an uncertain tenure; so that they would lose it ere long, if they ignored the possibilities of competition, direct and indirect (1920, p. 397).

Marshall's concern with realism finds an echo in Chamberlin's work. Chamberlin undoubtedly recognised the need for empirical research, so that Georgescu-Roegen was surely correct in emphasising his concern with 'the actual' (in Kuenne, 1967, p. 38). Chamberlin's concern with the actual had an interesting consequence. This relates to the introduction of the curve of marginal revenue. Something of the flavour of the period is to be gained by reference to Joan Robinson's introductory remarks: 'There are many occasions when several explorers are surprised, on meeting each other at the pole. Of such an occasion the history of the marginal revenue curve presents a striking example' (1933, pp. vi–vii). Mrs Robinson then went on to identify some eight authorities who were involved in these discussions, including Roy Harrod and Jacob Viner.

Interestingly enough, Chamberlin, while aware of the importance of the margin, did not employ these curves in his thesis of 1927. But writing in the *Theory* (1933), Chamberlin made it clear that unlike Mrs Robinson, he did not regard marginal revenue curves as the ' heart of the matter' (1957, pp. 274–75). As he observed: 'in my own attempt to blend monopoly and competition, the marginal revenue curve was discovered at an early stage and seen for what it is – a piece of pure technique unrelated to the central problem'. He added:

> A major deficiency in the marginal revenue technique is that it does not by itself reveal the price. This means that the discussion of equilibrium takes place primarily in terms of *output*, the category so neatly determined by the intersection of the two marginal curves, instead of in terms of *price*, the category with reference to which business decisions are usually taken (1957).

In addition to the above, Chamberlin cited three practical sources of inspiration. First, there was the Taussig–Pigou controversy as to whether or not charging what the market will bear in railway rates was to be explained in terms of joint costs (1961, p. 517). Second, he drew attention to the influence of Allyn Young, who had given particular attention to trade marks and patents in so far as they confer a monopoly power which is, however, consistent with competition (1961, p.525). A third source of stimulus was found in the literature of business. This point is confirmed by the extensive bibliography attached to the thesis (1927).

THE PRELIMINARY ARGUMENT

Chamberlin's task was to give the theory of value a different orientation – having first defined the extremes of competition and monopoly, and explored some of the ground between them (duopoly).

Having defined pure monopoly (1948, p. 63) as involving 'control over the supply of all economic goods' he concentrated attention on the case of the single seller who comprises the industry, making the point that in this type of case there is 'always competition between the product concerned and others' (ibid., p. 64). This is the familiar example involving control over price in a situation where there are no close substitutes. Chamberlin's solution is now well known, making it necessary only to recall the state of knowledge in the 1920s; a state of knowledge which is reflected in the care with which marginal revenue and marginal cost are defined (1948, pp. 14 and 24) and in the significance of their deployment in a single diagram (Figure 18.1).

Pure competition, a term which Chamberlin may have introduced to the literature (Schumpeter, 1954, p. 973n):

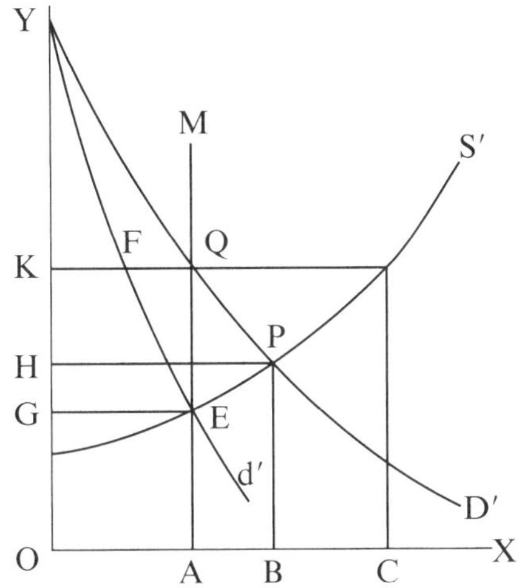

Source: Chamberlin (1948, p. 13)

Figure 18.1 Monopoly

> is taken as a point of departure, the adjective 'pure' being chosen deliberately to describe competition unalloyed with monopoly elements. It is a much simpler and less inclusive concept than perfect competition, for the latter may be interpreted to involve perfection in many other respects than in the absence of monopoly. (1948, p. 6).

Thus defined, pure competition is of interest 'because it describes a portion of economic activity' in the context of a highly organised market (1948, pp. 9, 11). Chamberlin went on to make the point that: 'in order to define the point of equilibrium . . . it is necessary to examine the demand and supply conditions for the group'. He then proceeded to deploy the now familiar diagrams (Figure 18.2) concerning the operation of the firm *and* the situation in the market as a whole (1948, p.17ff).

Commonplace as the example now is, there are a number of points of interest arising from the concern with pure rather than with perfect competition. First, Chamberlin conducted his treatment of equilibrium by reference to the marginal producer, noting that the cost curves for intra-marginal firms will have the same minimum point, if their rents are included as costs. Second, he allows for the fact that if the minimum point of the average cost curve will be the same distance from the X axis, the curves for different producers may vary in their location with reference to the Y axis. Thirdly, formal allowance is made for the possibility that the process of new entry may affect the position of the average cost curve facing the firms.

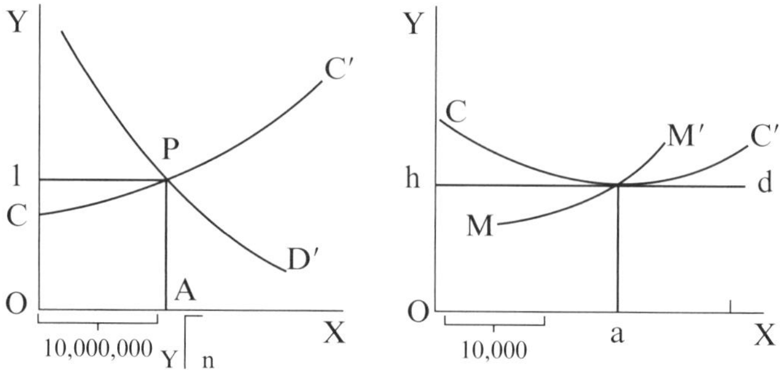

Source: Chamberlin (1948, p. 21)

Figure 18.2 Pure competition

However, to the modern reader, as for Chamberlin himself, the third chapter on 'Duopoly and Oligopoly' remains the most interesting. A version appeared in the *Quarterly Journal* for 1929, when Chamberlin was obliged to strike out the reference to oligopoly at the insistence of F.W. Taussig, the then editor, who 'thought the term a monstrosity' (1957, p. 33) – a decision which must have caused the author some pain since he was unaware at that time of any prior use of the term in print. In discussing the Cournot model of two sellers offering an identical product, Chamberlin concluded that duopoly is not one problem but several. The solution varies depending upon the extent to which sellers recognise their influence upon price and the presence of uncertainty.

ESSENTIALS OF THE THEORY

Chamberlin's main interest was in that situation where the pairing of buyers and sellers is no longer random; that is, where goods are differentiated in the mind of the consumer. Here the firm may control price, product specification and selling costs where the latter are 'incurred to alter the position or shape of the demand curve'(1948: 117). The problems which are exposed by such a perspective are wide ranging, so that it is important to note at the outset that Chamberlin concerned himself almost solely with *intra* rather than *inter*-industry competition and that he retained something very like the Marshallian industry in so doing.

Even this restricted perspective, however, meant that the technical apparatus had to be altered as compared to the treatment of pure competition. The firm now has a choice of cost curve arising from the capacity to alter product specification (1948, pp. 94–100), while in addition, selling costs have to be added to costs of production. Chamberlin thought that it would be difficult to generalise about the curve of selling costs since its shape would be affected by the nature of the product, the level of planned expenditure and the choice of media, but gave it a U shape in both the short and long run (1948, pp. 133–35, 138).

Perhaps the most important innovation resulted from Chamberlin's appreciation of the point that: 'A monopoly of Lucky Strikes does not constitute a monopoly of cigarettes, for there is no degree of control whatever over the supply of other substitute brands' (1948, p. 65). He thus introduced *two* revenue curves. The DD curve is defined as the fractional part of the Market Demand curve (for example, for cigarettes) and 'shows the demand for the product of any one seller at various prices on the assumption that his competitor's prices are always identical with his' (1948, p.90).

In contrast, the dd curve provides 'a rough index of buyers' preferences for the product of one seller over that of another' (1948, p. 93) and indicates the 'increase in sales which he could realise by cutting his price *provided* others did not also cut theirs' (1948, p. 90). In the context of the large group, the relatively elastic (as compared to DD) dd curve is relevant since it is legitimate to assume that any adjustment 'by a single producer spreads its influence over so many of his competitors that the impact felt by any one of them is negligible' (1948, p. 83) – i.e., the diffusion effect.

To ease the task of exposition, Chamberlin proceeded under the heroic assumption that both demand and cost curves for all products 'are uniform throughout the group' (1948, p. 82) thus permitting the use of a single set of revenue and cost functions – and further heightening the misleading impression that the reader confronts a minor variant of the earlier treatment of pure competition.

Methodologically, the technique is classically Marshallian in that Chamberlin assumed price and product, product and selling costs, selling costs and price to be given, before allowing the third element in each case to vary (1948, chapters 5 and 7). In fact, Chamberlin spent a great deal of time in discussing product variation and selling costs, although there is little doubt that the analysis of price adjustment attracted most attention – perhaps because of the obvious parallels and contrasts with pure competition.

The procedure is familiar: if the typical seller faces a dd curve which is consistent with excess profits, new entry will force the curve to a position of tangency, with the cost curve thus yielding an equilibrium under conditions of decreasing cost (Figure 18.3). Tangency holds provided there are many sellers. If there are not sufficient sellers and it does not hold, there are excess profits and inefficient production.

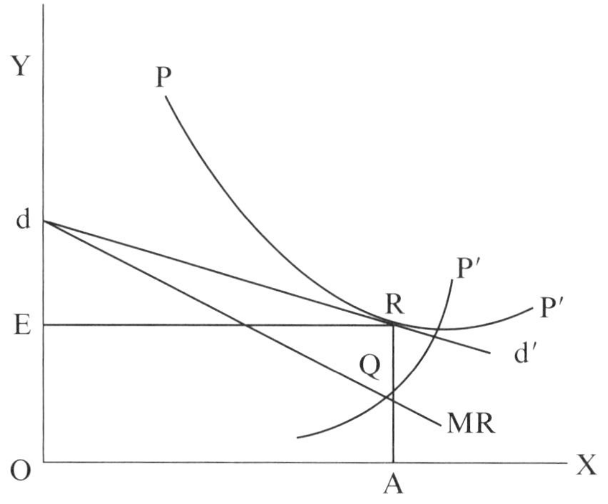

Source: Chamberlin (1948, pp. 75–76)

Figure 18.3 The large group

However the emphasis on tangency obscures the real purpose. One must sympathise with Chamberlin's repeated complaint that this solution had come to be regarded as the 'central principle involved' (1948 p. 195). In fact, Chamberlin recognised that decisions on cost, price and selling outlay were closely linked, and therefore that the relevant functions facing the firm were interdependent. The reader is, in fact, presented with a market situation where change is endogenous, so that in practice the result is heterogeneity of prices, and variation over a wide range of outputs (scales of production) and in profits (1948, p. 81), which is unlikely to be completely eliminated even in a competitive environment. Variation arising from the active pursuit of differentiation is the theme. It is hardly surprising that Chamberlin, with his emphasis on the process of creative destruction, should have likened his position to that of Schumpeter (1957, pp. 62–3). As he noted in an article first published in 1951: 'To many, certain features of monopolistic competition would indicate that it is necessarily a theory of change to be associated with dynamics rather than circular flows'.

THE SMALL GROUP

Chamberlin's treatment of the small group was no less dramatic at the time of writing, particularly since the argument brought to the fore a problem which is implicit in the large group case (with its interdependent functions)

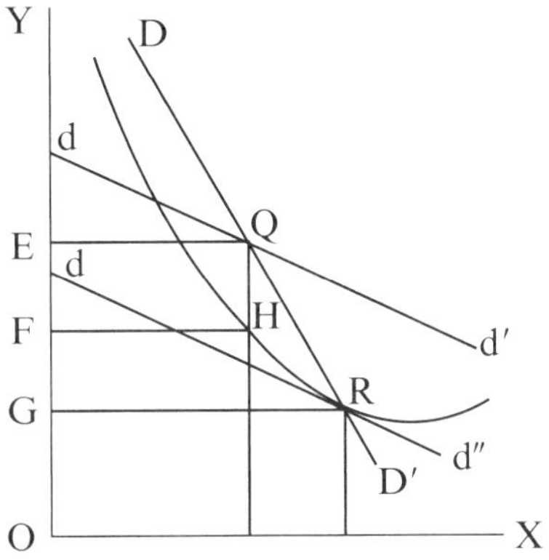

Source: Chamberlin (1948, p. 91)

Figure 18.4 The small group

– that of determinacy. Building on the analysis of Chapter 3, Chamberlin argued that the particular outcome would depend on the behavioural assumptions made. The monopoly (Figure 18.4) solution would obtain if each seller 'sought to maximise his profit with regard to his full influence, direct and indirect, upon the situation' (1948, p. 100), that is, at point Q in the figure. The competitive solution will obtain 'if sellers neglect their indirect influence upon the price, each assuming the others to be unaffected by his own actions' but forcing a reaction which results in each firm arriving at the point R. The most probable solution (dependence recognised) might be expected within these extremes (with dd lying at a point intermediate between Q and R, but with its stability affected by uncertainty:

> the same elements of uncertainty are present here as under the simpler hypothesis of a standardised product . . . Each seller may be in doubt as to his rival's policy, and therefore as to his own, because he does not know (a) whether, if his rival's present policy continues, it will continue with respect to his price or with respect to his output, (b) how intelligent and far-seeing his rival is, and (c) how large would be the incursions made upon him by his own price cut. This last factor is augmented by a new unknown – the extent of the buyer's preferences for his own product over others, expressed by the shape of the demand curves for individual products (1948, p. 101).

But concentration on an identifiable range within which a solution may be found (e.g. RQ in figure 18.4) is itself misleading, depending as it does on the 'heroic assumption' of similar cost and revenue functions. The material point is that there are as many solutions as there are behavioural assumptions to be made.

While it seems a short step from the analysis just considered to the 'kinked' demand curve model, Chamberlin did not take this step although he did argue that the version associated with Hall and Hitch was merely ' a combination of my own d and DD curves'. But at the same time it must be observed that Chamberlin did not link the two marginal revenue curves which are associated with the average curves.

This development was not confirmed until 1939 with the analyses of Sweezy and of Hall and Hitch, which had the effect of identifying a range of discontinuity in the composite MR curve, thus exposing not only a range of possible results but also the fact that a number of marginal cost curves may pass through the relevant range for any given position of the latter (see, for example, Skinner *et al.*, 1996, pp. 180, 183).

But Chamberlin did add a further dimension to the argument by addressing the issue of the spatial distribution of firms, the phenomenon of oligopolistic interdependence. When Chamberlin completed his thesis in 1927, he included within the main body of the argument three sections on space, sections IV.2. on spatial differentiation; V.2. on 'pure spatial differentiation' and V.6. on monopoly and urban rent. The last two sections were to appear in modified form as Appendices C and D in the book. The section on pure spatial competition is reprinted in Skinner (2001).

The problem which arises may affect firms which are members of a large group. For example, retail stores or filling stations may form a network of interwoven markets where action taken by one seller may impinge on the fortunes of others in a different place – the 'chain linking effect', which suggests that even where a number of firms are selling physically similar (or even identical) products, consideration of indirect influence may enter the calculation. Chamberlin thus concluded that: 'oligopolistic elements are very general in the economic system and that economic study must be increasingly concerned with their influence upon prices and other economic categories' (1948, p. 61). In all of these cases, we confront the problem of interdependence and a situation where the curves of revenue (and of revenue product) are conjectural, based as they are upon judgements with regard to the future performance of rivals. In the situation described above there is no clearly defined path to equilibrium (Loasby, 1976).

Chamberlin's modelling of monopolistic competition had a profound effect on the way economists view competition when sellers are interdependent. Later generations have modified his assumptions. Following Dixit and Stiglitz (1977), the demand side is often modelled as a group of close substitutes nested together in a sub-utility function which is CES in form. Krugman (1979) combined the Dixit-Stiglitz specification with the assumption on the supply side that there are fixed set-up costs, giving unit costs which are everywhere decreasing rather than U-shaped. As in the Chamberlin model, the cost functions of all firms are identical and monopoly power is restrained by the existence of the differentiated but closely substitutable products. A large number of models in both industrial organisation and international trade are based on this version of monopolistic competition. Another generation is building models with new features such as heterogeneous firms. But all of these models build on the enduring insights of the Chamberlin model.

REFERENCES

Chamberlin, E. H. (1927), *The Theory of Monopolistic Competition*, thesis dated 1 April, (Cambridge, MA: Harvard Rd Archives).

Chamberlin, E. H. (1948), *The Theory of Monopolistic Competition*, 6th Edition, Cambridge, MA: Harvard University Press (1st edition published 1933).

Chamberlin, E. H. (1957), *Towards a More General Theory of Value*, Oxford: Oxford University Press.

Chamberlin, E. H. (1961), 'The Origin and Early Development of Monopolistic Competition Theory', *Quarterly Journal of Economics*, 75, 515–543.

Dixit, A. and Stiglitz, J. (1977), 'Monopolistic Competition and Optimum Product Diversity', *American Economic Review*, 67, 297–308.

Hall, R. L. and Hitch, C. J. (1939), 'Price Theory and Business Behaviour', *Oxford Economic Papers*, 2, 12–45.

Krugman, P. R. (1979), 'Increasing Returns, monopolistic Competition and International Trade', *Journal of International Economics*, 9, 469–79.

Kuenne, R. E. (1967), *Monopolistic Competition Theory: Studies in Impact*, London: John Wiley.

Loasby, B. J. (1976), *Choice, Complexity and Ignorance*, Cambridge: Cambridge University Press.

Marshall, A. (1920), *Industry and Trade*, London: Macmillan.

Robinson, J. (1933), *The Economics of Imperfect Competition*, London: Macmillan.

Schumpeter, J.A. (1954), *History of Economic Analysis,* London: Allen and Unwin.

Skinner, A. S. (with Hay, F. and Oughton, C.) (1996), *Contributions to a Perspective on Intermediate Price Theory*, Manchester: Manchester University Press.

Skinner, A. S. (2001), 'E. H. Chamberlain: Oligopoly and Oligopolistic Interdependence: The Issue of Space' in *Economics Broadly Considered*, Biddle, J. E., Davis, J. B. and Medema, S. G. (eds), London: Routledge.

19. Kinked demand curves

R. Rothschild

The 'kinked demand curve' (KDC) is one of several early attempts to characterize the demand for the output of a firm under oligopolistic market conditions. Although it holds relatively little appeal for modern writers who work within a game-theoretic framework, it remains an intuitively plausible explanation of firms' behavior in practice.

Early discussions of the concept that underlies the KDC can be found in the work of Hayes (1928), Kahn (1929) and Sweezy (1937, 1938), amongst others (for an excellent survey, see Reid, 1981). However, its formalization – or at least the version that will be familiar to contemporary students – is to be found in work published almost simultaneously by Sweezy (1939) in the USA, and Hall and Hitch (1939) in the UK. While Sweezy's contribution to the articulation of what he termed the 'imagined demand curve' was an essentially theoretical one based on informal interviews with businessmen, that of Hall and Hitch was based upon the results of a detailed study of costing and pricing behavior carried out in 38 firms. However, in both cases it is apparent that the motivation for the model rests upon a recognition of the practical considerations that surround the setting of prices in oligopolistic industries.

The most familiar variant of the KDC diagram is made up of two figures that appear in Sweezy's 1939 article. The model focuses on a single firm in an N-firm oligopoly, in which all competitors have identical costs and produce varieties of a product that are, in some sense, equally differentiated. The firm's demand curve is made up of parts of two distinct curves, a 'share of the market' curve (a simple leftward translation of the market demand curve to represent the demand facing the seller when all firms set the same price), and a curve that reflects the firm's expected demand if it were the only one to change its price, either upward or downward, from some initial common level.

In this figure, the curve AB represents the price-quantity pairs that the firm would face if all in the industry set the same price; CD is the 'ceteris paribus' demand curve, reflecting the anticipated outcome for the firm when it undertakes a unilateral price change upward or downward from

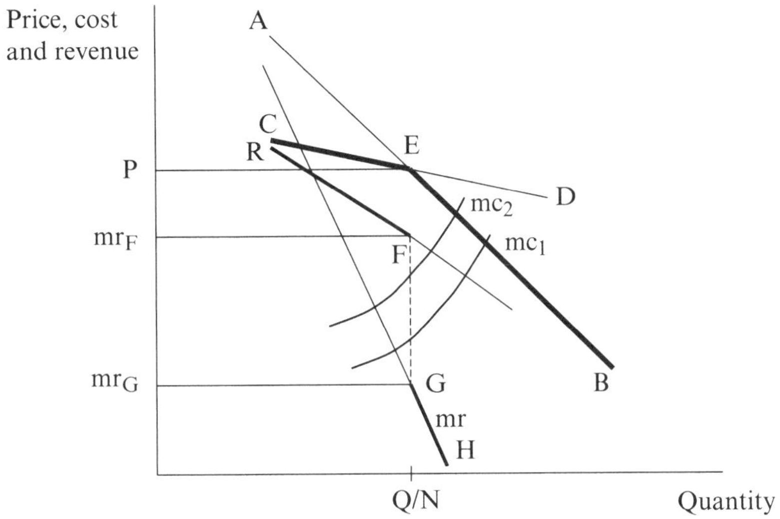

Figure 19.1 The kinked demand curve

P. The quantity sold at P is Q/N, where Q is total market demand at P. The firm conjectures that in the absence of any change in industry costs, competitors will not follow a departure from P in the upward direction, since by keeping their prices unchanged they will take business from it. Consequently, if the firm undertakes such an increase it will expect to face the relatively elastic segment CE. Conversely, since competitors should be expected to follow a departure from P in the downward direction in order not to lose business, the firm in undertaking such a decrease will not expect to face the segment ED, but rather the relatively inelastic share-of-the-market demand segment EB. Sweezy's 'imagined demand curve', viewed from the common price P, is therefore CEB. Since any firm contemplating a unilateral increase from P would expect to lose revenue, while a decrease from P would be expected to yield only a proportionate share of the increase in demand along the relatively inelastic segment of the curve – and thus result in a decrease in revenue – any unilateral deviation from P will be deemed to be profit decreasing and all firms will therefore stick at P.

It is important to stress that the 'kink' at the prevailing price P occurs because firms conjecture that competitors will behave in the manner described above. In Sweezy's model, firms are in no sense agreed – as they might be in a formal cartel – that such behavior will necessarily occur. In contrast to behavior that reflects formal agreement, actions predicated upon conjectures that give rise to the KDC are deemed by some writers to reflect 'tacit' collusion.

The existence of the kink implies a discontinuous 'marginal revenue' curve comprising the segment RF – the marginal revenue associated with curve CE – and the segment GH, the marginal revenue associated with the curve AB below E. Mathematically speaking, the region FG between the two components exists because the first derivative of the total revenue (that is, marginal revenue) associated with the demand function CEB is discontinuous at E. The marginal revenue in FG is therefore not defined. This means that if all firms' marginal costs were to rise or fall by the same amount in FG, there would be no clear incentive for any firm to depart from P. But if all firms' marginal costs were to rise by the same amount to a point above F, or fall to a point below G, the common price should be expected to change, though the model offers no insight into how or the extent to which it might do so.

The KDC analysis can in a sense be thought to reconcile the marginalist principle that marginal revenue should equal marginal costs if profits are to be maximized, with the empirical observation that, in oligopolistic industries, price stability or, alternatively, 'sticky prices', can often be observed even in the face of changes in costs. If marginal costs lie anywhere in FG, marginal revenue everywhere to the left of F is greater than these costs, and marginal revenue everywhere to the right of G is less than these costs. It can be argued therefore that given any increase or decrease in marginal costs in the interval FG, there are compelling reasons for keeping the common price at P. It is important to emphasize that this does not imply an 'equality' between marginal revenue and marginal costs at Q/N. Here, the familiar condition for profit maximization is replaced at that output by the weak inequality $mr_F \geq mc \geq mr_G$.

An implication of the discontinuity in marginal revenue is that the marginal revenue product of labor – and, hence, the firm's demand curve for labor – can also be discontinuous. In Sweezy's view, this possibility was of central importance, since it means that an increase in wages at the firm level would not necessarily imply a change in output, employment or price, even though profits might fall.

Although the concept of asymmetrical price responses by competitors to changes in own price has a certain intuitive appeal to practitioners, the model has been subjected to several criticisms. Of these, the most widely rehearsed in undergraduate textbooks is the fact that the conjectures that underpin firms' pricing behavior must be expected to hold at *any* arbitrarily chosen price. That is to say, the model explains why P may be stable but fails to predict where it will materialize. Indeed, P can lie anywhere between marginal cost and the monopoly price.

However, as at least one author – Rothschild (1992) – has noted, this criticism may be unfair. In a paper that retains the spirit of Sweezy's model, he shows that if all varieties of the good produced in the industry are (symmetrically) differentiated to some degree, then a departure by a firm from P in the downward direction will not necessarily be followed by its competitors. This is because for each such firm, depending upon the degree of variety substitutability, the sales gained by matching the move away from P may be insufficient to offset the loss in revenue resulting from the decrease in price. Conversely, any departure by a firm from P in the upward direction might be followed by competitors if their gain in revenue from the price increase is proportionately larger than their gain in sales from sticking at P. The implication is that if the kink is to occur, the potential for these two effects on revenue should not exist, and this requirement, in turn, restricts the set of prices at which the kink is likely to be found. Indeed, since, for a given N, the precise gains and losses in firms' revenues from undertaking matching changes away from P will depend upon (a) the degree of variety substitutability and (b) the location of the initial P on AB, it is quite possible that under certain demand and cost conditions, there will exist a unique price at which the conditions for the existence of the kink will be satisfied.

Another criticism of the model is that it is essentially 'static', while the process it seeks to describe is inevitably dynamic. Consequently, even though, as Tirole (1988) has observed . . .. '(t)he modelling of dynamic features in a static framework is, *a priori,* very appealing', recent work by Bhaskar (1988), Maskin and Tirole (1988) and Sen (2004) amongst others has focused on the kink as an outcome to a repeated game amongst players of either the Bertrand or Stackelberg types. These contributions, while of considerable interest in themselves, move the analysis away from the original conceptualization.

Despite its weaknesses, the KDC concept survives, at least in undergraduate texts in microeconomic theory. Moreover, the idea that prices might be 'inflexible' when costs change has a role in contemporary macroeconomics: rigidity in the face of changes in costs or demand prevents smooth adjustments in times of boom or recession and this, inter alia, can affect the distribution of income between wage earners and the owners of capital over the business cycle.

ACKNOWLEDGEMENT

I thank J. E. King for helpful comments on an early draft.

REFERENCES

Bhaskar, V. (1988), 'The kinked demand curve: A game-theoretic approach', *International Journal of Industrial Organization*, 6, 373–84.

Hall, R. E. and C. J. Hitch (1939), 'Price theory and business behaviour', *Oxford Economic Papers*, 2, 12–45.

Hayes, H. G. (1928), *Our Economic System*, New York: Holt.

Kahn, R. F. (1929), *The Economics of the Short Period*, Unpublished Fellowship Dissertation, King's College, Cambridge.

Maskin, E. and J. Tirole (1988), 'A theory of dynamic oligopoly, II: Price competition, kinked demand curves, and Edgeworth cycles', *Econometrica*, 56, 571–99.

Reid, G. C. (1981), *The Kinked Demand Curve Analysis of Oligopoly*, Edinburgh: Edinburgh University Press.

Rothschild, R. (1992), 'A simple proof of Sweezy's "kinked demand" conjecture', *Scottish Journal of Political Economy*, 39, 69–75.

Sen, D. (2004), 'The kinked demand curve revisited', *Economics Letters*, 84, 99–105.

Sweezy, P. M. (1937), 'Discussion on wage policy and investment', *American Economic Review (Papers and Proceedings)*, 27, 156–7.

Sweezy, P. M. (1938), *Monopoly and Competition in the English Coal Trade, 1550–1880*, Cambridge MA: Harvard University Press.

Sweezy, P. M. (1939), Demand under conditions of oligopoly', *Journal of Political Economy*, 47, 568–73.

Tirole, J. (1988), *The Theory of Industrial Organization*, Cambridge MA: MIT Press.

Special markets and topics

20. Backward-bending labour supply curves

John E. King

The backward-bending labour supply curve is a staple feature of labour economics textbooks (Borjas 2005, Figure 2.11b, p. 44), and is also found both in advanced handbooks on labour market theory (Killingsworth 1983, Figure 1.5, p. 13) and in introductory principles texts (Samuelson and Nordhaus 1998, Figure 13–4, p. 229). It is derived from a simple application of neoclassical consumer theory to the individual's labour supply decision.

In Figure 20.1A, the individual has to choose between two goods, leisure and income. Leisure is measured in hours per day; the term is used to denote all uses of time other than paid work. Income represents all other goods; it is obtained by supplying hours of labour (non-leisure) in return for a wage. The individual's preferences are illustrated by the indifference curves in Figure 20.1A, which take the standard form: they are downward-sloping, convex to the origin (since the marginal rate of substitution of income for leisure declines as income increases), and do not touch either axis ('man cannot live by leisure – or income – alone'). The budget constraint is illustrated by the straight lines DA, DB and DC, with a slope equal to the hourly wage rate (Ow_1, Ow^* and Ow_2). The vertical intercept shows the income that individuals would earn if they took no leisure and worked for 24 hours a day, while the horizontal intercept shows that zero work means zero income.

The analysis can be made more realistic, and the diagram very much more complicated, by allowing for (i) the payment of overtime at premium rates; (ii) alternative uses of time, such as domestic chores and commuting; (iii) alternative sources of (non-wage) income; and (iv) the fact that time is needed to consume goods. To derive the backward-bending labour supply curve, however, it is convenient to ignore these complications. Consider the effect of reductions in the hourly wage rate, from Ow_2 to Ow^* to Ow_1. This reduces the slope of the budget constraint, which pivots from DC to DB to DA. There is a reduction in the price of leisure (less wage income must be given up to 'buy' each hour of leisure).

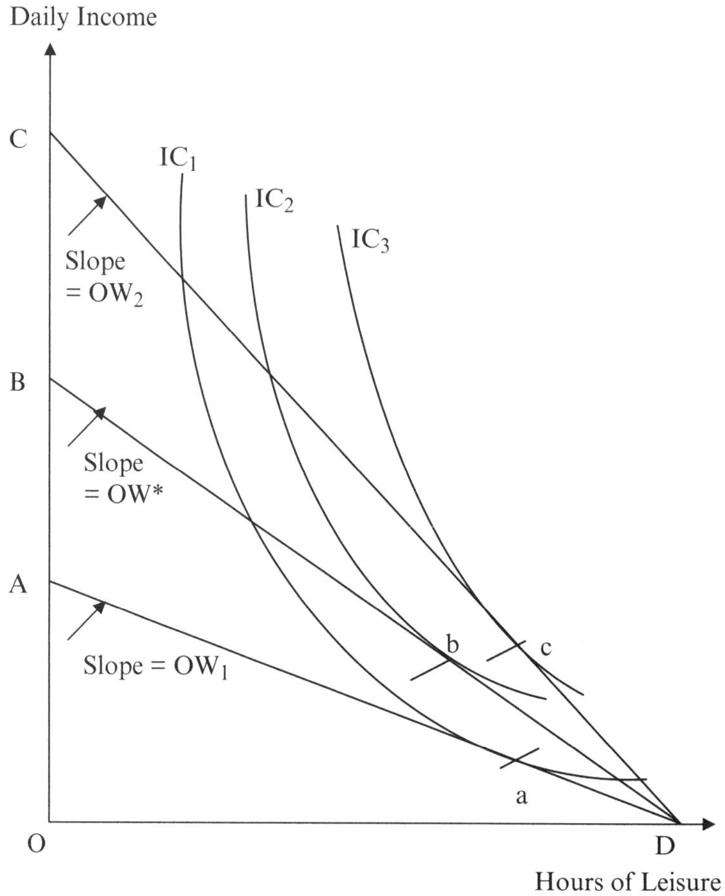

Figure 20.1A The individual labour supply decision

As in neoclassical consumer theory more generally, the price effect is the sum of the substitution effect and the income effect. Leisure is now cheaper, relative to all other goods (the substitution effect), but the individual's real income has also fallen, reducing the capacity to buy both leisure and consumer goods (the income effect). The substitution effect is always positive: as leisure becomes cheaper, more will be consumed, and fewer hours of labour will be supplied. If leisure is assumed to be a normal (non-inferior) good, the income effect is always negative: less income, less leisure demanded, more hours of work. Thus the substitution and income effects of a wage cut operate in opposite directions, and the net effect or *price effect* is unpredictable. More precisely, it depends on the

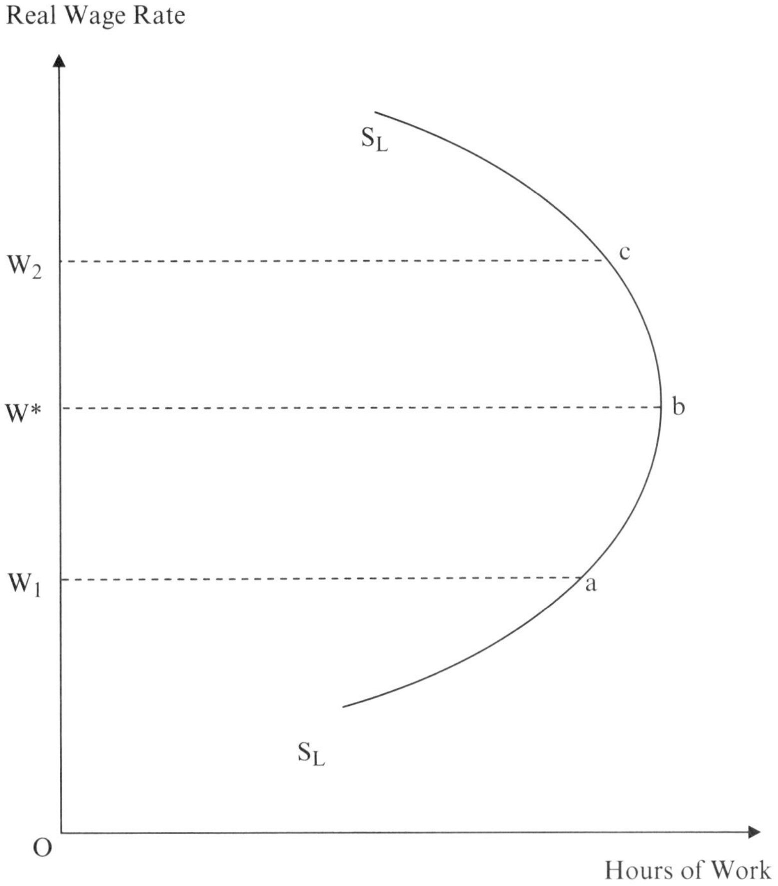

Figure 20.1B The individual labour supply curve

specific nature of the individual's preference function. The individual's labour supply curve may thus slope upwards, or downwards, or it may be backward-bending, as shown in Figure 20.1B, where it is drawn in wage rate/hours of work space. The points a, b and c in Figure 20.1B correspond to the points a, b and c in Figure 20.1A. The labour supply curve is backward-bending because the substitution effect dominates the income effect at low wage rates ($Ow < Ow^*$), while the income effect dominates the substitution effect at higher wage rates ($Ow > Ow^*$).

To keep the diagram uncluttered, only the price effect is shown in Figure 20.1A; readers may draw the substitution and income effects for themselves, preferably using a soft pencil. Note that one important, implicit and highly questionable assumption has been made in this analysis. Individuals are assumed to be completely free to choose the hours of paid work (and hence also the hours of leisure) that they prefer. In practice, of course, many employees do not have this freedom. Jobs are commonly offered on a 'take it or leave it' basis, with the hours of work specified by the employer. Individuals may thus find themselves 'under-employed', working fewer hours (and 'enjoying' more leisure) than they themselves would have chosen, or 'over-employed', with the opposite implications (see Killingsworth 1983, pp. 48–50).

In modern textbooks, the backward-bending labour supply curve sometimes appears with a gender gloss, with the female labour supply curve depicted as upward-sloping and the male curve either backward-bending or downward-sloping over a substantial range of wage rates; this is the case, for example, in Hamermesh and Rees (1993, pp. 48–55), where the backward-bending curve applies to 'Max' but not to 'Maxine'. There is some empirical support for this, or at least for the slightly weaker proposition that the wage elasticity of labour supply is much greater for women than for men (Killingsworth 1983, p. 432).

The origins of neoclassical labour supply theory are disputed (Derobert 2001). The story of the backward-bending labour supply curve diagram is more straightforward. It begins, perhaps surprisingly, with a practical problem of economic policy posed by the theory of public finance. The father of neoclassical welfare economics, A.C. Pigou, was a liberal socialist who never doubted the possibility of interpersonal comparisons of utility and was a resolute defender of redistributive taxation. Since the marginal utility of a dollar to a poor person was much greater than its marginal utility to a rich person, he argued, fiscal policy should take from the rich and give to the poor. Pigou believed that there was no need to worry about the effect on incentives. Progressive income taxation would drive a wedge between the pre-tax and post-tax wage rate (and it is the post-tax wage rate that is illustrated in Figures 20.1A and 20.1B). This, he thought, would necessarily lead taxpayers to supply *more* labour, to make up for their loss of disposable income (Pigou 1920, p. 593; this claim is rather weaker in later editions of the book).

It was a much more conservative economist, Lionel Robbins, who spotted the mistake (Robbins 1930). Pigou had assumed that the individual's labour supply curve was always downward sloping. But this is true only if the income effect of a wage cut is always greater than the substitution effect, which is not plausible. Robbins put the case against Pigou in what now seems rather archaic language (but, according to James Buchanan (1971), was entirely appropriate for its purpose). Everything depends on the elasticity of demand for income in terms of effort. In Figure

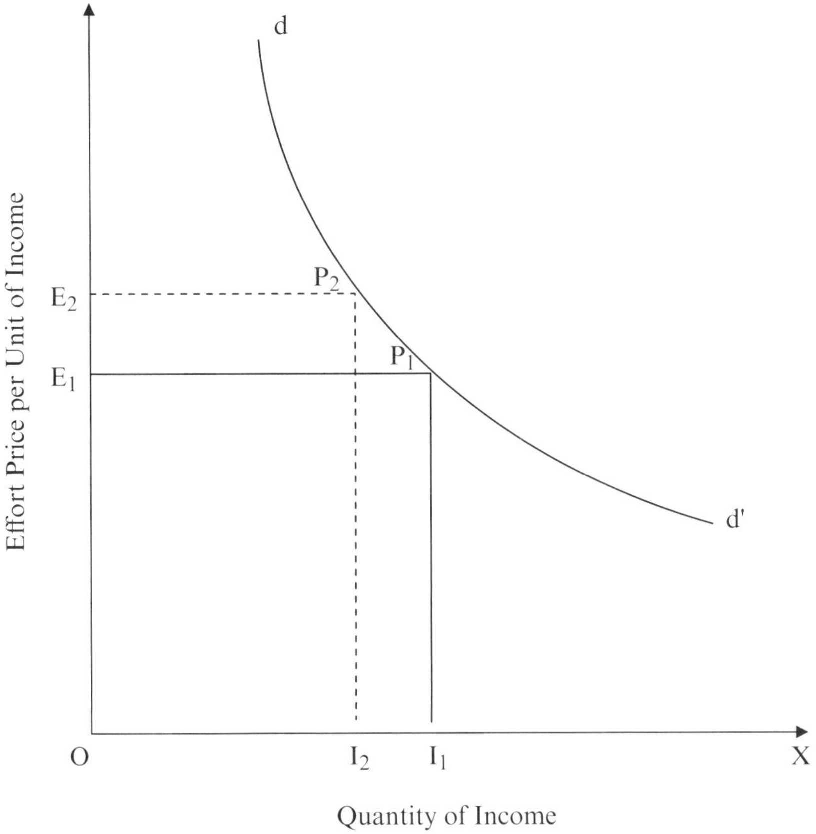

Figure 20.2A Lionel Robbins's first diagram

20.2A, the effort price per unit of income is measured on the vertical axis (this may be thought of as the inverse of the post-tax wage rate), and the quantity of income on the horizontal axis. The individual's demand for income in terms of effort is shown by dd'. An increase in the income tax rate increases this price from OE_1 to OE_2 (and reduces the post-tax wage rate accordingly), leading to less income being demanded; the individual moves from P_1 to P_2 on the demand curve. Whether or not more effort will be supplied depends on the elasticity of dd', which can be inferred by comparing the areas $O\,E_1\,P_1\,I_1$ and $O\,E_2\,P_2\,I_2$. The implications of this are illustrated in Figure 20.2B, where the quantity of effort (that is, hours of work) is now measured on the vertical axis, and the slope of the rays OG_1 and OG_2 shows the post-tax wage rate before and after the increase in taxation. In this case, a reduction in the wage leads to more work being

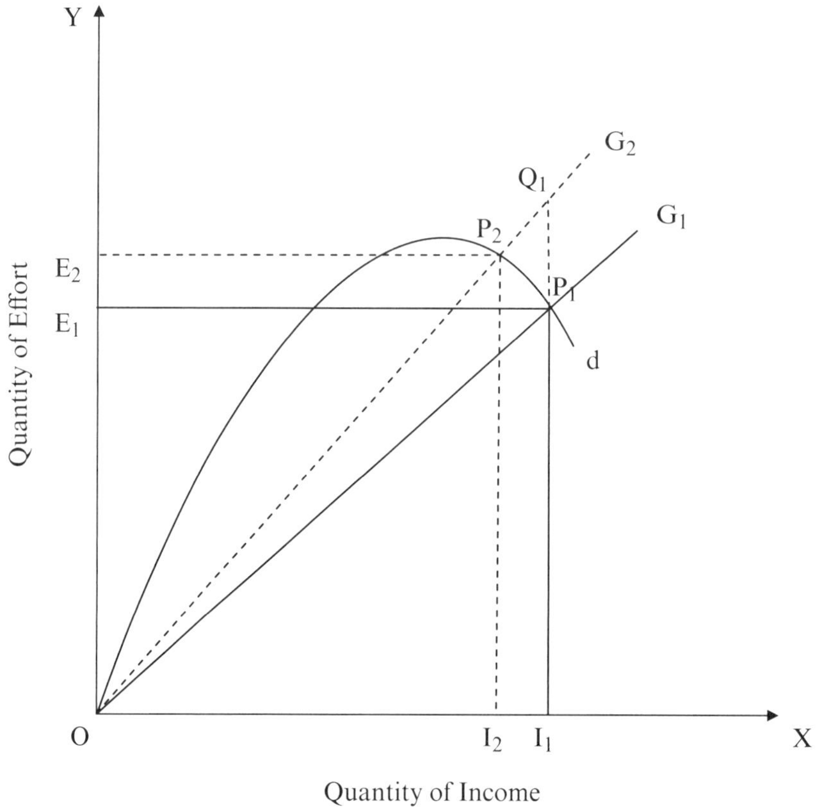

Figure 20.2B Lionel Robbins's second diagram

done (as Robbins put it), but there is no a priori reason why this (or any other special case) should be so.

Six years later, Henry Phelps Brown (1936, Figure 5, p. 155) almost became the first to draw a backward-bending labour supply curve like that in Figure 20.1B, but he inverted the axes, as shown in Figure 20.3. It seems that the author of the first version of Figure 20.1B to appear in print was Joan Robinson, in the 'diagrammatic illustrations' chapter of her *Essays in the Theory of Employment*, written in 1935 but published two years later (Robinson 1937, Figure 1, p. 166). In *Value and Capital*, J. R. Hicks (1939, pp. 36–7) restated the arguments in terms of the income and substitution effects, thereby establishing the backward-bending labour supply curve in the canon of mainstream microeconomics.

For a while it also featured prominently in development economics. In Robbins's original formulation, it was the supply of productive *effort*

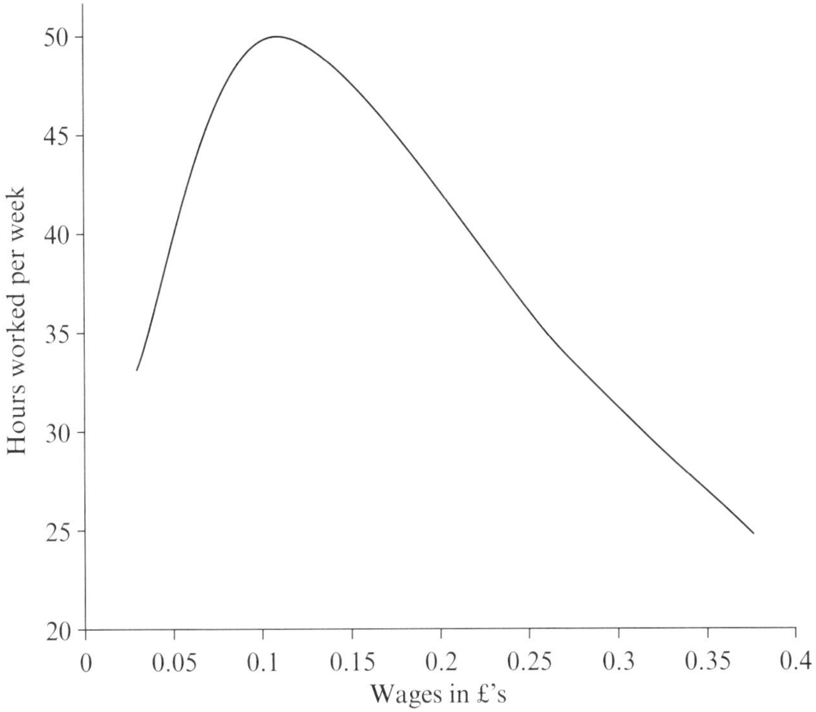

Figure 20.3 Henry Phelps Brown's version with axes inverted

– not restricted to hours of work – that was being analysed. Neoclassical economics has always had great difficulty in saying anything sensible about work effort in paid employment (Spencer 2008), but Robbins's analysis does have an obvious bearing on the decisions of self-employed people, who have some direct control over the pace and intensity at which they work as well as the number of hours that they devote to it. The most numerous self-employed producers, of course, are farmers, and in the early days of development economics as a separate academic (sub-) discipline, it was often suggested that a downward-sloping or backward-bending labour supply curve could be observed in peasant agriculture. Sometimes this was associated with the theory of economic dualism, according to which human motivation and behaviour was quite different in the 'traditional' or backward sector from that in the 'modern' sector of underdeveloped countries (Berg 1961). This, however, carried deliberate or unintended connotations of cultural condescension, verging on racism, and by the early 1970s, it was being severely criticised. The

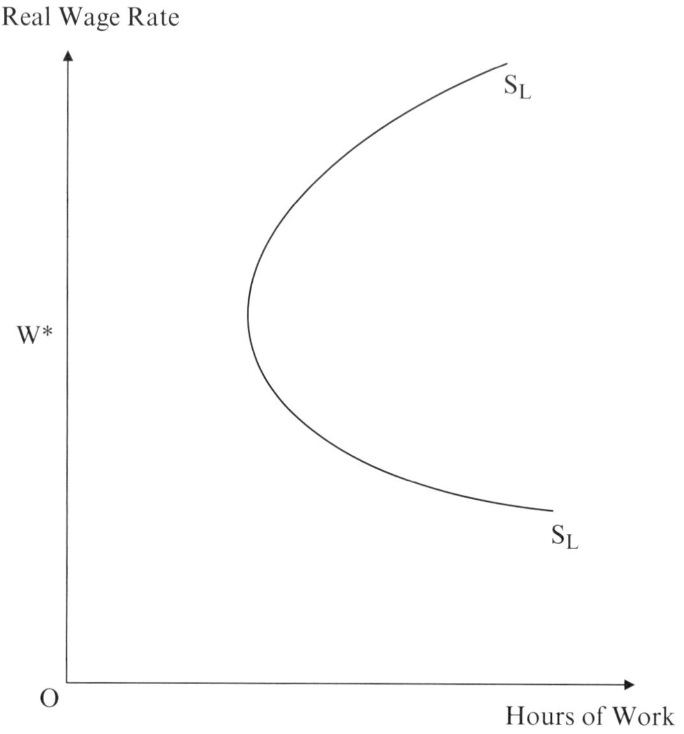

Figure 20.4 Backward-bending labour supply curve (conservative version)

backward-bending labour supply curve is no longer found in introductory development economics texts.

There is, finally, a (contentious) macroeconomic dimension. The policy prescriptions of 'supply-side economics', and especially of its extreme version, the Laffer curve (see Chapter 54), depend on a strongly upward-sloping labour supply curve. As J.K. Galbraith noted, however, neo-liberal policy rhetoric often seemed to take a slightly different line: 'In recent years, the rich have not been working because they have had too little money, and the poor have not been working because they have had too much' (quoted in Parker 2005, p. 577). This implies the dominance of the income effect over the substitution effect for the poor (whose wages are low), and the dominance of the substitution effect over the income effect for the rich (whose wage rates are high). This is illustrated in Figure 20.4, which is the opposite of Figure 20.1B. No evidence has ever been adduced in its favour, although the leftward-sloping section, showing falling work effort as the wage increases from very low levels up to Ow*, was a staple theme of eighteenth-century writers, who feared the consequences of encouraging idleness among the poor (Furniss 1965).

REFERENCES

Berg, E. 1961. 'Backward-sloping labour supply functions in dual economies: the African case', *Quarterly Journal of Economics* 75(3), August, pp. 468–92.

Borjas, G.J. 2005. *Labour Economics*. Boston, MA: McGraw-Hill/Irwin, third edition.

Brown, E.H. Phelps. 1936. *The Framework of the Pricing System*. London: Chapman and Hall.

Buchanan, J.M. 1971. 'The backwardbending supply curve of labour: an example of doctrinal retrogression?' *History of Political Economy* 3(2), Fall, pp. 382–90.

Derobert, L. 2001. 'On the genesis of the canonical labour supply theory', *Journal of the History of Economic Thought* 23(2), June, pp. 197–215.

Furniss, E.S. 1965. *The Position of the Laborer in a System of Nationalism: A Study in the Labor Theories of the Later English Mercantilists*. New York: Kelley.

Hamermesh, D.S. and Rees, A. 1993. *The Economics of Work and Pay*. New York: HarperCollins, fifth edition.

Hicks, J.R. 1939. *Value and Capital*. Oxford: Clarendon Press.

Killingsworth, M.R. 1983. *Labor Supply*. Cambridge: Cambridge University Press.

Parker, R. 2005. *John Kenneth Galbraith: His Life, His Politics, His Economics*. Toronto: HarperCollins.

Pigou, A.C. 1920. *The Economics of Welfare*. London: Macmillan.

Robbins, L. 1930. 'On the elasticity of demand for income in terms of effort', *Economica* 29, June, pp. 123–9.

Robinson, J. 1937. *Essays in the Theory of Employment*. London: Macmillan.

Samuelson, P. and Nordhaus, W. 1998. *Economics* (International edition). Sydney: Irwin/McGraw-Hill, 16th edition.

Spencer, D.A. 2008. *The Political Economy of Work*. London: Routledge.

21. Location theory: the contributions of von Thünen and Lösch

B. Curtis Eaton and Richard G. Lipsey

VON THÜNEN'S CIRCLES

Figure 21.1 was produced by a friend of von Thünen's to illustrate the main results in his book, *The Isolated State* (see Von Thünen, 1966, page 216). The first edition of this remarkable book was published in German in 1826 but was not translated into English until 1966. This diagram, and another that illustrates some comparative static properties of von Thünen's model, appear in the notes at the end of Section Three, Part One. His model was designed to explore the allocation of land to alternative agricultural uses and is, surely, one of the earliest explicit optimising models in economics.

The pattern of rings in the top half of the figure is the equilibrium allocation of Thünen's model. It illustrates the way in which the land surrounding the town at the centre of the diagram is allocated to various agricultural activities. Moving from the centre of the diagram outward, the first two rings are devoted to free cash cropping and forestry, then come three rings devoted to the production of grain using different methods of cultivation, the crop alternation system, the improved system and the three-field system, and finally the outermost ring is devoted to stock farming. Land beyond the outer ring is, in Von Thünen's words, an 'uncultivated wilderness'. The bottom half of the figure illustrates the alterations to this pattern caused by the presence of a navigable river that meanders through the semicircle and a small town located as indicated.

In the first two chapters of *The Isolated State*, von Thünen describes the model, the questions he addresses and the mode of analysis, as well as providing an intuitive summary of the results. His words are worth reproducing in their entirety (1966, pp. 7–8).

> Imagine a very large town, at the centre of a fertile plain which is crossed by no navigable river or canal. Throughout the plain the soil is capable of cultivation and the same fertility. Far from the town, the plain turns into an uncultivated wilderness which cuts off all communication between this State and the outside world.

Fig. I

Fig. II

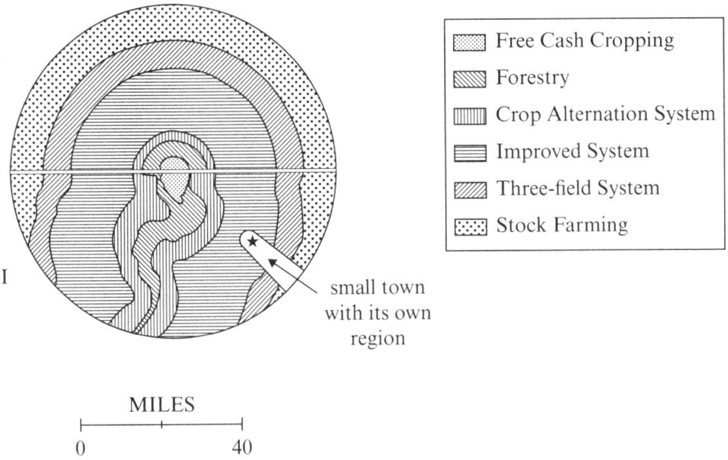

Source: Von Thünen (1966, p. 216). Permission granted by Peter Hall

Figure 21.1 Allocation of land in von Thünen's model around a single city (top half) and as distorted by an additional small town and river (bottom half)

> There are no other towns on the plain. The central town must therefore supply the rural areas with all manufactured products, and in return it will obtain all its provisions from the surrounding countryside.
>
> The mines that provide the State with salt and metals are near the central town which, as it is the only one, we shall call simply 'the Town'.
>
> The problem we want to solve is this: What pattern of cultivation will take shape in these conditions?; and how will the farming system of the different districts be affected by their distance from the Town? We assume throughout that farming is conducted absolutely rationally.
>
> It is on the whole obvious that near the Town will be grown those products which are heavy or bulky in relation to their value and hence so expensive to transport that the remoter districts are unable to supply them. Here too we shall find the highly perishable products, which must be used very quickly. With increasing distance from the Town, the land will progressively be given up to products cheap to transport in relation to their value.
>
> For this reason alone, fairly sharply differentiated concentric rings or belts will form around the town, each with its own particular staple product.
>
> From ring to ring the staple product, and with it the entire farming system, will change; and in the various rings we shall find completely different farming systems.

Von Thünen defines the bid rent for any activity as the maximum surplus or profit that the land would generate if it were devoted to that activity. Because transport is costly, bid rent is a function of the distance from the central

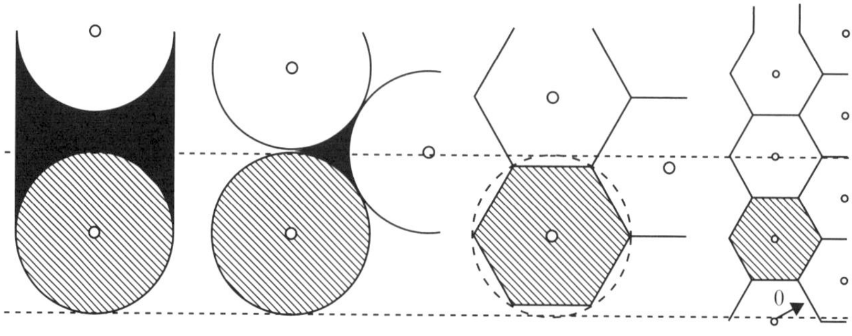

Source: Lösch (1954, p. 110). Permission granted by Yale University Press.

Figure 21.2 Lösch market areas: circles and hexagons

market located in the Town. In the equilibrium illustrated in Figure 21.1, land at any given distance from the Town is allocated to the activity with the highest positive bid rent. On the outside edge of the last ring, the highest bid rent is 0, so beyond this last ring the land remains an uncultivated wilderness. This approach provides not only a theory of the location of activities and land rent, but also a theory of factor intensities. Because prices of goods in the Town are taken as given, the analysis is partial equilibrium.

Although not expressed in elegant mathematics, von Thünen's conceptualisation and analysis of the problem are remarkably modern. Although it was published in 1826, it is thoroughly neoclassical in conception. It has been the foundation of a large literature on land use (see, for example, Chapter 3 of Fujita and Thisse, 2002). The monocentric models of cities in particular, developed by Alonso (1964), Mills (1972) and others in the 1960s, owe a heavy debt to von Thünen's *The Isolated State*.

LÖSCH'S HEXAGONS

Figure 21.2 illustrates the hexagonal market areas made famous by August Lösch in his book *The Economics of Location*, first published in German in 1940 and in English in 1954 (p. 110). The dots in the figure represent the locations on a homogeneous plane of firms selling a single good to customers who have identical demands and who are uniformly distributed on the plane. The boundaries delineate sets of consumers who, in the equilibrium of Lösch's model, buy the good from the firms located at the centres of the circles on the left side of the figure, or the centres of the hexagons on the right side of the figure.

As Von Thünen did, Lösch starts with a clear statement of his problem and the model he uses to address it (p. 105).

> Among all the factors that can create an economic region we shall select the economic. We shall consider market areas that are not the result of any kind of natural or political inequalities but arise through the interplay of purely economic forces, some working toward concentration and others toward dispersion. In the first group are the advantages of specialization and of large-scale production; in the second, those of shipping costs and of diversified production.
>
> In the following derivation we start from radical assumptions in order that no spatial differences may lie concealed in what we assume: that economic raw materials are evenly and adequately distributed over a wide plain. Our area shall be homogenous in every other respect as well, and contain nothing but self-sufficient farms that are regularly distributed. How can this starting point lead to spatial differences?
>
> Let us select any one of these farms, and ascribe to its owner the wish to produce manufactured goods over and above his own needs. Will he be able to sell them? The savings due to mass production will favour his enterprise, whereas transportation costs will hamper it. How large will his market eventually be? Suppose his neighbours are of the same stamp and live similarly, so the demand curve for one is typical of all.

Suppose, with Lösch, that the good in question is beer. For this one firm, Lösch then aggregates demand for beer from the surrounding plane, assuming that the firm's customers buy beer from the firm at a common price and then bear the cost of transporting it to their individual locations. Lösch then observes that if the aggregated demand curve intersects the firm's declining average cost curve, which he calls the firm's supply curve, the firm is a viable enterprise. This results in a circular market area centred on the enterprise, the size of which is inversely related to the firm's price. At the boundary, the price of beer inclusive of transport costs is so high that the quantity demanded is zero. Assuming that the firm chooses the price that yields the largest possible profit, if there is just one or a small number of firms, portions of the market will not be served. The un-served part of the market is the black area on the left side of the figure. He continues (1954, pp. 109–110):

> The deduction so far would be relevant if economic regions were circular in form [as in the far left hand part of the figure]. But they are not. Even if our district were full of breweries lying so closely together that their sales areas touched [as in the second part of the figure], one or another farmer would still be tempted to start a brewery for himself. And he could do so. First, because all the corners between the circles would not yet have been fully turned to account: and second, because the size of the individual brewery could be reduced . . . without making the plant unprofitable.

> The corners can be utilized by pressing the circles together until a honeycomb results [as in the third part of the figure]. As a consequence of this diminution in regional size the total demand curve . . . will be shifted downward. But the hexagon can be made even smaller, until the total demand curve . . . just touches the supply curve . . . Then the market is full [as in the final, right hand, part of the figure].'

In this derivation, Lösch is consciously applying Chamberlin's logic of monopolistic competition to his model of spatial competition by assuming that entry will continue until a zero profit Chamberlinian tangency solution occurs. Lösch does point out elsewhere in his book that the hexagonal or honeycomb pattern of market areas is somewhat arbitrary. He says that identical triangular, square and rectangular market areas are also possible. Lösch prefers the hexagonal market areas because they are the most efficient way to serve the entire market, but acknowledges that the others are possible. Many subsequent writers assumed that because the tightly packed hexagonal pattern of market boundaries was the most efficient way to serve the market, it would also be the pattern that would emerge as the free entry equilibrium.

It is surprising that although Lösch was offering a theory of location, nowhere in his book do firms explicitly choose either their locations or their time of entry. They are assigned locations by Lösch in accordance with what he believes is an equilibrium configuration – the pattern of locations necessary to support the Chamberlinian tangency solution with hexagonal, rectangular or triangular market areas. However, the dynamic of entry that is implicit in Lösch's argument requires that the entrant must anticipate a very complex and instantaneous pattern of relocation that will accommodate its entry. For example, if one firm enters an existing hexagonal set of markets, all existing firms must relocate to produce a tighter pattern of market hexagons.

There are several problems with this treatment. First, the triangular pattern of market areas is not a Nash equilibrium. If firms are located in this pattern, and one of them considers relocating, it will break the pattern. Second, in a growing market, the only pattern that is dynamically stable in the sense that it reproduces itself as new entrants choose the locations that offer the highest profits is rectangular rather than hexagonal, square or triangular. (See Eaton and Lipsey (1976) for discussion of both of these points.) Third, if there are significant location-specific sunk costs, and/or significant relocation costs, and/or if the relocation process takes a significant amount of time, the Chamberlinian tangency solution is not well founded, in the sense that foresighted free entry will not necessarily drive profit to zero. A new entrant into an established market structure must initially expect a significantly smaller market share, and hence significantly lower profits, than existing firms. As a result, the equilibrium density of packing of firms has an upper bound that depends on the zero profit Chamberlinian solution and a lower bound that depends on the size of the fixed costs of entry (see Kaldor, 1935, and Eaton and Lipsey, 1978).

The hexagonal construction was apparently first discussed in Launhardt (1885). Among geographers, it was Walter Christaller who made the hexagonal pattern of market areas famous, through his book *Central Places in Southern Germany*, published in German in 1933 and in English not until 1966. As Lösch generously acknowledges, Christaller's construction predates his own. If this were a book on famous diagrams in geography, we would be talking about Christaller's hexagons, not Lösch's. Lösch added to Christaller's analysis the explicit recognition that the size of equilibrium market areas in models of spatial competition is determined by opposing forces, one set that works to create agglomeration and another that works to create dispersion. This is a clear plus. In addition, Lösch embraces Chamberlin's zero profit logic in locational situations where, as observed in the previous paragraph, it is not appropriate. As with Lösch, Christaller does not articulate the process by which the hexagonal pattern emerges.

For both Christaller and Lösch, the hexagonal market areas diagram was merely a beginning, for the objective of both of these wonderful books was to advance the understanding of spatial patterns of central places. Their theories of the hierarchy of central places take somewhat different approaches, but hexagonal market areas are prominent in both. Christaller's theory is somewhat simpler. The fundamentals are these: the higher the order of a central place, the larger the range of goods offered for sale in it; a central place of a given order sells all the goods that are available in central places of lower orders; market areas of all goods are hexagonal. Christaller assumed that the sizes of market areas increase from one level of the hierarchy to the next by an integer multiple, K. Different values of K generate a variety of hierarchies of central places and patterns of nested hexagonal market areas. The seeds sown by both Lösch and Christaller flourish in more recent work on central places (see Berry, 1988).

Both the hexagons of Lösch and Christaller and the circles of von Thünen are driven by an assumption that the cost of transporting goods from one point in the plane to another is proportional to the Euclidian distance between the two points. In fact, much transportation occurs over road networks. Given that many road networks are rectangular, particularly in urban areas, an alternative distance metric is more appropriate. Under what has been called the 'block metric', the distance between two points in the plane is the sum of the absolute values of the differences in their x and y coordinates. Here the assumption is a dense network of roads that run parallel to the x and y axes.

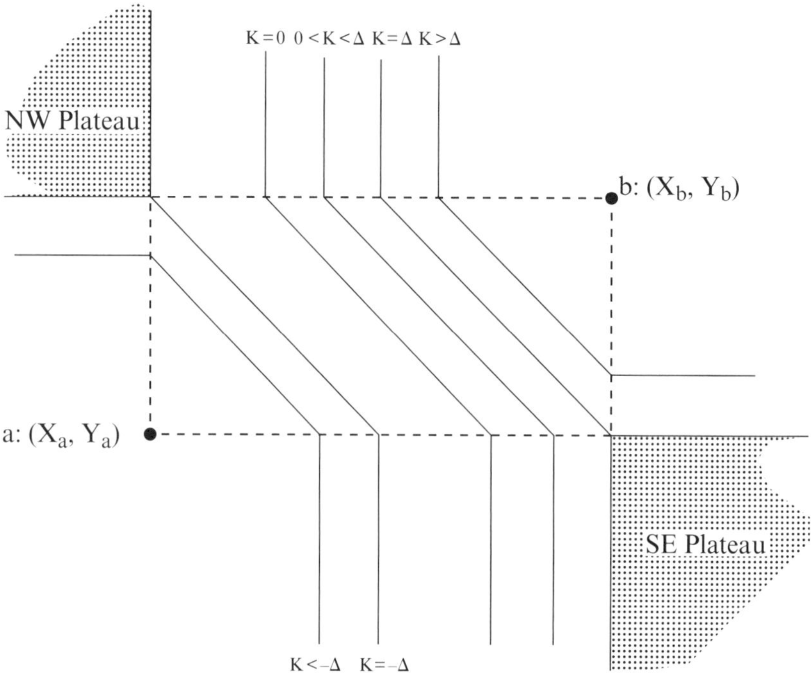

Source: Eaton and Lipsey (1980, Figure 1, p. 136). Permission granted by the *Journal of Urban Economics*

Figure 21.3 Market boundaries under the block metric

Now consider the two firms *a* and *b* shown in Figure 21.3 (which is Figure 1 from Eaton and Lipsey 1980). Their locations define the rectangle in Cartesian space shown by the dashed lines in the figure. Denote the firms' mill prices by p_a and p_b and the transport costs per unit of commodity per unit of distance by *t*. Now define firm *a*'s *net margin of advantage* by $K = (p_b - p_a)/t$. When p_a is equal to p_b, *K* is equal to 0, and the market boundary between the two firms is the locus of points that are equidistant from the two firms – in Figure 21.3, this boundary is the line that is labelled $K = 0$. Inside the rectangle the slope of the boundary is -1 and outside of the rectangle the boundary is vertical. Other boundaries shown in the figure refer to cases in which firm *a*'s margin of advantage, *K*, differs from zero. As *K* increases, the market boundary shifts rightward and firm *a*'s market increases. For all customers in the area of Figure 21.3 labelled 'SE Plateau' firm *b* is the nearer firm. It is closer to any of the customers in the SE Plateau than is firm *a* by the constant distance $\Delta = (x_b - x_a) - (y_b - y_a)$.

Thus, when firm *a*'s margin of advantage, *K*, is equal to Δ, customers in the SE Plateau are indifferent between the two firms. Similarly, when *K* is equal to – Δ customers in the NW Plateau are indifferent between the two firms. Notice also that if the locations of the two firms define a square rather than a rectangle, then Δ =0, and consequently customers in the two plateaus are indifferent between the two firms when their mill prices are identical ($p_b = p_a$).

Three interesting implications follow if we use the block metric instead of the Euclidean metric and assume that there is a dense network of roads that run parallel to the *x* and *y* axes in the Cartesian plane. First, von Thunen's circles are transformed into squares – because under the block metric, the set of points that are equidistant from a given point is a square, whereas it is a circle under the Euclidean metric. Since roads run parallel to the *x* and *y* axes, the squares are oriented in a diamond fashion and are, of course, all centered on Thunen's isolated town. Second, Lösch's efficient hexagonal market areas are transformed into square market areas. To picture the efficient configuration of firms under the block metric, imagine tiling Lösch's infinite plane with identical square tiles arranged in a diamond pattern, so that two sides of each tile run in a north-easterly direction and two in a north-westerly direction. A firm is located at the centre of each tile, and its market area is the square tile within which it is located. Third, if we consider price competition among any two arbitrarily located firms in Lösch's framework, there are two large plateaus located outside the rectangle defined by the firms' locations for which the difference in the distance between the two is a constant. These plateaus create discontinuities in the function relating either firm's market area to its price. These discontinuities create an incentive for destabilising behaviour in the firms' choices of prices, and call into question the existence of a stable price equilibrium. (See Eaton and Lipsey (1980) for proofs and further elaboration.)

REFERENCES

Alonso, William (1964), *Location and Land Use: Toward a General Theory of Land Rent*, Cambridge, MA: Harvard University Press.

Berry, Brian J. L. (1988), *Market Centers and Retail Location: Theory and Applications*, Englewood Cliffs, NJ: Prentice-Hall.

Christaller, Walter (1933), *Die zentralen Orte in Süddeutschland*, Jena, Germany: Fischer.

Christaller, Walter (1966), *Central Places in Southern Germany*, Englewood Cliffs, NJ: Prentice-Hall.

Eaton, B. Curtis and Richard G. Lipsey (1976), 'The Non-Uniqueness of

Equilibrium in the Löschian Location Model', *The American Economic Review*, **66** (5), 77–93.
Eaton, B. Curtis and Richard G. Lipsey (1978), 'Freedom of Entry and the Existence of Pure Profit', *The Economic Journal*, **88** (315), 455–69.
Eaton, B. Curtis and Richard G. Lipsey (1980), 'The Block Metric and the Law of Markets', *Journal of Urban Economics*, **7** (3), 337–47.
Fujita, Masahisa and Jacques-François Thisse (2002), *Economics of Agglomeration: Cities, Industrial Location, and Regional Growth*, Cambridge: Cambridge University Press.
Kaldor, N. (1935), 'Market Imperfections and Excess Capacity', *Economica*, **2** (5), 35–50.
Launhardt, Wilhelm (1885), *Mathematische Begründung der Volkswirtschaftslehre*, Leipzig: B.G. Teubner.
Lösch, August (1940), *Die räumliche Ordnung der Wirtschaft*, Jena, Germany: Fischer.
Lösch, August (1954), *The Economics of Location*, New Haven, CT: Yale University Press (English translation of the 2nd revised edition).
Mills, Edwin S. (1972), *Studies in the Structure of the Urban Economy*, Baltimore, MD: Johns Hopkins University Press.
Thünen, Johann Heinrich von (1826), *Der isolierte Staat in Beziehung auf Landwirtschaft und Nationalökonomie*, Hamburg: Perthes.
Thünen, Johann Heinrich von (1966), *The Isolated State*, Oxford: Pergamon Press (English translation of Thünen, 1826).

22. Hotelling's model of spatial competition

Nisvan Erkal

Seventy years ago, Harold Hotelling's paper 'Stability in Competition' was published in the *Economic Journal*. It represents a seminal contribution to the theory of spatial competition. Providing an appealing framework to address the nature of competition in characteristics as well as geographical space, it has resulted in a vast amount of academic research. In fact, Hotelling's line has become the single most popular model of horizontal differentiation in economics.

Product selection is a critical decision for firms. Firms differentiate their products to decrease the competition between them and to have some market power. Following Lancaster (1979, ch. 2), it is common to distinguish between two cases of product differentiation. Models of product selection typically involve either vertical or horizontal product differentiation. Two products are horizontally differentiated when there is no ranking among consumers based on their willingness to pay for the products. Both products have a positive demand whenever they are offered at the same price and heterogeneity in preferences over characteristics explains why both products are present in the market. Two products are vertically differentiated if one product captures the whole demand when both are supplied at the same price. Hence, all consumers have the same ranking between the different products offered at the same price.

In the standard Hotelling model of horizontal differentiation, consumers are defined by their ideal products (locations) in characteristics (geographical) space and by a disutility for not consuming their ideal product. It was Hotelling himself who emphasized the similarity between characteristics and geographical space, quoting the case of different types of cider, some sweeter than others (p. 54). The space corresponds to a linear market of length l, as shown in Figure 22.1 (a variation of the figure in Hotelling, 1929). Consumers are distributed uniformly along this space in terms of their tastes for an ideal product. The disutility they suffer from buying a variant which differs from their ideal is increasing in the distance between their ideal product and the product they consume. It is represented by a

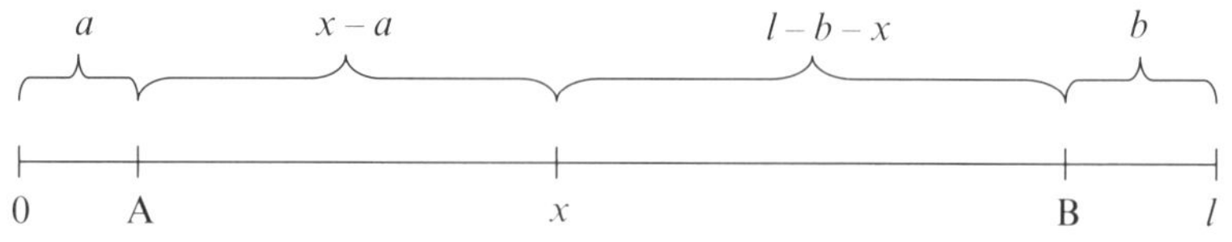

Figure 22.1 Hotelling's line

constant transportation cost t per unit of distance. Consumers buy from the producer whose delivered price (price charged by the firm plus the disutility cost) is the lowest. Demand is completely inelastic, at one unit per consumer.

On the supply side, market structure is given, allowing for no entry. In Figure 22.1, there are two firms (A and B) and each firm produces a single product. The firms' products are located at distances a and b from the two ends of the market. Firms can costlessly change their locations. Marginal costs of production are constant.

The firms play the following game. In the first stage, they choose their locations in the market place. In the second stage, they simultaneously and independently choose their prices. Hence, there is no scope for collusion.

Let p_A and p_B stand for the prices charged by firms A and B, respectively. The portion of the market that firm A serves is determined by finding the location of the consumer who is indifferent between the two firms' products. In Figure 22.1, x stands for the location of this consumer. The consumer has to travel $x - a$ and $l - b - x$ to purchase the product of firms A and B, respectively. Hence, for this consumer, the delivered price of purchasing the product of firm A is given by $p_A + t(x - a)$. Similarly, the delivered price of purchasing the product of firm B is $p_B + t(l - b - x)$. The location of the indifferent consumer can be found by setting these two delivered prices equal to each other and solving for x. Normalizing the mass of consumers to 1, the demand of firm A is given by x and the demand of firm B is given by $l - x$. Because of product differentiation, a firm is not necessarily deprived of all its potential customers as soon as its rival undercuts its price. Moreover, what matters for firms is local competition. Nearby products represent closer substitutes for consumers than distant ones.

Hotelling's goal in his model was to show that price stability was possible in a duopoly without collusion. This was in response to the thinking of Cournot (1897), Bertrand (1883) and Edgeworth (1925) that a price cut by one firm would capture the entire market, which results in price instability until the prices are driven down to marginal cost. Hotelling challenged this view, arguing that a price cut would cause a firm to lose only a few of its customers to its rival because many customers prefer to purchase from the same firm even if there are price differences.

Hotelling's main conclusion from his framework was that firms competing in prices and products tend to supply identical products: 'Buyers are confronted everywhere with an excessive sameness' (p. 54). This idea became known among economists as the 'Principle of Minimum Differentiation'. However, it was shown 50 years later by d'Aspremont, Gabszewicz and Thisse (1979) that Hotelling's analysis was flawed. No price equilibrium exists in pure strategies unless the firms are sufficiently far apart. D'Aspremont *et al.* demonstrated that altering the transportation cost from linear to quadratic yields a tractable model which produces a result of maximum differentiation. While getting closer to a rival attracts more customers, moving away relaxes price competition. In equilibrium, this second effect dominates in location choice.

Hotelling's model of spatial competition has been thoroughly explored by altering its basic assumptions to generalize and extend the analysis. For example, various authors have considered different numbers of firms, alternative transport cost and demand formulations, and different assumptions regarding consumer density over space.[1] His one-dimensional model has also been extended to the case of multiple dimensions. For example, Neven and Thisse (1990) have analysed a duopoly model of product selection where products are both horizontally and vertically differentiated. Tabuchi (1994) has analysed competition with two horizontal characteristics and Irmen and Thisse (1998) have analysed competition with *n* characteristics. The main result emerging from these papers is that firms will agglomerate in one dimension if they are differentiated enough in the other dimensions. In contrast to the one-dimensional models of horizontal or vertical product differentiation, prices do not necessarily fall when variants get closer. The reason for this is that variants are sufficiently separated along the other dimensions. Hence, these models show how Hotelling's Principle of Minimum Differentiation can be restored in one dimension in a multi-dimensional framework.

One of the most famous extensions of the Hotelling model is Salop's (1979) model of a circular city. Salop's assumptions are very similar to those discussed above. However, firms are assumed to be located around a circle. Since the emphasis of Salop (1979) is on optimal diversity, assuming a circular model makes the analysis more tractable. He assumes that entrants locate equidistant from each other (hence there is no location choice) and shows that there is excessive entry relative to the social optimum.

As Hotelling himself noted, an important application of the Hotelling model beyond industrial organization exists in political science. In such models of political competition, parties compete for voters by choosing their platforms within an ideological spectrum (Downs, 1957).[2]

Launhardt (1885, ch. 29) had a similar paradigm for studying product differentiation 44 years before Hotelling.[3] In fact, he is sometimes credited with anticipating Hotelling's spatial model and analysing oligopolistic competition with product differentiation. His formulation combines the concepts of horizontal and vertical differentiation by considering a model where firms locate at different points along a street, but have access to different transportation costs. The assumption of different transportation costs allows one to capture vertical as well as horizontal differentiation. This is because if both firms are located at the same place, the firm with the lower transportation cost would supply the whole population of consumers if the firms were to charge the same price. Launhardt treated locations as exogenous and focused on the impact of the differences in transportation costs.[4] Hence, as discussed in Dos Santos Ferreira (1998), Hotelling's important contribution lies in endogenizing locations as strategic variables. Moreover, it was Hotelling who extended the spatial analysis of strategic competition from a geographical space to an abstract characteristics space and a political space.

NOTES

1. See, for example, Eaton and Lipsey (1975), d'Aspremont, Gabszewicz and Thisse (1979), Denzau, Kats and Slutsky (1985), Kats and Neven (1990), Anderson, Goeree and Ramer (1997). See Anderson, de Palma and Thisse (1992), ch. 8 for a review.
2. See Enelow and Hinich (1984 and 1990) for recent surveys of this literature.
3. Launhardt's book has recently been published in English under the title of *Mathematical Principles of Economics* (1993). See Pinto (1977) for a discussion of the contribution of this book.
4. Dos Santos Ferreira and Thisse (1996) contains a presentation of Launhardt's ideas in terms of modern economic theory. Dos Santos Ferreira (1998) discusses the relation between Hotelling's (1929) paper and the corresponding passages of Launhardt's (1885) book.

REFERENCES

Anderson, S. P., A. De Palma and J. F. Thisse. 1992. *Discrete Choice Theory of Product Differentiation*, Cambridge, MA: MIT Press.

Anderson, S. P., J. K. Goeree and R. Ramer. 1997. 'Location, location, location', *Journal of Economic Theory*, 77, 102–127.

Bertrand, J. 1883. 'Revue de la théorie mathématique de la richesse sociale et des recherches sur les principes mathématiques de la théorie des richesses', *Journal des Savants*, 48, 499–508.

Cournot, A. 1897. *Recherches sur les Principes Mathématiques de la Théorie des Richesses*, New York: Macmillan. Translated by N. Bacon.

D'Aspremont, C., J. J. Gabszewicz and J. F. Thisse. 1979. 'On Hotelling's stability in competition', *Econometrica*, 47, 1145–1150.

Denzau, A., A. Kats and S. Slutsky. 1985. 'Multi-agent equilibria with market shares and ranking objectives', *Social Choice and Welfare*, 2, 95–117.

Dos Santos Ferreira, R. 1998. 'Launhardt and Hotelling', *Recherches Économiques de Louvain*, 64, 97–109.

Dos Santos Ferreira, R. and J. F. Thisse. 1996. 'Horizontal and vertical differentiation: The Launhardt model', *International Journal of Industrial Organisation*, 14, 485–506.

Downs, A. 1957. *An Economic Theory of Democracy*, New York: Harper and Row.

Eaton, B. C. and R. G. Lipsey. 1975. 'The principle of minimum differentiation revisited: Some new developments in the theory of spatial competition', *Review of Economic Studies*, 42, 27–49.

Edgeworth, F. 1925. 'The pure theory of monopoly', in *Papers relating to Political Theory*, Vol. 1, London: Macmillan, 455–469.

Enelow, J. M. and M. J. Hinich. 1984. *The Spatial Theory of Voting: An Introduction*, Cambridge: Cambridge University Press.

Enelow, J. M. and M. J. Hinich, eds. 1990. *Advances in the Spatial Theory of Voting*, Cambridge: Cambridge University Press.

Hotelling, H. 1929. 'Stability in Competition', *The Economic Journal*, 39(153), 41–57.

Irmen, A. and J. F. Thisse. 1998. 'Competition in multi-characteristics spaces: Hotelling was almost right', *Journal of Economic Theory*, 78, 76–102.

Kats, A. and D. Neven. 1990. 'Oligopoly equilibrium in Hotelling's model', Virginia Polytechnic Institute, Department of Economics, Mimeo.

Lancaster, K. J. 1979. *Variety, Equity and Efficiency*, New York: Columbia University.

Launhardt, W. 1885. *Mathematische Begründung der Volkswirtschaftslehre*, Leipzig: B. G. Teubner.

Launhardt, W. 1993. *Mathematical Principles of Economics*, Cheltenham: Edward Elgar.

Neven, D. and J. F. Thisse. 1990. 'On quality and variety competition', in J. J. Gabszewicz, J. F. Richard and L. Wolsey, eds, *Economic Decision Making: Games, Econometrics, and Optimization*. Amsterdam: North-Holland, 175–199.

Pinto, J. V. 1977. 'Launhardt and location theory: Rediscovery of a neglected book', *Journal of Regional Science*, 17(1), 17–29.

Salop, S. 1979. 'Monopolistic competition with outside goods', *Bell Journal of Economics*, 10, 141–156.

Tabuchi, T. 1994. 'Two-stage two-dimensional spatial competition between two firms', *Regional Science and Urban Economics*, 24, 207–227.

23. Cobweb diagrams

Marc Nerlove

HISTORY AND BACKGROUND

Mordecai Ezekiel's 1938 paper made 'The Cobweb Theorem' and his famous diagram well-known to every student of economics. Ezekiel was attempting to explain apparently self-perpetuating fluctuations in the prices of some agricultural commodities observed by Hanau (1927), Schultz (1930), and Coase and Fowler (1935). Tinbergen (1930), Ricci (1930), Leontief (1934), Kaldor (1934), and Lange (1935) drew similar diagrams. Kaldor gave the name 'Cobweb Theorem' to the phenomenon.

Kaldor (1934, p. 132) writes:

> once allowance is made for the fact that in the real world functional adjustments take time and different forces in the system may operate with different 'velocities of adjustment' it may become possible to construct cases – *under the assumption that ruling prices are always expected to remain in operation . . .* where the successive reactions lead away from, rather than approach, an equilibrium position.

As Kaldor points out, the most important assumptions underlying cobweb phenomena are lags in responses and so-called 'static expectations'.[1]

Hanau's aim (1927) was to forecast the price of hogs at the Berlin market. The period of gestation for a piglet is 114 days, or approximately 3.75 months; the period from birth (farrowing) until the hog is ready to be marketed (finished) is approximately six months in the U. S., but it was considerably longer in the Germany of Hanau's time, on the order of twelve months.[2] Allowing for some time to breed a sow, and after some experimentation, Hanau settled on a relation between the supply of hogs for slaughter, and the ratio of the price paid and an index of feed prices eighteen months previously. Since the current price revealed a negative correlation with the number of hogs brought to market in Berlin, Hanau concluded that hog prices followed a cyclical path. Ezekiel knew Hanau's work well, having reviewed his monograph in the *Journal of the American Statistical Association* (1928).

Schultz (1930) was interested in interpreting the statistical relation between the price of an agricultural commodity and its quantity marketed in terms of demand functions. His work and that of Henry Moore (1925, 1929) met with a great deal of criticism.[3] The basic question was how to interpret observations on market prices and quantities in terms of supply and demand equilibria. Tinbergen (1930) suggested a solution to the problem in terms of discontinuous supply adjustment, instantaneous demand adjustment and static expectations. Ezekiel (1938) tried to synthesize all this into a general theory of cobweb phenomena.

EZEKIEL'S DIAGRAM

Ezekiel's famous diagram (1938, pp. 262 and 264) is reproduced here in a single figure (Figure 23.1) with four panels: the basic set-up; case 1, permanent oscillation; case 2, explosive oscillation; case 3, convergent oscillation. There are several points to note about this sequence of diagrams. The supply and demand curves, labeled respectively, $S_TS'_T$ and D'_TD_T are so-called 'total' demand and supply curves. These 'relate the total supplies on the market in a succession of periods to prices prevailing in

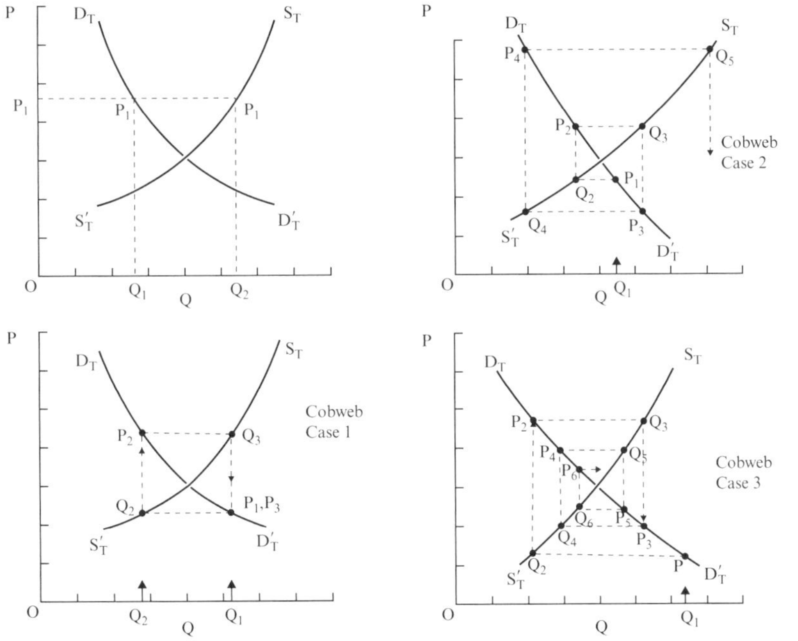

Figure 23.1 Ezekiel's diagram

each of those periods, and determine a curve describing that relationship . . .. *if* the total supply of the commodity cannot be changed within each period with which they are dealing in response to the prices of that period' (Ezekiel, 1938, p.259). Note that, in this case, demand includes reservation demand for an amount to be held in storage until the next period, and the total supply for this period includes any carry-over from the last period. If the commodity is perishable and cannot be stored, these quantities are zero. Let the quantity supplied in the first period be Q_1. The price for the first period, P_1, must be such as to clear the market in the first period. If producers have static expectations, that is, if they expect the price in the first period to hold forever, and can adjust in the next period, then supply, which includes carry-over from the first period, will be Q_2, and the price, P_2, must clear the market, including reservation demand, in the second period, and so on *ad infinitum*. The panel labeled 'Cobweb Case 1' depicts a total supply curve which is the mirror of the demand curve; in this case, no matter what the starting point, the prices and quantities will oscillate endlessly about the equilibrium intersection of the two curves, unless of course the starting point is exactly there. The third panel, labeled 'Cobweb Case 2', depicts a total supply curve which is everywhere of greater slope than the total demand curve; in this case, if the starting point is anywhere other than the equilibrium, prices and quantities over time will diverge from the equilibrium. The fourth panel, labeled Case 3, depicts a supply curve which is everywhere of lesser slope than the demand curve; in this case, prices and quantities will converge from any point to the equilibrium. Within any period, the quantity is fixed and the price determined by demand; the supply curve, however, reflects producers' plans during this period, only to be realized in the subsequent period. Ezekiel tries to suggest this by drawing the curves not as 'intersecting, but rather lapping over one another without real contact' (Ezekiel 1938, p. 263)

Ezekiel himself discusses a number of limitations and difficulties with the cobweb theory applied to agricultural commodities. Production must be determined completely by producers' response to price under conditions in which individual producers expect their individual actions to have no effect on the price they will obtain in the market and on the assumption that the current price will hold when their production comes to market (static expectations). Prices must be set by the supply available; the time needed for changes in production requires at least one full period and is not a partial response occurring over several periods of time. These assumptions are obviously unrealistic for most agricultural commodities. Moreover, in the case of crops, weather may greatly alter actual production from that which is planned. Of course, in general, both supply and demand may be affected by stochastic shocks.

CRITICISM AND EXTENSIONS

The cobweb theorem was subject to considerable criticism following Ezekiel (1938). Buchanan (1939) examined more closely the implications of the underlying assumptions for the supply response of producers of a disturbance in equilibrium. He questioned the assumption that 'while output changes according to the assumption that producers always expect the price ruling in the last period to prevail in the next, the supply curve remains unaltered. In other words, the supply curve is completely reversible throughout its whole length with respect to each period' (p. 68). Supply response is assumed to occur fully over one period; there is no partial adjustment and no difference between long-run and short-run supply response. With no entry and exit, producers always lose more net revenues in a period of low prices than they gain in a period of high prices. Eventually they must cease production altogether. Free entry only complicates matters. But the implication is that perpetual or divergent fluctuation cannot persist. Buchanan's careful examination of previous writers on the cobweb suggests a diversity of views on just what kind of supply response is consistent with the theorem (pp. 77–78). He also questions the assumption of no partial adjustment either over many periods or within one period (p. 79). Finally he says, 'the inviolable assumption that people never learn from experience, no matter how protracted, is at least debatable' (p. 81). To say the least!

Åkerman (1957) introduced a difference between long- and short-run supply functions:

> If a farmer has experienced an appreciable price change for one of his products . . . and, therefore, wants to extend its cultivation during the following year, he will meet with greater immediate difficulties than if the extension could be brought about gradually over a period of years. . . . All [earlier authors assume] . . . one unique normal supply schedule without distinguishing between short- and long-term schedules. This is the main reason why they have ascribed quite exaggerated properties to the cobweb phenomena (p. 154–155) Åkerman regards the possibility of a growing disequilibrium rather improbable (p.158).

Until Nerlove (1958a), almost all studies of agricultural supply response were based on the two questionable assumptions underlying Ezekiel's (1938) presentation of the Cobweb Theorem: static expectations and full adjustment to price changes within one period.[4] Nerlove (1958a, 1958b) introduced adaptive expectations and partial adjustment models of farmers' response to price in a cobweb model.[5] Nerlove found that the ratio of the slope of the demand curve to the slope of the supply curve would have to be larger in absolute value as the adaptive expectations model approached the traditional static expectations. Partial adjustment has the same effect. Thus, while the scope of stability of equilibrium is enhanced by adaptive expectations or partial adjustment or the two in combination, the possibility of theoretical instability and continuing losses by producers is by no means eliminated. Nerlove's study of agricultural supply response (1958a) was successful in demonstrating that farmers were indeed responsive to prices; it accounted for the great surpluses that were built up in the post-war years, and was indirectly but nonetheless deeply influenced by Ezekiel's famous diagram.

In his paper, 'Rational Expectations and the Theory of Price Movements', Muth (1961) advances the theory that expectations 'are essentially the same as the predictions of the relevant economic theory. In particular, the hypothesis asserts that the economy generally does not waste information, and that expectations depend specifically on the structure of the entire system.' Under this hypothesis, he describes producer behavior for a simple model of supply and demand with fixed production lag, that is, the model on which Ezekiel based his cobweb theorem. He finds that with positively serially correlated shocks to the supply function, rational price expectations are a weighted average of past prices in which the weights depend upon the parameters of both the demand and supply functions. When shocks persist forever (that is, a unit root in supply shocks), the model reduces to adaptive price expectations of the sort used by Nerlove (1958a), except that the coefficient of expectations is now a simple function of both the slopes of the supply and demand functions.[6]

CONCLUSION

The cobweb theorem is fatally flawed as a theory of agricultural price movements; it has little empirical relevance, nor is it supported by any empirical evidence. Ezekiel's famous diagram has nonetheless had a profound and lasting influence on the development of dynamic models of agricultural supply and other dynamic economic models and of the rational expectations hypothesis.

NOTES

1. Arrow and Nerlove (1958, p. 297). As they point out, however, this is far from a realistic assumption in any real-world context.
2. USDA/ERS, http://www.ers.usda.gov/Briefing/hogs/background.htm (accessed 10/15/2008).
3. See E. J. Working (1927) and Ricci (1930).

4. See Nerlove (1958a, pp, 66–82) for a review of these studies.
5. Various models of expectation formation, extrapolative, adaptive, implicit, futures-based, and rational are discussed by Nerlove and Bessler (2001, pp. 166–177) and related to models of partial adjustment.
6. Nerlove and Fornari (1998) have applied an econometrically feasible variant of rational expectations to explain stocks and prices in the U. S. cattle industry and find it works quite well.

REFERENCES

Åkerman, Gustav (1957), 'The Cobweb Theorem: A Reconsideration', *Quarterly Journal of Economics*, 71, 151–160.

Arrow, Kenneth J. and Marc Nerlove (1958), 'A Note on Expectations and Stability', *Econometrica*, 26, 297–305.

Buchanan, N. S. (1939), 'A Reconsideration of the Cobweb Theorem', *Journal of Political Economy*, 47, 67–81.

Coase, R. H. and R. F. Fowler (1935), 'Bacon Production and the Pig Cycle in Great Britain', *Economica*, New Series, 2, 142–167.

Ezekiel, Mordecai (1928), Review of Hanau (1927), *Journal of the American Statistical Association*, New Series, 23, 205–208.

Ezekiel, Mordecai (1938), 'The Cobweb Theorem', *Quarterly Journal of Economics*, 52, 255–280.

Hanau, Arthur (1927), *Die Prognose der Schweinepreise*, Vierteljahrshefte zur Konjunkturforschung, Institut für Konjunkturforschung, Sonderheft 2, Berlin: Reimar Hobbing.

Kaldor, Nicholas (1934), 'A Classificatory Note on the Determinateness of Equilibrium', *The Review of Economic Studies*, 1, 122–136.

Lange, O. (1935), 'Formen der Angebotsanpassung und wirtschaftliches Gleichgewicht', *Zeitschrift für Nationalökonomie*, 6, 358–365.

Leontief, Wassily W. (1934), 'Verzögerte Angebotsanpassung und partielles Gleichgewicht', *Zeitschrift für Nationalökonomie*, 5, 670–676.

Moore, H. L. (1925),'Moving Equilibrium of Demand and Supply', *Quarterly Journal of Economics*, 34, 357–371.

Moore, H. L. (1929), *Synthetic Economics*, New York: Macmillan.

Muth, John F. (1961), 'Rational Expectations and the Theory of Price Movements', *Econometrica*, 29, 315–335.

Nerlove, Marc (1958a), *The Dynamics of Supply: Estimation of Farmers' Response to Price*, Baltimore, MD: Johns Hopkins University Press.

Nerlove, Marc (1958b), 'Adaptive Expectations and Cobweb Phenomenon', *Quarterly Journal of Economics*, 72, 227–240.

Nerlove, Marc and D. A. Bessler (2001), 'Expectations, Information and Dynamics', *Handbook of Agricultural Economics*, Volume l, edited by B. Gardner and G. Rausser, 156–206.

Nerlove, Marc and I. Fornari (1998), 'Quasi-Rational Expectations, An Alternative to Fully Rational Expectations: An Application to Modeling U.S. Beef Cattle Supply', *Journal of Econometrics*, 83, 129–161.

Ricci, Umberto (1930), 'Die 'Synthetische Ökonomie' von Henry Ludwell Moore', *Zeitschrift für Nationalökonomie*, 1, 649–668.

Schultz, Henry (1930), 'Der Sinn der statistischen Nachfragen', *Veröffentlichungen der Frankfurter Gesellschaft für Konjunkturforschung*, Volume 10, Bonn: Kurt Schroeder Verlag.

Tinbergen, J. (1930), 'Bestimmung und Deutung von Angebotskurven, ein Beispeil', *Zeitschrift für Nationalökonomie*, 1, 669–679.

Working, Elmer J. (1927), 'What Do Statistical Demand Curves Show?', *Quarterly Journal of Economics*, 41, 212–235.

24. Reswitching and reversing in capital theory

Avi J. Cohen and Geoffrey C. Harcourt

Reswitching and capital reversing – anomalies contradicting the neoclassical marginal productivity theory of income distribution – figured prominently in the Cambridge capital theory controversies (Blaug 1975; Bliss 1975; Cohen and Harcourt 2003, 2005; and Harcourt 1969, 1972). These anomalies in the measurement of capital, particularly in aggregate production functions, gained prominence with the 1966 'Paradoxes in Capital Theory: A Symposium' in the *Quarterly Journal of Economics*. Both sides of the controversy came to agree on the existence of reswitching and capital reversal, and aggregate production functions fell into disrepute in the 1970s and early 1980s. However, there has been no agreement on the significance of the controversies, and aggregate production functions have been revived with theories of real business cycle and endogenous growth.

CONTEXT

Since the first pure exchange models of the marginal revolution, price has been explained as an index of scarcity. Price is proportional to marginal utility, which depends on scarcity. Neoclassical capital theory is the arena for extending the general principle of relative scarcity to explain all prices, including factor prices in models with production and time.

A common starting point for the neoclassical perspective on capital is a one-commodity Samuelson/Solow/Swan aggregate production function model: $Q = f(K, L)$, where the one produced good (Q) can be consumed directly or stockpiled for use as a capital good (K). With the usual assumptions, like exogenously given resources and technology, constant returns to scale, diminishing marginal productivity and competitive equilibrium, this simple model exhibits what Samuelson (1962) called three key 'parables':

1. The real return on capital (the rate of interest) is determined by the technical properties of the diminishing marginal productivity of capital;
2. a greater quantity of capital per head leads to a lower marginal product of additional capital and thus to a lower rate of interest, and the same inverse, monotonic relation with the rate of interest also holds for the capital/output ratio and sustainable levels of consumption per head;
3. the distribution of income between laborers and capitalists is explained by relative factor scarcities/supplies and marginal products. The price of capital services (the rate of interest) is determined by the relative scarcity and marginal productivity of aggregate capital, and the price of labor services (the wage rate) is determined by the relative scarcity and marginal productivity of labor (L).

The three parables of this one-commodity model depend on a physical conception of capital (and labor) for their one-way causation – changes in factor quantities cause inverse changes in factor prices, allowing powerful, unambiguous predictions like parable 2.

But problems for these parables arise in more general models with heterogeneous capital goods. As Wicksell (1911 [1934]), p. 149) pointed out, heterogeneous capital goods cannot be measured and aggregated in physical units; instead, capital valuation must be used. Their value can be measured either as the cost of production, which takes time, or the present value of the future output stream they produce. In either case, since the measure involves time, it presumes a rate of interest – which, in the simple model, is determined in a one-way manner by the quantity of capital. This additional circularity, or interdependence, causes Wicksell effects. These involve changes in the value of the capital stock associated with different interest rates, arising from either inventory revaluations of the same physical stock due to new capital goods prices (price Wicksell effects) or differences in the physical stock of capital goods (real Wicksell effects).

In the Cambridge controversies, the problems created for the neoclassical parables by Wicksell effects were termed reswitching and capital reversing. Reswitching occurs when the same technique – a particular physical capital/labor ratio – is preferred at two or more rates of interest while other techniques are preferred at intermediate rates. At lower values of the interest rate, the cost-minimizing technique 'switches' from *a* to *b* and then 'reswitches' back to *a*. The same physical technique is associated with two different interest rates, violating parables 1 and 2.

With capital reversing, a lower capital/labor ratio is associated with a lower interest rate. In comparing two steady-state equilibrium positions, it is as though capital services have a lower price when capital is 'more scarce'. Capital reversing implies that the demand curve for capital is not always downward sloping, violating parables 2 and 3.

Because of Wicksell effects, in models with heterogeneous capital goods (or heterogeneous output), the rate of interest depends not only on exogenous technical properties of capital, but also on endogenously determined prices like the interest rate. The endogeneity of prices allows multiple equilibria, which complicates the one-way parable explanations of income distribution. Differences in quantities no longer yield unambiguously signed price effects. The power and simplicity of one-commodity models emanates from eliminating these endogenous price effects and measurement problems.

As early as 1936, Piero Sraffa wrote a letter to Joan Robinson explaining the essence of this complication for neoclassical capital theory. Reswitching and capital-reversing were noted in the 1950s by Robinson (1953–54) and David Champernowne (1953–1954), but their full significance was realized only with Sraffa's 1960 book (Ch. 12, 'Switches in Methods of Production'), which eventually led to the 1966 *QJE* Symposium. Sraffa (1962, p. 479) posed the key question regarding the measurement of capital: 'What is the good of a quantity of capital . . . which, since it depends on the rate of interest, cannot be used for its traditional purpose . . . to determine the rate of interest[?]'

DIAGRAMS

Reswitching and capital reversing appeared in diagrams by Robinson (1953–54), Champernowne (1953–54), Sraffa (1960), Samuelson (1962, 1966), Garegnani (1970, but first drawn in 1963), Pasinetti (1966) and Bhaduri (1969). The diagrams by Harcourt, (Figure 24.1 and 24.2) which synthesize the aggregate production function results of these other authors, appeared in a survey on capital theory in the newly created *Journal of Economic Literature*, and were reproduced in his 1972 book, *Some Cambridge Controversies in the Theory of Capital*.

The diagrams focus on the factor price frontier, or the wage (w) – rate of interest/profits (r) relationship. Given different techniques of production (a, b, c) – each of which uses different capital goods with homogeneous labor – for any given wage, the firm chooses the technique yielding the highest rate of interest/profits. The (absolute value of the) slope of the w–r line for each technique measures the technique's capital/labour ratio. The outer 'envelope' of the intersecting w–r lines shows the dominant technique(s) for each possible value of w (or r).

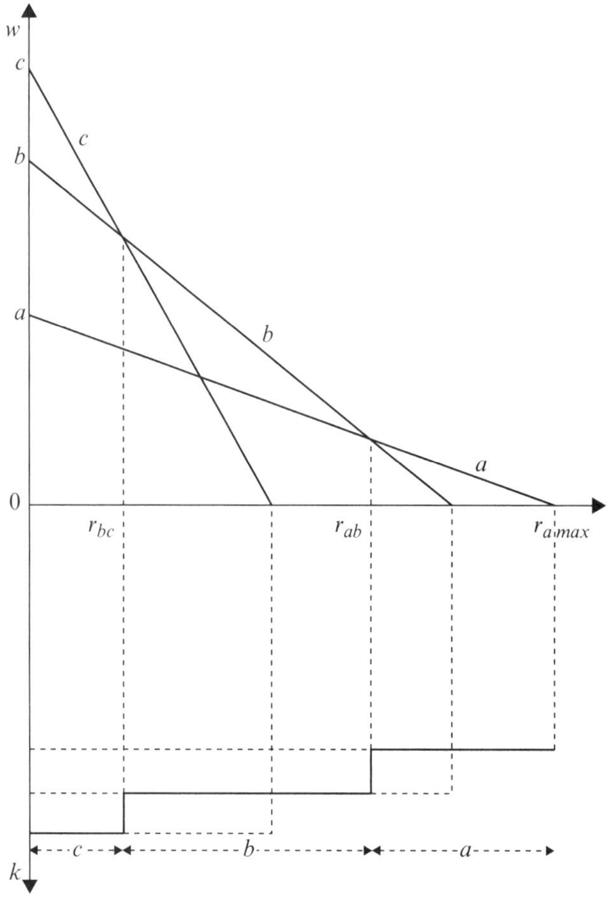

Figure 24.1 Straight line w–r *relationships for neoclassical parable*

Figure 24.1, based on Samuelson (1962), illustrates the case where the three parables of the neoclassical marginal productivity theory of distribution hold true, and reswitching and capital reversing are ruled out. The *w–r* lines are linear because Samuelson assumes equal factor proportions in the consumption and capital-goods industries. As higher values of *w* are considered, firms 'switch' from technique *a* to *b* to *c*, each with a higher capital/labor ratio and lower *r*. On the bottom half of the diagram, note that the lowest quantity of capital (*k*) – measured in terms of consumption goods – for technique *a* is associated with the highest rate of interest/profits, and there is a inverse, monotonic relationship between *k* and *r* as firms 'switch' through techniques *b* and then *c*.

Notice that the value of k for each single technique does not change with changes in factor prices. Samuelson's equal factor proportions assumption makes the relative prices of consumption and capital goods independent of changes in the distribution of income between wages and profits. As in a one-commodity model, capital can be measured independently of distribution and has an unambiguous physical marginal product that can explain the rate of interest/profits.

Figure 24.2 illustrates the more general case where factor proportions for the consumption and capital-goods industries may differ. Those difference account for the non-linearity of the w–r line for technique a.

As higher values of w are considered, firms 'switch' from technique b to a, and then 'switch' back to b. This is the reswitching violation of parables 1 and 2. (In early, simple examples with only two techniques, reswitching was called 'double-switching'.) On the bottom half of the diagram, as the technique 'switches' from b to a at r_{ba}, a decrease in the rate of interest/profits is associated with a decrease in the quantity of capital. This is the capital-reversing violation of parables 2 and 3. (Joan Robinson credited the recognition of this result to Ruth Cohen, labeling it the 'Ruth Cohen Curiosum (RCC)'.) Notice also that for technique a, even though the physical quantity of capital is unchanged between r_{ba} and r_{ab}, the measurement of the value of the capital (k) decreases as we consider lower values of the rate of interest/profits (the negatively sloped line segment on the bottom half of the diagram), reflecting price Wicksell effects. Capital cannot be measured independently of distribution.

The reswitching and capital reversing results have proven to be quite general, extending beyond aggregate production functions. Bliss (1975, p. 85) concludes that 'there is no support from the theory of general equilibrium for the proposition that an input to production will be cheaper in an economy where more of it is available'. This raises questions about the marginal productivity theory of income distribution, and the extent to which the returns to capital can be explained using usual scarcity theory of relative prices.

HISTORY AND SIGNIFICANCE

Karaswarmy Velupillai (1975) discovered a numerical example of reswitching in Irving Fisher's *The Rate of Interest* (1907, 353–53), which Fisher noted as odd, but did not pursue. Violations of the three neoclassical parables arose in many earlier capital controversies, involving Eugene von Böhm-Bawerk, J.B. Clark, Irving Fisher, Thorstein Veblen, Frank Knight, Friedrich von Hayek and Nicolas Kaldor – see Cohen and

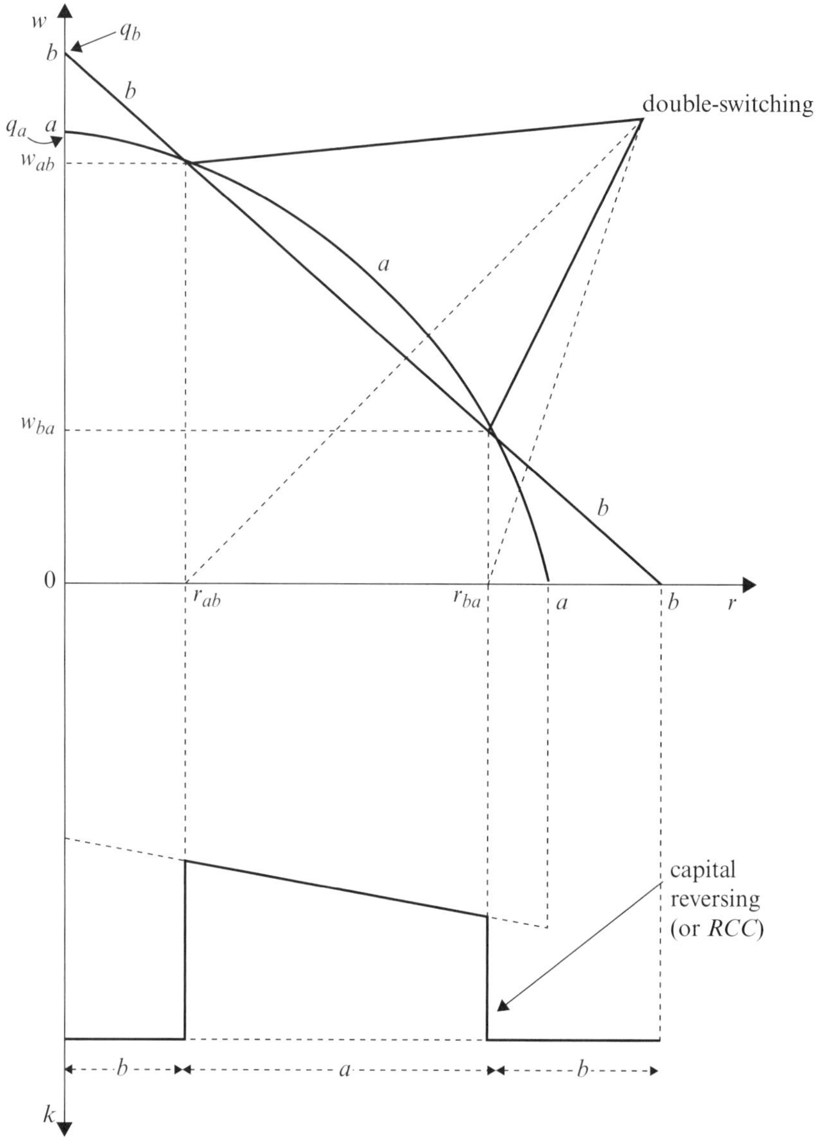

Figure 24.2 Non-linear w–r *relationships and capital values with reswitching and capital reversing*

Harcourt (2005) for an overview. Related criticisms around the measurement and aggregation of capital in aggregate production functions appear in the works of Franklin Fisher (1992) and Jose Felipe and Fisher (2003). Felipe and Fisher follow in the footsteps of similar criticisms made by E.H. Phelps-Brown, Anwar Shaikh and Herbert Simon. In his Nobel lecture, Simon (1979, p. 497) noted that the good statistical fits to the Cobb-Douglas production function 'cannot be taken as strong evidence for the [neo-]classical theory, for the identical results can readily be produced by mistakenly fitting a Cobb-Douglas function to data that were in fact generated by a linear accounting identity (value of output equals labour costs plus capital cost).'

On the remaining disagreements about the significance of reswitching and capital reversal, both for the scarcity theory of price and more generally, see Cohen and Harcourt (2003).

REFERENCES

Bhaduri, A. (1969), 'On the significance of recent controversies on capital theory: a Marxian view', *Economic Journal*, 79 532–9.

Blaug, M. (1975), *The Cambridge Revolution: Success or Failure? A Critical Analysis of Cambridge Theories of Value and Distribution*, Revised Edition, London: Institute of Economic Affairs.

Bliss, C.J. (1975), *Capital Theory and Distribution*, Amsterdam: North-Holland.

Bliss, C.J., A.J. Cohen and G.C. Harcourt (eds) (2005), *Capital Theory*, 3 vols, Cheltenham, UK: Edward Elgar.

Champernowne, D.G. (1953–54), 'The production function and the theory of capital: a comment', *Review of Economics Studies*, 21, 112–35.

Cohen, A.J. and G.C. Harcourt (2003), 'Whatever happened to the Cambridge capital theory controversies?' *Journal of Economic Perspectives*, 17, 199–214.

Cohen, A.J. and G.C. Harcourt (2005), 'Introduction: capital theory controversy: scarcity production, equilibrium and time', in *Capital Theory* (3 Volumes), edited by C. Bliss, A.J. Cohen and G.C. Harcourt, Cheltenham, UK: Edward Elgar, Vol. I, xxvii–lx.

Felipe, J. and F.M. Fisher (2003), 'Aggregation in production functions: what applied economists should know', *Metroeconomica*, 54, 208–62.

Fisher, F.M. (1992), *Aggregation: Aggregate Production Functions and Related Topics*, Cambridge, MA: MIT Press.

Fisher, I. (1907), *The Rate of Interest: Its Nature, Determination and Relation to Economic Phenomena*, New York: Macmillan.

Garegnani, P. (1970), 'Heterogeneous capital, the production function and the theory of distribution', *Review of Economic Studies*, 37, 407–36.

Harcourt, G.C. (1969), 'Some Cambridge controversies in the theory of capital', *Journal of Economic Literature*, 7, 369–405.

Harcourt, G.C. (1972), *Some Cambridge Controversies in the Theory of Capital*, Cambridge: Cambridge University Press.

'Paradoxes in capital theory: a symposium' (1966), *Quarterly Journal of Economics*, 80, 503–83.
Pasinetti, L.L. (1966), 'Changes in the rate of profit and switches of technique', *Quarterly Journal of Economics*, 80, 503–17.
Robinson, J. (1953–54), 'The production function and the theory of capital,' *Review of Economic Studies*, 21, 81–106.
Samuelson, P.A. (1962), 'Parable and realism in capital theory: the surrogate production function', *Review of Economic Studies*, 29, 193–206.
Samuelson, P.A. (1966), 'A summing up', *Quarterly Journal of Economics*, 80, 568–83.
Simon, H.A. (1979), 'Rational decision making in business organizations', *American Economic Review*, 69, 493–513.
Sraffa, P. (1936), Letter to Joan Robinson, October 1936. Archives, King's College, Cambridge.
Sraffa, P. (1960), *Production of Commodities by Means of Commodities: Prelude to a Critique of Economic Theory*, Cambridge: Cambridge University Press.
Sraffa, P. (1962), '*Production of Commodities*: a comment', *Economic Journal*, 72, 477–79.
Velupillai, K. (1975), 'Irving Fisher on switches of techniques: a historical note', *Quarterly Journal of Economics*, 89, 679–80.
Wicksell, K. (1911) [1934], *Lectures on Political Economy, Volume 1*, London: George Routledge and Sons.

25. The Markowitz mean-variance diagram

Fiona Maclachlan

The Markowitz mean-variance diagram plays a central role in the development of theoretical finance. In setting the foundation for the capital asset pricing model, it represents the beginning of modern portfolio theory. Prior to Harry Markowitz's contribution, the field of finance relied much less on mathematical technique. Contributions to the literature tended to be descriptive, or involved only simple operations applied to accounting data. The principle of diversification, while accepted as a rule of thumb, was not well understood. Markowitz's mean-variance paradigm, summed up succinctly in his famous diagram, set finance on the path to becoming a technical scientific discipline, more a branch of economics than of business administration.

The Markowitz diagram is based on the idea that all the information about a portfolio of risky assets that is relevant to a risk-averse investor can be summed up in the values of two parameters: the standard deviation and the expected value of the portfolio's return, briefly stated as the risk and return. The diagram, presented in Figure 25.1, contains four essential features: i) the set of parameter pairs of feasible portfolios represented by the shaded area, ii) the efficient frontier along the upper edge of the feasible set, iii) the linear asset allocation line running from the point on the vertical axis at the rate of return on the risk-free asset and tangent to the efficient frontier, and iv) the super-efficient portfolio parameter pair located at the point of tangency. The feasible portfolios are constructed by considering an initial endowment that can be spread across different risky assets in a multitude of ways. The efficient frontier represents those portfolios for which the expected return is the highest for any level of risk, and for which the risk is the lowest for any level of expected return. Its curvature, in bending towards the vertical axis, is the result of the benefit of diversifying among assets whose returns are not perfectly correlated.

Points on the asset allocation line represent the parameter pairs associated with portfolios made up of a combination of the super-efficient portfolio and the risk-free asset. Points on the line to the left of the efficient

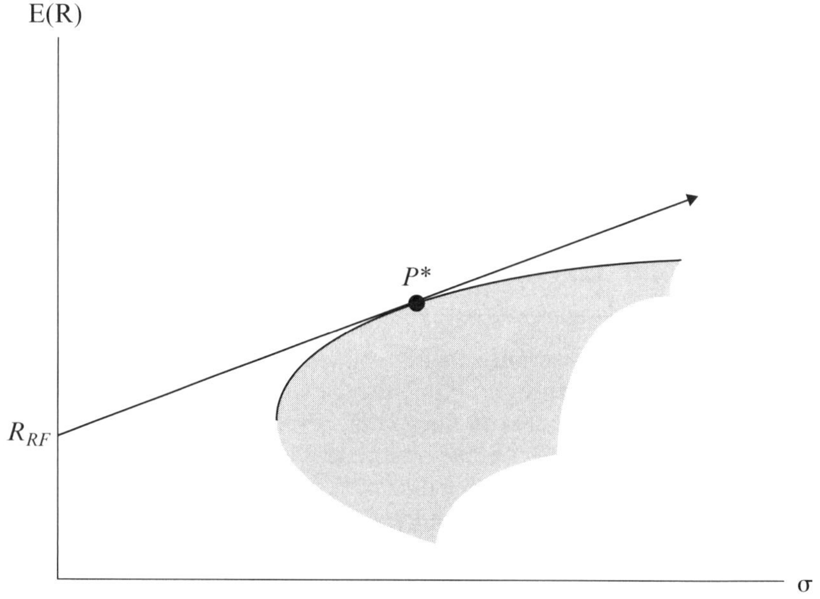

Note: The shaded area is the feasible set and the upper boundary is the efficient frontier. P* marks the super-efficient portfolio located at the point of tangency between the asset allocation line and the efficient frontier. R_{RF} represents the risk-free rate of return.

Figure 25.1 The Markowitz mean-variance diagram

frontier are associated with portfolios that combine long positions in both the super-efficient portfolio and the risk-free asset, while points to the right are associated with a leveraged long position in risky assets created through borrowing at the risk-free rate. If investors have access to risk-free borrowing and lending, the optimal portfolio will lie along the asset allocation line, since portfolios below and to the right will be inefficient and portfolios above and to the left will not be feasible.

The origin of the mean-variance paradigm is recounted in vivid detail by Markowitz (1999).[1] As a PhD student in economics at the University of Chicago, he went to see Jacob Marschak for advice on a topic for his dissertation. While waiting in the anteroom, he happened to meet a stockbroker, also waiting to see Marschak, who suggested that he write his dissertation on the stock market. Markowitz relayed the suggestion to Marschak and found him receptive to the idea. Both men were members of the Cowles Commission, as it was called at the time, and econometric investigations of the stock market was of special interest to their benefactor, Alfred Cowles. Marschak sent Markowitz to a professor in the business school for advice on background reading in the current literature on investments.

Markowitz recalls that it was sometime in 1950, while going through the books on investments suggested by the business school professor, that he hit on his seminal idea regarding diversification. The presumption of previous writers had been that, through the law of large numbers, diversification could eliminate all risk as long as one had a large enough number of stocks in one's portfolio. The advice that followed was to invest in those assets with the highest expected return. Markowitz recognized the error in the implicit assumption that stock returns were uncorrelated and sought to discover a measure of risk for a portfolio of assets with imperfectly correlated returns. The idea of using variance as a measure of risk came to him independently, although Irving Fisher and others had previously thought of it. Next, he found the formula for the variance of the returns of a portfolio of risky assets in a book on probability.

> On examining the formula for the variance of a weighted sum of random variables (found in Uspensky 1937 on the library shelf), I was elated to see the way covariances entered. . . . Dealing with two quantities—mean and variance—and being an economics student, I naturally drew a trade-off curve. Being, more specifically, a student of T. C. Koopmans . . ., I labeled dominated *EV* combinations 'inefficient' and the undominated ones 'efficient.' (Markowitz 1999, p. 8)

By a curious coincidence, in April of the same year that Markowitz made his original sketch in the library at the University of Chicago, an article by Marschak appeared in *Econometrica*, which while not actually showing the diagram, sketches out some of the essential details. In summarizing the state of the art in the 'theory of assets', Marschak writes:

> [I]f more than one commodity or time-point is considered, say $\gamma(\tau + 1) = \varepsilon$ quantities, each prospect may be characterized by ε means, ε variances, $\varepsilon(\varepsilon - 1)/2$ correlations, etc. Each distribution parameter was regarded as being a 'good' (or possibly a 'bad') in the eyes of the man. . . . Tastes were described by indifference surfaces drawn in parameter space *P*, and the empirical properties of these surfaces were discussed. For example, the risk-aversion (risk-discount), i.e., the rate of substitution between the mean and the variance of income, expressed by the relevant slope of an indifference surface, was stated to be positive. (Marschak 1950, p. 118–19)

Markowitz's diagram of the efficient frontier first appeared in print in the *Journal of Finance* in 1952. Unlike the now standard depiction presented in Figure 25.1, Markowitz's construction had the axes reversed and used variance rather than standard deviation as the measure of risk.

The story of the history of the diagram is complicated by the appearance of a competing diagram, also in 1952, in an *Econometrica* article by Cambridge economist A. D. Roy. Roy's diagram has the axes orientated in their now usual fashion, and has the standard deviation rather than variance as the risk measure. Moreover, he identifies the boundary of the feasible set as an envelope curve and, presaging the capital market line and the super-efficient portfolio, he draws a ray from a point on the vertical axis tangent to the efficient frontier, albeit giving it a different interpretation from that of the capital market line. The point of tangency in Roy's diagram coincides with the portfolio that maximizes the probability that the portfolio return will be above the level at which the line meets the vertical axis.

Roy includes Marschak (1950) in his list of references so it is plausible that he was following up on the hints provided in that article. Given that Marschak was Markowitz's dissertation adviser, it would be ironic if his competitor for claims of primacy for the diagram was given an edge from reading Marschak's article. Markowitz (1999, p. 5) notes that Roy should share with him the honor as the father of modern portfolio theory but, in truth, Roy's contribution remained obscure and did not inspire further developments, despite his writing an additional article on the topic in 1956.

Markowitz, on the other hand, teamed up with William Sharpe, who went on to make major strides in theoretical finance. Markowitz served as Sharpe's unofficial dissertation adviser in the early sixties. A key innovation introduced by Sharpe (1964) was to recognize that in a world with a risk-free asset, the investor's optimal portfolio would lie, not necessarily on the efficient frontier, but instead on a line tangent to the efficient frontier and intersecting the vertical axis at the risk-free rate of return. The portfolio corresponding to the point of tangency is known as the super-efficient portfolio, and the optimal risk return combination for an investor could be achieved by combining an investment in the super-efficient portfolio with a position in the risk-free asset. This position could be long or short depending on one's risk preferences. The idea of the asset allocation line comes from the Tobin (1958) separation theorem that states that one can think of a portfolio in two parts: one part invested in risky assets and one part invested in the risk-free asset. The decision regarding the best combination of risky assets can be made separately from the decision regarding one's level of investment in the risk-free asset.

Once all the pieces of the Markowitz mean-variance diagram were in place, Sharpe (1964) was able to draw out the full economic implications in his formulation of the capital asset pricing model, for which he, along with Markowitz, was awarded the Nobel prize in economics in 1990. It is a good example of the power of a simple diagram to illuminate the way to an important discovery.

When Markowitz defended his dissertation on portfolio diversification at the University of Chicago in 1955, Milton Friedman gave him a hard time, claiming that his contribution was not economics and that the university could not grant a PhD in economics for a dissertation that was not economics. Markowitz recalls: 'he kept repeating that for the next hour and a half. My palms began to sweat. At one point he says, you have a problem. It's not economics, it's not mathematics, it's not business administration' (Buser 2008, p. 5). Friedman, who was committed to the stance he had recently taken in his famous essay on the methodology of positive economics, could not see how the discovery of a new paradigm for analyzing investment decisions could qualify as a contribution to the discipline. Fortunately though, Markowitz was ultimately successful in his defense, much to the benefit of the field of financial economics.

NOTE

1. See also Bernstein (1992) and Buser (2008).

REFERENCES

Bernstein, P. (1992), 'Capital Ideas: The Improbable Origins of Modern Wall Street', New York, NY: The Free Press.

Buser, S. (2008), 'Markowitz: Interview at Rady School of Management at the University of California San Diego', *History of Finance, American Finance Association*, http://www.afajof.org/association/historyfinance.asp, accessed 8 January 2010.

Markowitz, H. (1952), 'Portfolio Selection', *Journal of Finance*, **7** (1); 77–91.

Markowitz, H. (1999), 'The Early History of Portfolio Theory: 1600–1960', *Financial Analysts Journal*, **55** (4): 5–16.

Marschak, J. (1950), 'Rational Behavior, Uncertain Prospects, and Measurable Utility', *Econometrica*, **18** (2): 111–141.

Roy, A. D. (1952), 'Safety First and the Holding of Assets', *Econometrica*, **20** (3): 431–449.

Roy, A. D. (1956), 'Risk and Rank or Safety First Generalised', *Economica*, **23** (91): 214–228.

Sharpe, W. (1964), 'Capital Asset Prices: A Theory of Market Equilibrium Under Conditions of Risk', *Journal of Finance*, **19** (3): 425–42.

Tobin, J. (1958). 'Liquidity Preference as Behavior Towards Risk', *The Review of Economic Studies*, **25** (1): 65–86.

26. Rent-seeking diagrams

Anne O. Krueger

INTRODUCTION

Rent seeking is a resource-using activity undertaken by individuals or groups from which they seek to profit, but from which activity there will be no increase in output. It is a socially unprofitable but privately profitable undertaking for successful rent seekers. Examples of such activities include lobbying to get a tariff increased, bribing to obtain a necessary license, and queuing to receive rationed goods when the quantity demanded at the ration price exceeds the supply. In the first case, the resource is the time of the lobbyist(s) and any capital and goods and services the lobbyist may employ to influence the decisions of the tariff-making body. In the second case, the resource, in the first instance, is the time of the briber and his money (or goods) paid as a bribe, but bribes make officials wealthier, and hence increase competition for entry into government service, which in turn may lead to multiple efforts to pass entrance examinations, more than needed years of schooling, and so on. Queueing to receive rationed goods requires the time of someone, often the servant of the eligible party. Not all rent seekers will be successful: some may not receive licenses or receive the rationed item, but the expected returns from the activity induce people to undertake it.

In each of these examples, and any other case of rent seeking, the critical points are two. First, whether the lobbyist obtains the tariff increase or not, whether the briber obtains the license or not, and whether the person queueing actually receives a ration portion, the activities devoted to doing so do not increase society's total output but use resources that could otherwise be employed elsewhere. Indeed, in the case of a tariff increase, successful lobbying will mean a reduced total bundle of goods and services available to society under standard (small country) assumptions, but if there is rent-seeking activity to influence tariff rates, the loss is increased.

Second, in each instance, resources are devoted to the activity (for which there is no product) which could otherwise be devoted to increasing output of one good or another. The individuals lobbying, bribing or queueing could otherwise use their time employed in an activity which increased total output.

In some circumstances, the value of the lost output is equal to the value of the rents in the activity undertaken. For this to be so, it requires that there be competition for the desired outcome (higher tariff, receipt of license or rationed item), and that the supply of the factor or factors seeking the rents be perfectly elastic. When the outcome of rent-seeking efforts is uncertain (as with receipt of a license), risk-neutrality must hold for equality. If the supply of the relevant factor is upward sloping or rent seekers are risk averse, the value of lost output becomes the quadrilateral. If there are ways that society can reduce rent seeking (perhaps by greater penalties for bribery, for example, making the expected gain less than the full value of the license) the foregone output can be reduced. At the extremes, when either the value of the item sought is equal to the price of acquiring it (rationed goods, import license) or the expected value of profiting from any wedge between the price at which the item is obtained and the market-clearing price is zero (as, perhaps, because the probability of being caught is too high), there will be no rent seeking and no foregone output.

The original rent-seeking diagram by the author (see discussion of history below) was intended to illustrate the proposition that rent-seeking activity uses resources without increasing output. This is reproduced as Figure 26.1. The basic setup is one in which food (F) is the only good produced. It can be exchanged for imports at a given international price, but in order to distribute goods on the domestic market, some workers must be reallocated from production of food to distribution. The consumption possibility frontier (see Chapter 42 in this volume) under free trade with no rent seeking is given by the $\hat{M}\hat{F}$ curve, where $\hat{F}$ is the amount of food that would be produced if there were no imports (and hence no consumption of the importable). A point such as C might be the chosen free trade equilibrium.

If imports were restricted with a tariff without rent seeking, the chosen consumption point would be at a point such as K, with more food produced and consumed, and fewer imports than at free trade (and consumer welfare would be lower than at free trade). If, however, instead of a tariff there were a quota restricting imports to the same quantity as under the tariff (where the import license recipient pays only the international price and can sell at the domestic price), additional resources are attracted away from food production. A tariff-ridden equilibrium that restricts imports to the amount $\overline{M}$ would result in a higher domestic price of the imported good (shown by the line D'D') relative to the other good, with reduced consumption of the import contrasted with free trade, greater consumption of the exportable good, but reduced overall welfare.

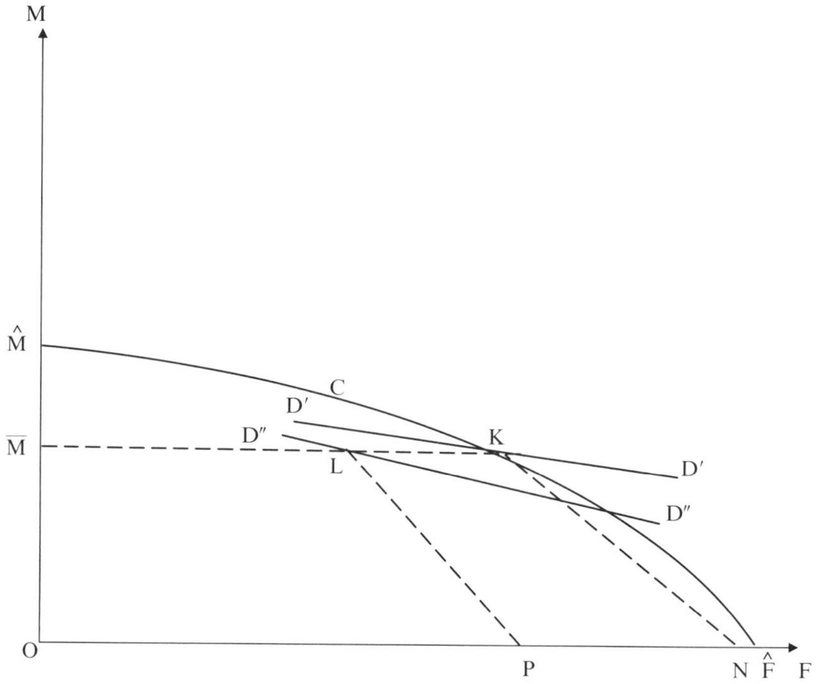

Figure 26.1 Rent-seeking import restrictions

But if imports of the quantity $\overline{M}$ are allocated by a system of import licenses and rent-seeking uses, resources that would otherwise produce the exportable good, F, consumption of F is reduced from K to L. The amount LK represents the value of resources withdrawn from F and used in rent seeking. It may be noted that if the authorities were to auction off the available import licenses (and no resources were used in lobbying or other efforts to affect the quantity of licenses issued), the rent seeking would disappear, as there would be no margin between the price paid for the license and the domestic price.

By assumption in this simple example, the quantity of imports (and hence the quantity of the good consumed) remains unchanged. Since consumption of the exportable falls below that which would take place with a tariff (instead of the quantitative import restriction), welfare is reduced even further than with a tariff. The domestic price of the import-competing good falls somewhat from its tariff-equivalent level, as demand shifts downward because of reduced output of the exportable good.

There are numerous theoretical extensions and variations of the basic model, along with a plethora of applications. Rent-seeking behavior can be modeled under uncertainty, and/or with additional factors of production or goods. In recent years, much effort has been devoted to game-theoretic formulations of particular aspects of rent seeking.

Likewise, there are numerous applications. Rent-seeking behavior can take place in efforts to affect government policy (as in tariff-seeking) or in response to government policy (as with quantitative restrictions on imports, although their quantity too could be influenced through rent seekers). Rent seeking can take place in the labor market (as when a minimum wage leaves many work seekers; the rate of unemployment is the equilibrating variable), in government regulation, in restrictions on international trade, in private and in public firms, and in much more (see Congleton, Hillman and Konrad (2008) for a survey). Rent seeking can be illegal (as in the case of bribes) or legal (as, for example, when regulators set a maximum rate of return allowable for a public utility and the quantity of capital used is above that which would be chosen by unconstrained profit maximizers).

HISTORY

For many years, economists regarded bribes and other corruption as transfer payments, treating them as if they affected income distribution but not production. This changed, in significant part because the visibility of rent-seeking activities increased enormously as many former colonies became independent in the several decades after the Second World War. An early model, which was later seen to be a case of rent seeking, was that of Harris and Todaro (1970), who were concerned with very high minimum wage rates legally mandated in Africa, with a large increase in migration into urban areas and urban unemployment when the minimum wage increased relative to the market-clearing wage. Barzel (1974) modeled queueing in Israel under meat price controls, where the length of the queue increased when the disparity between the controlled price and the market-clearing price increased.

Then came three contributions which pointed to the more general nature of the phenomenon that these, and other researchers had identified. Tullock (1967) argued that there was competition for monopoly rents. Krueger (1974) pointed to the excess of the welfare cost of quantitative restrictions over the cost of tariffs when rent seekers used resources to attempt to gain favorable treatment for import licenses and pointed out that the phenomenon took place when there was a government action or regulation that meant that markets did not clear at the prevailing price (legally zero in the case of license issuance). Posner (1975) analyzed the social costs of attempted regulation of private monopolies, concluding that the resources and waste expended on regulation might exceed that of private monopolies. A natural extension was to recognize that rent seekers might not only expend resources for regulatory favors, receipt of relevant licenses and other valuable permissions, but they could use resources to influence policy makers to decide on regulations and laws that would be to their benefit.

The key feature of all these contributions was the dissipation of resources in the rent-seeking process because a barrier of some kind was set between the apparent cost to an individual or group of obtaining something and its market-clearing price. Subsequent research has considerably enriched the analysis and broadened the applications. The rent seeking notions have been applied to a number of topics in economic history, law, sociology and other fields. Much recent work on institutional design is also informed by insights from the rent seeking literature.

REFERENCES

Barzel, Yoram, 1974, 'A Theory of Rationing by Waiting', *Journal of Law and Economics*, Vol. 17, No. 1 (April), pp. 73–95.

Congleton, Roger D., Ayre L. Hillman and Kai A. Konrad, 2008, 'Forty Years of Research on Rent-Seeking: An Overview', pp. 1–42 in R.D. Congleton, A.L. Hillman and K.A. Konrad, editors, *Forty Years of Research on Rent Seeking*, Vol. 2, Springer-Verlag, Berlin.

Harris, J.R. and M.P. Todaro, 1970, 'Migration, Unemployment, and Development: A Two-Sector Analysis', *American Economic Review*, Vol. 60 (March), pp. 126–42.

Krueger, Anne O., 1974, 'The Political Economy of the Rent-Seeking Society', *American Economic Review*, Vol. 74, No. 3 (July), pp. 291–303.

Posner, Richard, 1975, 'The Social Costs of Monopoly and Regulation', *Journal of Political Economy*, Vol. 83, No. 4 (July), pp. 807–47.

Tullock, Gordon, 1967, 'The Social Costs of Tariffs, Monopolies, and Theft', *Western Economic Journal*, Vol. 5 (June), pp. 224–32.

27. The logistic growth curve

J. S. Cramer

The logistic curve was devised in the 19th century to describe the time path of a growing human population. It was first proposed (and named) by Verhulst, a pupil of the Belgian statistician and demographer Quetelet, forgotten until the 1920s, and is now mainly used as an instrument of market research.

In order to describe the course over time of a quantity $W(t)$ consider its rate of change $\dot{W} = dW(t)/dt$. The simplest assumption is that this is proportional to the size already attained, or $\dot{W}(t) = \beta\, W(t)$, which leads of course to exponential growth, as in Malthus's famous dictum that population, if unchecked, will increase at a geometric rate. For the greater part of the nineteenth century, this was not a bad approximation for the immigrant population of continents like Northern America and Australia, yet it was clear that the process could not continue indefinitely. Verhulst (1838, 1845) therefore modified the differential equation by introducing an upper limit or saturation level Ω, writing

$$\dot{W}(t) = \beta\, W(t)\,(\Omega - W(t)) \qquad (27.1)$$

so that the rate of growth is proportional to both the level attained and the remaining room for further expansion. If we consider the proportion $Y(t) = W(t)\,/\Omega$ we have $\dot{Y}(t) = \beta\, Y(t)\,(1 - Y(t))$ and the solution of this differential equation is

$$Y(t) = \exp(\alpha + \beta t)/\{1 + \exp(\alpha + \beta t)\}$$

or

$$Y(z) = \exp z/(1 + \exp z) \qquad (27.2)$$

with $z = \alpha + \beta t$. This is the logistic curve of Figure 27.1, which rises monotonically along an S-shaped trajectory from zero to 1 as z moves with t through the time axis. The curve is symmetrical around $z = 0$, where

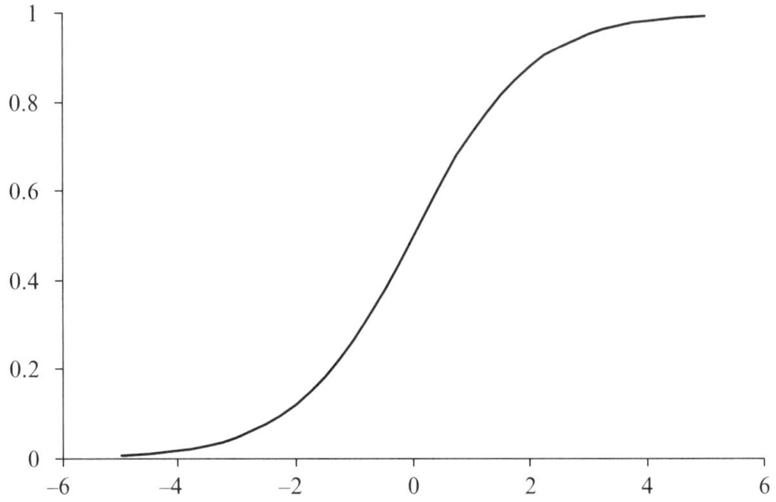

Figure 27.1 The logistic curve y(t)

Y(0)= *0.5*. In applications, the parameters α and β determine the position and slope of the curve in respect of historical time *t*.

Verhulst applied the curve to statistics of the Belgian population, estimating the three parameters α, β and Ω by equating the values of the curve to the population figures in three selected years. His work passed largely unnoticed, while in the first decades of the 20th century the idea of (27.1) and its concomitant (27.2) was reinvented independently by several scholars and applied to a variety of subjects, like the course of autocatalytic chemical processes and the growth of living organisms. Pearl and Reed (1920) used it once more for population growth, and a few years later, Yule (1925), in his Presidential address to the Royal Statistical Society, took up the same theme and at last gave due credit to Verhulst and his naming of the curve. For more on this see Cramer (2004).

The major interest of Verhulst and Pearl was the estimate of Ω, the limiting value of the population of Belgium and the United States respectively. By now it is generally recognized that population growth is a complex process that demands more sophisticated models. The logistic is still popular in market research, however, where it serves, using various names (like the S-curve), to model the introduction and adoption of new products and technologies.

An entirely different and separate usage of the logistic has sprung up in the statistical analysis of discrete choice. Since the curve rises monotonically from zero to one, it can be regarded as the distribution function of a random variate, and in this guise it very closely resembles the distribution function of a normal distribution. Although there is no known statistical experiment that would generate logistic variates, the distribution provides a ready alternative for the normal as used in probit analysis and then gives rise to logit analysis or logistic regression. In this role, the logistic function has been amazingly fruitful in interpretations and generalizations. But this paradigm stands entirely apart from the growth curve of the same name.

REFERENCES

Cramer, J.S. (2004), 'The early origins of the logit model', *Studies in History and Philosophy of Biological and Biomedical Sciences*, 35, 613–626.
Pearl, R. and Reed, L.J. (1920), 'On the rate of growth of the American population since 1870 and its mathematical representation', *Proceedings of the National Academy of Sciences*, 6, 275–288.
Verhulst, P.-F. (1838), 'Notice sur la loi que la population suit dans son accroissement', *Correspondance Mathématique et Physique*, 10, 113–121.
Verhulst, P.-F. (1845), 'Recherches mathématiques sur la loi d'accroissement de la population', *Nouveaux Mémoires de l' Académie Royale des Sciences, des Lettres et des Beaux-Arts de Belgique*, 18, 1–32.
Yule, G.U. (1925), 'The growth of population and the factors which control it', *Journal of the Royal Statistical Society*, 138, 1–59.

28. Graph theory and networks

Cassey Lee

The economy is obviously a complex entity characterized by interactions between multiple and heterogenous agents over time. Many attempts have been made to visually represent and model such interactions. One approach that has been increasingly used involves the use of tools and concepts from a branch of mathematics known as graph theory. Its origin dates back to Euler's solution of the 'Königsberg Bridge Problem' in 1736. In the social sciences, sociologists have been early enthusiasts of graph theory. The history of 'social network analysis' (SNA) dates back to the 1930s, with significant breakthroughs in the 1960s (Scott, 1991). In economics, some of the early studies employing graph theory can be traced back to the second half of the 1990s. It took roughly another 15 years before it became the basis of a new field of study in economics under the banner of 'social networks'.

The term 'graph theory' should not be confused with the economists' common use of the word 'graph', which usually refers to a two-dimensional Cartesian representation of equations. Graph theory is a study of the properties of graphs, where a graph is a set of vertices (dots) connected by edges (lines). Figure 28.1 provides a depiction of a graph with five vertices.

For a graph with n vertices, the maximum number of edges m is given by the formula:

$$m = \frac{n(n-1)}{2}$$

In the example shown in Figure 28.1, the five vertices are connected by ten edges. Beyond such basics, various mathematical properties of graphs are studied in graph theory, such as tree structures (a graph without cycles, that is, it does not loop back), polyhedral (a graph with flat surfaces) and colourings (partitioning of vertex sets).

In economics, graph theory has been used in a number of areas. One of the most common applications is the use of tree diagrams (which are acyclic connected graphs) in modelling sequential decision making. Figure 28.2 provides a graphical representation of an extensive form game where

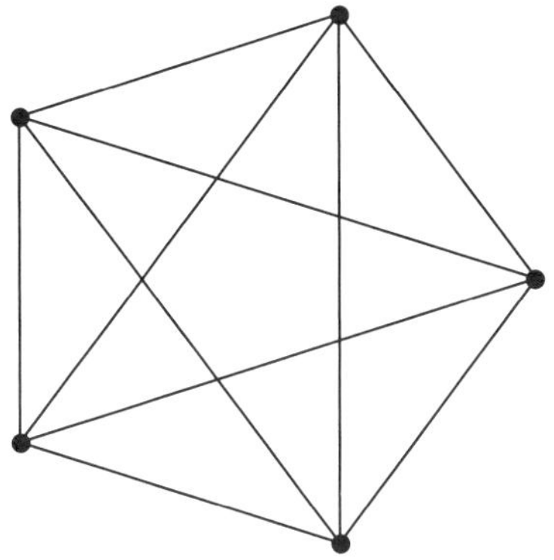

Figure 28.1 Graph with five vertices

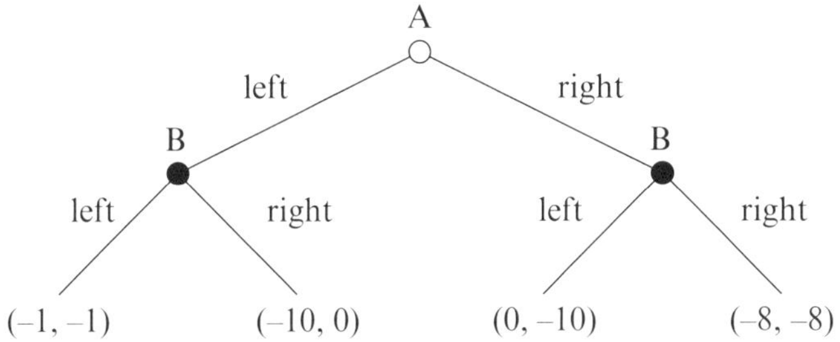

Figure 28.2 Decision tree

driver A makes a decision before driver B to keep to the left lane or right lane (with payoffs (π_A , π_B) indicated in parentheses).

Graph theory has also been used to model and analyse interactions that occur in a network setting. In this respect, there appears to be at least two distinct areas of applications in economics. The first is in the area of economics of network industries such as computer software and hardware, telecommunications, water distribution and gas distribution (Economides, 1996, Crampes, 1999 and Shy 2001). Here, the network characteristics of industries are sometimes visually represented using graph-theoretic types of representation. Figure 28.3 provides an example from Economides (1996) of a telecommunications network. However, much of the literature in this area focuses on economic aspects of such industries (such as externalities, complementarity and compatibility), using very simple network diagrams for analytical purposes. The mathematical properties of networks are usually not an important part of analysis in this literature.

A more recent and powerful application of graph theory in economics

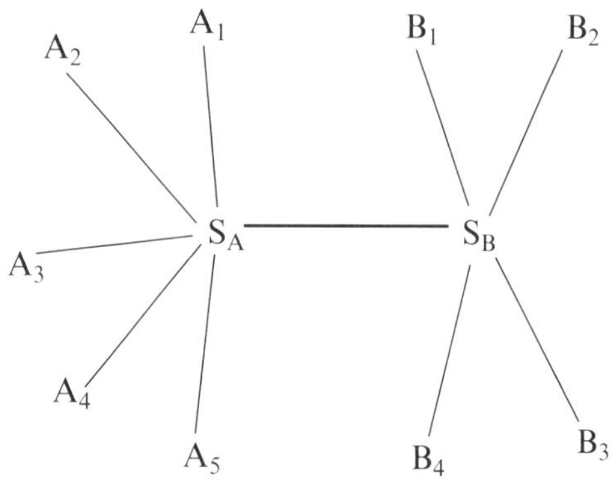

Source: Economides 1996, p.676

Figure 28.3 Local and long-distance telephone network

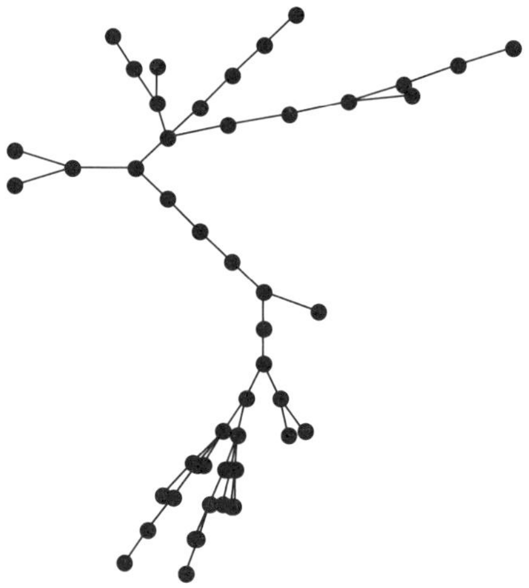

Figure 28.4 A random graph

is in the study of what is known today as 'social networks' (Goyal 2007, Vega-Redondo 2007 and Jackson 2008). The studies in this area have been undertaken against the backdrop of more complex graphical theoretic representations such as random graphs, where networks are generated randomly. Figure 28.4 is a depiction of a random graph.

A number of interesting empirical works on social networks using graph theory have emerged in recent years. One such study is that of Goyal *et al.* (2006), who studied the change in social distance among economists over the

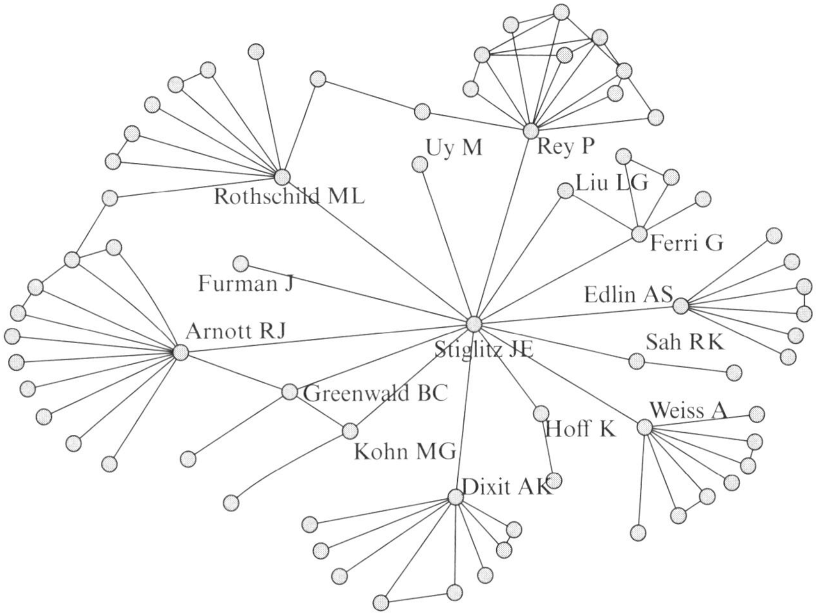

Source: Goyal *et al.* 2006, p.410

Figure 28.5 Local network of collaboration of Joseph E. Stiglitz in the 1990s

period 1970–2000. They found that the network of collaborating economists is far from random, with the distance between economists becoming smaller over time due to the presence of 'star' economists, each co-authoring with many other economists. Figure 28.5 provides an illustration of the network of collaboration of one such star – the Nobel laureate Joseph E. Stiglitz.

Another intriguing application of graph theory is the analysis of the rise of the Medicis' influence in the fifteenth century, which is related to their ability to engineer marriages with other influential families (see Figure 28.6). Underlying such visual representations are various graph theoretic measures of the connectedness of the Medici family in the network.

The spatial nature of the graph theoretic representation has also made it amenable to a variety of applications in economics. Many of these applications are embedded in game theoretic settings. They include information diffusion, social learning and network/coalition formation. Different types of network topologies have been used in these studies (for example, chains, grids, lattices, connected graphs). A survey of the application of graph theory in other disciplines (for example, Strogatz 2001), such as biology,

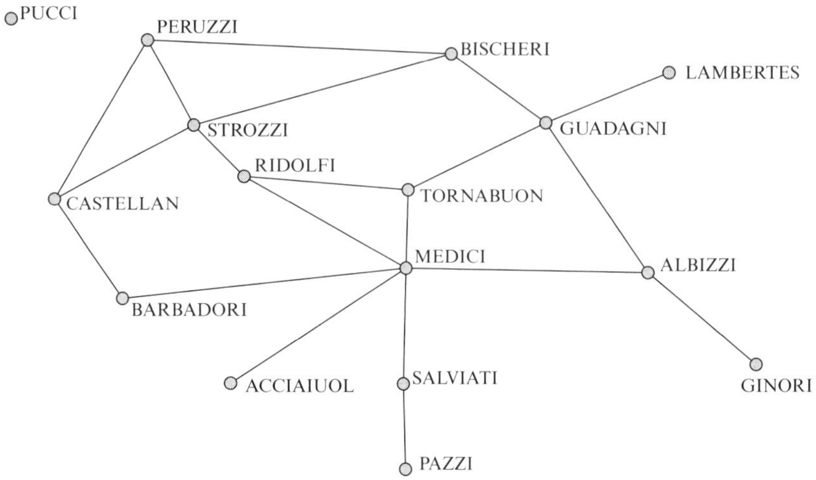

Source: Jackson 2008, p.4

Figure 28.6 Network of fifteenth-century Florentine marriages

physics, chemistry and engineering, suggests that this area is likely to remain a treasure trove for economists for years to come.

REFERENCES

Crampes, Claude (1999). 'Network Industries and Network Goods', *European Economy*, Vol. 4, pp. 81–99.

Economides, Nicholas (1996). 'The Economics of Networks', *International Journal of Industrial Organization*, Vol. 14, pp. 673–699.

Goyal, Sanjeev (2007). *Connections: An Introduction to the Economics of Networks*. Princeton, NJ: Princeton University Press.

Goyal, Sanjeev, Marco van der Leij and José Luis Moraga-Gozález (2006). 'Economics: Emerging Small World', *Journal of Political Economy*, Vol. 114, pp. 403–412,

Jackson, Matthew O. (2008). *Social and Economic Networks*. Princeton, NJ: Princeton University Press.

Scott, John (1991). *Social Network Analysis: A Handbook*. London: Sage Publications.

Shy, Oz (2001). *The Economics of Network Industries*. Cambridge: Cambridge University Press.

Strogatz, Steven H. (2001). 'Exploring Complex Networks', *Nature*, Vol. 410, pp. 268–276.

Vega-Redondo, Fernando (2007). *Complex Social Networks*. Cambridge: Cambridge University Press.

PART II

General equilibrium analysis

Basic tools of general equilibrium analysis

29. Circular flow diagrams

Roger E. Backhouse and Yann Giraud

The circular flow diagram occurs in virtually all modern introductory economics textbooks as a way of explaining flows of income between firms and households and their measurement in the national accounts. More complicated versions of the diagram then provide the justification for analysing income determination in terms of leakages from and injections into the circular flow of income, which can be analysed using the so-called Keynesian cross.

1. THE DIAGRAM

The crucial element in all circular flow diagrams is symbols representing firms and households, which may be drawings of factories and residential houses (usually suburban detached houses) or may involve photographs. One arrow is then drawn running from firms to households, representing the flow of factor payments (wages and profits), with a second arrow on the other side of the diagram going from households to firms, representing spending on goods and services produced by firms. This simplified form of the diagram is represented by the solid lines in Figure 29.1. Sometimes, there will also be arrows going in the opposite direction, denoting the goods and services, including factor services, for which these expenditure flows are payments. The lesson to be drawn from this is that incomes must be exactly equal to expenditure: they measure the same flows of money but at different points in the circuit. It is also possible to measure production of goods and services by firms; because there is nowhere else for this output to be sold, this shows the product measure of national income to equal the other two measures.

The diagram is then made more complicated in a number of ways. One possibility is to add arrows representing flows of expenditure between firms (see the dotted line at the top of Figure 29.1). These represent purchases of intermediate goods. Though few introductory textbooks use this terminology, it is possible to draw a 'production boundary' around the firms.

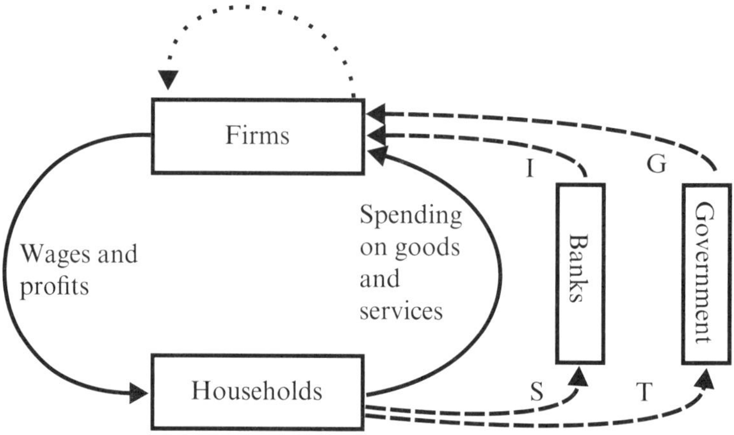

Note: S = savings T = taxes, G = government spending, I = investment.

Figure 29.1 The circular flow diagram of contemporary textbooks

Payments enter national income if and only if they cross this boundary. That means that just as purchases of intermediate goods do not enter national income, neither do payments within the household sector, such as payments by parents of pocket money to their children (which are not shown).

More important is the addition of the income flows shown using dashed lines on the right-hand side of Figure 29.1. These decompose households' expenditure flows into the categories in which they occur in the national accounts. Savings (S) are assumed to flow into banks and taxes (T) are paid to government. Each of these purchases goods and services from firms, giving rise to investment (I) and government spending (G). International trade could be added, but is omitted here for simplicity. This provides a justification for the equations:

$$Y = C + I + G$$

$$C = Y - T - S$$

This decomposition matters because it explains the analysis of national income in terms of 'leakages' from and 'injections' into the circular flow. This involves a conceptual jump, because up to this point, the diagram, which derives its persuasive power from the fact that there is nowhere else for income to go, has been used to prove national income identities. Once the possibility of leakage is allowed for, we jump to a world in which equilibrium, and a constant flow round the system, will occur only if there is a balance between these flows.

2. THE CIRCULAR FLOW DIAGRAM AND KEYNESIAN ECONOMICS

The canonical instance of the diagram is Paul Samuelson's *Economics* (1948), which became the dominant textbook in the 1950s. This had much in common with the diagrams shown above but differed in a way that carried different metaphorical baggage. Instead of the pictures of factories and houses, there were what appear to be two tanks, labelled 'Business' and 'Public', linked by pipes through which water (income) could flow, as shown in Figure 29.2. A closed loop was used to explain the national accounts, and in the next chapter it was modified to show water/expenditure leaking out through an open pipe at the bottom, with additional water/expenditure being pumped into another opening at the top. Though it is not clear that the diagram depicts a possible real system, Samuelson is clearly using the analogy of a hydraulic machine to make his argument. It also makes the point that the circular flow is driven by investment, for the pump in the top right corner, interestingly powered by 'Technical change, etc.' (hardly a Keynesian view of investment), is the only explicit mechanism for moving water round the system. The use of this analogy illustrates what Coddington (1983) termed hydraulic Keynesianism.

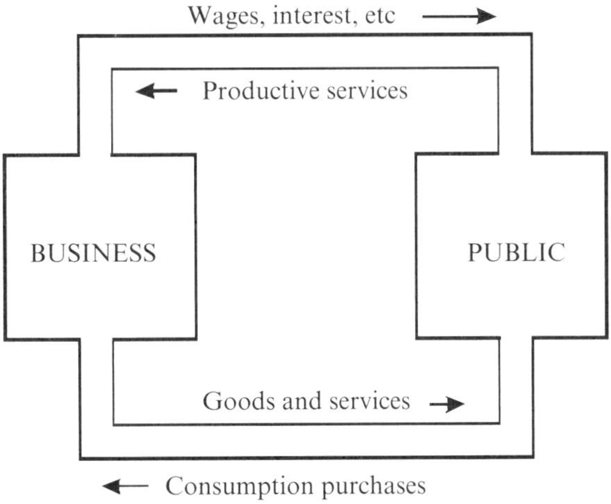

Figure 29.2 Samuelson's circular flow diagram

Source: Photograph by R.E. Backhouse

Figure 29.3 The Phillips machine

Whereas it is not clear in Samuelson's diagram what mechanism causes water/expenditure to flow round the system, the same cannot be said of the machine that A. W. Phillips built, in which the circular flow of income was represented by coloured water flowing round a real system of pipes and cisterns. This went significantly beyond textbook diagrams in that it showed stocks (the level of water in various tanks) as well as flows: the circular flow diagram had become an analogue computer that could be used to measure responses to external shocks. The pump was still there, behind the model, but once water entered the system, gravity and carefully designed valves ensured that it offered an exact representation of the economy – leakages were no longer a feature of the economy but a sign of mechanical failure!

In his highly influential *Introduction to Positive Economics* (1963), Richard Lipsey used the circular flow diagram as his main device to explain core macroeconomic principles, instead of the more common 45-degree diagram used by Samuelson. This unusual choice reflected his use of the Phillips machine at the LSE during the writing of his book. Lipsey's circular flow diagrams contained numerical examples that the student was expected to use as exercises to produce his own understanding of the theory. On the other hand, Campbell McConnell's *Economics* (1966), the first American textbook to outsell Samuelson, displayed a series of circular flow diagrams to represent the building of a capitalist society from transactions between self-interested individuals to a whole monetary economy, and did not make use of the diagram in explaining macroeconomic principles. In the mid-1980s, the circular flow diagram was frequently used as an introductory device in non-Keynesian textbooks, such as Edmund Phelps's *Political Economy: An Introductory Text* (1985), or in microeconomic texts such as Jack Hirshleifer's *Price Theory and Applications* (1988).

A circular flow diagram can be used whenever it is necessary to explain the relationships between income flows in the economy as a whole that underlie the national accounts. A good illustration of the distance the diagram could travel is its use to explain the structure of computable general equilibrium models of international trade flows (see Hertel 1997). Consequently, the diagram lost its relation to Keynesian economics.

3. THE EARLY HISTORY OF THE DIAGRAM

Whilst Samuelson's may be the canonical version of the diagram, it was not the first. His teacher, Frank Knight, had used a circular flow diagram, which he described as 'the familiar figure of the "wheel of wealth"', shown in Figure 29.4 (Knight 1933, pp. 60–1, quoted in Patinkin 1973b, p. 1037). Yet, unlike Samuelson, Knight did not use his 'wheel of wealth' to represent macroeconomic flows but to show the allocative functions of the price system in a capitalist society in which families and households specialised in different activities. Seemingly similar flow diagrams may be found in the economic literature of the late 19th and early 20th centuries, but generally their role was merely to indicate the role of money

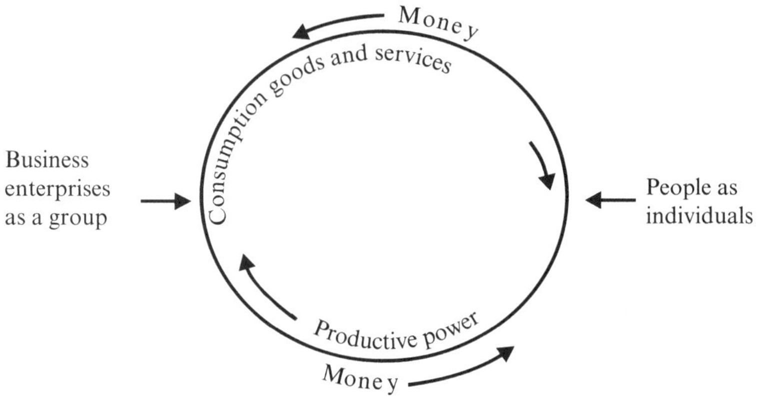

Source: As in Knight's original manuscript, circa 1926

Figure 29.4 Knight's wheel of wealth

as a medium of exchange. For example, Nicholas Johannsen had shown money circulating in a circle between businesses, with contributions flowing to and from a financial system located in the centre (Patinkin 1973b).

According to Patinkin (1973b), the true origin of Knight's diagram could be Foster and Catchings's (1925) 'Circuit Flow of Money', found in *Profits*, which Knight reviewed in 1926 when he began working on his *Economic Organization*. Though it looks like a hydraulic machine, Foster and Catchings' diagram is different from the canonical circular flow diagram: the tanks merely denote aggregates of payment flows. Their failure to distinguish stocks (water in tanks) and flows (water flowing through pipes) is in dramatic contrast with the Phillips machine, the essence of which was a precise relation between the properties of the hydraulic system and those of the economic system.

It has also been claimed that circular flow diagrams originated with the Physiocrats, in François Quesnay's *Tableau économique*, the third edition of which, dated 1759, is shown in Figure 29.5. The three columns are labelled 'Productive expenditure' (in agriculture), 'Expenditure of the revenue' (by landowners) and 'Sterile expenditure' (by artisans or manufacturers). Spending is initiated by landowners, who start out with rental income of 600, which they spend equally on agricultural and manufactured goods. These sectors then spend half of the income they receive on products from the other sector, generating further spending in what we would now describe as a multiplier process. Because agriculture is productive,

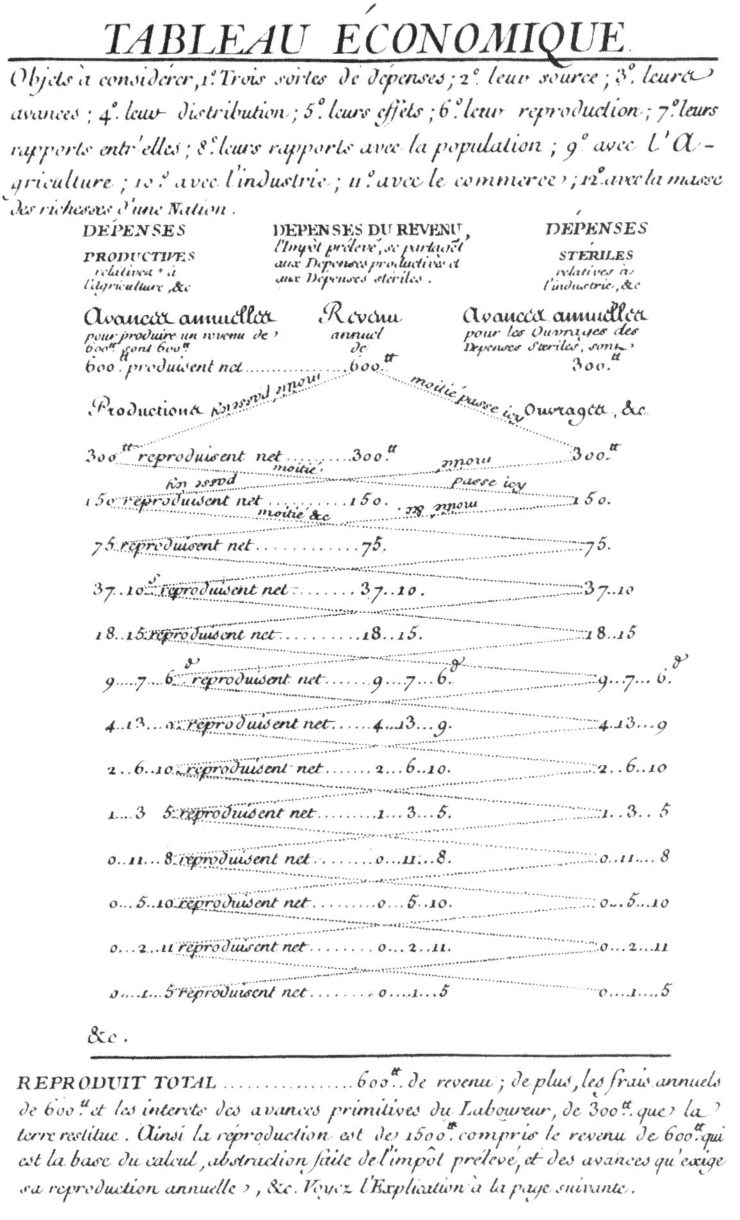

Source: M 184 n° 57-2 Centre Historique des Archives Nationales ds Paris

Figure 29.5 Quesnay's Tableau économique

it produces a surplus, assumed to be at the rate of 100 per cent, which is shown in the centre column (for a fuller account see Kuczynski and Meek 1972, or Blaug 1997).

Quesnay concludes, adding up the figures in the three columns, that this initial expenditure of 600 will produce a total revenue of 1500: the farmers will have their stocks restored to 600, artisans will have theirs restored to 300, and the landlords will have another 600 in rent, so that the process can start over again. Though this was not Quesnay's purpose – for him the tableau was a visual calculating machine (see Charles 2004) – economists have read this as a circular flow diagram, for it represents flows of income between different parts of the economy, the money ending up where it started. Hector Denis' *Histoire des systèmes économiques et socialistes* (1904) used a circular flow diagram, as understood here, to represent this theory and it is not unusual to encounter similar treatments of Quesnay in contemporary economics (see for example Gilibert 2008). Patinkin, however, was introduced to Denis' exposition through William Jaffé only after the publication of his 1973 article, which suggests that Knight was probably ignorant of it as well. It would thus appear that Knight's use of the diagram was original.

Samuelson's indebtedness to Knight is also rather difficult to assert with certainty (it is discussed in Patinkin 1973a, p. 791, footnote 8). Actually, Samuelson did not mention Knight in conjunction with his circular flow diagram but only in the course of explaining (in the second edition) the functions of an economic organisation (*What*, *How* and *For Whom*). In addition, it must be noted that the idea of an economy represented by a circular diagram was 'in the air' during the early years of the Great Depression outside academia. For example, in 1933, the cartoonist Hendrik Willem van Loon drew for the magazine *Survey Graphic* two circular figures, with which he showed that the deflationist spiral could be reversed with higher wages and higher spending. The period was also marked by a change in visual culture in the United States as artists, propagandists and social scientists made an extensive use of visual representation to diffuse knowledge to a large audience. Consequently, the invention and diffusion of graphic design had a notable impact on textbook publishing in the postwar period. Samuelson – intentionally or not – picked up on that larger visual culture, allowing for the dissemination of economic knowledge to an increasing number of students (Giraud, 2010). Therefore, it can be asserted that the circular flow diagram, unlike many other visual representations, is not only a tool devoted to professional economists but also a device of visual communication and mass education.

REFERENCES

Blaug, M. (1997). *Economic Theory in Retrospect* (5th edition). Cambridge: Cambridge University Press.
Charles, L. (2004). 'The Tableau Économique as Rational Recreation', *History of Political Economy* 36 (3), pp. 445–474.
Coddington, A. (1983). *Keynesian Economics: The Search for First Principles*. London: George Allen and Unwin.
Denis, H. (1904). *Histoire des systèmes économiques et socialistes*. Paris: Giard et Brière.
Foster, W. and Catchings, W. (1925). *Profits*. Boston: Houghton Mifflin.
Gilibert, G. (2008). 'Circular Flow'. In Durlauf, S. N. and Blume, L. E., eds, *The New Palgrave Dictionary of Economics* (2nd ed.). London: Palgrave Macmillan. Volume 1, pp. 790–794.
Giraud, Yann B. (2010). 'The Changing Place of Visual Representation in Economics: Paul Samuelson between Principle and Strategy, 1941–1955', *Journal of the History of Economic Thought* 32 (2), pp. 175–97
Hertel, T. W. (1997). *Global Trade Analysis: Modeling and Applications*. Cambridge: Cambridge University Press.
Hirshleifer, J. (1988). *Price Theory and Applications* (4th ed.). Englewood Cliffs, NJ: Prentice Hall.
Knight, F. H. (1933). *The Economic Organization*. Chicago, IL: Chicago University.
Kuczynski, M. and Meek, R. L. (1972). *Quesnay's Tableau Économique*. London: Macmillan.
Lipsey, R. G. (1963). *Introduction to Positive Economics*. London: Weidenfeld and Nicolson.
McConnell, C. (1966). *Economics* (3rd ed.). New York: McGraw-Hill.
Patinkin, D. (1973a). 'Frank Knight as Teacher', *American Economic Review* 63 (5), pp. 787–810.
Patinkin, D. (1973b). 'In Search of the 'Wheel of Wealth': On the Origins of Frank Knight's Circular-Flow Diagram', *American Economic Review* 63 (5), pp. 1037–1046.
Phelps, E. S. (1985). *Political Economy: an Introductory Text*. New York: Norton and Company.
Samuelson, P. A. (1948). *Economics*. New York: McGraw Hill.

30. The unit simplex

John Whalley

The unit simplex diagram (Figure 30.1) became a central part of modern economics with the development of general equilibrium theory in the 1950s, and is particularly associated with the proofs of existence of equilibrium following the pioneering work of Arrow and Debreu (1954). The diagram shows the coordinates of relative prices in a three-good economy in which only relative prices matter and in which the absolute price level is of no consequence: the traditional pure barter economy widely used in economics. It is drawn in three-dimensional space, with three axes of prices of goods. The feature that relative prices are all that matters reflects the common assumption made in general equilibrium analysis of homogeneity of degree zero of continuous excess demand functions in the pure exchange economy case. As Arrow showed, this follows directly from an assumption of utility-maximizing behaviour. This implies that the absolute price level plays no role in economic behaviour. Put differently, if all prices were to double, the incomes of households selling endowments of goods would double and at the same time the acquisition prices of goods would double. In relative terms, prices would be unchanged.

This central proposition that only relative prices matter is the long-standing feature of microeconomic analysis going back many hundreds of years, but its representation in this diagram was central to mathematical economics literature and discussion of the existence of the equilibrium which followed Arrow and Debreu. The original Walrasian formulation of general equilibrium asserted that a system of intertwined demand and supply functions, where outcomes in one market depended on prices in another market, would automatically have a solution just by counting numbers of equations and numbers of unknowns.

This was contested in the 1930s by Menger and the Austrian school, and this was to lead to discussions on whether or not a consistent equilibrium solution must necessarily exist. The concern was that prior to any policy or other application of such models, the logical consistency of the models should first be demonstrated.

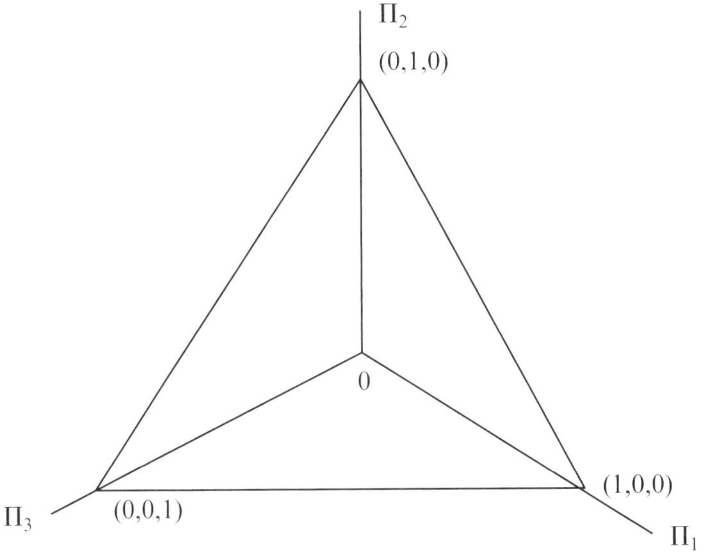

Figure 30.1 The unit simplex

This issue was later discussed by Abraham Wald and then taken further by Arrow & Debreu in their classic work (see Weintraub 1983). They demonstrated the existence of a competitive equilibrium by applying the Brouwer fixed point theorem to models of pure exchange (Gale and Nikaido 1965), and Debreu later also applied the Kakutani fixed-point theorem to models of production which involved point-to-set mappings. In the case of point-to-point mappings, a simple transformation of the excess demand function, pioneered by Nikaido in 1956, was used to show that a fixed point under the mapping due to Nikaido must inevitably imply that the conditions for a competitive equilibrium were satisfied. This was demonstrated using a continuous mapping of the unit simplex into itself as drawn in Figure 30.1. This same diagram was later to become pivotal in discussions of computation of economic equilibrium which are now associated with the pioneering work of Herbert Scarf in 1973 in his book and earlier papers on computing an equilibrium.

The unit simplex remains as a central and pivotal diagram in general equilibrium theory and still fulfils a central role in coursework in the area.

REFERENCES

Arrow, K. J. and Debreu, G. (1954), 'Existence of an Equilibrium for a Competitive Economy', *Econometrica*, Vol. 22, Issue 3, pp. 265–290.
Gale, D. and Nikaido, H. (1965), 'The Jacobian Matrix and Global Univalence of Mappings', *Mathematische Annalen*, Vol. 159, Issue 2 / April, 81–93.
Nikaido, H. (1956), 'On the Classical Multilateral Exchange Problem', *Metroeconomica*, Vol. 8, Issue 2, pp. 135–145.
Scarf, H. E. (1973), *The Computation of Economic Equilibria*, Yale University Press, New Haven and London.
Weintraub, E. R. (1983), 'On The Existence of a Competitive-Equilibrium: 1930–1954' *Economic Literature*, Vol. 21, Issue 1, pp. 1–39.

31. The Edgeworth box

John Creedy

The Edgeworth box, with its associated concepts of indifference maps and the contract curve, provides one of the most widely used diagrammatic tools in economics. Taking Jevons's (1871/1957) basic two-person two-good exchange model as his starting point, Edgeworth (1881) showed that for two individuals engaged in barter there is a range of efficient trades: these define the contract curve.[1] If a settlement is not on the contract curve, movement to it can make one person better off without the other being worse off. Movement along the contract curve involves one trader becoming worse off while the other gains. Defining indifference curves as showing combinations of amounts consumed for which utility is constant, the contract curve is the locus of points of tangency between traders' indifference curves, between limits given by their pre-trade curves (those going through the endowment point). The resulting 'indeterminacy' regarding the 'final settlement' gave rise, in Edgeworth's view, to a need for arbitration. He showed that the utilitarian optimal position (which maximises total utility) is on the contract curve. This led to his 'neocontractarian utilitarianism' argument: risk-averse traders who consider all outcomes as equally likely would accept the utilitarian arbitration because it corresponds to their long-run expected position.[2] The same diagram illustrates a price-taking equilibrium, whereby one or more of the mutual tangency positions also corresponds to tangency with a straight line going through the endowment point, whose slope represents the exchange ratio (and hence relative price). Individuals acting in isolation, taking prices as given in contrast to those engaged in barter, have mutually consistent demands and supplies. A price-taking equilibrium must correspond to a point on the contract curve. Edgeworth was thus able to clarify the sense in which a competitive equilibrium is 'optimal', fully recognising that it is just one of many (Pareto) optimal points. Furthermore, Edgeworth showed how Marshall's 'offer curves' can be derived from the indifference map, so that a point of intersection of offer curves is precisely a price-taking equilibrium.[3]

Edgeworth's diagram was drawn with the origin as the endowment

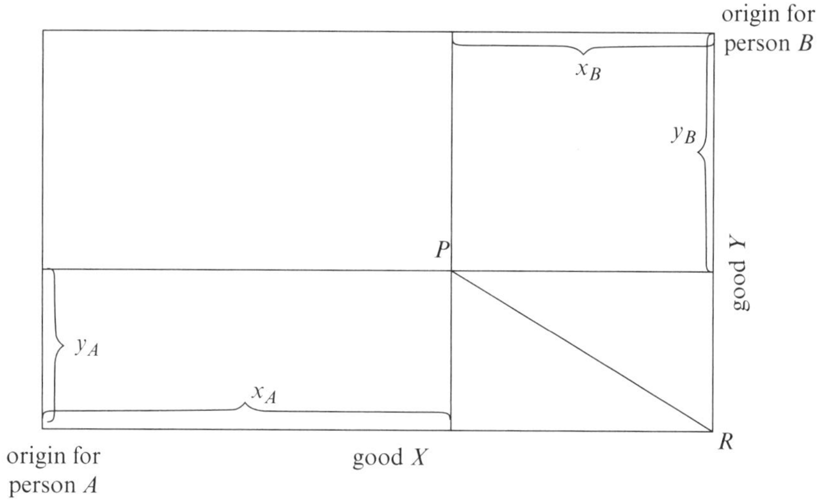

Figure 31.1 The Edgeworth box

point, corresponding to his emphasis on the amounts exchanged as the variables of interest. This meant that he did not actually draw two of the edges of the 'box'. The way in which the two sets of indifference curves and their related axes are related was later clarified by Bowley (1924). The discussion here uses the more familiar textbook form of the box, shown in Figure 31.1. The initial endowments of good *X* and good *Y* define the lengths of the base and height respectively, and the amounts consumed by persons *A* and *B* are measured respectively from the south-west and north-east corners of the box. Any point within the box represents a possible allocation of the available amounts of *X* and *Y* between the individuals. Thus at point *P* in Figure 31.1, person *A* is shown to consume x_A and y_A of goods *X* and *Y* respectively, while person *B* consumes x_B and y_B of the goods.

Suppose *A* holds all the initial amount of good *X* and none of good *Y*, and can obtain y_A of good *Y* only by giving up some of good *X* to person *B*: person *A* gives up an amount x_B of *X*, in order to obtain y_A of good *Y*. Conversely, *B* gives up y_A of *Y* in order to obtain x_B of *X* from person *A*. In the context of barter, the implied rate of exchange of *X* for *Y* is y_A/x_B. This is the slope of the line from *P* to *R*, which is the initial endowment position at which the individuals would consume if no exchange were to take place. The rate of exchange of *Y* for *X* is x_B/y_A; that is, the reciprocal of the rate of exchange of *X* for *Y*.

Although all points in the box represent feasible allocations, a more

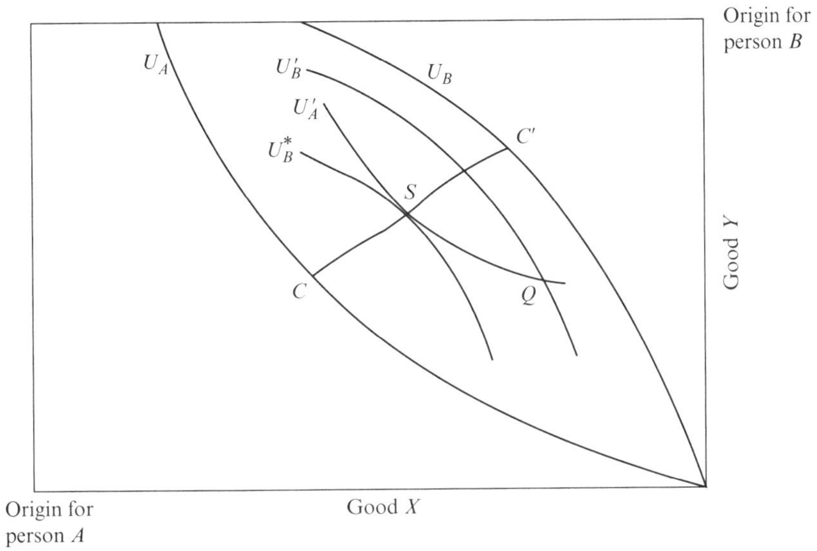

Figure 31.2 The contract curve

limited range is relevant when considering amounts exchanged. First, individuals will not trade if the resulting allocation places them on a lower indifference curve than the one passing through the endowment point. Consider point Q in Figure 31.2. The indifference curves of persons A and B which pass through the point Q are shown as U'_A and U'_B respectively. Both individuals are better off than they would be in isolation. However, there is a further opportunity for improvement. For example, person A may remain on U'_A, while B could move to the highest indifference curve consistent with U'_A. This is shown as U^*_B in Figure 31.2. Here U'_A is tangential to U^*_B at point S. This type of tangency is also characteristic of points C and C'. Any movement away from S would involve at least one of the individuals being made worse off by the movement. The reallocation from Q to S represents an improvement for person B without person A becoming worse off. There are many points of tangency between the sets of indifference curves between C and C'. The locus of these points is the contract curve. It is thus a locus of Pareto-efficient allocations: it is not possible to move away from any point on the contract curve without making at least one person worse off.

Consider an exchange where the individuals take prices as being outside their control: they are said to be 'parametric'. Since person A holds all the initial supply of good X, the budget of A is the price per unit of X multiplied by the endowment of X. The budget line must pass through point P in

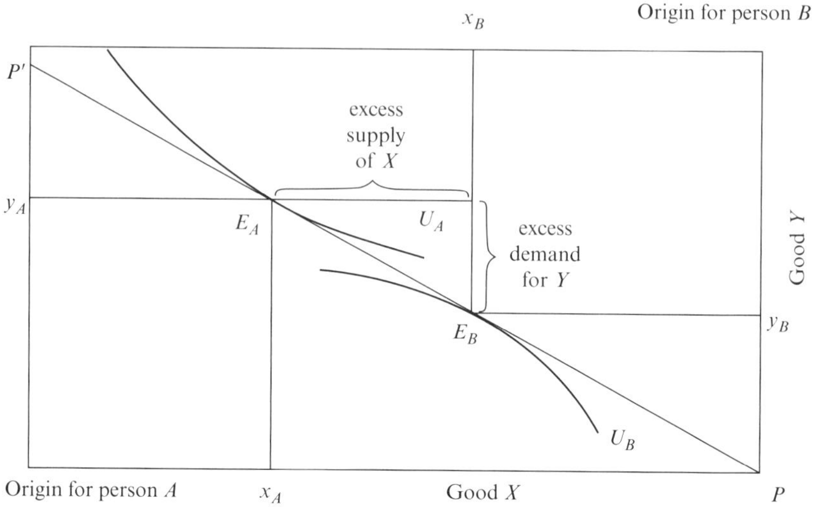

Figure 31.3 A disequilibrium price ratio

the south-east corner of the Edgeworth box in Figure 31.3. This is shown as PP', and the slope is given by the price ratio p_x/p_y. Similarly, person B is endowed with the initial supply of good Y, is initially also at point P and faces the same prices as person A, so the constraint is represented by the same line PP'. Person A must remain on or to the south-west, while B must remain on or to the north-east of the line.

Acting in isolation persons A and B would attempt to reach E_A and E_B, on indifference curves U_A and U_B respectively. With this arbitrary price ratio, person A would hope to retain x_A of good X and use the remainder of the endowment to purchase y_A of good Y. Also, person B would hope to retain y_B of Y, and to purchase x_B of X. Figure 31.3 shows that these plans are not compatible; there is an excess demand for Y and an excess supply of good X. The price ratio shown in this figure cannot be regarded as an equilibrium price ratio.

Equilibrium is a situation in which no individual's plans are frustrated, that is where there are no excess demands or supplies. In the present context this must imply that both individuals plan to consume at precisely the same point in the Edgeworth box. The price ratio which solves the problem of avoiding any excess demands is shown in Figure 31.4.

The important feature of the price line PP' in Figure 31.4 is that it is tangential to both individuals' indifference curves at the same point. At this price ratio, individual A plans to consume at E on indifference curve U_A. Person B also plans to consume at the same point E, but on

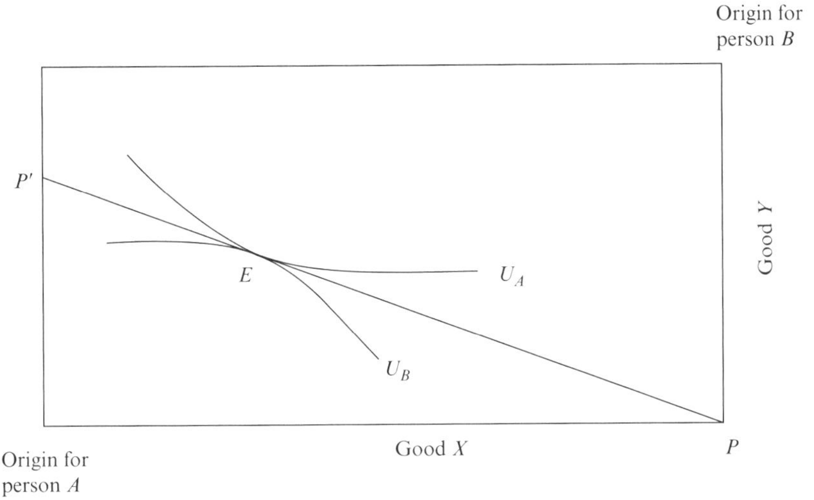

Figure 31.4 The price-taking equilibrium

indifference curve U_B. The amount of good X which A wishes to sell at that price ratio precisely matches the amount of good X which B wishes to buy. Similarly, the amount of Y which B wishes to sell is equal to the amount desired by person A. The prices which give rise to PP' in Figure 31.4 is therefore a price-taking equilibrium set. The respective indifference curves are tangential to the common budget line at E and therefore must also be tangential to each other. The equilibrium point is thus by definition on the contract curve, so the price-taking equilibrium is Pareto-efficient. This gives rise to what is now referred to as the 'First Fundamental Theorem' of welfare economics – that a price-taking equilibrium is Pareto-efficient. The use of price taking also provides a considerable reduction in the amount of information required by traders compared with barter. Individuals only need to know the equilibrium prices, whereas in barter they have to learn a considerable amount of information about other individuals' preferences and endowments.

NOTES

1. For further details of Edgeworth's original contributions to economics, see Creedy (1986).
2. This argument therefore united the 'economical' and 'utilitarian' calculus, and was of considerable significance to Edgeworth.
3. Edgeworth's demonstration that, in a barter context, the introduction of additional

traders eliminates the indeterminacy and replicates price taking, is discussed in Chapter 32, *The Role of Numbers in Competition.*

REFERENCES

Bowley, A. L. (1924), *The Mathematical Groundwork of Economics*, Oxford: Clarendon Press.
Creedy, J. (1986), *Edgeworth and the Development of Neoclassical Economics*, Oxford: Basil Blackwell.
Edgeworth, F. Y. (1881), *Mathematical Psychics: An Essay on the Application of Mathematics to the Moral Sciences*, London: Kegan Paul.
Jevons, W. S. (1871/1957), *The Theory of Political Economy*, 5th edition, edited by H. S. Jevons. New York: Augustus Kelly.

32. The role of numbers in competition

John Creedy

Edgeworth (1881) began his analysis of exchange by considering barter between two individuals. His model was based on the framework introduced by Jevons (1871/1957), who restricted his attention to price-taking equilibria where all units are exchanged at the same price ratio. Jevons confessed that he was unable to represent the model diagrammatically, but Edgeworth rapidly introduced the concepts of indifference curves and the contract curve, specifying a range of 'efficient exchanges' of goods between individuals.[1] The essential feature from Edgeworth's point of view is precisely that there is a range, rather than a unique point: 'the settlements are represented by an indefinite number of points' (1881, p.29). Hence in barter the rate of exchange is 'indeterminate'. The rate of exchange achieved in practice will thus depend to a large extent on bargaining strength.

The central problem that Edgeworth tried to resolve concerned the conditions necessary to remove this indeterminacy. The question naturally arises as to the extent to which it results from the absence of competition in the simple two-person market. Edgeworth thus quickly moved on to the introduction of further pairs of traders. His analysis involved the use of his 'Edgeworth box' apparatus, but was extremely terse. The following discussion does not therefore follow his own presentation.

The analysis of barter with numerous traders involves Edgeworth's stylised description of the process of barter: this is the famous 'recontracting' process. He supposed that transaction costs can be ignored and that knowledge of the other traders' dispositions and resources can be obtained by the formation of tentative contracts. These do not involve actual transfers and can be broken when further information is obtained. The importance of the recontracting process, apart from allowing the dissemination of information, lies in the fact that it makes it possible to analyse the use of collusion among some of the traders. Individuals are allowed to form coalitions in order to improve bargaining strength. Recontracting enables the coalitions to be broken up by outsiders who may attract members of a group away with more favourable terms of exchange.

The initial two traders are referred to as A_1, who holds all the initial stocks

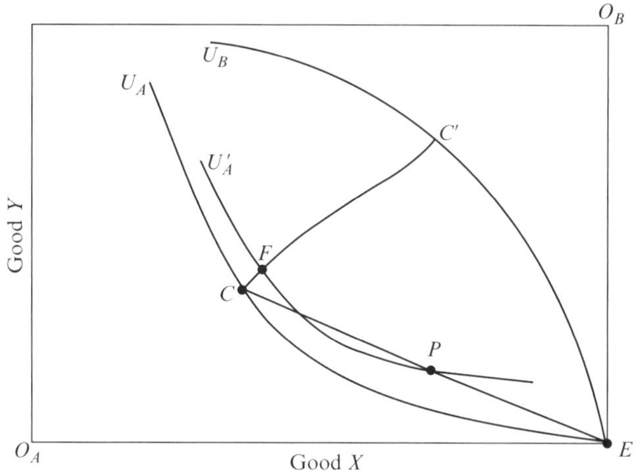

Figure 32.1 Two pairs of traders

of good X, and B_1, who holds all the stocks of good Y. The analysis begins by introducing a second person A_2 and a second person B_2, where the new traders are exact replicas of the initial pair, with the same tastes and endowments. This simplification is useful because the dimensions of the Edgeworth box and the indifference curves are identical for each pair of traders. Hence, it enables the same diagram to be used as in the case when only two traders are considered in isolation. Two basic points can be stated immediately. First, in the final settlement all individuals will be at a common point in the Edgeworth box, because if two individuals have identical tastes, their total utility is maximised by sharing their resources equally. Second, the settlement must be on the contract curve, otherwise there are wasted opportunities for one party to gain, without anyone losing.

It is useful to consider various contracts which will eventually be broken, in order to illustrate the way in which the introduction of additional traders provides a role for some kind of competitive process. Consider Figure 32.1 and suppose that when A_1 and B_1 are trading independently of A_2 and B_2, trader B_1 has all the bargaining power and is able to push A_1 to the limit of the contract curve at point C. Suppose also that the same applies to A_2 and B_2. If the two pairs of traders are then able to communicate with each other, A_2 can simply refuse to trade with B_2 at C. With no transaction costs, A_2 was previously indifferent between trading at C and consuming at the endowment point, E. This endowment position is effectively the 'threat point' of the As: it is the position in which they would find themselves if the bargaining process were to break down. But A_2 no longer needs to remain in isolation after refusing to trade with B_2, and instead can trade with A_1, after A_1 has traded with B_1 at C and has therefore obtained some of good Y. The two As can share their stocks of X and Y equally, arriving at point P; such an equal division maximises their total utility.

By reaching point P, half way between C and E, the convexity of the indifference curves implies that they are both better off than anywhere on the no-trade indifference curve. The two As would be on a higher common indifference curve, and thus better off, if they could consume at a point along the line CPE which is to the north-west of point P. However, they do not have enough resources to move beyond the half-way point P.

Trader B_2, who has been isolated, cannot prevent such a bargain. Thus B_1 is at C, both As are at P and B_2 is at the initial endowment point E. In this situation B_1 has no incentive to change, but B_2 has a strong incentive to offer a better deal to one of the As than the one offered by trader B_1. So long as B_2 offers one of the As, say A_2, a trade on the contract curve which allows A_2 to reach a higher indifference curve than U'_A, the initial agreement with B_1 will be broken and recontracting will take place.

The implication is that the ability of the As to turn to someone else, rather than deal with a single trader, means that the Bs now compete against each other. However trader B_1, who cannot prevent the recontracting, has an incentive to make yet a better offer. Hence, the recontracting process continues. The stylised process of recontracting with the two Bs competing against each other will produce a final settlement at the point C^* in Figure 32.2. This has the property that the indifference curve U'''_A passes through C^* and P^*, where P^* is half way between C^* and E. This means that the two As are indifferent between C^* and P^*, and since they cannot both reach any point between C^* and P^* along the line C^*E, they are unable to improve on C^*. Hence there is no need to leave one of the Bs in isolation and the two Bs will trade with the two As at point C^*.

This argument has shown that at the final settlement all traders are at a common point on the contract curve and the limit has moved inwards along the old contract curve. The analysis can be repeated by starting with an alternative situation whereby the As are initially assumed to be able to appropriate all the gains from trade. The point C' would then no longer qualify as a point on the new contract curve. The introduction of the additional pair of traders means that the contract curve shrinks, and the range of indeterminacy involved in barter is correspondingly reduced.

The extent to which the contract curve shrinks when the additional pair of traders is introduced is influenced by the fact that the As cannot get further than half way along a ray from a point on the contract curve to the endowment position. However, if there are three pairs of As and three pairs of Bs, the repetition of the above analysis involves two of the

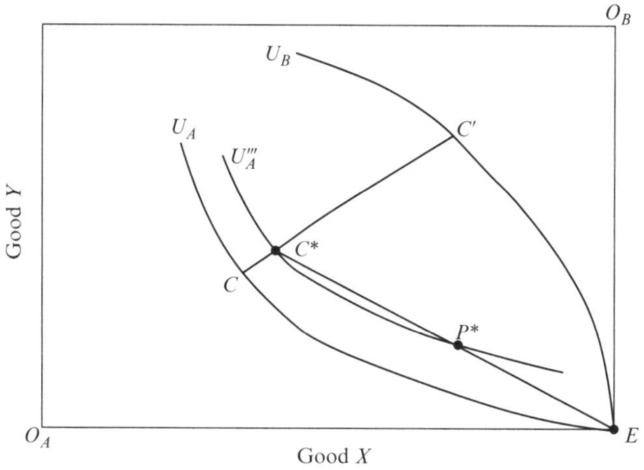

Figure 32.2 The new limit to the contract curve

*A*s dealing with two of the *B*s at a point on the contract curve. The two *A*s then share their resources equally with the remaining *A* while the third *B* is isolated. The *A*s are able to consume together at a point which is two-thirds of the way along the ray from the initial endowment position to the point on the contract curve where the trade involving the two *A*s and two *B*s takes place.

With N pairs, the *A*s can reach a proportion $(N-1)/N$ of the way from the endowment point to the contract curve: as N increases, this approaches unity. This means that the *A*s can reach all the way from E to the contract curve, so that the final settlement must be such that the indifference curve is tangential to the ray from the origin. A final settlement with many traders is therefore shown in Figure 32.3 as point P on the contract curve. The effect of working in from the point C' would lead to an equivalent result for an indifference curve of the *B*s, shown as U_B^*.

The result is that the final settlement looks just like a price-taking equilibrium. The figure illustrates the case where there is a single price-taking equilibrium. If there are multiple equilibria, the recontracting process causes the number of final settlements, with sufficiently large N, to shrink to the number of price-taking equilibria. This argument relating to the shrinking contract curve, first established by Edgeworth, is often referred to as the limit theorem.

Given that coalitions among traders are allowed in the recontracting process, a price-taking equilibrium cannot be blocked by a coalition of traders. In this sense the competitive equilibrium is robust. The argument

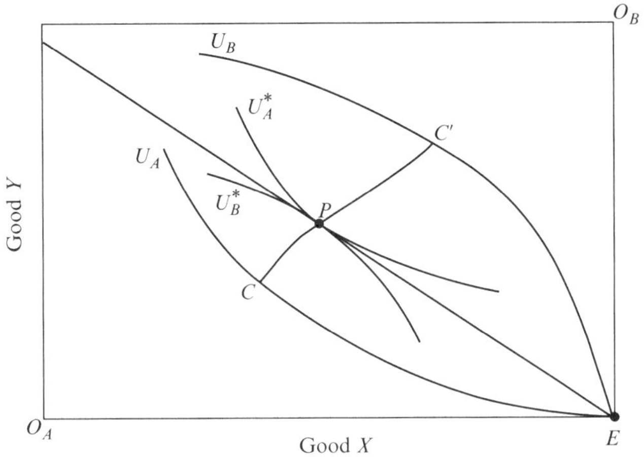

Figure 32.3 Final settlement with many traders

that a complex process of bargaining among a large number of individuals produces a result which replicates a price-taking equilibrium, allowing for the free flow of information using recontracting and enabling coalitions of traders to form and break up, is an important result that is far from intuitively obvious. The recontracting process can be said to represent a competitive process, and the contract curve shrinks essentially because of the competition between suppliers of the same good, although it is carried out in a barter framework in which explicit prices are not used.

The price-taking equilibrium, in contrast, does not actually involve a competitive process. Individuals simply believe that they must take market prices as given and outside their control. They respond to those prices without any reference to other individuals. But the result is that the price-taking equilibrium looks just like a situation in which all activity is perfectly co-ordinated.

NOTE

1. See *The Edgeworth box diagram*, and on further background, see Creedy (1986).

REFERENCES

Creedy, J. (1986), *Edgeworth and the Development of Neoclassical Economics*, Oxford: Basil Blackwell.

Edgeworth, F. Y. (1881), *Mathematical Psychics: An Essay on the Application of Mathematics to the Moral Sciences*, London: Kegan Paul.
Jevons, W. S. (1871/1957), *The Theory of Political Economy*, 5th edition, edited by H. S. Jevons, New York: Augustus Kelly.

33. Production possibilities frontiers

Ronald W. Jones

The concept of a production possibilities frontier is frequently used in applied areas of general equilibrium theory (such as international trade). It is the locus of maximal production points in an economy with a given technology and resource (input) base. References to the frontier were made in the early 1930s by Viner (1937), Lerner (1932), Leontief (1933), and Haberler (1936), but credit for its use two decades previously should go to Barone (1908) and, in a different context, to Irving Fisher (1907).[1]

Figure 33.1 illustrates the concept by the curve *FAIDBG* for the case in which two goods, *X* and *Y*, are produced by an economy, with flexible constant returns to scale technology.[2] Along this curve there is full employment (here this assume a pair of mobile factors, labor and capital). Points lying northeast of the curve (for example, *C*) denote outputs unattainable given the resource limitations. At any point, the slope of the production possibilities frontier shows literally how much of commodity *Y* must be sacrificed in order to produce another unit of commodity *X*, that is, the marginal opportunity cost of producing *X*. In competitive markets, this slope reveals the relative commodity price, p_X/p_Y.

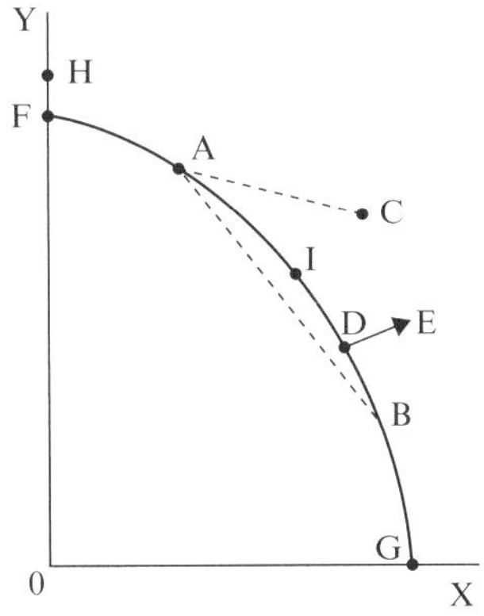

Figure 33.1 The production possibilities curve

The curvature of the frontier can be established in Figure 33.1 by considering an arbitrary pair of points, *A* and *B*. Techniques of production for both commodities at these points are assumed to be different. Consider any point on the connecting chord, say the midway point, obtained by using half the resource base with techniques used at *A* and the remaining half using techniques found at *B*. Such an allocation would not be optimal. The reason? Convex technologies (bowed-in isoquants) imply that it never pays to produce a commodity with two different techniques at the same time – an intermediate capital/labor ratio would be superior, for example, with production at point *I*. As a consequence, the production possibilities curve is strictly bowed out in this case.

SPECIAL SHAPES FOR PRODUCTION POSSIBILITIES FRONTIERS

There are several special shapes for production possibilities frontiers:

1. The Ricardian case: If there is only a single homogenous production factor required (say labor) and constant returns prevail, production possibilities are shown by a downward-sloping straight line, for example, a line connecting points *F* and *G* in Figure 33.1.
2. The 'endowment' case: If there are two productive factors, fixed in supply, and each is used exclusively in a single sector, the transformation curve is box-shaped, for example, formed by a horizontal line to point *I* in Figure 33.1, and a vertical drop from point *I*.
3. The case of increasing returns to scale: If *X* and *Y* both have increasing returns to scale technologies, and if there is a single factor (such as labor), the production possibilities frontier is bowed in towards the origin. However, if there are two (or more) productive factors and flexible technology, the tendency for the transformation schedule to be bowed out in the constant returns to scale case (as along *FAIDBG* in Figure 33.1) works against the bowed-in shape. A simple case: Increasing returns in the *X*-sector, the outcome of a fixed cost and a constant marginal cost of production, and constant returns to scale in the *Y* sector. Both sectors use only a homogeneous labor input. Maximal *Y* production is *0H*, which must be lowered to *0F* before any positive production of *X* can take place (the fixed costs of producing *X*), with constant marginal costs in *X* and in *Y* leading to a straight line connecting *F* and *G*. The locus would possess the 'bowed-in' shape, *HFG*.[3]
4. Higher Dimensions: Figure 33.2 illustrates production possibilities for a country in the three-dimensional case with constant returns to scale.

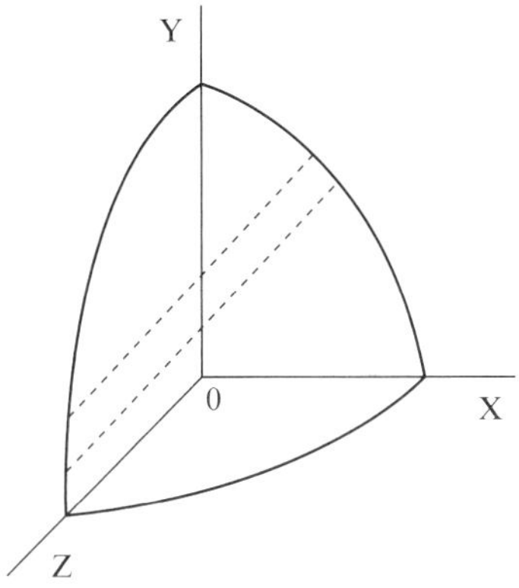

Figure 33.2 A ruled surface: three goods, two inputs

If there were only one homogenous input, the frontier would be a plane and positive production of all three commodities would only be possible if both commodity price ratios correspond to the slope of the plane. If there were three (or more) inputs required, the surface would be strictly bowed out. However, if there were only two inputs, the transformation surface would be ruled: A price plane would be tangent to the surface not at a single point, but along a linear 'rule' as illustrated by the dashed loci in Figure 33.2, with factor prices, and thus techniques, completely determined by a given set of commodity prices.

SHIFTS IN PRODUCTION-POSSIBILITIES CURVES

Changes in endowment levels, technology, or factor mobility all affect the position of a country's production-possibilities frontier:

1. If returns to scale are constant and techniques unchanged, a proportional increase in all endowments will alter commodity outputs by the same proportional amount.
2. In the 2x2 case with no joint production (each output is produced in a separate process), how do outputs adjust if there is an expansion in only a single input? If commodity prices are given, techniques are uniquely determined and therefore as a single input grows, the commodity using that input relatively intensively must expand, with the other commodity actually contracting to free up more of the non-expanding input (*A* to *C* in Figure 33.1). This is the famous Rybczynski Theorem (1955) in the theory of international trade.

3. In the Specific Factors Model (Jones, 1971 and Samuelson, 1971), production in each of a pair of sectors requires a type of capital not used in the other sector as well as labor drawn from a national labor market. If the labor endowment were to expand, so would production of both commodities if prices were constant. If one sector's capital stock could, over time, be converted into the type used in the other sector, the production possibilities frontier changes position. The envelope of such specific-capital frontiers would resemble the frontier shown in Figure 33.1, a Heckscher-Ohlin 2x2 model with mobile capital. The argument is made by Mayer (1974) and Neary (1978).

COMMODITY AGGREGATES OR COMPOSITES

A Composite Traded Commodity

Suppose a country can produce many goods (here limited to two: 1,2) that are traded at fixed prices on world markets, along with a commodity that cannot be traded internationally (call it *N*). For traded commodities, it is possible to consider a (Hicksian) composite traded commodity, (call it *T*), for convenience taken to be the value (at world prices) of the composite. Depending on the relative price of *N*, only one or both tradeables may be produced. Figure 33.3 illustrates that there is a commodity price ratio (p_N/p_T) for which both traded goods can be produced, thus locking in the wage/rental ratio for finite changes in the volume of the non-tradeable, leading to a changed composition of production of the two tradeables along a flat.

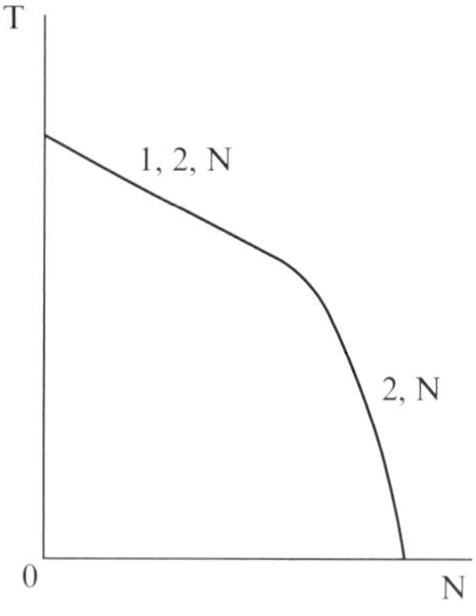

Figure 33.3 Traded and non-traded goods

Monopolistic Competition and the Gains from Trade

So-called 'New Trade Theory' (see for example Helpman and Krugman, 1985) highlights the case in which a country produces a number of varieties of the commodity in each sector (say two, *X* and *Y*), with a Chamberlinian type of monopolistic competition. Indeed, suppose a composite aggregate is possible for each sector, assuming the costs of any variety are identical – a fixed cost element and constant marginal costs. In autarky, suppose technology and endowments yield production point *D* in Figure 33.1. A move to free trade allows consumers a wider variety of goods in both the *X* and *Y* sectors, and for this given bundle of resources, forces a lowering of the number of varieties in each sector, thus reducing aggregate fixed costs and lengthening production runs. The consequence: aggregate production of the *X* and *Y* sectors expands with trade, from point *D* to, say, point *E* in Figure 33.1. That is, trade not only allows movements along budget lines to attain higher utility levels, it also makes possible an expansion of the production possibilities frontier.[4]

COUNTRY AGGREGATES: WORLD PRODUCTION POSSIBILITIES CURVES

Production possibilities frontiers can be constructed for country aggregates. Figure 33.4 illustrates for the Ricardian case a world production possibilities frontier for three countries, A, B, and C.[5] Inter-country mobility of some one or more factors can be accommodated in a world frontier, with not only each country producing commodities efficiently but each

Figure 33.4 Multi-country schedule

producing according to comparative advantage for factors not mobile internationally and factors with such mobility located according to absolute advantage (Jones, 2000, ch. 2).

NOTES

1. See the defense of Barone's claim presented by Maneschi and Thweatt (1987).
2. Although absent in traditional discussions, the possibility of joint production techniques as well as background integrated intermediate production is consistent with the concept of the production possibilities curve. As mentioned later, here there is no international trade in intermediates or factor movements.
3. An early discussion of the shape of the production possibilities frontier when there are increasing returns to scale is that of Herberg and Kemp (1969).
4. See Caves, Frankel and Jones (2007, ch. 7).
5. See McKenzie (1954) and Jones (1961), for illustrations of world production possibilities for the three-commodity case. Ruffin (1988) has a reinterpretation of the Ricardian model. There may be many varieties of labor in the world economy, and a single country may have, say, endowments of three such varieties, with a country transformation curve such as in Figure 33.4. This version of Ricardo leads to a simple Heckscher-Ohlin setting.

REFERENCES

Barone, Enrico (1908): *Principi di economia politica*, Tipografia Nazionale di G. Bertero, Rome.

Caves, Richard, Jeffrey Frankel and Ronald Jones (2007): *World Trade and Payments*, Addison Wesley, Boston, MA.

Fisher, Irving (1907): *The Rate of Interest*, Macmillan, New York.

Haberler, Gottfried (1936): *The Theory of International Trade*, Wm Hodge and Co, London.

Helpman, Elhanan and Paul Krugman (1985): *Market Structure and Foreign Trade*, MIT Press, Cambridge, MA.

Herberg, Horst and Murray Kemp (1969): 'Some Implications of Variable Returns to Scale', *Canadian Journal of Economics*, v. II, n. 3, pp. 413–15.

Jones, Ronald W. (1961): 'Comparative Advantage and the Theory of Tariffs: A Multi-Country Multi-Commodity Model', *Review of Economic Studies*, v. 28, pp. 161–75.

Jones, Ronald W. (1971): 'A Three Factor Model in Theory, Trade and History', Ch. 1 in Bhagwati, J. N., R. W Jones, R. A. Mundell and J. Vanek (eds), *Trade, Balance of Payments and Growth*, North-Holland, Amsterdam.

Jones, Ronald W. (2000): *Globalization and the Theory of Input Trade*, MIT Press, Cambridge, MA.

Leontief, Wassily (1933): 'The Use of Indifference Curves in the Analysis of Foreign Trade', *Quarterly Journal of Economics*, v. 47, pp. 493–503.

Lerner, Abba (1932): 'The Diagrammatic Representation of Cost Conditions in International Trade', *Economica*, N.S. v. 1, pp. 319–34.

Maneschi, Andrea and William Thweatt (1987): 'Barone's 1908 Representation

of an Economy's Trade Equilibrium and the Gains from Trade', *Journal of International Economics*, v. 22, pp. 375–82.
Mayer, Wolfgang (1974): 'Short-run and Long-run Equilibrium for a Small Open Economy', *Journal of Political Economy*, v. 82, pp. 955–67.
McKenzie, Lionel (1954): 'Specialization and Efficiency in World Production', *Review of Economic Studies*, v. 21, pp. 165–80.
Neary, J. Peter (1978): 'Short-run Capital Specificity and the Pure Theory of International Trade', *Economic Journal*, v. 88, pp. 488–510.
Ruffin, Roy J. (1988): 'The Missing Link: The Ricardian Approach to the Factor Endowments Theory of Trade', *American Economic Review*, v. 78, pp. 759–72.
Rybczynski, T. M. (1955): 'Factor Endowments and Relative Commodity Prices', *Economica*, v. 22, pp. 336–41.
Samuelson, Paul A. (1971): 'Ohlin was Right', *Swedish Journal of Economics*, v. 73, pp. 365–84.
Viner, Jacob (1937): *Studies in the Theory of International Trade*, Allen and Unwin, London.

34. The utility-possibility frontier

John S. Chipman

The concept of a utility-possibility frontier was defined independently by Allais (1943, pp. 640–2) and Samuelson (1947, pp. 244–5).[1] Allais's work, which contained numerous diagrams, did not become publicly available until the 1954 edition. Samuelson's 1947 exposition defined a 'possibility function' $P(U^1, U^2, \ldots, U^S) = 0$, which 'says that we may specify at will the levels of well-being of all but one of the individuals, and the last one's well-being is uniquely determined'. It did not include a diagram, but it led to three diagrams subsequently introduced by Graaff (1949–50), followed (evidently quite independently of Graaff) by three diagrams containing utility-possibility curves introduced by Samuelson himself (1950). Since the diagrams of Graaff and Samuelson have proved to be the most influential in the subsequent literature, they and the expositions that they stimulated will be discussed first. Three expositions by Allais will be discussed in the following section, and some later developments in the final section.

1. THE CONTRIBUTIONS AND INFLUENCE OF SAMUELSON AND GRAAFF

Stimulated by Samuelson (1947), Graaff (1949–50) used the concept of a 'possibility locus' to show that an 'optimal tariff' policy (of course barring foreign retaliation) would unambiguously improve a country's 'potential welfare', in the sense that with the possibility of lump-sum distributions of taxes and tariff revenues, all individuals' welfares could be improved. He illustrated (Figure 1, p. 48) Samuelson's 'possibility locus' by a two-dimensional graph. He contrasted a case of a 'twist' in which two of the possibility loci intersect, with a 'shift' in which one of them lies wholly outside of the other (Figure 2, p. 50). His paper showed that the possibility locus corresponding to the optimal tariff lies entirely outside that of free trade, whereas the criterion introduced by Scitovsky (1941), for example, would have allowed the curves to cross.

Samuelson's seminal 1950 treatment emerged from his dissatisfaction

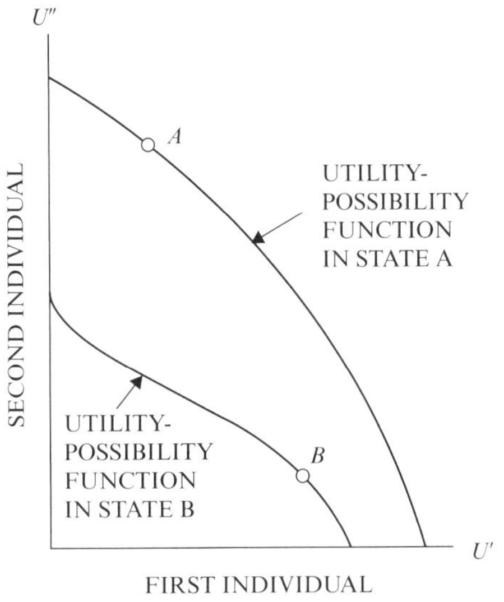

Source: Adapted from Samuelson (1950)

Figure 34.1 Graaff's depiction of Samuelson's 1947 'possibility locus'

with the debate between Hicks (1940) and Kuznets (1948), and others, concerning the proper way to gauge a change in a country's prosperity through measures of 'real social income'. To gauge what could be meant by an increase in this concept he produced the famous diagram (Figure 4 in Samuelson 1950, adapted in Figure 34.1 here) depicting for the two-person case the utility levels U' and U'' of the two individuals on the two axes, corresponding to a case (denoted A) in which more of fixed quantities of both goods are available for distribution to the two individuals than in the other case (denoted B), even though the two individuals are not necessarily both better off in state A than in state B, it being assumed that in each case the individuals at the observed time are in competitive equilibrium. He showed that in general, if more of one good were available under one alternative than another for allocation between the two individuals, but less of the other good under the other alternative, then the utility-possibility curves would necessarily cross (Figure 6 in Samuelson 1950, adapted in Figure 34.2 here), and no unequivocal statement could be made. He emphasized (p. 5) that if an ethical judgment, could be expressed in terms of a Bergsonian social welfare function, then from different ethical judgment contradictory conclusions could be drawn in the case in which the curves cross. He based his analysis on the assumption

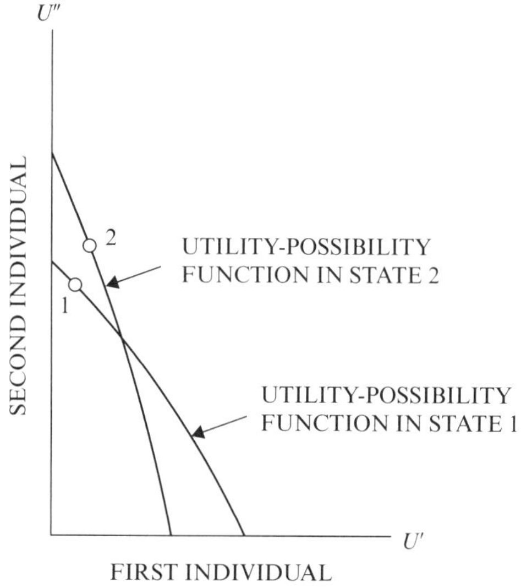

Source: Adapted from Samuelson (1950)

Figure 34.2 Samuelson's 1950 depiction of crossing 'utility possibility functions'

that the observed data points refer in each case to a regime of competitive equilibrium; thus, the points on a utility-possibility frontier correspond to points on Edgeworth's 'contract curve' in the so-called Edgeworth box, all of which are Pareto-optimal competitive equilibria.

The above analysis applies to what Samuelson called a 'point' utility-possibility curve corresponding to distribution of fixed quantities; but he also introduced the concept of a 'situation' utility-possibility frontier in which one is comparing two alternative sets of available quantities, for example, production-possibility sets.

These concepts were soon applied by Samuelson (1955, p. 352, Chart 4, Figure 34.3 here) to the theory of optimal public expenditure, in which one of the two goods is a 'public good' which is shared by all. Here, he displayed a utility-possibility set (containing non-Pareto optimal points) with a partially concave frontier and three superimposed social indifference curves, one of which was tangential to this set, corresponding to the so-called Lindahl-Bowen optimal solution.

The foremost subsequent applications of this methodology were to the theory of international trade. Kenen (1957), who allowed for production adjustments, defined a 'situation' utility-possibility curve as an envelope

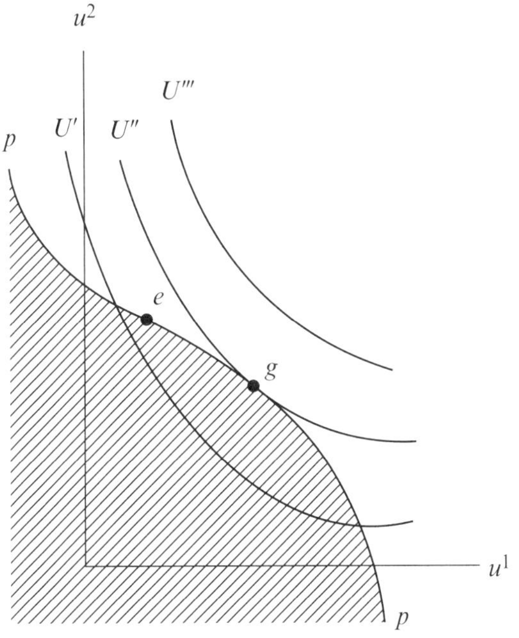

Source: Samuelson (1955)

Figure 34.3 Samuelson's 1955 depiction of a utility possibility set with superimposed social indifference curves

of 'point' utility-possibility curves. He also used this technique to prove the superiority of free trade to autarky; this was done (p. 440) by maximizing one person's utility whilst assuming the other's to remain constant, in accordance with Samuelson's 1947 definition (and consistently with Lange's 1942 procedure). Kenen's analysis was followed by those of both Kemp (1962) and Samuelson himself (1962), showing that the utility-possibility frontier corresponding to a country's free-trade situation lies outside that of autarky. In the latter paper (p. 823*n*) Samuelson cited Graaff's attribution (1957, p. 59) of the 'utility-possibility function' independently to Allais (1943) and to Samuelson (1947).

2. THE CONTRIBUTION OF MAURICE ALLAIS

Allais (1943, p. 616bis) introduced a concept of 'social return' (*rendement social*), which he said was of 'qualitative order' and not expressible

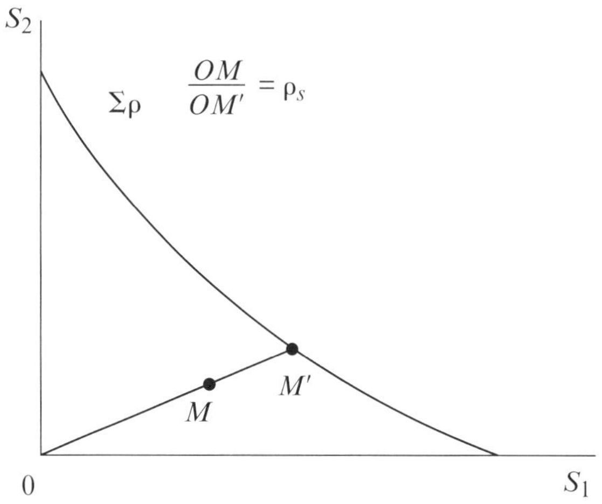

Source: Allais (1943)

Figure 34.4 Allais's 1943 depiction of a 'surface of maximum return'

numerically, but whose use was 'particularly convenient', and which on Paretian principles should be maximized. Later (p. 641) he remarked that an 'intrinsic definition' of social return was impossible owing to the lack of a criterion for comparing different individuals' satisfactions, but that it would be useful to provide a 'conventional definition' of the social return as follows: in the space of the 'satisfactions' S_i of n individuals (his terminology for utilities, assumed to be positive), given a 'representative point' M of (positive) satisfactions, the maximum possible point M' along a ray through M defines a point on the 'surface of maximum return' (his Figure 2 on p. 641, Figure 34.4 here). This defines that surface, and is thus equivalent to Samuelson's utility-possibility frontier. He defined the ratio $\rho_S = M/M'$ as the 'social return'; it formed the basis for the 'coefficient of resource utilization' introduced by Debreu (1951). Note from Figure 34.4 that Allais gave this surface a convex shape. A Benthamist might thus conclude that the social optimum was one of complete inequality (of this, more below).

Allais's analysis was further developed in Allais (1947, pp. 151–167). His diagram (p. 158), reproduced in Figure 34.5, which he described as the 'curve of social return', now dispensed with the ray from the origin, and he described this curve as the limit of the set of economically possible states R' (p. 157n), the region R'' by implication being the set of impossible ones. The curve retained the convex shape.

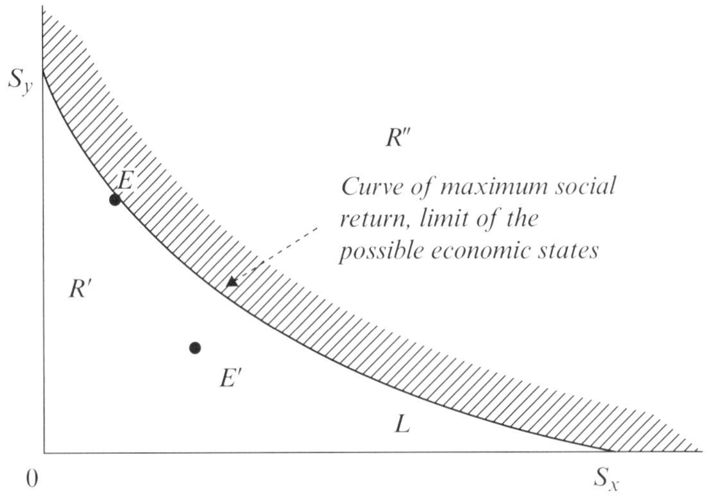

Source: Allais (1947)

Figure 34.5 Allais's 1947 depiction of a 'curve of maximum social return'

Allais's 1978 essay contains (pp. 176–7) a striking attack on Samuelson, condemning him for not, except in a footnote (Samuelson 1962, p. 823n3), having referred directly to Allais's diagrams of 1943 and 1947:

> In 1950 . . ., then in 1955 . . ., and again in 1956 . . ., Samuelson made extensive use of the graphical representation that I published in 1943. He made no reference to my two books (1943) . . .and (1947) . . ., which I sent him during the summer of 1947 and which we discussed in October 1947 during my visit to his M.I.T. office.

One can sympathize with Samuelson's not having taken the time to go through the 920 pages of Allais (1943) and the 800 pages of Allais (1947) as a precondition of commenting on the controversies of the time concerning 'real social income'. But it may be significant that the diagram presented in Allais (1978, p. 176, Figure 34.6 here) was substantially different from the two previous ones in not retaining the convexity and in emphasizing the zones of possibility and impossibility. But Samuelson's concept was not, unlike Allais's, intended only as a property of a Pareto-optimal state of a stationary closed economy with given factor endowments, but rather as a property of a particular state of a changing economy at a particular time under particular institutional conditions. Samuelson's and Graaff's central themes were the comparison of alternative states (such as countries

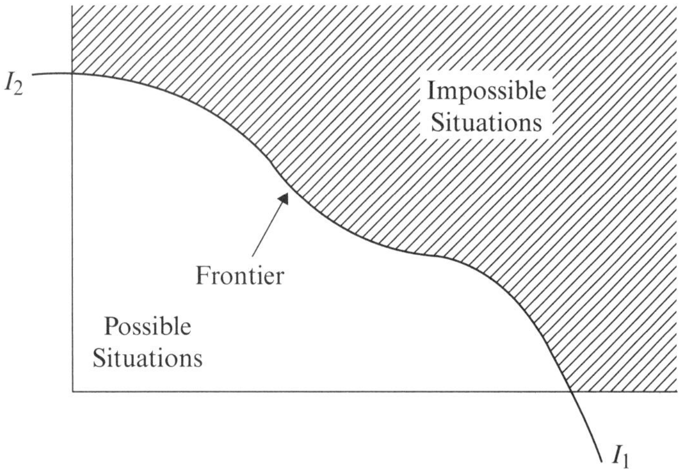

Source: Allais (1978)

Figure 34.6 Allais's 1978 depiction of the frontier separating possible from impossible situations

at different times and free trade versus autarky) and the ranking of different (Pareto-optimal) utility-possibility frontiers corresponding to such different times or institutional arrangements. Samuelson's concept was thus a tool for comparing different arrangements rather than a way of describing a particular one. Comparisons of alternative states were indeed discussed by Allais (1943, p. 645), and his 'social-return ratio' provided such a comparison, but limited to a particular ray from the origin as opposed to comparisons of alternative utility-possibility frontiers.

3. SUBSEQUENT CONTRIBUTIONS

As mentioned above, if the utility-possibility frontier has a convex rather than concave shape as in Allais (1943, 1947), then maximization of a linear Benthamist social-welfare function would lead to complete inequality as an optimal social solution. Since both Allais and Samuelson assumed utilities to be ordinal, the question arises as to what constraints can be imposed on the shapes of both the utility-possibility frontiers and the social indifference curves so as to avoid this dilemma.

Samuelson had argued (1950, p. 29) that his social indifference curves are quasi-concave. But Graaff (1957, pp. 48–51, 163) showed that a social-welfare function need not be quasi-concave even if the individual utility functions are. Later, Samuelson mentioned (in Stiglitz 1966, p. 1072) that Graaff had pointed out to him that he 'must introduce an extra (and arbitrary) axiom' to ensure this result. Gorman (1959, p. 489) introduced such an axiom, namely that the individual utility functions be not only quasi-concave, but actually concave (which is a cardinal property). Negishi (1963) provided a succinct argument, referring to Arrow and Hurwicz (1960, p. 72n46) for 'weak regularity conditions' under which a quasi-concave function can be represented by a concave one – conditions due to De Finetti (1949), who provided an example of a quasi-concave function which is not 'concavifiable' (see Kannai, 1977, p. 5), namely $U(x_1, x_2) = x_1/(2 - x_2)$ for $0 \leq x_1 < \infty$ and $0 \leq x_2 < 2$. A similar problem arises with the utility-possibility sets themselves, that is, the sets of possible points in the utility space, bounded by the utility-possibility frontier. Kannai and Mantel (1978) produced an example in the three-individual case in which these sets are not 'convexifiable', hence maximization of even a quasi-concave social utility function might still lead to an inegalitarian solution.

In short, one must return to cardinal utility in welfare economics in order to ensure plausible egalitarian results with the techniques of utility-possibility frontiers and social welfare functions.

ACKNOWLEDGEMENTS

I thank Augustine Mok and Heidi Weitzer for composing the diagrams.

NOTE

1. Of course, the concept goes back to Pareto (1902, p. 422), who spoke of the 'locus of maximum ophelimities', though his diagrammatic analysis was in the space of trades, as in Edgeworth. More explicitly, Lange (1942, p. 216), who did not use diagrams, defined welfare to be a maximum 'when it is impossible to increase the utility of any person without decreasing that of others', which of course is the Pareto criterion. Samuelson (1955, p. 352) correctly described the utility-possibility frontier as the 'utility frontier of Pareto-optimal points'. The set of possible points has come to be known as the 'Pareto set' (Kannai and Mantel 1978).

REFERENCES

Allais, Maurice (1943), *A la recherche d'une discipline économique*, Vol. I and Annexes, mimeo. Reissued with a printed introduction as *Traité d'Économie Pure*, [Paris]: Imprimerie Nationale, 1954, 5 volumes.

Allais, Maurice (1947), *Économie et intérêt*, 2 vols. Paris: Imprimerie Nationale.
Allais, Maurice (1978), 'Theories of General Economic Equilibrium and Economic Efficiency', in Gerhard Schwödiauer (ed.), *Equilibrium and Disequilibrium in Economic Theory*, Dordrecht: D. Reidel Publishing Company, 129–201.
Arrow, Kenneth J. and Hurwicz, Leonid (1960), 'Decentralization and Computation in Resource Allocation', in R. W. Pfouts (ed.), *Essays in Economics and Econometrics: A Volume in Honor of Harold Hotelling*, Chapel Hill, NC: The University of North Carolina Press, 34–104.
Debreu, Gérard (1951), 'The Coefficient of Resource Utilization', *Econometrica*, 19 (July), 273–92.
De Finetti, Bruno (1949), 'Sulle stratificazioni convesse', *Annali di Matematica Pura ed Applicata* [4], 30, 173–83.
Gorman, W. M. (1959), 'Are Social Indifference Curves Convex?' *Quarterly Journal of Economics*, 73 (August), 485–96.
Graaff, J. de V. (1949–50), 'On Optimal Tariff Structures', *Review of Economic Studies*, 17 (No. 1), 47–59.
Graaff, J. de V. (1957), *Theoretical Welfare Economics*, Cambridge: Cambridge University Press.
Hicks, J. R. (1940), 'The Valuation of the Social Income', *Economica*, N.S., 7 (May), 105–24.
Kannai, Yakar (1977), 'Concavifiability and Constructions of Concave Utility Functions', *Journal of Mathematical Economics*, 4, 1–56.
Kannai, Yakar and Rolf Mantel (1978), 'Non-Convexifiable Pareto Sets', *Econometrica*, 46 (May), 571–75.
Kemp, Murray C. (1962), 'The Gain from International Trade', *Economic Journal*, 72 (December), 803–19.
Kenen, Peter B. (1957), 'On the Geometry of Welfare Economics', *Quarterly Journal of Economics*, 71 (August), 426–47.
Kuznets, Simon (1948), 'On the Valuation of Social Income: – Reflections on Professor Hicks' article', *Economica*, N.S., 15 (February, May), 1–16, 116–31.
Lange, Oscar (1942), 'The Foundations of Welfare Economics', *Econometrica*, 10 (July–October), 215–28.
Negishi, Takashi (1963), 'On Social Welfare Function', *Quarterly Journal of Economics*, 77 (February), 156–8.
Pareto, Vilfredo (1902), 'Di un nuovo errore nello interpretare le teorie dell'economia matematica', *Giornale degli Economisti* [2], 25 (November), 401–33. English translation, 'On a New Error in the Interpretation of the Theories of Mathematical Economics', *Giornale degli Economisti e Annali di Economia*, 67 (December 2008), 515–44.
Samuelson, Paul A. (1947), *Foundations of Economic Analysis*, Cambridge, MA: Harvard University Press.
Samuelson, Paul A. (1950), 'Evaluation of Real National Income', *Oxford Economic Papers*, N.S., 2 (January), 1–29. Reprinted (with an addition) in Stiglitz (1966), 1044–72.
Samuelson, Paul A. (1955), 'Diagrammatic Exposition of a Theory of Public Expenditure', *Review of Economics and Statistics*, 37 (November), 350–56.
Samuelson, Paul A. (1956), 'Social Indifference Curves', *Quarterly Journal of Economics*, 70 (February), 1–22.
Samuelson, Paul A. (1962), 'The Gains from International Trade Once Again', *Economic Journal*, 72 (December), 820–29.

Scitovsky [de Scitovszky], Tibor (1941), 'A Note on Welfare Propositions in Economics', *Review of Economic Studies*, 9 (November), 77–88.
Stiglitz, Joseph E. (ed) (1966), *The Colleted Scientific Papers of Paul A. Samuelson*, Vol. 2, Cambridge, MA: MIT Press.

35. The factor price frontier

Alan D. Woodland

1. INTRODUCTION

The factor price frontier diagram had its origins in the theory of growth but has become a useful tool in the theory of international trade. The factor price frontier is a relationship between factor prices that are consistent with equilibrium in an economy. It has different levels of sophistication and interpretation. It can simply refer to the combinations of factor prices that yield zero profit for a single good, in which case it is an isocost curve in factor price space. It can also be combinations of factor prices that are consistent with equilibrium in the production sector of an economy, this manifestation being used extensively in the theory of international trade. More generally, it can be combinations of factor prices consistent with a general equilibrium for a closed economy or a closed world economy. Its most common use was to illustrate the relationship between the rate of profit and the wage rate in the steady state of a growth model.

2. THE FACTOR PRICE FRONTIER DIAGRAM

In this section, the factor price frontier diagram is constructed, and discussed, for the case of a competitive equilibrium in the production sector of a small open economy. The equilibrium conditions for the production sector are presented and described first. Then the diagram is constructed and discussed.

Assuming that goods are produced with factors only, and not intermediate inputs (which can be incorporated at the cost of simplicity), the equilibrium conditions for the production sector may be expressed as

$$c^j(w_1, w_2, \ldots, w_n) - p^j \geq 0 \leq y^j,\ j \in J \tag{35.1}$$

$$v_i - \sum_{j \in J} a_{ij} y^j \geq 0 \leq w_i,\ i \in I, \tag{35.2}$$

where $a_{ij} \equiv \partial c^j(w_1, w_2, \ldots, w_n)/\partial w_i$ is, assuming differentiability and by Shephard's (1953) Lemma, the cost-minimizing input of factor i per unit output of good j, $I = \{1, 2, \ldots, n\}$ is the set of factors of production, $J = \{1, 2, \ldots, m\}$ is the set of goods, and the double inequalities of the form $x \geq 0 \leq z$ is the convention for the complementary slackness condition $x \geq 0$, $z \geq 0$ and $xz = 0$. Together, these conditions determine factor prices $(w_1, w_2, \ldots, w_n)$ and product outputs $(y_1, y_2, \ldots, y_m)$ given the product prices $(p_1, p_2, \ldots, p_m)$ and the factor endowments $(v_1, v_2, \ldots, v_n)$. The first set comprise the profit maximization conditions for firms, while the second set (discussed further below) constitute the factor market equilibrium conditions.

The first set of conditions (35.1) constitute the profit maximization conditions for firms operating in perfectly competitive input and output markets. Condition (35.1) states that the unit cost of production of good j must be at least as great as the unit price of that good, meaning that profit cannot be positive. The Kuhn-Tucker (complementary slackness) conditions imply that goods actually produced yield zero profit and that goods yielding a negative profit will not be produced.

The second set of conditions (35.2) constitute the factor market equilibrium (market clearing) conditions. Thus, (35.2) states that the demand for factor i, given by $\Sigma_{j \in J} a_{ij} y^j$, cannot exceed the fixed endowment, v_i, of that factor. The complementary slackness conditions imply that demand will exactly equal the available supply for a factor when the equilibrium factor price is positive; and an excess supply for factor i is only consistent with equilibrium if its price is zero ($w_i = 0$).

Together, conditions (35.1) and (35.2) describe the equilibrium for the production sector. All firms maximize profits and factor markets clear, thus determining the factor prices and output levels.

The factor price diagram for the production sector summarizes the relationship between factor prices that are consistent with equilibrium in the production sector. Accordingly, this diagram is derived primarily from the profit maximization conditions (35.1). For consistency with production sector equilibrium, it is evident from (35.1) that the factor price vector $w = (w_1, w_2, \ldots, w_n)$ must be such that $c^j(w_1, w_2, \ldots, w_n) - p^j \geq 0$ for all goods $j \in J$. For a given vector of product prices $p = (p_1, p_2, \ldots, p_m)$, the factor price vector must be in the factor price set defined as

$$W(p) \equiv \{w\colon c^j(w) - p^j \geq 0, \quad j \in J, \quad w \geq 0\}. \tag{35.3}$$

This is the set of all factor prices that do not yield a positive profit in the production of any good.

The lower boundary of this set is what can be called the factor price

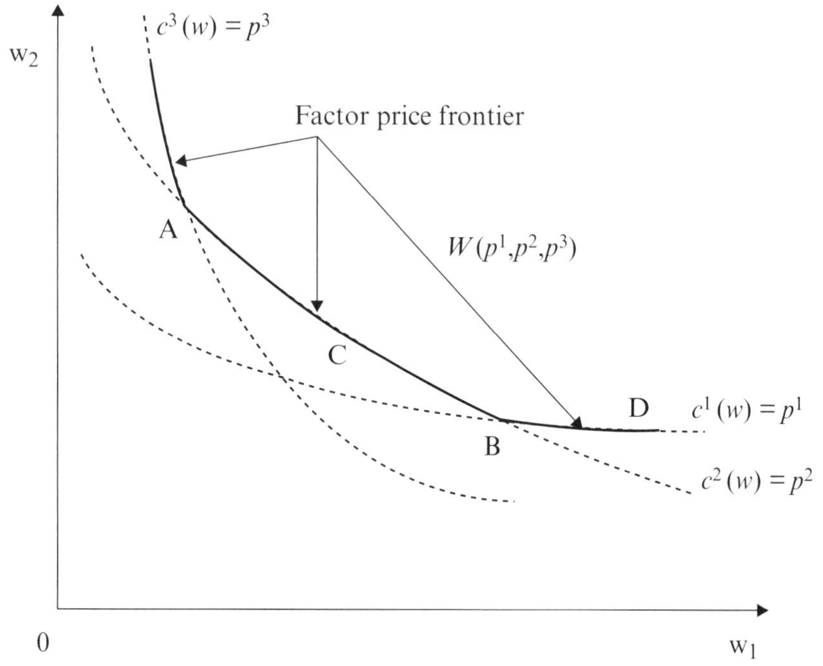

Figure 35.1 Factor price frontier with three goods and two factors

frontier, which may be interpreted as the smallest factor prices that are consistent with no good being producible at a positive profit. The frontier may be characterized formally as the solution to a family of constrained optimization problems. Thus

$$F(p, v) \equiv \arg\min_{w} \{w'v \colon c^j(w) - p^j \geq 0, \quad j \in J, \quad w \geq 0\} \qquad (35.4)$$

traces out the loci of factor price points that constitute the factor price frontier when the endowment vector $v \geq 0$ is varied parametrically. Alternatively, it can also be obtained by minimizing one factor price in the factor price set, conditional on the others being given, to yield the frontier in the form $w_1 = \omega(w_2, \ldots, w_n)$.

Figure 35.1 presents the factor price frontier for the special case where there are three goods and two factors of production. The figure represents equilibrium in the production sector of the economy. The diagram is drawn in factor price space, here (w_1, w_2). Depicted are three (dashed) curves, showing combinations of the two factor prices that yield zero profit (unit cost equal to price, $c^j(w) = p^j$) for each of the three goods.

These curves are isocost loci in factor price space. Factor prices northeast of these loci incur a loss while those southwest yield a profit.

The solid curve is the factor price frontier. Factor prices on and northeast of the factor price frontier constitute the factor price set $W(p)$ comprising factor price vectors that yield zero or negative profits, while those southwest allow a positive profit for at least one good. At point A on the factor price frontier, the factor price vector is such that goods 2 and 3 earn a zero profit (A is on the zero profit loci), while production of good 1 would incur a loss (A is above the zero profit locus for good 1). At this point, goods 2 and 3 can be produced in equilibrium. Similarly, at point B, goods 1 and 2 can be produced at zero profit, but production of good 3 incurs a loss. At points C and D, only one good can be produced (yields a zero profit), namely goods 2 and 1 respectively.

In summary, the factor price frontier is the set of factor prices that are consistent with profit maximization in a perfectly competitive context when the factor endowment vector is not known or specified. Above the frontier, factor prices are too high; production of any good entails a loss and so competitive forces will bid factor prices down until zero profits occur for at least one good. Below the frontier factor, prices are too low; production of some goods produces a positive profit and so competition amongst firms will bid up factor prices until the frontier is reached. Only on the frontier is it the case that competitive production sector equilibrium can occur.

The discussion thus far has focused on the profit maximization conditions (35.1) without explicit reference to the factor market equilibrium conditions (35.2). Clearly, factor price vectors on the factor price frontier are only interesting from an economics viewpoint if they are equilibrium factor price vectors and, in the present context, this also requires the factor market equilibrium conditions to be satisfied.

It turns out that the constrained optimization problem (35.4) provides the equilibrium factor price vector corresponding to the product price and factor endowment combination (p, v). This is illustrated in Figure 35.2. If the endowment vector is v (as shown with origin placed at point B), then the objective function in (35.4) reaches its smallest feasible value at point B where the line depicting the iso-objective function (perpendicular to v) touches the factor price frontier. That is, the constrained optimization problem (35.4) yields the solution for w at point B. At this solution, the equilibrium vectors of factors used in the two industries are shown in the figure as v^1 and v^2. By Shephard's Lemma, these vectors are normal (at right angle) to the respective isocost curves at the equilibrium price vector w. They sum to the endowment vector, v, thus forming the familiar parallelogram. In short, at point B, there is equilibrium in the production sector. Firms in industries 1 and 2 earn zero profits, while firms in industry

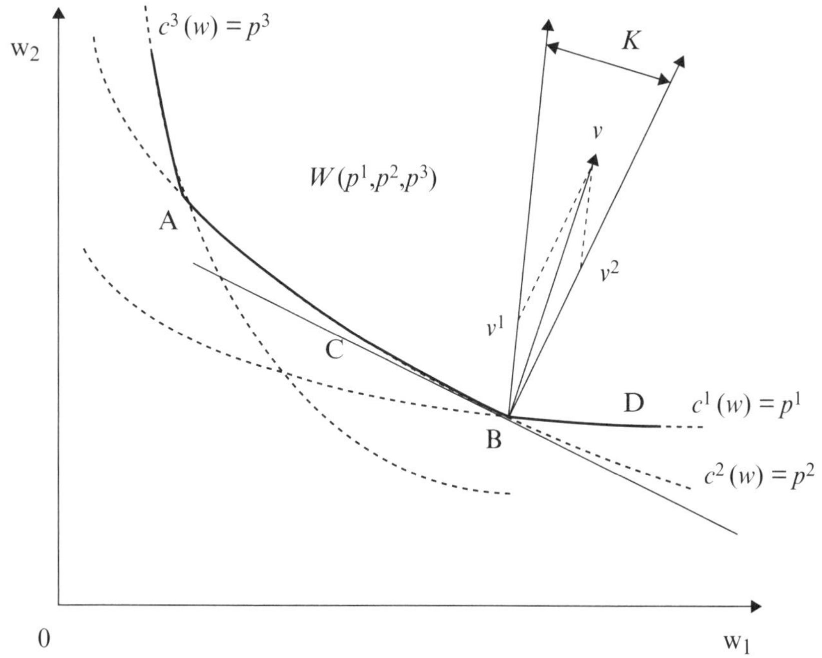

Figure 35.2 Factor market equilibrium with three goods and two factors

3 are unprofitable; and factor markets are in equilibrium since aggregate factor demand by industries 1 and 2 ($v^1 + v^2$) equals the factor endowment, v, meaning that factor markets clear.[1]

It should also be evident from this demonstration that each factor price vector on the factor price frontier will be an equilibrium factor price vector for some appropriate choice of the endowment vector. In other words, by varying the endowment vector, the solution to the constrained optimization problem (35.4) moves along the factor price frontier; conversely, for any factor price vector on the frontier, there is an endowment vector for which there is production sector equilibrium.

3. AN APPLICATION OF THE FACTOR PRICE FRONTIER

To illustrate the power and usefulness of the factor price frontier, consider how the frontier shifts in response to a change in one of the product prices.

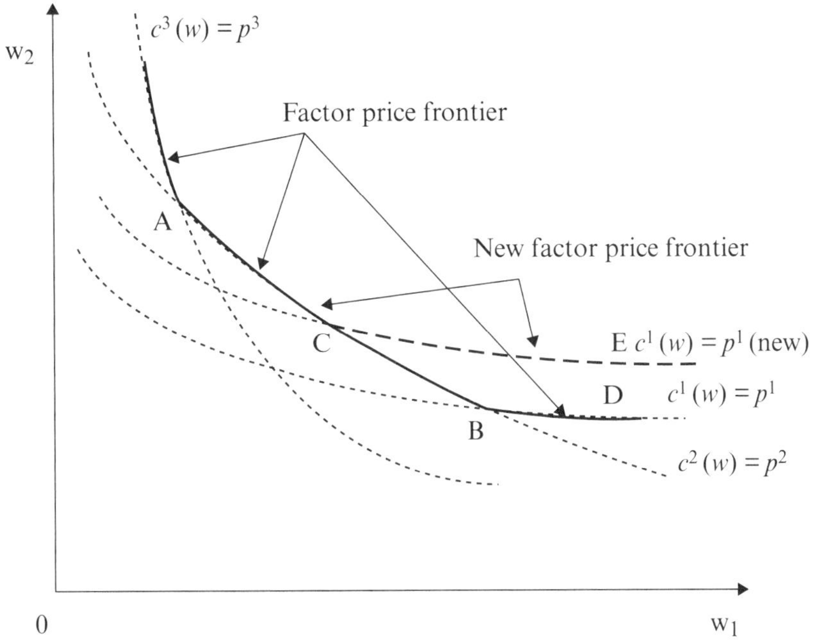

Figure 35.3 *Effect of a product price change on the factor price frontier with three goods and two factors*

This is depicted in Figure 35.3, which is derived from Figure 35.1. The additional contribution of Figure 35.3 is that it shows how the frontier shifts (partially) in response to an increase in the price of good 1. This increase in price shifts the isocost curve for good 1 upwards and to the right (specifically equi-proportionally outwards from the origin), meaning that higher factor prices are now required to prevent positive profits being made. The isocost curves for the other goods are unaffected, of course. The upshot is that the factor price frontier also (partially) shifts northeast and is now given by the old (solid) frontier through point *A* as far as point *C* and by the new dashed curve to the right of point *C* and passing through point *E*. The old portion from *C* to *B* to *D* is no longer relevant, as these factor prices would generate profits in the production of goods 1 and 2.

To illustrate how the diagram helps to demonstrate the Stolper-Samuelson theorem, suppose that the economy is initially at point *B* and that goods 1 and 2 are both produced (good 3 is not produced). The factor price vector on the new frontier allows these same two goods to be produced after the price change has moved to point *C*. Suppose further that the country's factor endowments are consistent with point C (see Woodland 1977 and 1982 for further details) so that point C constitutes the new equilibrium solution for factor prices. Then it follows that the increase in the price of good 1 has led to an increase in the price of factor 2 and a decrease in the price of factor 1. Since the proportionate increase in the price of factor 2 must be greater than the proportionate increase in the price of good 1, the Stolper-Samuelson theorem has been established; the real income (measured in either product price) has increased for the factor used relatively intensively in the production of the good experiencing the price rise (here factor 2), while the real income of the other factor falls.

If the initial equilibrium is at point A (or anywhere to the left of C), the increase in the price of good 1 (of the size depicted) has no effect on factor prices. Between B and C there will obviously be an effect on factor prices (and the production pattern) for a sufficiently large increase in the price of product 1.

4. EXTENSION TO GROWTH MODEL

To show how the factor price frontier diagram arises in a steady state growth context, consider a simple heterogeneous capital goods model. In this model, it is assumed that the production sector can produce a single consumption good (labelled 0) and m capital goods using labour and the capital goods as inputs using constant returns to scale technologies. Technical progress is ignored for simplicity. The unit cost functions are denoted $c^j(w_0, w_1, \ldots, w_m)$ for $j \in J = \{0, 1, \ldots, m\}$, where w_0 is the wage rate and w_i is the rental price of capital input i. The gross own rate of return to capital type i is denoted by $\rho_i = w_i/p^i$, which is the rental divided by the price. The net own rate of return to capital type i is given by $r_i = \rho_i - \delta_i$, where δ_i is the rate of depreciation. Thus, the rental rate arguments in the unit cost functions can be written as $w_i = (r_i + \delta_i)p^i$.

The profit maximization conditions may now be expressed as

$$c^j(w_0, (r_1 + \delta_1)\, p^1, \ldots, (r_m + \delta_m)\, p^m) - p^j \geq 0 \leq y^j, \quad j \in J. \tag{35.5}$$

If product prices are given (by world markets or by elsewhere in the economy), the factor price set can now be defined as

$$W(w_0, r) \equiv \{(w_0, r_1, \ldots, r_m): c^j(w_0, (r_1 + \delta_1)\, p^1, \ldots, (r_m + \delta_m)\, p^m) - p^j \geq 0, \; j \in J, \; (w_0, r) \geq 0\}, \tag{35.6}$$

which is the set of wages and net own rates of return that yield zero or negative profits and where $r = (r_1, r_2, \ldots, r_m)$ is the vector of rates of return. The factor price frontier is defined as

$$F(p, v) \equiv \arg\min_{w_0, r} \{ (w_0, r)'v \colon c^j(w_0, (r_1 + \delta_1)\, p^1, \ldots, (r_m + \delta_m)\, p^m) - p^j \geq 0,\ \ j \in J,\ \ (w_0, r) \geq 0 \}, \tag{35.7}$$

with v changing parametrically. It gives the wage rate and the net own rates of return that are consistent with equilibrium in the production sector.

In the steady state, the net rates of return have to be equal to the rate of interest on bonds, which is denoted as r (think of vector r above now becoming a scalar). Thus, in the steady state the factor price set reduces to

$$W(w_0, r) \equiv \{ (w_0, r) \colon c^j(w_0, (r + \delta_1)\, p^1, \ldots, (r + \delta_m)\, p^m) - p^j \geq 0,\ \ j \in J,\ \ (w_0, r) \geq 0 \}, \tag{35.8}$$

which is the set of wages and the common net own rate of return on capital that yield zero or negative profits in the production of every good. Each zero profit condition generates a downward sloping locus in the two dimensional (w_0, r) space. By analogy with the previous development, the factor price frontier for the steady state may be defined as the solution to the minimization problem for all two dimensional vectors v given by

$$F(p, v) \equiv \arg\min_{w_0, r} \{ (w_0, r)'v \colon c^j(w_0, (r + \delta_1)\, p^1, \ldots, (r + \delta_m)\, p^m) - p^j \geq 0,\ \ j \in J,\ \ (w_0, r) \geq 0 \}. \tag{35.9}$$

It gives the wage rate and the common net own rate of return on capital that are consistent with equilibrium in the production sector.

Figure 35.1 may now be straightforwardly reinterpreted to illustrate the factor price frontier in a steady state growth context. The axes now represent the wage rate and the rate of return to capital. One of the goods is a consumption good and the other two are capital goods, with cost functions redefined as $\tilde{c}^j(w_0, r) \equiv c^j(w_0, (r + \delta_1)\, p^1, \ldots, (r + \delta_m)\, p^m)$. The reinterpreted figure thus shows a negative relationship between the wage rate and the rate of return to capital in the steady state.

5. LITERATURE REVIEW

The origin of the concept of a factor price frontier lies in the early theoretical analysis of growth. It is generally accepted that the concept originated with Samuelson (1957), though Kurz (2008) suggests that Ricardo had the basis of the idea. Subsequently, Samuelson (1962, p.196) acknowledges that the idea of a trade-off between wages and the rate of profit in capital models can also be found in works by von Thünen, Joan Robinson and Paul Sraffa.

It seems that the diagram itself originated in Samuelson's (1962) paper on the surrogate production function in capital theory. Samuelson says that 'a good name for this fundamental trade-off relation would be the Factor-price Frontier' – a name that has stuck. However, it has also been variously called the 'wage frontier' (Hicks, 1965), the 'wage-profit frontier' (Kurz and Salvadori, 1995), the 'optimal transformation frontier' (Bruno, 1969) and the 'efficiency curve' (Hicks, 1973).

The use of the factor price frontier in capital theory has been thoroughly surveyed by Kurz (2008). Of particular note are papers by Bruno (1969) and Burmeister and Kuga (1970a, 1970b) on the duality between the production possibilities frontier and the factor price frontier.

In the international trade context, Samuelson's (1953–54) famous paper on the prices of factors and goods in general equilibrium seems to be the first to show that the equilibrium factor price vector can be determined as the solution to the problem of minimizing the value of the factor endowments subject to the no-profit conditions (as expressed above in (35.4)). This idea was used intensively by Woodland (1977) to illustrate the usefulness of the factor price diagram in the interpretation and demonstration of various theorems, such as the Stolper-Samuelson theorem, in international trade. Ikema (1978) has a related discussion.

NOTE

1. Indeed, any endowment point in the diversification cone K in Figure 35.2 that contains v also yields this same solution. This result is at the heart of the famous factor price equalization theorem. If two free-trading countries have the same technology (hence the same factor price frontier), and have their (different) endowment vectors in the same cone of diversification, then they will have the same factor price vectors despite the (limited) difference in endowments.

REFERENCES

Bruno, M., 1969, 'Fundamental Duality Relations in the Pure Theory of Capital and Growth', *The Review of Economic Studies*, 36, 39–53.
Burmeister, Edwin and Kiyoshi Kuga, 1970a, 'The Factor-Price Frontier in a Neoclassical Multi-Sector Model', *International Economic Review*, 11, 162–174.
Burmeister, Edwin and Kiyoshi Kuga, 1970b, 'The Factor-Price Frontier, Duality and Joint Production', *The Review of Economic Studies*, 37, 11–19.
Hicks, J.R., 1965, *Capital and Growth*, Oxford University Press, Oxford.
Hicks, J.R., 1973, *Capital and Time: A Neo-Austrian Theory*, Oxford University Press, Oxford.
Ikema, Makoto, 1978, 'On the Factor-Price Frontier in the Pure Theory of International Trade', *Hitotsubashi Journal of Economics*, 18(2), 62–75.
Kurz, Heinz D, 2008, 'Factor Price Frontier', in *The New Palgrave Dictionary of Economics*, eds. Steven N. Durlauf and Lawrence E. Blume, Palgrave Macmillan, Basingstoke. Sourced at The New Palgrave Dictionary of Economics Online, 15 January 2009, DOI:10.1057/9780230226203.0545.
Kurz, H.D. and N. Salvadori, 1995, *Theory of Production: A Long-period Analysis*, Cambridge University Press, Cambridge, UK.
Samuelson, Paul A., 1953–54, 'Prices of Factors and Good in General Equilibrium', *The Review of Economic Studies*, 21, 1–20.
Samuelson, Paul A., 1957, 'Wages and Interest: A Modern Dissection of Marxian Economic Models', *The American Economic Review*, 47, 884–912.
Samuelson, Paul A., 1962, 'Parable and Realism in Capital Theory: The Surrogate Production Function', *The Review of Economic Studies*, 29, 193–206.
Shephard, R.W., 1953, *Cost and Production Functions*, Princeton University Press, Princeton, NJ, USA.
Woodland, A.D., 1977, 'A Dual Approach to Equilibrium in the Production Sector in International Trade Theory', *Canadian Journal of Economics*, 10(1), 50–68.
Woodland, A.D., 1982, International Trade and Resource Allocation, Advanced Textbooks in Economics, Vol. 19, North-Holland Publishing Company, Amsterdam.

36. Pareto efficiency

Peter Lloyd

Pareto efficiency is a concept that is central to general equilibrium theory and has wide applications in welfare economics and games theory. It is a general equilibrium concept applied to an economy with multiple agents making individual choices. Its attraction is that it avoids comparisons of the utilities or welfare levels between individual consumers. The concept is named after its inventor, the Italian economist Vilfredo Pareto.

1. THE CONCEPT OF PARETO EFFICIENCY

Consider an allocation in some economy. This may be an allocation of a fixed bundle of consumer goods among a fixed number of consumers, or an allocation of a fixed supply of factors of production among a fixed number of goods. In general equilibrium, there are many possible allocations in each case and we seek an allocation or allocations which are best in some unambiguous and useful sense.

Take, for example, the consumption allocation. Given the set of alternative allocations of the goods among the consumers, we say that there is a Pareto improvement if a movement from one allocation to another within this set makes at least one individual better off and does not make any other worse off. An allocation is said to be Pareto-efficient if there is no allocation which is a Pareto improvement.

This definition has the very considerable advantages that it utilises only an ordinal concept of individual (or household) utility and it avoids interpersonal comparisons of levels of utilities. In general, there is more than one Pareto-efficient allocation and typically there are many, possibly infinitely many. Yet it shows that some allocations are efficient and some are inefficient. Inefficient allocations are to be avoided. They are an indication of slack in the organisation of the economy.

The minimum number of agents in an allocation problem is two. The problem of finding efficient allocations among two agents lends itself to geometry. From the time of Pareto himself, efficient allocations have almost invariably been illustrated in this way.

2. AN EXCHANGE ECONOMY

The standard illustration of the concept is that of an exchange economy. This is an economy in which a pre-existing quantity of goods is to be allocated among a number of consumers. Consider that there are only two goods to be allocated among only two consumers. Let the goods be labelled 1 and 2 and the consumers A and B. In this case, we can use the Edgeworth box, whose dimensions are given by the fixed quantities available for allocation. Any point in the box is a feasible allocation of 1 and 2 between A and B. The preferences of individuals A and B are given by their indifference maps, which are assumed to have the usual properties; in particular the indifference map of an individual is everywhere dense and indifference curves are continuous and concave from above (see Chapter 3, on indifference curves and isoquants). These maps can be shown within the box by using the lower left-hand corner of the box as the origin for individual 1 and the upper right-hand corner as the origin for individual 2 in the familiar manner (see Chapter 31, on the Edgeworth Box). We can then compare any two allocations and say whether individuals 1 and 2 are better or worse off or possibly indifferent if we move from one allocation to the other.

Take an initial allocation such as P' (Figure 36.1). The indifference curves passing through this point are I'_A and I'_B respectively. If the two indifference curves intersect, they form a lens-shaped area. The points in the interior and on the boundary of this lens are the set of allocations which are Pareto improvements over the initial allocation. (The points in the interior of this lens are the set of allocations which satisfy the stronger criterion that all individuals are strictly better off.) Within this set, there is a subset of allocations which are Pareto-efficient. However, the choice of initial allocation was arbitrary. If we consider all possible allocations, there will be a set of Pareto-efficient allocations, including the subset in the lens described but not confined to it. The locus of all such points is called the contract curve. It necessarily slopes upwards and is continuous, assuming continuity of utility functions, and contains the two corners of the box where all of the quantities are allocated to one individual.

If, given a choice of ordinal utility functions to represent the preference orderings of each of the two individuals, the utility levels at each point on the contract curve are mapped into utility 2-space, we obtain the utility possibility curve (see Chapter 34, on utility possibility frontier). This shows the maximum utility for one individual, given a utility level for the

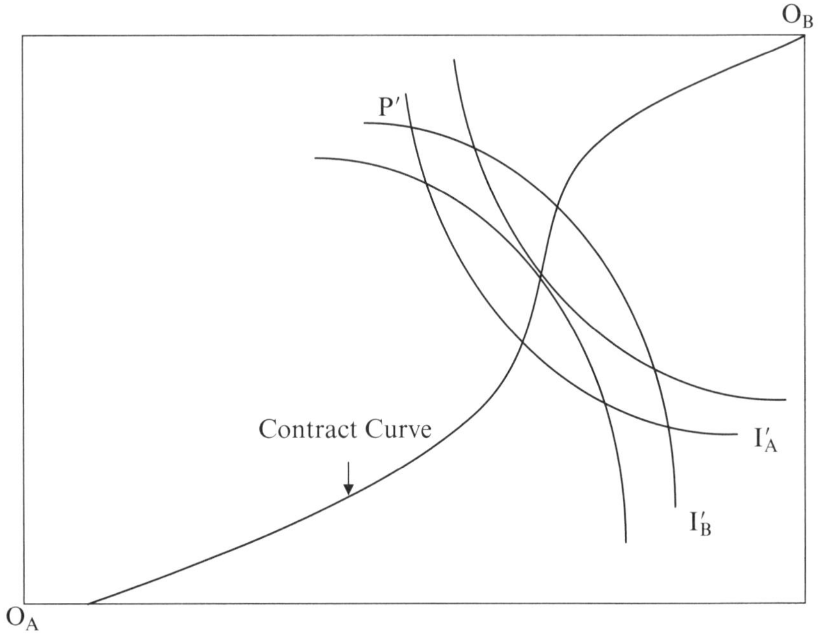

Figure 36.1 Pareto efficiency

other. This curve has a negative slope. In any economy, we can increase the utility of one individual by transferring quantities of the goods from the other. The curve shows the efficient boundary of such possibilities.

Sometimes the concept is referred to as Pareto optimality. However, by itself it does not produce an optimal allocation. Some Pareto-efficient allocations may produce a distribution of goods among the households of the society which many consider highly inequitable or unjust; for example, in the extreme case where all of both goods are allocated to one individual. Consequently, the term Pareto-efficiency is now the description preferred by almost all economists.

Clearly under these assumptions, the Pareto-efficient allocations have the property that the marginal rates of substitution between the two goods of the two individuals are equal. If these rates are not equal, a Pareto improvement is possible; for example, if the marginal rate of substitution of A is greater than that of B, the welfare of one or both can be improved by reducing A's consumption of good 1 and increasing A's consumption of good 2. (If the lens intersects a boundary of the box, that is, if there are Pareto-efficient allocations in which the quantity consumed of one good by one household is zero, the equality is replaced by an inequality.)

Geometrically, the indifference curves of the two individuals are tangent to each other. This geometric property allows us to determine the set of Pareto-efficient allocations and makes the geometry such a powerful exposition of the concept of Pareto efficiency. This is remarkable, as the allocation requires two individuals simultaneously changing their consumption of two goods, subject to the constraint of a fixed availability of each good, with consequential changes in their utilities. All of these variables are in the box.

This approach can be readily extended to an economy which can produce alternative amounts of the two goods.

3. AN ECONOMY WITH PRODUCTION

Consider an economy which can produce a fixed number of goods using a fixed number of primary factors and distribute the resulting output among a fixed number of consumers. In this model, there are two allocation problems, one the problem of allocating primary factors among alternative industries and the other the consumption allocation problem. Or better, we have a single allocation of factors among industries and the outputs among consumers. To illustrate the allocation choices, the minimum number of goods, factors and households is two apiece. This gives us the 2x2x2-dimensional version of the model that is the standard illustration of the neoclassical general equilibrium model. In this model, producer agents have to decide on the allocation of inputs between industries and consumer agents must decide on the allocation of these outputs between consumers. It turns out that there are three marginal conditions that must be satisfied for Pareto efficiency.

The production allocation set is shown by the production box (see Chapter 40, on the Stolper-Samuelson production box.) This box (Figure 40.2) and the solution to the production allocation problem are isomorphic to those in the consumption box considered above. The factors are labelled K (for capital) and L (for labour). The dimensions of the box are given by the fixed quantities of the factors available in the economy. Any point in this box is a feasible allocation of K and L between the industries producing goods 1 and 2. Production functions for goods 1 and 2 represent the technologies. The level surfaces of these functions, the isoquants, show in the box space the different combinations of K and L that can produce a given quantity of the output of each good. As with the indifference curves, it is usual to give these curves convenient properties; in particular, the isoquants are everywhere dense, continuous and concave from above. We can compare any two allocations and say whether the outputs of goods 1 and 2 have increased, decreased or remained constant.

The Pareto-efficient subset of allocations is obtained in the same manner as in the consumption box. For all points in the interior of the box, these allocations are determined geometrically by the tangency of the isoquants, that is, by the first-order condition that the marginal rate of substitution between capital and labour in the production of the two goods is equal (or on the boundary, by an inequality). The locus of Pareto-efficient points is the production contract curve.

Given the production functions, the output levels at each point on the contract curve are mapped into output 2-space to give the production possibility or transformation curve. This shows the maximum output of one good, given the output level for the other. In any economy, we can increase the output of one good by transferring quantities of the inputs used in the production of the other. This curve shows the efficient boundary of such possibilities. It has a negative slope. If, further, the technologies are restricted to constant returns to scale, the curve is concave provided there is some substitutability between inputs in the two industries.

For each point on the production contract curve, the outputs can be allocated among consumers in an infinity of ways. For a fixed output of the two goods, this consumption allocation problem is the same as above.

Clearly both first-order conditions have to be satisfied simultaneously. But the two problems are not independent of each other. There is a third condition required for Pareto-efficiency in the economy. Take the transformation curve resulting from efficient production in the economy. The slope of any point on this curve is the marginal rate of transformation between the two goods. The marginal rates of substitution in production between the two goods must be equal to the marginal rate of substitution in consumption of the goods. Otherwise, the mix of outputs and consumption bundles can be changed so as to bring about a Pareto improvement.

When these three conditions hold simultaneously, they trace out the set of Pareto-efficient allocations for the economy. Together they determine a set of local maxima. If there is enough regularity in the model, they also determine a set of global maxima. If there is not enough regularity, supplementary conditions are required to locate global maxima.

While this model conveys great insights into the general equilibrium of an economy, it is a simple model. It can be extended in two basic ways. First, the dimensions of the model can be extended to deal with any fixed number of goods, factors and consumers. A more recent extension of the model is to introduce a continuum (infinity) of agents or goods. Second, the structure of the model can be relaxed in various ways. We can allow a labour-leisure choice for consumers, joint production or intermediate inputs. The model can also be extended to many time periods and to an economy which trades with other economies. The latter extension takes us into the pure theory of international trade. The Heckscher-Ohlin model of international trade is the neoclassical model of international trade, the extension of the model above for a closed economy to multiple national economies which trade with each other. The standard textbook version of this model, with two countries, two factors and two goods (and a representative household in each country or some other assumption that determines the demand side of the model) is the staple of international trade theory. In all of these extensions, the concept of Pareto efficiency is used to determine efficient allocations.

4. PARETO EFFICIENCY AND THE PRICE SYSTEM

From the time of Pareto himself, the concept of Pareto efficiency has been linked to analysis of the efficiency and equity of the allocation resulting from a price mechanism in a capitalist society. Pareto believed that his analysis shows that a price system fulfils the conditions of Pareto efficiency and leads to a 'maximum ophelimity' for the economy, but it is unclear what is being maximised. Moreover, the distributional aspects of the performance of the economy are unclear, as Pareto explicitly eschewed interpersonal comparisons. After Pareto, there is a long history of attempts to resolve this problem (see Samuelson, 1947, chapter VIII). Lange (1938), following a lead provided by Pareto himself, examined the efficiency of a socialist economy. A number of authors demonstrated the Pareto efficiency of a price system in an economy that is perfectly competitive and free of market failures. Yet, in the absence of an acceptable social welfare criterion to evaluate different situations with different utilities of the members of the society, the desirability of unhindered allocation by a price system remained unclear.

This issue was resolved by the Two Fundamental Theorems of Welfare Economics (see Blaug, 2007, for a history of these two theorems). The essence of these theorems had been lurking in the analysis for some time. A precise statement and proof of the theorems for a general specification of an economy with many agents, goods and factors and a general production structure was provided by Arrow (1951). The first theorem states that every competitive equilibrium is Pareto-efficient. The second theorem states that every Pareto-efficient allocation can be achieved as a competitive equilibrium after a suitable lump sum redistribution of initial endowments of factors or of income. Of course, these results hold only under a number of conditions, including perfect competition everywhere, a complete set of markets, selfish consumers and the absence of market failures. These requirements aside, the two theorems show, as Pareto believed, that one can demonstrate the meaning and implications of efficiency in an economic system without making interpersonal comparisons of utility. Given the impracticability of lump sum redistributions, however, governments still need to exercise some value judgements when deciding between two alternative allocations.

5. A SHORT HISTORY

The concept of Pareto efficiency originates chiefly in Pareto (1906, chapter VI), but see also Pareto (1911). He built on the work of Edgeworth (1881) on recontracting, in which the concept is implicit. Pareto developed the concept initially for a pure exchange economy:

> These are the considerations that lead us to define maximum ophelimity as that from which it is impossible to change by a slight amount in such a way that the ophelimities enjoyed by each individual, neglecting those that remain constant, all increase or all decrease. (Pareto, 1911, p. 82)

It is not clear why he includes the case of a decrease in utilities, but otherwise this definition is almost identical to the modern definition and it launched an enormous literature on the properties of general equilibria. In his use of an ordinal utility function and his unwillingness to add or compare the utilities ('ophelimities') of individuals, Pareto is quite modern.

For an exchange economy with two goods and two consumers, Pareto has both an algebraic and a geometric treatment of the concept. In the latter he uses the Edgeworth box to locate and describe the marginal conditions in the same way as we do today. Pareto extends his discussion to a model with production but his treatment of production is rudimentary and unsatisfactory. Samuelson (1947, pp. 212–14) provides an excellent discussion of Pareto's method of analysis. Pareto's contribution was clarified and extended by Barone (1908).

The first use of the box to examine the production allocation was by Lerner in 1933 (though it was not published until 1952), after it was used famously by Stolper and Samuelson (1941). The first person to look at the combined production and consumption allocation was Burk (Bergson) (1938). He derives all of the marginal conditions algebraically, for an economy which is more general in some respects than that discussed in Section 4 above; for example, it has a labour–leisure choice for households which both consume and supply labour to the production sector.

The presentation in terms of boxes for both consumption and production allocations and the derivation of the three marginal conditions in the manner above emerged shortly after: Reder (1947) and Bator (1957). The first model with a continuum, in this case a continuum of traders in a pure exchange economy, was that of Aumann (1964).

REFERENCES

Arrow, K. (1951), 'An extension of the basic theorems of classical welfare economics' in J. Neyman (ed.), *Proceedings of the Second Berkeley Symposium on Mathematical Statistics and Probability*, Berkeley: University of California Press, 507–32.

Aumann, R. J. (1964), 'Markets with a continuum of traders', *Econometrica*, 32, 39–50.

Barone, E. (1908), *Principi di economia politica*, Rome: Tipografia Nazionale di G. Berteno.

Bator, F. M. (1957), 'The simple analytics of welfare maximisation', *American Economic Review*, 47, March, 22–59.

Blaug, M. (2007), 'The fundamental theorems of modern welfare economics, historically contemplated', *History of Political Economy*, 39, 185–207.

Burk (Bergson), A. (1938), 'A reformulation of certain aspects of welfare economics', *Quarterly Journal of Economics*, 52, 310–34.

Edgeworth, F. Y. (1881), *Mathematical Psychics: An Essay on the Application of Mathematics to the Moral Sciences*, London: Kegan Paul.

Lange, O. (1938), *On the Economic Theory of Socialism*, Minneapolis, MN: University of Minnesota Press.

Lerner, Abba P. (1952), 'Factor prices and international trade', *Economica*, 19, 1–15.

Pareto, V. (1906), *Manual of Political Economy*, 1971 translation of 1927 edition, New York: Macmillan.

Pareto, V. (1911), 'Mathematical economics', reprinted and translated in W. J. Baumol and S. M. Goldfeld (eds), *Precursors in Mathematical Economics: An Anthology*, London: The London School of Economics and Political Science.

Reder, M. W. (1947), *Studies in The Theory of Welfare Economics*, New York: Columbia University Press, 52–95.

Samuelson, P. A. (1947), *Foundations of Economic Analysis*, Cambridge, MA: Harvard University Press.

Stolper, W. F. and P. A Samuelson (1941), 'Protection and real wages', *Review of Economic Studies*, 9, 58–73.

37. The phase diagram technique for analyzing the stability of multiple-market equilibrium

D. Wade Hands

The phase diagram technique is a tool for analyzing the stability of equilibrium (or equilibria) in a two-variable economic model. The technique starts from a standard two-variable diagram, but adds arrows to indicate the direction of movement away from any non-equilibrium position. As a tool of mathematical analysis, the phase diagram is a rather blunt instrument; it is limited to two-dimensional models (or those that can be reduced to two dimensions) and only captures the rough qualitative properties of the underlying dynamic model. If the dynamics are given explicitly by a system of differential (or difference) equations, more detailed information can be obtained by solving or integrating the dynamic system and directly analyzing the time-path of the variables. Nonetheless, the phase diagram technique provides a very convenient and intuitive way of deriving a wealth of information about the dynamics of a wide range of multiple-market economic models.

The phase diagram has been used in the analysis of multi-market stability since Alfred Marshall introduced it into economics in his *Pure Theory of Foreign Trade* during the 1870s, and it played an important role in the literature on the stability of Walrasian general equilibrium during the late 1950s and 1960s. Over the years, the phase diagram technique has also been employed in many other areas of economic theory, including macroeconomics, growth theory, development economics and a number of areas within applied microeconomics. The technique has also been used to analyze economic models using modern mathematical software programs (Shone 2002).

1. ALFRED MARSHALL IN THE PURE THEORY OF FOREIGN TRADE

Alfred Marshall introduced the phase diagram technique in his analysis of two-country two-good international trade in *The Pure Theory of Foreign*

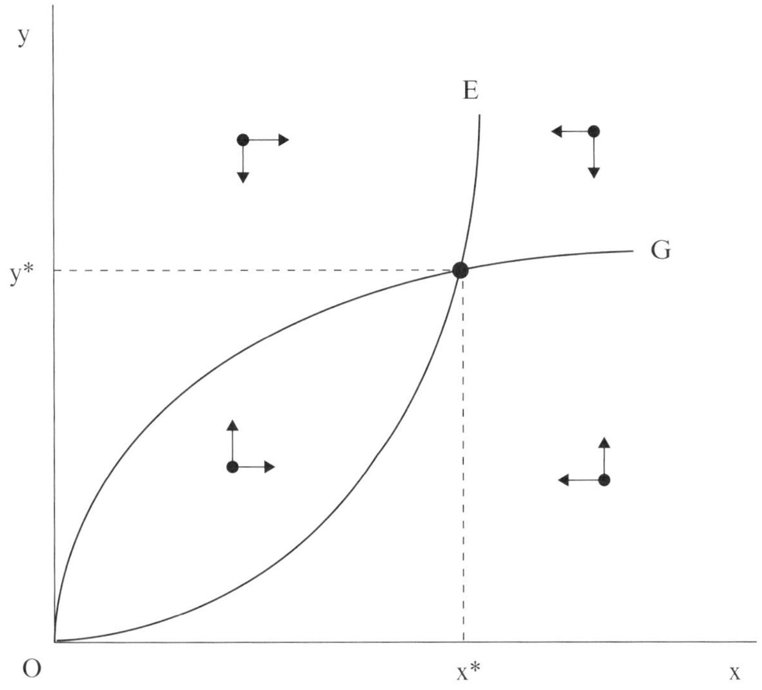

Source: Marshall (1949)

Figure 37.1 Marshall's trade diagram

Trade (1949). As John Whitaker explains, this 'is the first known application to economic theory of the phase-diagram method of handling a system of differential equations' (Whitaker, 1975, p. 115). Marshall had begun writing the international trade text at some point during 1873 (Groenewegen, 1995, p. 169) and the manuscript was privately circulated by Henry Sidgwick in 1879. The essay was first reprinted along with *The Pure Theory of Domestic Values* by the London School of Economics in 1930 and parts of the essay were also included as Appendix J of Marshall's *Money, Credit and Commerce* (1960). Marshall's model became a core part of the neoclassical theory of international trade and his discussion of stability was a precursor to many later theoretical developments (Chipman 1965).

Marshall's model involved international trade in linen and cloth between England and Germany. Figure 37.1 reproduces a version of Marshall's figure 7 from *The Pure Theory of Foreign Trade*. Each point on the curve OE shows the amount of cloth (x) that England would export in exchange for a particular amount of imported linen (y); and similarly, each point on OG shows the amount of cloth Germany would import (x) in exchange for a given export of linen (y). The equilibrium combination of cloth and linen is given by (x*, y*). Marshall explained the dynamics in the following way:

> In order to determine the directions in which the amounts of the exports of cloth and linen are tending to change at any time, it is requisite . . . to draw arrowheads – an arrowhead pointing towards the right if the exchange-index lies on the left of OE, towards the left if this point lies on the right of OE; and an arrowhead pointing upwards if the exchange-index lies below OG, downwards if this point lies above OG. (Marshall, 1949, p. 19)

The equilibrium of the two curves in Figure 37.1 is stable in the sense that starting from any non-equilibrium import-export combination, the dynamics of the system will generate a path through (x, y) space that converges to the equilibrium values (x*, y*). The equilibrium is globally stable if the entire domain of the two functions is that which is shown in the diagram; if the functions OE and OG extend beyond what is shown, then the phase diagram in Figure 37.1 only guarantees the local stability of the equilibrium.

Marshall also applied the phase diagram technique to discuss the stability of international trade models with multiple equilibria. For example, Figure 37.2 – a version of Marshall's Figure 8 – shows a model with three equilibria, two stable and one unstable.[1]

2. THE PHASE DIAGRAM TECHNIQUE IN WALRASIAN GENERAL EQUILIBRIUM THEORY

The analysis of the 'true dynamic stability' multiple market competitive equilibrium began with Samuelson (1941) – reprinted as chapter nine of *Foundations* (1947). In that paper, Samuelson discussed Marshall's diagrammatic approach to the stability of international trade equilibria – and even provided a differential equation version of Marshall's model – but he analyzed the (local) stability of the general equilibrium price vector directly by analyzing the real parts of the characteristic roots of the excess demand Jacobian matrix, and did not provide a phase diagram for the Walrasian system.

The key contribution to the literature on the global stability of competitive equilibrium came in Arrow and Hurwicz (1958). Although the main result of that paper was to prove the global stability of an m-good Walrasian general equilibrium model under the gross substitute assumption using 'Liapounoff's second method', they also employed the phase

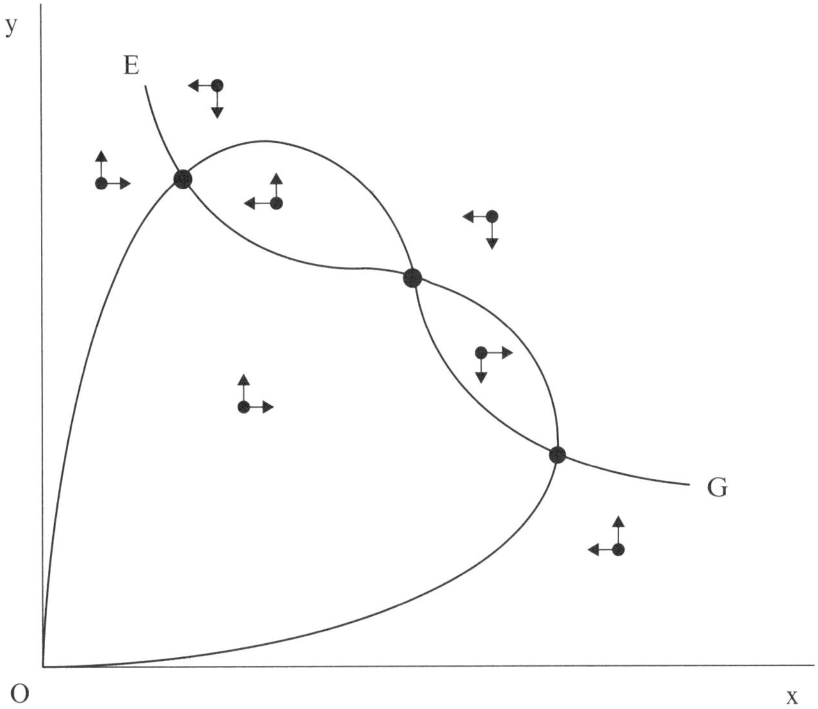

Source: Marshall (1949)

Figure 37.2 Marshall's multiple equilibria diagram

diagram technique to demonstrate the general result for the 3-good case. Since Walras's Law implies that if two out of the three markets are in equilibrium, then the third market will be in equilibrium as well, the 3-good model reduces to the following 2-good dynamic system:

$$\frac{dp_1}{dt} = \overset{\circ}{p_1}(t) = f_1[p_1(t), p_2(t)],$$

$$\frac{dp_2}{dt} = \overset{\circ}{p_2}(t) = f_2[p_1(t), p_2(t)],$$

with $f_{12} = \partial f_1/\partial x_2 > 0$ and $f_{21} = \partial f_2/\partial x_1 > 0$ under the gross substitute assumption.

The stability of general equilibrium for this system is shown in Figure 37.3 (a version of Arrow and Hurwicz's Figure 1, p. 547).

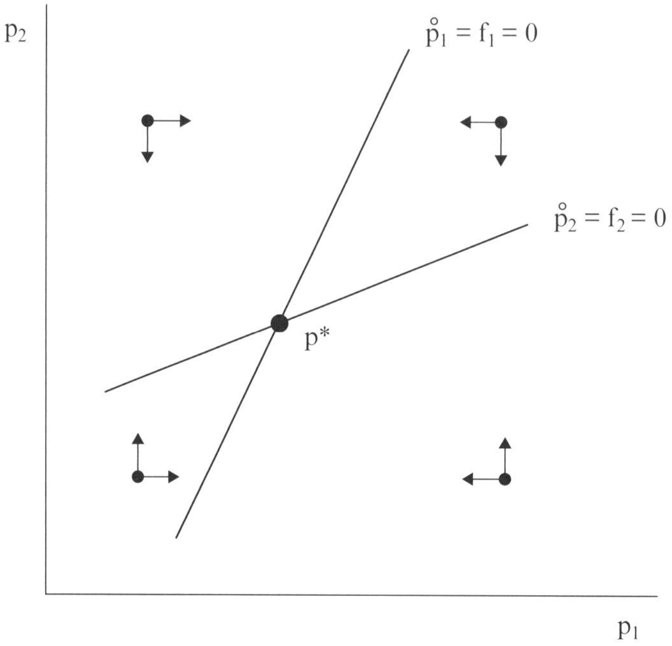

Source: Arrow and Hurwicz (1958)

Figure 37.3 The gross substitute system

These two examples – Marshall's international trade model and the gross substitute Walrasian system – represent only a small sample of the many ways that the phase diagram technique has been used, and continues to be used, to analyze the stability of multiple-market equilibrium.

NOTE

1. It is interesting to note that Marshall anticipated (1949, p. 25) some of the later results on the number of stable and unstable equilibria (such as Varian 1975).

REFERENCES

Arrow, Kenneth J. and Hurwicz, Leonid (1958), 'On the Stability of the Competitive Equilibrium', *Econometrica*, 26, 522–552.

Chipman, John (1965), 'A Survey of the Theory of International Trade: Part 2, The Neo-Classical Theory', *Econometrica*, 33, 685–760.

Groenewegen, Peter (1995), *A Soaring Eagle: Alfred Marshall 1842–1924*. Cheltenham: Edward Elgar.
Marshall, Alfred (1949), *The Pure Theory of Foreign Trade and The Pure Theory of Domestic Values*. London: The London School of Economics and Political Science.
Marshall, Alfred (1960), *Money, Credit and Commerce*. New York: Augustus M. Kelley.
Samuelson, Paul A. (1941), 'The Stability of Equilibrium: Comparative Statics and Dynamics', *Econometrica*, 9, 97–120.
Samuelson, Paul A. (1947), *Foundations of Economic Analysis*. Cambridge, MA: Harvard University Press.
Shone, Ronald (2002), *Economics Dynamics: Phase Diagrams and Their Economic Applications*, Second Edition. Cambridge: Cambridge University Press.
Varian, Hal R. (1975), 'A Third Remark on the Number of Equilibria of an Economy', *Econometrica*, 43, 985–986.
Whitaker, John K. (1975), *The Early Economic Writings of Alfred Marshall, 1867–1890*, Volume Two. New York: The Free Press.

38. The theory of second best and third best

Wai Chiu Woo

The generalized theory of second best developed by Lipsey and Lancaster (1956) not only creates a devastating effect on welfare economics but also a challenge on how to draw a simple diagram to express the theory.

The central message of the theory is simple: Pareto optimality in the first-best situation (absence of constraints additional to those of limited resources and given technology) requires the equality of marginal rate of substitution (MRS) for consumers and marginal rate of transformation (MRT) for any pair of commodities. Suppose in one (or some) sector(s) there is some irremovable distortion (due to, say, an unbreakable monopolist, tariff or other reasons) so that a (some) first-best optimality condition(s) cannot be fulfilled. Subject to this extra constraint, to attain the (second-best) welfare optimum, should we fulfil as many remaining first-best conditions as possible? The answer from the second-best theory is 'no'.

The challenge to graphical economists is that the problem involves at least three sectors. Optimum condition is not fulfilled in one sector. We would like to see if attaining one or more equality conditions in the remaining sectors is welfare-improving. However, a diagram simultaneously portraying three sectors is normally three-dimensional and difficult to read and draw.

McManus (1959) pioneered a two-dimensional diagram, using a right triangle, to illustrate the problem. Winch (1971) modified it to a normal triangle (although looks like an equilateral) and Ng (1979 and also 2004) explicitly used an equilateral triangle, taking advantage of the property that, at any point in the triangle (such as point P in Figure 38.1[1]), perpendicular distances (PA, PB and PC) to the three sides must sum to be a constant. We can then use the perpendicular distance to indicate the quantity of a good (such as PA as the quantity for x). Assume a linear production constraint, x + y + z = constant. An equilateral triangular plane can be used to represent a production possibility set as any points in it satisfy the constraint.

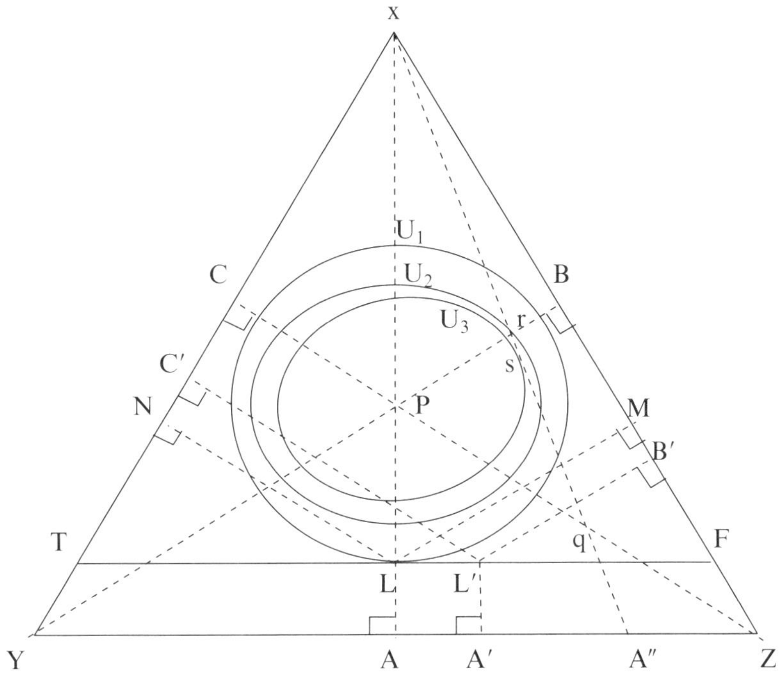

Source: Adapted from Ng (2004)

Figure 38.1 Second best policy in a triangle

TF in Figure 38.1 is thus analogous to a linear transformation curve on the (Y, Z) plane conditional on the quantity of X fixed at LA. Along the line, the quantity of X is fixed (LA = LA'), but the combination of Y and Z can differ (LN < C'L' for Z; LM > L'B' for Y). Similarly, any lines parallel to any sides of the triangle represent a conditional transformation curve.

Following Lipsey and Lancaster, social welfare can be captured by a representative consumer's utility. Assuming interior solution and uniqueness, there is a point inside the triangle giving rise to the highest utility level. Let this be point P. Since this is the Pareto optimum, all the optimum conditions are fulfilled here. Given continuity and convexity of preference, lower levels of utility can be represented by some indifference 'rings' such as U_1 (not necessarily a circle), where any points on the ring imply a constant utility level. TF is the transformation curve on the (Y, Z) space conditional on the quantity of X and it touches the highest indifference ring at L. Therefore, at point L, $MRS_{YZ} = MRT_{YZ}$ with X fixed at LA. If we choose another quantity of X and draw another transformation curve parallel to TF, we can locate another tangency point to the indifference ring, which also implies $MRS_{YZ} = MRT_{YZ}$ at another quantity of X. So, we can identify a locus such as XA (whose shape is dependent on the shape of the rings and not necessarily a line), indicating that $MRS_{YZ} = MRT_{YZ}$. Similarly, locus YB and locus ZC represent $MRS_{XZ} = MRT_{XZ}$ and $MRS_{XY} = MRT_{XY}$ respectively. Obviously, the three loci must cross at the optimum point P, where the three optimum conditions are fulfilled together.

Consider a typical second-best environment: one of the optimum conditions cannot be fulfilled, say, if $MRS_{YZ} = kMRT_{YZ}$ (then $P_Y/P_Z = kMC_Y/MC_Z$) with $k > 1$. The locus representing $MRS_{YZ} = kMRT_{YZ}$ is XA″. So, should we try satisfying as many remaining optimum conditions? If we can only select points on XA″, we cannot also select points at the same time on both YB and ZC, but only on one of them. So, should we select points on either YB or ZC, that is, either point r or point q. The answer is no. Point q gives rise to a utility lower than U_1. It would be beneficial to move along XA″ (the constraint) closer to U_1. Point r gives rise to the higher utility $U_2 > U_1$. But the best attainable point under the constraint XA″ is at s, where all the first-best conditions are violated. So, the second-best conclusion is demonstrated in this simple diagram.

The conclusion of the theory of second best is devastating as it implies that Pareto optimum conditions no longer provide a good guide to policy makers. The theory of second best also implies that simple piecemeal policies based on first-best conditions are not desirable, making the study useless in each special environment, unless we can jump right to the summit of first best, which, given the second-best constraint, is not possible. There are suggestions that the second-best theory is not applicable on some occasions (making the first-best rules still useful), say, a separable economy (when there are no externalities and goods are neither substitutes nor complements), but these scenarios do not seem very realistic (see Lipsey 2007). Furthermore, we cannot expect all the first-best conditions to be always attainable. So, does it make the study of first-best Pareto optimality conditions completely useless? A more constructive approach is offered by the theory of third best by Ng (1977). The second-best-type distortions (such as the presence of monopoly power) prevent some first-best conditions from being fulfilled. Another type of constraint for policy may be called 'informational constraint', but that is not a concern for second-best theorists. Implementing the second-best policy is usually very complicated, involving knowledge of the first-order as well as the second-order derivatives of the relevant objective and constraint functions. To see how the informational constraint matters, consider a 'relation curve'

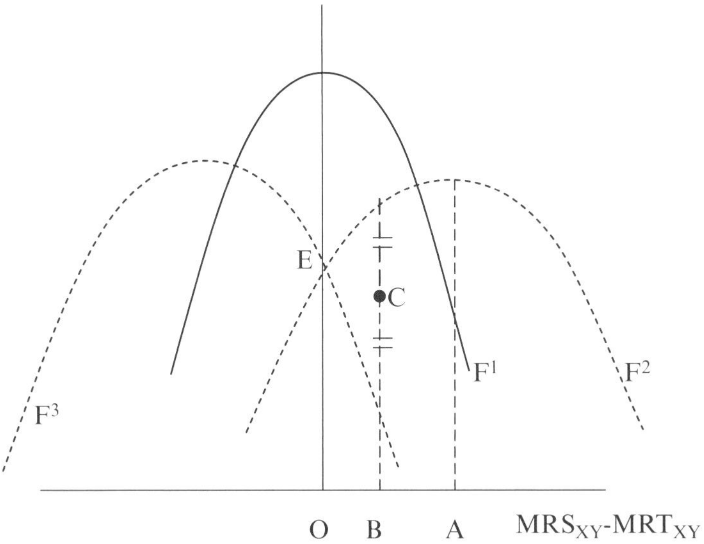

Source: Adapted from Ng (2004)

Figure 38.2 *Third best policy*

that relates the level of social welfare and the degree of departure from the first-best rule, say, $MRS_{XY} - MRT_{XY}$. F^1 in Figure 38.2 illustrates a concave relation curve. For most cases, the relation curve may be expected to be concave, at least over the relevant domain of distortion, as a higher degree of departure is more harmful. For example, the first-best rule is attained when price equals marginal cost. If the slope of demand curve is everywhere smaller than the marginal cost curve, the relation curve is concave. F^1 is maximized when we do not depart from the first-best rule $MRS_{XY} - MRT_{XY} = 0$. This simply means that the first-best rule should be adopted in the first-best world (in the absence of irremovable distortions).

With a second-best distortion in some part of the economy, the relation curve for the pair X and Y will change. With sufficient information, we know how the relation curve is changed. For instance, if we know it is changed to F^2, we choose the optimal degree of departure at OA. But a more realistic scenario may be that we are poorly informed. We do not know the direction and degree of departure of the second-best optimum from that resulting from the application of the first-best rule. Furthermore, we do not know the shape and skewness of the relation curve apart from its concavity property. To reflect this situation, F^2 and F^3 are drawn as equally likely to appear in the presence of the second-best distortion. They are drawn to be symmetrical, reflecting our ignorance about the sign of skewness. With such poverty of information, the expected welfare level is OE if we stick to the first-best rule. Departing from this rule, the expected welfare level is lower, say, at BC. Thus, the third-best policy in this situation is not to depart from the first-best rule.

Of course, the above result is partly dependent on the assumption of a concave relation curve, which could be criticized. Lipsey (2007) argues that the curve will not be concave throughout. Based on the Cobb-Douglas utility function, he also establishes that the relation curve under the second-best environment is concave at first but then becomes convex with further deviations from the first-best rule. In this situation, the third-best policy above still applies for non-drastic deviation but not for drastic deviation. More importantly, the theory of the third best is proposed especially for a situation where a poorly-informed policy maker does not know which direction the first-best condition is violated in. If we know the concrete shape of the relation curve, then the second-best policy should be adopted instead. The third-best theory indicates when the first-best or second-best policy should be adopted based on information availability. Although there is no guarantee that the curve must be concave, it can be adopted as a benchmark case and, in the absence of precise information, concavity over the relevant domain can be considered as an average case.

Lipsey is right:

> Since the competitive market economy is the best known method of allocating resources, departures from it through either public policy or private behaviour, are regarded as prima facie undesirable, unless justified by well-reasoned and persuasive arguments . . .. Useful piecemeal policy advising is not impossible . . . it is an art, assisted by good economics, both theoretical and empirical. (p.362)

In fact, it is precisely the third-best theory that provides a good support for this conclusion and a good guide to the useful piecemeal policy that Lipsey is in favour of.

NOTE

1. The figure is adapted from Figure 9.1 of Yew-kwang Ng's (2004) *Welfare Economics*, which was adapted from McManus (1959) and Winch (1971). Figure 38.2 is adapted from Figure 9.2, also from Ng. Professor Ng has kindly permitted me publish the adapted versions of the figures.

REFERENCES

Lipsey, R.G. (2007), 'Reflections on the general theory of second best at its golden jubilee', *International Tax and Public Finance*, 14: 349–364.
Lipsey, R.G. and Lancaster, K. (1956), 'The general theory of second best', *Review of Economic Studies*, 24(1): 11–32.
McManus, M. (1959), 'Comments on the general theory of second best', *Review of Economic Studies*, 26(3): 209–224.
Ng, Yew-Kwang (1977), 'Towards a theory of third best', *Public Finance/Finances Publiques*, 32: 1–15.
Ng, Yew-Kwang (1979), *Welfare Economics: Introduction and Development of Basic Concepts*, London: Macmillan.
Winch, D.M. (1971), *Analytical Welfare Economics*, Harmondsworth Penguin Education.

Open economies

39. The offer curve

Murray Kemp

The offer curve (or reciprocal demand curve) diagrammatically relates the imports and exports of a single country to the world prices of the traded goods. The diagram accommodates only two traded goods and is therefore of limited use in analyzing many policy issues, but it has been immensely useful in introducing students to some of the fundamental propositions of the modern theory of international trade. Its potential usefulness was first convincingly displayed by Marshall (1879).

In Figure 39.1, alternative terms of trade (the world price of a country's exported commodity in terms of its imported commodity) are represented by the positive slopes of the dashed straight lines through the origin; and the amount offered of each commodity at any particular terms of trade is indicated by the point of intersection of the relevant price line and the offer curve GOG'. For example, at the terms of trade represented by the slope of the line POQ, neither commodity is offered, so autarky prevails in the country under study; at the terms of trade represented by the slope of the line $P'OQ'$, the country offers the first commodity in exchange for the second; and, at the terms of trade represented by the slope of the line $P''OQ''$, the country offers the second commodity in exchange for the first.

The offer curve is usually drawn on the basis of several assumptions:

1. All agents (households) are identical in all respects (preferences, endowments and information), that is, all agents are representative.
2. The amounts of (the two or more) factors of production supplied to the market are given constants, independent of commodity and factor prices.
3. All produced goods are internationally tradeable.
4. The country can survive without international trade.
5. In each industry, returns to scale are constant.
6. There is neither international borrowing and lending nor international transfers (in the form of freely given aid or in the form of war indemnities).

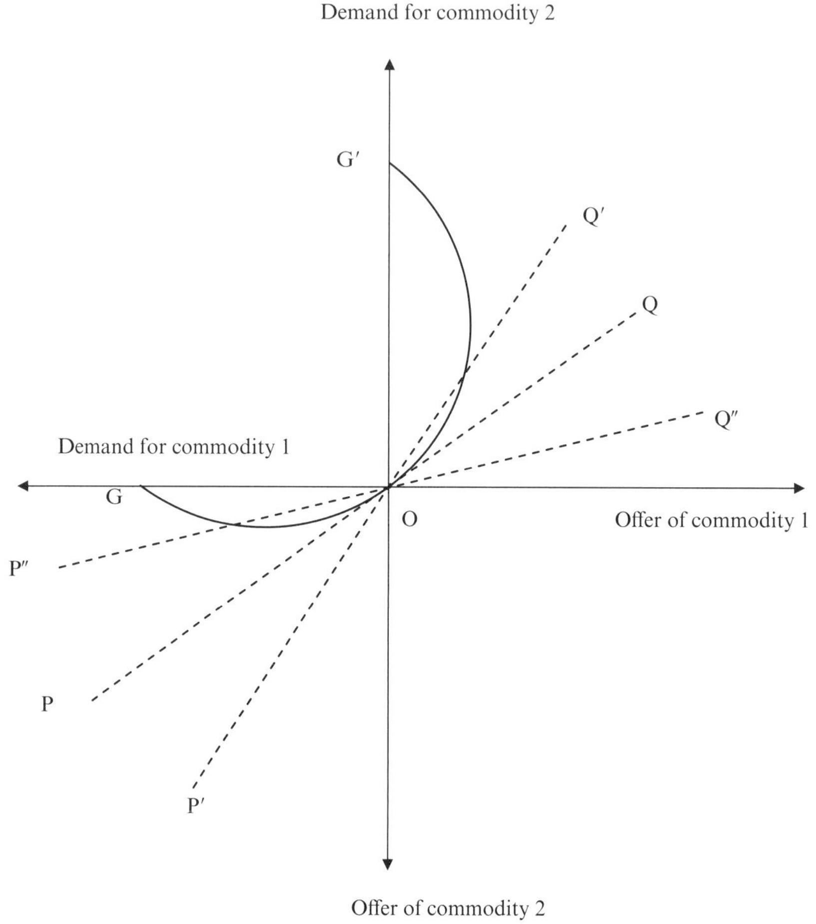

Figure 39.1 Offer curves of H and G derived from their terms of trade

Given these assumptions, it is usually taken for granted that the offer curve has the curvature of *GOG′* in Figure 39.1. However, intervals of reverse curvature are compatible with assumptions (1)–(6).

If each of the two trading countries (say *G* and *H*) has an offer curve with the properties of *GOG′*, it is a simple matter to align the two curves, as in Figure 39.2, and conclude that there is a unique free-trade world equilibrium with the equilibrium terms of trade indicated by the slope of *OP*. Equipped with Figure 39.2, the student can tackle many of the conventional comparative statical questions concerning the effects (on the equilibrium terms of trade and the international distribution of income)

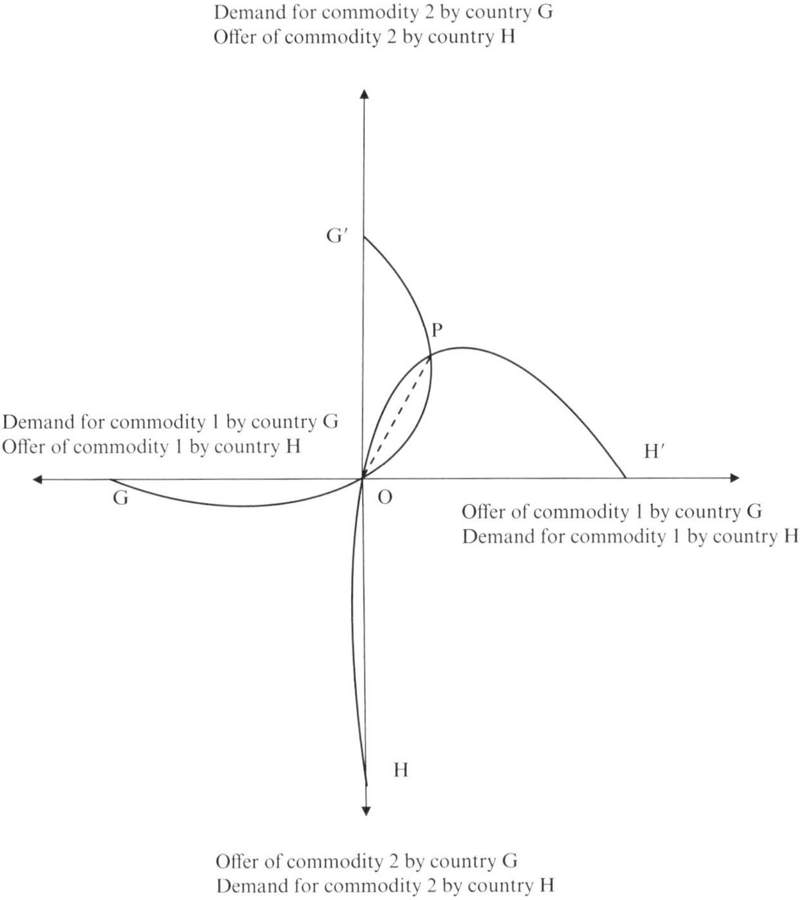

Figure 39.2 *Offer curves of H and G determine the equilibrium traded quantities*

of the imposition of tariffs and subsidies, of international transfers (aid and indemnity payments), of international borrowing and lending, and of technical improvements in one of the trading countries.

However assumptions (1)–(6), on which Figures 39.1 and 39.2 rest, are quite strict. If the assumptions are relaxed, one must be prepared to redraw the offer curves and qualify many of the propositions cherished by trade theorists. For example, it is now well known that if, contrary to assumption (2), the supply of labour or any other factor of production is sensitive to changes in commodity or factor prices, the offer curve of a country might bend back on itself, so that a greater quantity of imports is demanded at a higher price and the possibility of multiple world equilibria must be recognized; see Kemp and Jones (1962). The same possibility emerges if, contrary to assumption (3), the country produces goods for which there is no international market. For the supply of non-traded goods, and therefore the flow of factors of production to industries producing traded goods, responds to changes in all prices, those of traded goods and those of non-traded goods; see Kemp (1969, Chapter 6).

Consider the next assumption (4), that each country can survive under autarky. It is possible that even a wealthy trading country has no autarkic equilibrium. It might lack the climate, land area, soil fertility and technology needed for the production of subsistence food and medical services. One thinks immediately of Holland, Belgium, Ireland, Singapore, Hong Kong and even Japan and the United Kingdom. But if a country has no autarkic equilibrium and if there are just two traded goods, the offer curve of that country consists of two disjoint segments, each confined to its own quadrant; or it reduces to the origin. This in turn suggests that, if there are just two countries, the offer curves of those countries may fail to intersect. Hence the depiction of the worldwide free-trade equilibrium by Figure 39.2 must be revised, as must the comparative static analysis based on that figure; for further details, see Kemp (2003).

Finally, if assumption (5) is abandoned and increasing returns to scale (supported by external economies of production) are admitted to both industries, the shape of the offer curve changes radically. A large part of the curve, containing the origin and extending into the first and third quadrants, must be redrawn with curvature opposite to that of GOG'. At any given terms of trade, in either country, there may be one, two or three potential equilibria. If there are three, one of them must involve incomplete specialization in production. However, in any potential equilibrium involving incomplete specialization, both outputs and offers respond perversely to small changes in the terms of trade; see Kemp (1969, pp. 167–169) and Wong (1995, pp. 229–233).

REFERENCES

Kemp, M.C. (1969), *The Pure Theory of International Trade and Investment*, Englewood Cliffs, NJ: Prentice-Hall.

Kemp, M.C. (2003), 'International Trade without Autarkic Equilibrium', *Japanese Economic Review* 54: 353–360.

Kemp, M.C. and R.W. Jones (1962), 'Variable Labor Supply and the Theory of International Trade', *Journal of Political Economy* 70: 30–36.

Marshall, A. (1879/1930), *The Pure Theory of Foreign Trade*, London: London School of Economics and Political Science.
Wong, K.-Y. (1995), *International Trade in Goods and Factor Mobility*, Cambridge, MA: MIT Press.

40. The Stolper-Samuelson box

Henry Thompson

General equilibrium economics stresses the interplay between output markets and input markets in the whole economy. The Stolper-Samuelson (1941) production box solidified the link between prices of products and prices of inputs in a competitive neoclassical economy examining the particular issue of a tariff and the real wage.

In the production box with two factors and two products, the intuitive property is that a higher price raises the demand and relative price of the factor intensive in that product. The Stolper-Samuelson theorem relates directly to the underlying theorem of Heckscher (1919) and Ohlin (1933) stating that a country would import the product using its relatively scarce factor intensively, a tariff reducing imports and making the scarce factor more expensive. The production box mirrors the exchange box of Edgeworth (1904) and Pareto (1906) that complete the general equilibrium economy conceptualized by Walras (1874).

Figure 40.1 is a production diagram with inputs of capital K and labor L for products 1 and 2. Cost minimization implies that the slope of the convex neoclassical isoquant for product 1 equals the slope of the isocost line. That is, the marginal rate of substitution equals the wage rent ratio w/r. Positive diminishing marginal productivity implies convexity of the isoquant. Product 2 has a similar cost-minimizing equilibrium.

The production box in Figure 40.2 combines the two products with the origin O_2 for product 2 in the upper right hand corner. The length of the box is the endowment of labor $L = L_1 + L_2$ and its height the capital endowment $K = K_1 + K_2$. Equilibrium in production determines factor prices and the distribution of factors between sectors.

With perfect factor mobility between sectors, the wage would be the same in each sector, as would the return to capital. Cost minimization and factor mobility together imply that the economy operates on the locus of tangencies of isoquants, namely the contract curve CC in Figure 40.2. Neoclassical homothetic production implies a unique contract curve. Product 1 is capital intensive with the contract curve above the diagonal, and K_1/L_1 greater than K_2/L_2. Moving northeast along the contract curve,

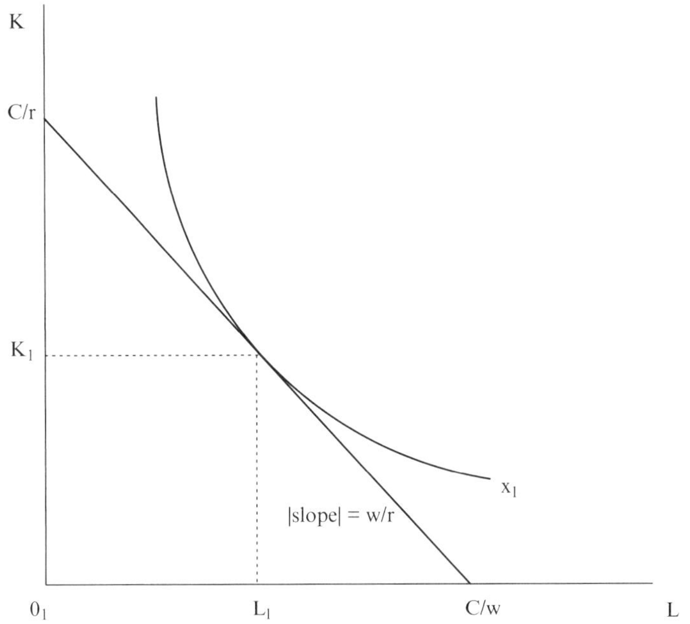

Figure 40.1 Cost minimization

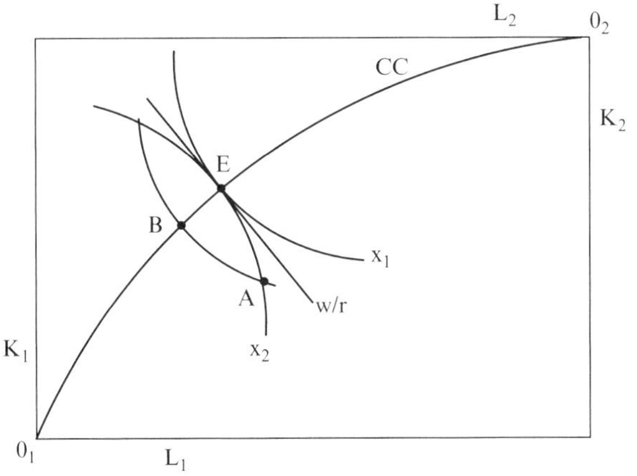

Figure 40.2 Equilibrium in the production box

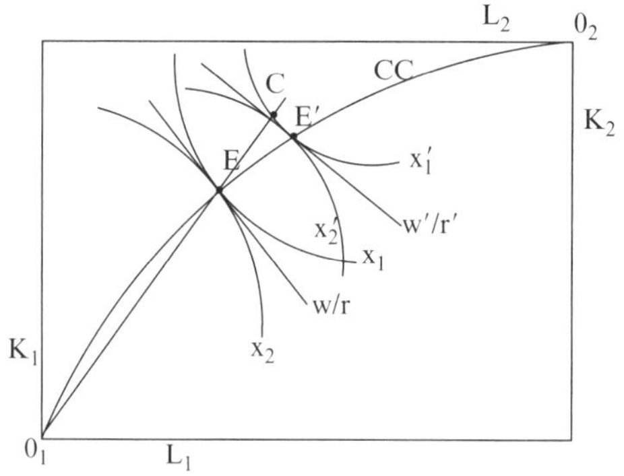

Figure 40.3 A tariff on product 1 and factor prices

the output of product 1 expands, and the wage/rent ratio w/r falls, but the capital/labor ratio remains higher in industry 1.

Homothetic production implies an equal slope of all isoquants along any ray from the origin. One implication is that the contract curve does not cross the diagonal. If a point on the diagonal is on the contract curve, every other point would be as well. This necessary lack of a factor intensity reversal, however, is unique to the two-dimensional model.

The two isoquants have the same slope and the production equilibrium point E in Figure 40.2. At any point such as A off the contract curve, the slopes of the isoquants are unequal. At point A, the marginal value of labor is higher in sector 2, labor is bid into that sector, capital is similarly bid into sector 1, and the economy converges to equilibrium at some point between B and E on the contract curve.

A tariff raises the price of the import-competing product, shifting production in its direction along the contract curve and leading to the Stolper-Samuelson factor price adjustment. Figure 40.3 illustrates the effect of a tariff on imported product 1. Output increases from x_1 to x_1' as sector 2 output declines from x_2 to x_2' and both capital and labor move to sector 1.

Expansion of capital-intensive sector 1 increases the relative demand for capital, lowering the wage/rent ratio. Homothetic production implies an equal w/r along ray O_1C in Figure 40.3 and the tariff-induced equilibrium at E' is below point C on isoquant x_1'. The relative wage falls from w/r to w'/r', demonstrating the Stolper-Samuelson theorem that an increase in the relative price of the capital-intensive product raises the relative price of capital.

This general statement shows that the Stolper-Samuelson theorem has application beyond tariffs, applying to any price change regardless of its source. Other applications include price changes induced by changes in domestic taxes, tastes, income, regulation, restructuring, monopoly power or technology. The model can also be modified to examine the impact of factor market distortions such as minimum wages, union contracts, labor subsidies and investment taxes.

As the expanding capital-intensive import-competing sector 1 becomes more labor intensive, sector 2 might be expected to become more capital intensive, but both sectors become more labor intensive. The decrease in labor-intensive production explains this paradox.

The algebra of the Stolper-Samuelson theorem developed by Samuelson (1953) and Jones (1965) lay the foundation for extending the general equilibrium model to include more inputs or products in Chipman (1966), Ethier (1974) and Jones and Scheinkman (1977). The rich possibilities of more factors are illustrated in the model with simply a third factor developed by Ruffin (1981) and Thompson (1985). Beyond the two-dimensional model, defining factor intensity is problematic, as illustrated by the 3x3 model of Thompson (2001). One consistent result is that a tariff must raise the real return to some factor of production and lower some other real return, the magnification effect of Jones (1965).

The algebraic model, along with improved production data, has led to highly detailed computable general equilibrium models that expose the myriad links between tariffs and wages. It is little exaggeration to say that the Stolper-Samuelson theorem was the stimulus for these advances in economic thought. Another advantage of the algebraic model is that the theoretical assumptions can be relaxed parametrically, as in Thompson (2003), who shows that the Stolper-Samuelson theorem is robust.

The Stolper-Samuelson production box provides underlying intuition on the link between product prices and factor prices, and keeps attention focused on cost minimization and substitution. The Stolper-Samuelson theorem also expands awareness from partial to general equilibrium, to include the secondary effects of changing prices on the economy. The Stolper-Samuelson production box will remain a crucial component of economic thought.

REFERENCES

Chipman, John (1966), 'A survey of the theory of international trade: Part 3, the modern theory', *Econometrica* 34, 18–76.

Edgeworth, Francis (1904), 'The theory of distribution', *Quarterly Journal of Economics* 18, 149–219.

Ethier, Wilfred (1974), 'Some of the theorems of international trade with many goods and factors', *Journal of International Economics* 13, 201–224.
Heckscher, Eli (1919), 'The effect of foreign trade on the distribution of income', *Ekonomisk Tidskrif*, reprinted in Harry Flam and June Flanders (eds) (1991) *Heckscher-Ohlin Trade Theory*, Cambridge, MA: The MIT Press.
Jones, Ron (1965), 'The structure of simple general equilibrium models', *Journal of Political Economy* 73, 557–572.
Jones, Ron and José Scheinkman (1977), 'The relevance of the two-sector production model in trade theory', *Journal of Political Economy* 85, 909–935.
Ohlin, Bertil (1933), *Interregional and International Trade*, Cambridge, MA: Harvard University Press, reprinted in Harry Flam and June Flanders (eds) (1991) *Heckscher-Ohlin Trade Theory,* Cambridge, MA: The MIT Press.
Pareto, Vilfredo (1906), *Manual of Political Economy*, 1971 translation of 1927 edition, New York: Augustus M. Kelley.
Ruffin, Roy (1981), 'Trade and factor movements with three factors and two goods', *Economics Letters* 8, 177–182.
Samuelson, Paul (1953), 'The prices of goods and factors in general equilibrium', *Review of Economic Studies* 21, 1–20.
Stolper, Wolfgang and Paul Samuelson (1941), 'Protection and real wages', *Review of Economic Studies* 9, 58–73.
Thompson, Henry (1985), 'Complementarity in a simple general equilibrium production model', *Canadian Journal of Economics* 18, 616–621.
Thompson, Henry (2001), 'International trade with three factors, goods, or countries', *Keio Economic Studies* 38, 43–52.
Thompson, Henry (2003), 'Robustness of the Stolper-Samuelson factor intensity price link', in Kwan Choi (ed.), *Handbook of International Trade*, Boston, MA: Blackwell.
Walras, Leon (1874), *Elements of Pure Economics: Or the Theory of Social Wealth.* 1954 translation of 1926 edition, Homewood, IL: Richard Irwin.

41. The Lerner diagram

Alan V. Deardorff

The Lerner Diagram was first drawn by Abba Lerner in an unpublished seminar paper in 1933. He used unit-value isoquants together with unit isocost lines to show the relationship between prices of goods and factors in what we now call the Heckscher-Ohlin model. That paper was reproduced, 'as it was originally written' according to the journal editor, as Lerner (1952). Since then, many others have used the diagram, attributing it to Lerner, for purposes well beyond Lerner's explication of good and factor prices. Notably, Findlay and Grubert (1959) used the diagram for analyzing the effects of technological progress on outputs and, in consequence, the terms of trade.

Some (including me, until I learned better) have called it the Lerner-Pearce Diagram, giving credit also to Pearce (1952a,b). In fact, although Pearce (1952a) was debating Lerner regarding the likelihood of factor price equalization, he used unit isoquants, not unit-value isoquants. Since these do not align in equilibrium with a single unit isocost line, they cannot be used in the same way, and they do not achieve the essential simplicity of Lerner's construction. Pearce (1952b) did use unit-value isoquants, but in context it is clear that he was simply copying Lerner.[1]

1. THE DIAGRAM

The essential Lerner Diagram is Figure 41.1. It is drawn for given constant-returns-to-scale technologies for producing two goods, X and Y, from two factors, capital K and labor L, and for given goods prices, p_X and p_Y. Technologies and prices together imply the two curved unit-value isoquants shown: the combinations of factors that will yield an output of a good worth one unit of value ($1). From these isoquants, one constructs the straight line that is tangent to both. For both goods to be produced in a competitive equilibrium, factor prices, w for L and r for K, must be such that factors worth $1 can produce output worth $1 and no more. The common tangent thus represents a unit-isocost line embodying such

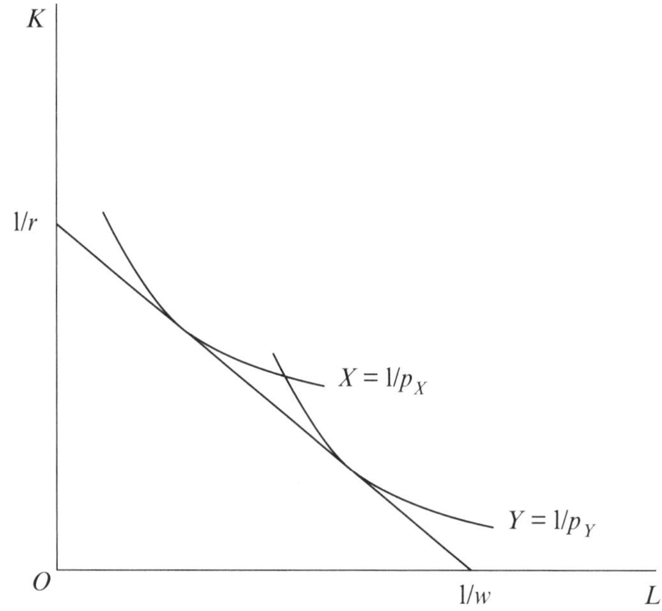

Figure 41.1 Prices of goods and factors in the Lerner diagram

equilibrium factor prices. Its intercepts are the quantities of the factors worth $1, and thus $1/w$ and $1/r$ as shown.

Lerner's purpose with this diagram was to show that, in this world of two factors and two goods, the prices of the goods determine the prices of the factors, which is the essential message of Samuelson's (1948, 1949) Factor Price Equalization Theorem. This is true, by this construction, only if the common tangent exists and is unique.[2]

2. EXTENSIONS

The importance of the Lerner Diagram in trade theory derives from far more than just its original use by Lerner. The diagram can be augmented to include information on factor intensities, factor endowments and factor allocations. The isoquants themselves can be shifted to represent changes in prices and/or changes in technologies. And the number of goods can be expanded beyond two, showing alternative equilibria that arise with and without factor price equalization when factor endowments do and do not lie within a common cone of diversification. Each of these extensions is illustrated here.

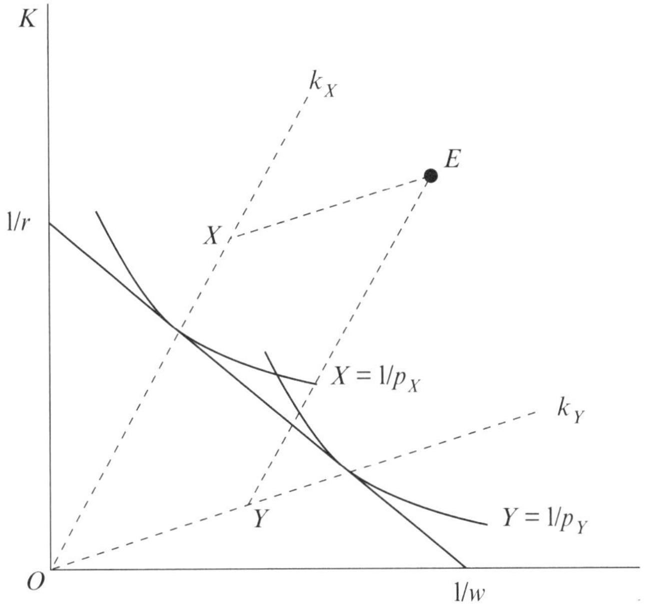

Figure 41.2 Factor intensities and allocations

Figure 41.2 includes, as Lerner did, the two straight lines from the origin through the points of tangency. These lines, labeled k_X and k_Y, show by their slopes the ratios of factors that must be employed in each industry if both face the common factor prices (w,r). The lines therefore also constitute the loci of possible allocations of the factors to the two industries under these circumstances.

By adding to the diagram a point E showing a country's factor endowments, lines k_X and k_Y can be used to construct a parallelogram between the origin, O, and E. Its two other corners then show the only allocations of factors to the two industries consistent with full employment. In effect, points O and E thus anchor a production Edgeworth Box, with the lines k_X and k_Y identifying a point on its efficiency locus. Points X and Y represent factors allocated to the industries, and their positions relative to both the origin and the isoquants imply the value of the economy's outputs of X and Y.

Figure 41.3 shows the effects of either an increase in the price of good X or a Hicks-neutral improvement in its technology. These changes imply that a smaller amount of factors will produce a dollar's worth of X, and the unit-value isoquant of X therefore shifts inward to X'. This shift requires that most of the rest of the figure be redrawn. First, a new common

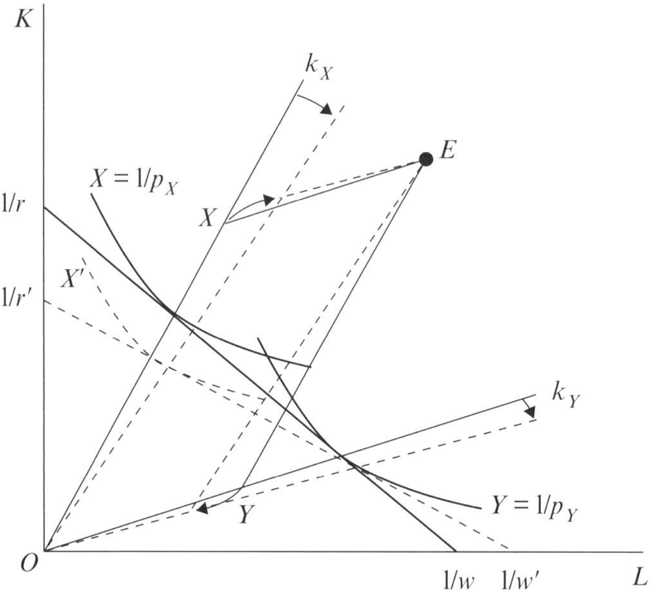

Figure 41.3 Effect of increase in price or technology for good X

tangent appears, flatter than before and tangent to both isoquants at lower ratios of capital to labor. The intercepts of this tangent show that the rental price of capital has risen, while the wage of labor has fallen. The lower capital–labor ratios imply flatter lines for k_X and k_Y, which therefore rotate clockwise, as shown. Finally, the new parallelogram constructed from these lines shows the *X* industry employing more of both factors, while the *Y* industry employs less. Thus output of *Y* falls while that of *X* rises (the latter due in one case to both the additional factors and the improved technology).

Finally, Figure 41.4 shows a version of the Lerner Diagram with three goods, *X*, *Y*, and *Z*. Like Figure 41.1, this takes as given the prices and technologies of all three goods. However, these are assumed here to conform to a particular configuration, in which all three goods can be produced somewhere, but not all in one country.[3] As a result, there is no common tangent to all three unit-value isoquants at once, but only to two at a time. The tangent to the *X* and *Y* isoquants determines the factor prices, w_1, r_1, consistent with producing both of them, without any output of good *Z*, production of which would lose money. The tangent to *Y* and *Z* similarly determines w_2, r_2 at which *Y* and *Z* can be produced. The points of tangency determine the factor ratios that will be

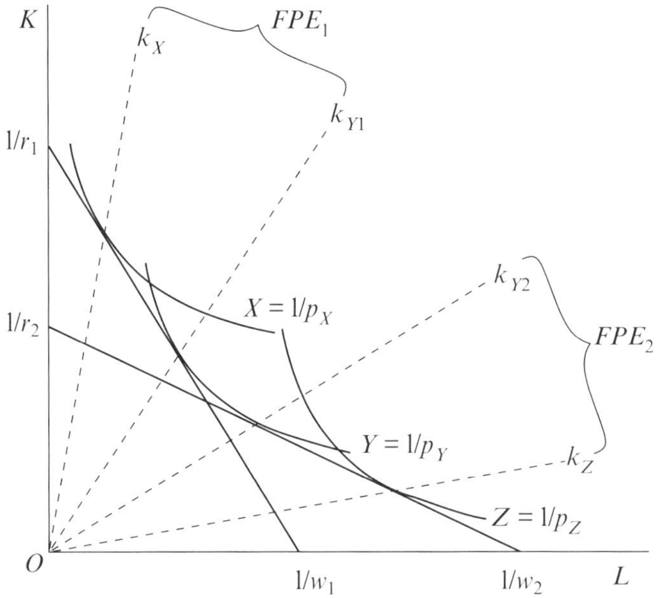

Figure 41.4 Two cones of diversification

employed in these two cases, k_X and k_{Y1} in the first case and k_{Y2} and k_Z in the second.

These ratios provide the bounds for two diversification cones. In Figure 41.4, these are labeled FPE_1 and FPE_2 to indicate that if two countries have factor endowments within the same one of these cones, they will have the same factor prices. Of course, in a two-country world, this could not happen, since both would produce the same two goods and nobody would produce the third. But if there are many countries (as the Lerner Diagram certainly allows), countries' factor endowments could be distributed across factor space in such a way that several would lie within each cone. In that case, there might also be countries with factor endowments lying between the cones, producing only good *Y*, and with factor prices somewhere between those shown (determined by an appropriate tangent to the *Y* isoquant).

This 'two-cone model' is highly abstract, like all of the models considered here. But it does a nice job of capturing a world in which groups of rich and poor countries have distinct factor prices and patterns of specialization. Recent empirical work suggests that this may fit the data from a range of countries better than the one-cone model.

NOTES

1. This is not to say that Pearce's substantive point about the likelihood of factor price equalization was incorrect; only that he seems not to deserve credit for introducing the diagram.
2. Lerner devoted much of his attention to the possibility of non-uniqueness, which requires what we would today call a factor-intensity reversal. He viewed this as unlikely.
3. That is, the price of the good of intermediate factor intensity, *Y*, must not be so low that producing a mixture of goods *X* and *Z* would always be at least as profitable.

REFERENCES

Findlay, R. and H. Grubert (1959), 'Factor Intensities, Technological Progress and the Terms of Trade', *Oxford Economic Papers* **11**, 111–121.
Lerner, Abba P. (1952), 'Factor Prices and International Trade', *Economica* N.S. **19** (February), 1–15.
Pearce, Ivor F. (1952a), 'The Factor Price Equalization Myth', *Review of Economic Studies* **19** (2), 111–120.
Pearce, Ivor F. (1952b), 'A Note on Mr. Lerner's Paper', *Economica* N.S. **19** (February), 16–18.
Samuelson, Paul A. (1948), 'International Trade and the Equalisation of Factor Prices', *Economic Journal* **58** (June), 163–184.
Samuelson, Paul A. (1949), 'International Factor-Price Equalisation Once Again', *Economic Journal* **59** (June), 181–197.

42. The trade theory diagram

Peter Lloyd

In international trade theory, a figure combining a concave transformation curve and a quasi-concave social indifference map has been widely used to show gains from trade and other welfare propositions for trading economies. Ronald Findlay described it as 'the sacred diagram of the international trade economist' (Baldwin, 1982, p. 142).

The model has one country producing, consuming and trading two goods. The country is assumed to be small in the particular sense of smallness used in the theory of international trade, that is, a price taker. Under these conditions, the country gains from trade. Extensions of the figure have been used to illustrate a variety of issues in the normative theory of trade policy. These figures are still used in almost every undergraduate text and many graduate texts on international trade.

1. THE DIAGRAM

Figure 42.1 presents the basic diagram. In it the production possibilities of the country are represented by a transformation curve PP′. This curve is drawn as strictly concave. It is assumed that a social indifference map representing the preferences of the community between all alternative combinations of aggregate consumption of the two goods exists. Furthermore this map is always drawn as if it is well-behaved, and in particular, the social or community indifference curves do not intersect and all curves are strictly concave from above. Thus, it is assumed that the map has all of the basic properties of a well-behaved indifference map representing the preferences of a single individual between bundles of the two goods.

The transformation curve and the social indifference map are combined to show the effects of international trade. It is assumed that the country concerned can trade freely at the fixed prices. Given the relative price of good 1, that is (p_1/p_2), the country chooses to produce at the point $y^f = (y^f_1, y^f_2)$ where y^f_i is the national output of good i =1 or 2. It trades

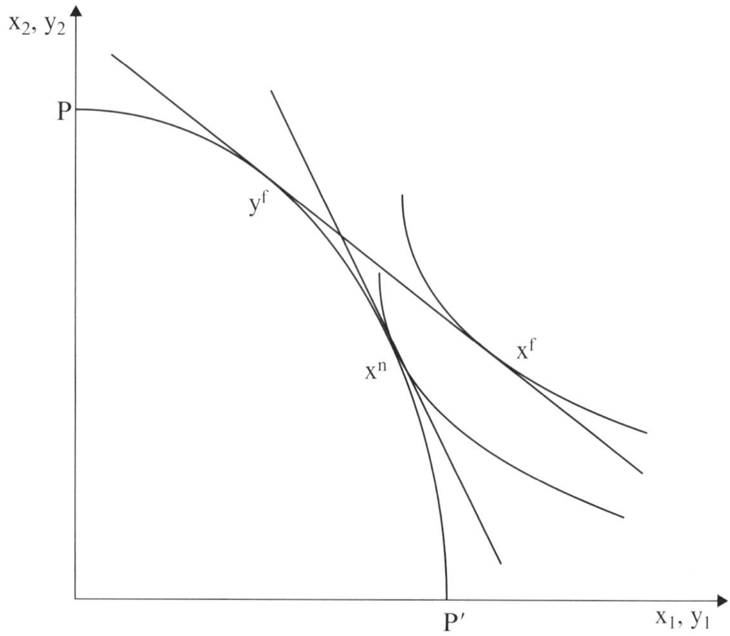

Figure 42.1 *Gains from trade*

along the line which is tangent to this point and chooses to consume an aggregate bundle $x^f = (x_1^f, x_2^f)$ where x_i^f is the aggregate national consumption of good $i = 1$ or 2. Through this point, there passes a social indifference curve which is tangential to the trade line.

These production and consumption points can be compared with the corresponding points when there is no trade. Under this condition, the country is constrained to the production possibilities given by its transformation curve. It would choose the consumption bundle x^n, which in this case is also the production point y^n. Through this point, there passes a social indifference curve. It follows immediately from the result that the free-trade consumption bundle lies in the set of bundles above the indifference curve of the no-trade situation, and that the free-trade consumption bundle is socially preferred to the no-trade bundle. Thus this simple diagram shows the gains from trade for a small country trading freely with the rest of the world. Indeed, free trade is the optimal policy for such a small country. This was the foundation of the argument by international economists for free trade.

2. ITS HISTORY

The history of this curve is tangled. There are numerous claims for the first discovery of the figure. There are also numerous antecedents with slightly different but closely related diagrams that preceded it. In these antecedents, however, the commodity traded may be an asset rather than a produced good, the entity trading may be an individual rather than a nation and the transformation curve may be concave, linear or a curve with concave and convex segments. Humphrey (1993) has given an excellent account of these precedents.

The first discovery of this international trade figure has been variously credited to Viner in 1931, Lerner (1932) and Leontief (1933). In his classic study of the theory of international trade theory, Viner (1937, Chart XI) presented a figure with all of the geometric features of Figure 42.1. In a footnote, he stated that this diagram was presented in a lecture at the London School of Economics in January 1931. The same footnote also refers to the constructions of both Lerner and Leontief, whose works had been published by the time of the publication of Viner's book. We cannot be sure how much of the text describing these curves and the gains from trade was present in the 1931 presentation.

Leontief (1933) developed the essential geometry of the transformation curve and the social indifference map and used these to show the nature of the equilibrium for a small price-taking country and gains from trade. He then extended the model to two countries trading freely with each other. Here he assumed explicitly that trade is balanced and implicitly that what are now called transfer costs are zero and, therefore, the Law of One Price holds. He presented another diagram showing the pattern of trade for the two countries. This is the antecedent of the modern textbook geometry of the Heckscher-Ohlin and other trade models. It illustrated the properties of the competitive equilibrium for a world economy consisting of two nations freely trading two goods.

Lerner (1932) contains a diagram showing the competitive equilibrium for a world economy in which there is a world transformation curve and a world indifference map. There are two countries and two goods. This yielded the same results as Leontief's 2-country diagram. His analysis was a quantum leap in the understanding of international trade and in several respects is more sophisticated than any account until the work of Samuelson some 15 years later. However, his paper does not contain Figure 42.1.

All three authors developed their geometry independently, but Leontief can be considered the originator of the diagram in the form of Figure 42.1. His paper is the one usually cited by subsequent writers.

Subsequently, the analysis was extended in two directions. First, the geometry was used to illustrate the general equilibrium behaviour of the two-country two-good version of the Heckscher-Ohlin model. The role of comparative advantage in determining the competitive equilibrium and the relationships between goods production and factor allocations and between goods prices and factor prices were developed. Second, in the 1950s, 1960s and 1970s, these diagrams were applied by leading international trade economists such as Harry Johnson, Jagdish Bhagwati, Max Corden and Ronald Findlay to a variety of policy issues. These include non-discriminatory or discriminatory tariffs, non-tariff measures, domestic distortions, non-economic objectives or growth in the production possibilities of the country due to factor accumulation or technological progress. This geometry became the way in which international trade economists of this and subsequent generations understand the basic issues of international trade policy.

As an example, consider the basic case of an *ad valorem* tariff levied on imports of good one, the import good in Figure 42.1. Figure 42.2 illustrates the loss of welfare. The free-trade equilibrium production and consumption points are y^f and x^f, as before. The line connecting these points has a slope given by the relative price of good 1 in the free-trade

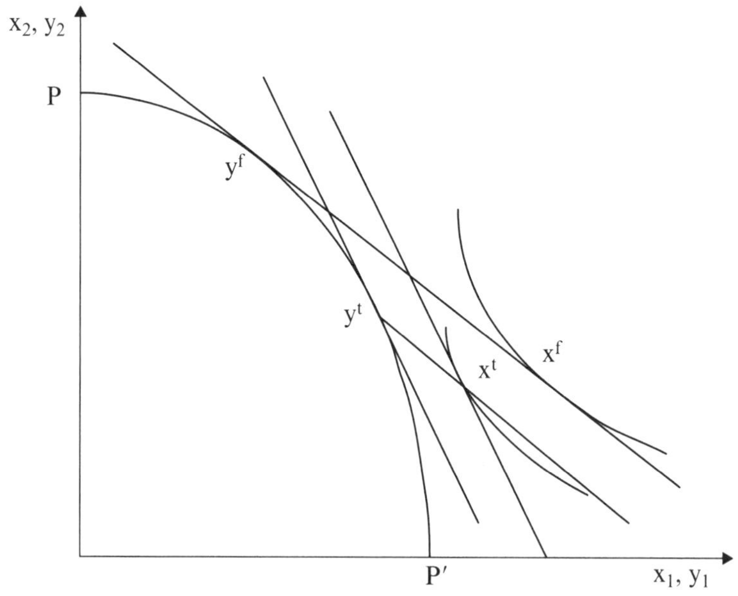

Figure 42.2 The welfare loss due to a tariff

situation. The production and consumption points in the tariff situation are y^t and x^t. The line connecting these points also has a slope given by the relative price of good 1 under free trade as the terms of trade are not affected by the imposition of the tariff. However, the steeper lines passing through these points have a slope given by the higher price of good 1 in the tariff situation. Consumers and producers make their choices in response to these post-tariff relative prices. Producers choose y^t, trade takes place at the fixed world prices and consumers choose x^t. The line tangential to y^t shows the national product valued at distorted prices. The line passing through x^t shows the value of national expenditure, including the tariff revenue that is redistributed to households. Social indifference curves are drawn through the consumption points in the free-trade and tariff situations. The free-trade consumption point lies on a higher indifference curve than the tariff-distorted point.

3. REVISITING THE SOCIAL INDIFFERENCE MAP

While, in the 1940s and 1950s, the transformation curve became grounded in the efficient allocation of resources which lies behind it (see Chapter 40, on the Stolper-Samuelson box), the social indifference map was increasingly questioned. The underlying problem we now know is that such a map exists only under very stringent and quite unrealistic conditions.

Samuelson (1956) showed that a social utility function exists for all feasible income distributions if situations can be compared by making lump-sum redistributions so as to maximise a Bergson-Samuelson social welfare function. The latter function has as its arguments the (ordinal) utility functions of individual households. This gives a social utility function that can rank alternative situations. It provides a solution to the problem that is elegant but quite unrealistic.

One alternative condition is to assume that all individuals have identical homothetic preferences. Under this condition, aggregate demand is independent of the distribution of income. A social utility function or social indifference map exists. This assumption is widely used today in international trade theory. However, this map can only be used as a generator of aggregate demand, given aggregate national income and prices. It can be used to obtain a competitive equilibrium and to test theories of comparative advantage but it has no welfare interpretation and cannot be used by itself to rank alternative situations.

Some of the early writers clearly had concerns over the use of a social indifference map. In particular, Lerner (1932) used his map as a function that generates aggregate demand but seems also to have believed that it can serve as a local welfare comparator. As 'the New Welfare Economics' gained acceptance in the 1950s and 1960s, international trade economists came to rely upon a national compensation test to compare situations. This enabled theorists to demonstrate that certain situations were welfare-improving in the Pareto sense that it would be possible by means of lump-sum redistributions of income to make at least some households better off and none worse off. These assumptions dispense with the need for a social indifference map. These tests can be easily extended to a world with many goods, factors, countries and trade policy interventions.

As an example of one policy choice and one compensation test, consider again the case of an *ad valorem* tariff as in Figure 42.1. The consumption possibility set in the free-trade situation is larger than that in the tariff situation. Observe that $p^f x^f > p^f x^t$. At free trade prices, there is an increase in real national income in the free-trade situation. Starting from the free-trade situation and moving to free trade, there will be gainers and losers, but the gainers can compensate the losers. (Note too that $p^t x^f > p^t x^t$. Hence, $p^t x^t \not> p^t x^f$. That is, starting from the free-trade situation, the gainers in moving to a protected trade situation cannot compensate the losers. Thus the movement to free trade satisfies the double Scitovsky test – see Chapter 14, on community indifferences curves and the Scitovsky paradox.) Contemporary graduate trade theory relies upon a test incorporating a Pareto improvement to illustrate propositions in international trade theory and policy.

REFERENCES

Baldwin, Robert E. (1982), 'Gottfried Haberler's contributions to international trade theory and policy', *Quarterly Journal of Economics*, 97, 141–48.

Humphrey, Thomas M. (1993), 'The trade theorist's sacred diagram: Its origin and early development' in Thomas M. Humphrey, *Money, Banking and Inflation: Essays in the History of Economic Thought*, Cheltenham: Edward Elgar.

Leontief, Wassily W. (1933), 'The use of indifference curves in the analysis of foreign trade', *Quarterly Journal of Economics*, 47, 493–503.

Lerner, Abba (1932), 'The diagrammatical representation of cost conditions in international trade', *Economica*, 12, 319–34.

Samuelson, Paul A. (1956) 'Social indifference curves', *Review of Economic Studies*, 9, 89–110

Viner, Jacob (1937), *Studies in the Theory of International Trade*, New York: Harper and Brothers.

43. The four-quadrant diagram for the two-sector Heckscher-Ohlin model

Arvind Panagariya

The four-quadrant diagram is remarkable for its ability to represent succinctly and precisely the full equilibrium in the two-good, two-factor, two-country Heckscher-Ohlin (H-O) model. With four factor allocations, two outputs and two factor prices in each country and the common goods price, the model has 17 variables in all. The diagram manages to show the equilibrium value of the key variables explicitly, with the remaining ones determined indirectly.

I first introduce the basic diagram as applied to the autarky equilibrium. I then extend it to the two-country equilibrium and briefly mention further applications. In the penultimate section, I give a brief history of the diagram.

1. THE BASIC DIAGRAM

Consider an economy producing two goods, 1 and 2, using two factors, labor (L) and capital (K). Production functions exhibit the standard properties, including constant returns to scale and diminishing returns to each factor. Cost minimization under these assumptions leads to a positive relationship between optimal capital–labor ratio and the wage–rental ratio in each good. Measuring the wage–rental ratio, w, along the horizontal axis and the capital–labor ratio in sector i, k_i, along the vertical axis, I depict the relationship for each good in the first quadrant of Figure 43.1.

The H-O model further assumes that one of the goods, say, good 2, is unambiguously capital intensive. This means that for each set of factor prices, the cost-minimizing capital-to-labor ratio is higher in good 2 than good 1. This is the reason I have drawn Ok_2 above Ok_1 everywhere in Figure 43.1. In principle, it is possible for Ok_1 and Ok_2 to cross such that good 2 is capital intensive for lower values of w and labor intensive (meaning it would exhibit lower capital–labor ratio than good 1) for higher values of it. I will briefly return to this 'factor-intensity reversal' later.

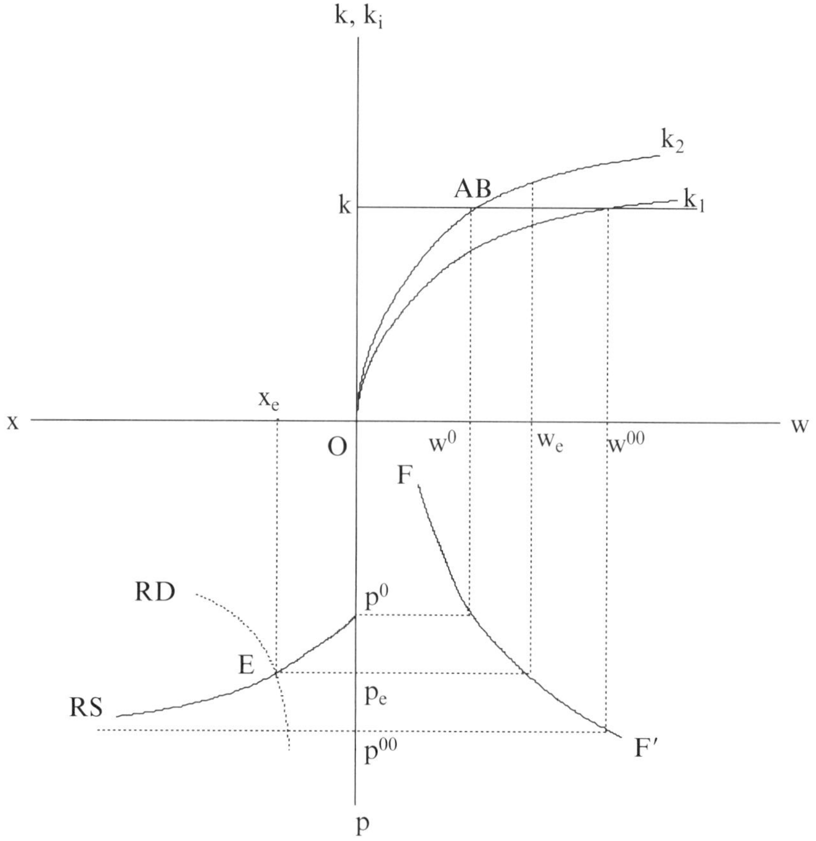

Figure 43.1 Autarky equilibrium in the H-O model

Ruling out the factor-intensity reversals, the Stolper-Samuelson (1941) property of the H-O model allows us to establish a one-to-one relationship between goods prices and factor returns. A higher relative price of good 1, the labor-intensive good, is associated with a higher wage–rental ratio. Intuitively, the increase in the relative price of good 1 leads to an expansion of good 1 and contraction of good 2. At the initial factor prices, good 1 demands more labor per unit of capital than good 2 releases. This change leads to an excess demand for labor and excess supply of capital, raising the wage–rental ratio. FF' in the fourth quadrant of Figure 43.1 depicts this positive relationship between w and p, where p denotes the relative price of good 1.

Next, let k on the vertical axis in the first quadrant of Figure 43.1

represent the capital–labor endowment ratio of the country. If the country specializes completely in good 2, we have $k_2 = k$, as shown by point A. Cost minimization then implies w^0 as the wage–rental ratio and p^0 as the corresponding price. At prices equal to or less than p^0, it is unprofitable to produce good 1 and the economy specializes completely in good 2. The equilibrium is characterized by $k_2 = k$, requiring $w = w^0$.

We can now turn to tracing the full relative supply curve in the third quadrant. Measure the ratio of output of good 1 to that of good 2 by x. We already know that at prices equal to or less than p^0, $x = 0$. Starting at p^0, suppose we increase p. Positive output of good 1 now appears with resources allocated from good 2 to good 1. As this happens, w and the capital–labor ratios in the two sectors rise. Both capital–labor ratios can rise despite a constant endowment ratio because of the shrinking output of the capital-intensive good. As expected, we have an upward-sloped relative supply curve RS. Eventually, as p reaches p^{00}, the output of good 2 drops to zero with $k_1 = k$ and $w = w^{00}$. The value of x approaches infinity as p approaches p^{00}.

The last step in completing the autarky equilibrium is to introduce demand. This is done most simply by assuming homothetic preferences; this ensures that the relative demand, depicted by RD in Figure 43.1, depends only on the relative price. The intersection of RS and RD gives the equilibrium price and relative output shown by p_e and x_e respectively. Given p_e, we can determine w_e as the wage–rental ratio in the fourth quadrant and given w_e, we can read the equilibrium k_1 and k_2 along Ok_1 and Ok_2, respectively, in the first quadrant. The values of k_1 and k_2 can be combined with full employment conditions to determine absolute levels of factor allocations. In turn, the factor allocations can be combined with the production functions to determine outputs and marginal products of labor and capital in each good. The latter equals the real factor returns in terms of the two goods.

2. THE TWO-COUNTRY EQUILIBRIUM

Let us think of the country just considered as Home and introduce a second country called Foreign. Identify the variables of Foreign by an asterisk. Although Ohlin (1933) did not originally assume this, to obtain precise predictions, assume Home and Foreign have identical tastes and technology and differ only in terms of relative factor endowments. Regarding the latter, assume that Foreign has a lower capital–labor endowment ratio than Home.

To avoid clutter, I depict the international equilibrium separately in

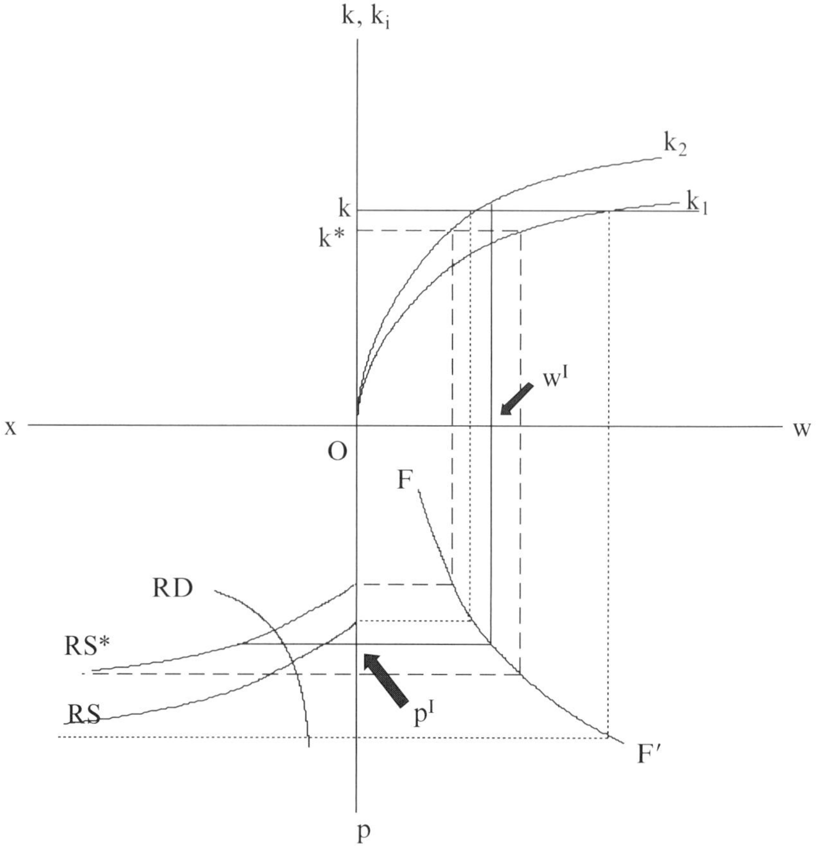

Figure 43.2 Two-country equilibrium in the H-O model

Figure 43.2, where I suppress the autarky equilibriums and some of the labeling. All curves associated with Home and Foreign are the same except the relative supply curves. With the endowment ratio of Foreign at k*, its supply curve is RS*. Consistent with the Rybczynski (1955) theorem, at a given goods price, labor-abundant Foreign produces relatively larger quantity of the labor-intensive good, good 1.

It is immediately clear from Figure 43.2 that under autarky, the good using the abundant factor more intensively will be cheaper in each country: good 2 in Home and 1 in Foreign. Therefore, consistent with the Heckscher-Ohlin theorem, each country will export the good using its abundant factor more intensively. Under autarky, the lower price of this good leads to a lower relative price of that factor in each country.

Therefore, under autarky, the wage–rental ratio is lower in the labor-abundant Foreign than Home. As trade equalizes the good prices between the two countries (p^I in Figure 43.2), it also equalizes the relative factor prices (w^I in Figure 43.2). But equal wage–rental ratios lead to equal capital–labor ratios in each good across countries. In turn, this equalizes the marginal products of each factor in each good across countries. Therefore, consistent with the Factor-Price Equalization theorem, trade equalizes not just the goods prices but real factor prices internationally as well.

3. FURTHER APPLICATIONS

Three further applications of the four-quadrant diagram may be noted. First, the reader may verify that if the endowment ratios were sufficiently different, trade would result in complete specialization by at least one country. In this case, trade would lead to a convergence of the factor prices but stop short of their complete equalization except in the borderline case in which the goods price is at the threshold of complete specialization.

Second, the diagram can also be employed to analyze factor-intensity reversals. Thus, for example, imagine that Ok_1 intersects Ok_2 from below at point Z so that good 2 is capital intensive for the wage–rental ratios to the left of Z and labor-intensive to the right of it. This will result in FF' in the fourth quadrant taking a U-shape, with the bottom of U being vertically below Z. FF' will have a positive slope to the left of Z and a negative slope to the right of it. Suppose further that the capital–labor endowment ratio of Home is above Z and of Foreign is below it. It is then clear that the wage–rental ratio of Home will be determined on the downward-sloping section of FF' and of Foreign on the upward sloping section of it. Equalization of goods prices in a free-trade equilibrium will now not result in the equalization of factor prices. Besides, given that good 1 is capital intensive in Foreign and labor intensive in Home, there is no meaningful way to relate exports to factor endowments and factor intensities.

Finally, technologies may differ between the two countries. For simplicity, suppose that the technology for good 2 is the same but Foreign has a slightly superiority technology in good 1 in the Hicks-neutral sense. The relationships for Home in Figure 43.2 remain unchanged. Given the Hicks-neutral difference in technology, the relationships for Foreign in the first quadrant of Figure 43.2 are also unchanged. But since good 1 is labor intensive, at a given price ratio, Foreign has a higher wage–rental ratio. Therefore, the relationship in the fourth quadrant for Foreign now lies to the right of FF'. The relative supply curve of Foreign in the third quadrant lies to the left of where it is shown in Figure 43.2. All results of the H-O still hold except that while trade leads to the convergence of factor prices, it falls short of equalizing them. At a common goods–price ratio, factor prices in Home and Foreign are determined along different FF' curves in the fourth quadrant. Other forms of technological differences can be similarly analyzed.

4. HISTORY OF THE DIAGRAM

Although the diagram is often associated with the names of Harrod (1958) and Johnson (1957), the constructions in the first and fourth quadrant in Figure 43.1 can be found in Samuelson (1949), who presents them in the first and second quadrants, respectively, with the wage–rental ratio shown on the vertical axis. Remarkably, in footnote 1 on p. 188, he even draws the two quadrants side by side, depicting the factor-intensity reversal. Harrod only presents the first quadrant, but elaborates on factor-intensity reversals. Johnson explicitly acknowledges building his analysis on the diagrams in Samuelson and Harrod; he places the relationship between the goods prices and the wage–rental ratio in the fourth quadrant, explicitly introduces countries' factor endowments and extensively applies the diagram to analyze the patterns of trade and the implications of trade for factor–price convergence and equalization across countries. I am unable to track down when the full four-quadrant diagram first appeared, though I saw it for the first time in 1975 in my graduate course in international trade by Professor Carlos Rodriguez of Columbia University, who drove down every Friday morning to teach the course at Princeton. I have subsequently used the four-quadrant diagram regularly in my own graduate courses.

REFERENCES

Harrod, Roy (1958). 'Factor Price Relations Under Free Trade', *Economic Journal* 68, pp. 245–55.

Johnson, Harry G. (1957). 'Factor Endowments, International Trade and Factor Prices', *Manchester School of Economic and Social Studies* 25(3), pp. 270–83.

Ohlin, Bertli (1933). *Interregional and International Trade*, Cambridge, MA: Harvard University Press.

Rybczynski, T.M. (1955). 'Factor Endowments and Relative Commodity Prices', *Economica* 22, pp. 336–41.

Samuelson, Paul (1949). 'International factor price equalization once again', *Economic Journal* 59, pp. 181–197.

Stolper, Wolfgang F. and Paul A. Samuelson (1941). 'Protection and Real Wages', *Review of Economic Studies* 9, pp. 58–73.

44. The integrated world equilibrium diagram

Avinash Dixit

Factor price equalization means that under certain conditions, unrestricted international trade in goods equalizes prices of factors across countries, even though the factors cannot move across borders so there are only separate national markets for them. When Victor Norman and I started our work on various generalizations of the 2-by-2 Heckscher-Ohlin-Samuelson model of trade, the dominant approach to the factor price equalization issue was 'univalence', namely whether the mapping from the prices of factors to the unit costs of goods was globally invertible. The mathematical conditions for this were stringent and abstruse, and relevant only in the case where the number of goods exactly equaled the number of factors. No one knows the exact number of either, but surely it is extremely unlikely that the two are equal. As Victor Norman remarked, what is really special about the 2-by-2 case is not that 2 is a small number, but that 2 = 2.

The univalence approach had an even more basic flaw. It enabled us to find unique factor prices *given* the prices of goods. But where do these prices of goods come from? Under free trade, they come from the equilibrium conditions of the world markets for goods. Trade theory has always prided itself on being a showcase for general equilibrium theory. The study of factor price equalization should not disregard the fact that a trading equilibrium is a *general* equilibrium.

This implies some restrictions on the prices of goods. We should look for solutions to the set of simultaneous equations 'Unit cost = Price' for all the goods, not for arbitrary prices on the right-hand side, but for equilibrium prices. How do we find them? The answer is immediate when we look back at the basic question in this light. If factor prices are equal across countries, no further trade in factors will occur even if country borders are opened up for factor movements. In other words, goods trade will achieve the same equilibrium as when factors are also internationally mobile, so that there is a world market for each factor. Therefore we should find that equilibrium, and the prices of goods it generates.

Once we set up that equilibrium, we realize that there is no need to

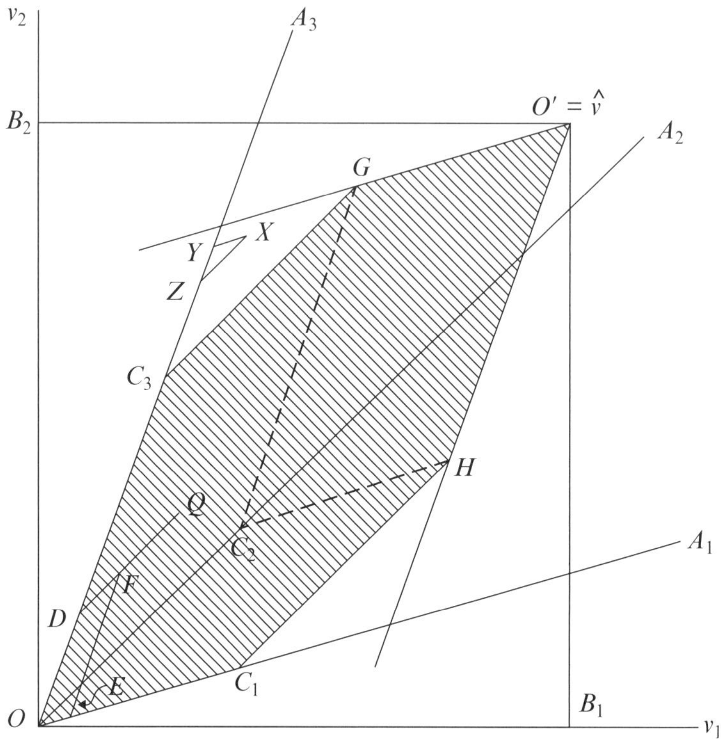

Source: Dixit and Norman (1980). Reproduced with permission from Cambridge University Press.

Figure 44.1 The integrated world equilibrium diagram

examine univalence. Instead, we can directly ask whether the equilibrium quantities of goods can be split up between the separate countries in such a way as to employ fully the endowments of factors in each country, making it unnecessary for factors to move.

The integrated world equilibrium diagram immediately emerges as a simple way to illustrate this process.[1] Figure 44.1 shows the case of three goods and two factors; this is a reproduction of Fig. 4.6 from Dixit and Norman (1980). The lengths OB_1 and OB_2 are the world's total endowments of the two factors v_1 and v_2; then OO' becomes the vector of these endowments. In a hypothetical equilibrium where factors can be traded freely across countries, suppose the directions OA_1, OA_2 and OA_3 represent the factor proportions used in the production of the three goods. (If input substitution in production is possible, these proportions are endogenous, being cost-minimizing at the equilibrium prices of factors. The figure merely illustrates the outcome of the equilibrium that has been calculated in the background.) Similarly, the vectors OC_1, OC_2 and OC_3 represent the factor quantities used in the production of the three goods in the equilibrium. For the world factor markets to clear, these vectors must add up to OO'. With GO' equal and parallel to OC_1, C_1H and C_3G each equal and parallel to OC_2, and HO' equal and parallel to OC_3, this completes a hexagon $OC_1HO'GC_3O$.

Now suppose factors are not internationally tradable. Consider a point Q inside the hexagon, and suppose OQ is the vector of factor endowments in one country, so that QO' is the vector of factor endowments in the other country. Now it is possible to split up the production of goods in the integrated equilibrium between the two countries in such a way as to clear the markets for factors in each country. In fact it is possible to do so in a continuous infinity of ways. The figure shows two examples. In the first way, one country produces enough of good 3 to use up factors OD, enough of good 2 to use up factors DQ, and nothing of good 1; the other country produces the rest. In the second way, one country produce enough of good 1 to use up factor endowments OE, good 3 to use up EF, and good 2 to use up FQ; again the other country produces the rest. Any of these assignments replicates the integrated equilibrium with separate factor markets in each country. Incidentally, the construction also shows how quantities of goods produced and traded cannot be determined uniquely when there are more goods than factors.

Next consider a point such as X outside the hexagon. If one country has the factor endowment OX, then any attempt to assign the quantities of goods in the integrated equilibrium will require this country to produce enough of the third good to use up factors somewhere between OY and OZ. But that will leave the other country producing negative amounts of the third good. This is not possible, therefore the integrated equilibrium cannot be replicated with separate factor markets in the two countries, and factor price equalization cannot occur.

It is even more evident that non-negative production quantities cannot be assigned to the two countries to replicate the integrated equilibrium if the factor endowment point lies outside the cone spanned by the directions OA_1 and OA_3. In other words, if the relative factor endowment composition of the two countries differs by more than the differences in the relative factor requirements of the goods' production, we cannot get factor price equalization. Point X lies inside this cone, yet it cannot be replicated; so factor price equalization in fact requires a little bit more.

Our construction is very similar to that in another showcase of general equilibrium, namely finance. In Arrow-Debreu theory, people trade in contracts for commodities contingent on each of the conceivable states of the world. In reality, markets exist only for various financial assets, which are particular linear combinations of the state-by-state contingent claims. Then the question is whether or when markets are complete, that is, trading in assets can replicate the equilibrium of an Arrow-Debreu world. The answer is that the Arrow-Debreu equilibrium can be replicated with trade in assets if the vectors of state-contingent payoffs to the available assets span the full space of state-contingent commodities.

In the standard model of international trade, countries differ in their factor endowments, and would like to trade factor services. They cannot do so directly, but can trade linear combinations of factors that are embodied in goods. The question is whether trade in these packages of factors can replicate direct trade in all individual factors. The analogy would suggest that the answer is yes if the vectors of factor proportions embodied in goods span the space of the factors. But there is a further complication. In finance, the packages of Arrow-Debreu state-contingent claims that constitute the assets can be traded in positive or negative amounts by taking long or short positions in the assets. But in international trade, a country cannot produce negative quantities of a good. Therefore, we need a theory of non-negative spanning. And that is exactly what the construction of the integrated world equilibrium diagram achieves.

This is how Victor Norman and I thought about factor price equalization and the integrated world equilibrium diagram. Let me say a little bit about precedents and subsequent developments. So much of modern international trade theory comes from Samuelson that it is hardly surprising to find a nice verbal statement of the idea in one of his early papers on the subject (Samuelson, 1949, p. 194):

> Let us suppose that in the beginning all factors were perfectly mobile and nationalism had not yet reared its ugly head. . . . [T]here would be one world price of food and clothing, one real wage, one real rent, and the world's land and labour would be divided between food and clothing production in a determinate way. . . . Now suppose that an angel came down from heaven and notified some fraction of all the labour and land units producing clothing that they were to be called Americans, the rest to be called Europeans; and some different fraction of the food industry that henceforth they were to carry American passports. Obviously, just giving people and areas national labels does not alter anything: it does not change commodity or factor prices or production patterns.
>
> But now turn a recording geographer loose, and what will he report? Two countries with quite different factor proportions, but with identical wages and rents and identical modes of commodity production.

Here is the integrated world equilibrium and its split into two national equilibria with factor price equalization for the 2-by-2 case, but in very simple words. Our diagram just shows how to do it for more goods and factors. Indeed, we later discovered that Travis (1964) had anticipated some simple cases of our general theory of the integrated world equilibrium and its diagrammatic representation.

What about subsequent developments? No new idea or technique can meet the fondest hopes of its authors without the work of others who use, extend, modify and improve upon it. We have been lucky. It would take too long to list all the advances, so we will mention just two. Helpman and Krugman (1985) used the integrated equilibrium to great effect in their analyses of trade under various kinds of imperfect competition. Deardorff (1994) produced an elegant generalization with many goods and factors, clarifying the general sense in which factor price equalization requires endowments to differ less across countries than factor intensities vary across industries.

The only correct answer to the question whether economics is a science or an art is 'Both'. Therefore, Victor Norman and I are especially pleased to have a contribution on the art side that is deemed worthy of inclusion in this volume, and to have the opportunity to tell the story behind it.

NOTE

1. The diagram gives an appealing visualization and intuition. Of course, the rigorous proof that the conditions that emerge from the procedure are both necessary and sufficient for factor price equalization requires algebraic reasoning; see Dixit and Norman (1980, pp. 108–110).

REFERENCES

Deardorff, Alan V. (1994), 'The possibility of factor price equalization, revisited', *Journal of International Economics*, 36(1–2), 161–175.

Dixit, Avinash and Victor Norman (1980), *Theory of International Trade*, Cambridge, UK: Cambridge University Press.

Helpman, Elhanan and Paul Krugman (1985), *Market Structure and Foreign Trade*, Cambridge, MA: MIT Press.

Samuelson, Paul A. (1949), 'International factor-price equalization once again', *Economic Journal*, 58(2), 181–197.

Travis, William P. (1964), *The Theory of Trade and Protection*, Cambridge, MA: Harvard University Press.

45. The optimal tariff

Murray Kemp

Any trading country, whatever its size, can move world prices in its favour by imposing restrictive tariffs (or quotas) on its imports or exports. That was recognized long ago by Torrens (1821, 1844) and J.S. Mill (1844, 1848). However, tariffs may be set at such high levels that trade disappears altogether. The task of any country is to choose tariffs not just to improve its terms of trade but to choose them optimally to maximize its wellbeing. It was left to Bickerdike (1906, 1907) and Edgeworth (1908) to provide governments with the necessary formulae.

From the foundation laid by Bickerdike and Edgeworth emerged the basic diagram, reproduced as Figure 45.1 and on display in nearly every modern textbook on the theory of international trade. The diagram is based on the assumption that just two countries, *G* and *H*, trade in just two commodities. Under free international trade, the world trading equilibrium is at point *P*, where the two offer curves, GOG' and HOH', intersect. The equilibrium terms of trade are represented by the slope of *OP*. However, by restricting its imports by means of an optimal import duty, country *G* can move the equilibrium to the preferred point P', where one of its trade indifference curves *uu*' is tangential to country *H*'s offer curve. (Bickerdike, 1907, recognized that if there are two traded commodities then only one tax is needed.) At P', country *G* enjoys improved terms of trade (represented by the slope of OP') and an improved level of wellbeing. The post-tariff equilibrium price ratio in *G* is represented by the slope of AP' and the optimal import duty is represented by OA/OB.

Given the persistent curvature of *H*'s offer curve, the optimal import duty for *G* is necessarily positive. In Figure 45.2, that feature of HOH' is abandoned and the possibility that the optimal tariff might be zero is recognized. It is worth emphasizing that the revised shape of *H*'s offer curve is quite compatible with the customary assumptions under which offer curves are drawn; see Kemp and Shimomura (2000) and Chapter 39 of this volume. To this point it is implicitly assumed that country *H* does not retaliate against *G*'s tariff. Under that assumption, country *H* must

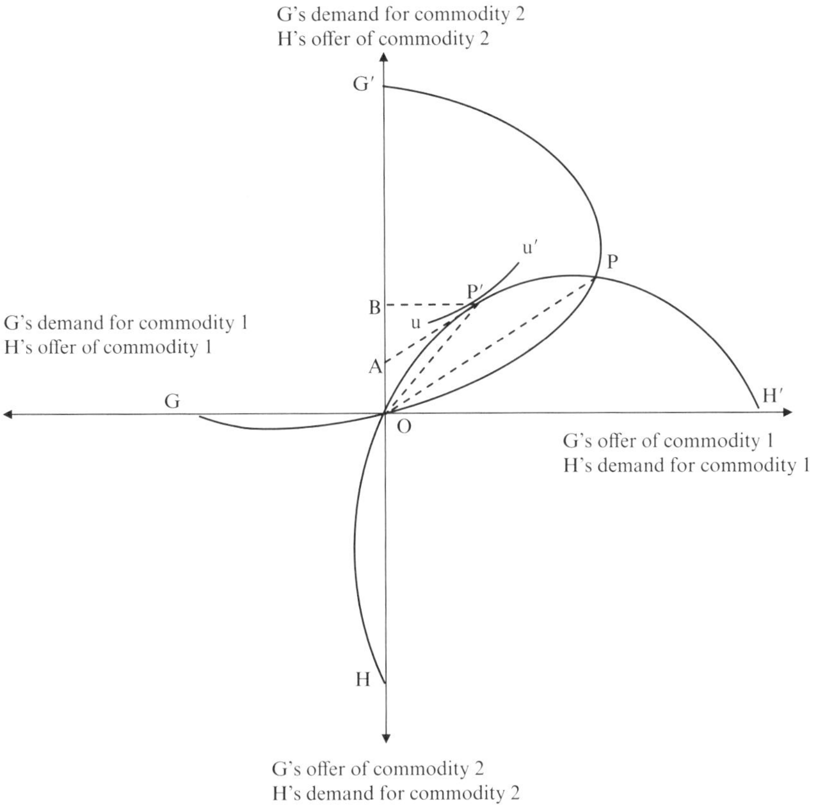

Figure 45.1 G's optimal tariff identified on H's offer curve

be worse off in the post-tariff situation than under free trade. If, on the other hand, each country chooses an optimal tariff of its own whenever its trading partner imposes a tariff (so that each country's optimal tariff is conditional on that of the other country) then it is possible that both countries will be worse off than under free trade; see, for example, Johnson (1953–4) and Wan and Zhou (2008).

I have referred to the assumptions under which offer curves are customarily drawn. Those assumptions are discussed in detail by Kemp and Shimomura (2000) and in Chapter 39 of this volume. For the present purposes, the most important of those assumptions is of price-taking representative households. Given that assumption, the purpose of the optimal tariff is clear: it is to maximize the utility of the representative household under the assumption that the tariff proceeds are evenly distributed over households. Without the assumption, one must find an alternative

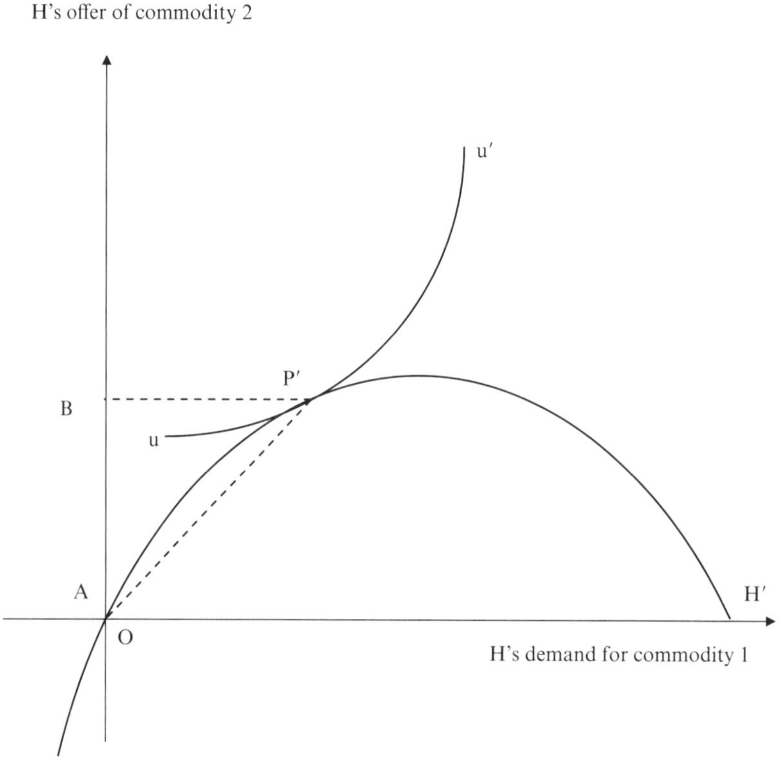

Figure 45.2 The possibility of a zero optimal tariff

social welfare function and an alternative distribution of tariff proceeds. Evidently the optimal tariff depends on the choices made.

REFERENCES

Bickerdike, C.F. (1906), 'The Theory of Incipient Taxes', *Economic Journal* 16: 529–535.

Bickerdike, C.F. (1907), 'Review of A.C. Pigou, *Preferential and Prospective Import Duties*', *Economic Journal* 17: 98–102.

Edgeworth, F.Y. (1908), 'Appreciations of Mathematical Theories III', *Economic Journal* 18: 392–403.

Johnson, H. (1953–4), 'Optimal Tariffs and Retaliation', *Review of Economic Studies* 21: 142–153.

Kemp, M.C. and K. Shimomura (2000), 'An Antiquarian Note on Optimal Tariffs', *History of Political Economy* 32: 415–420.

Mill, J.S. (1844), *Essays on Some Unsettled Questions of Political Economy*,

London: John W. Parker, West Strand. Reprinted by the London School of Economics and Political Science, *Reprints of Scarce Works on Political Economy*, no. 7, 1948.
Mill, J.S. (1848), *Principles of Political Economy with Some Applications to Social Philosophy*, Book III, Chapter XVIII, Section 5, 1st edition, London: John W. Parker.
Torrens, R. (1821), *An Essay on the Production of Wealth*, London: Longman, Hurst, Rees, Orme and Brown.
Torrens, R. (1844), *The Budget: On Commercial and Colonial Policy*, London: Smith, Elder and Co.
Wan, H.Y., Jr and Y. Zhou (2008), 'Trade Liberalization as a Game of Decision under Uncertainty', in B. Tran-Nam, N.V. Long and M. Tawada, eds, *Globalization and Emerging Issues in Trade Theory and Policy*, Bingley, UK: Emerald, pp. 15–28.

PART III

Macroeconomics

Macroeconomic analysis and stabilisation

46. Keynesian income determination diagrams

Michael Schneider

In the *General Theory*, Keynes summarised his income determination theory, which he made clear applies only to a period short enough for the capacity-creating effects of investment to be ignored, as stating: (i) that '[i]n a given situation of technique, resources and costs' (Keynes, 1936, p.28) income depends on the volume of employment; and (ii) that employment depends on an aggregate supply function Z = φ(N), where N stands for employment and Z stands for the aggregate supply price of the output from employing N men, and an aggregate demand function D = f(N), where D stands for the sum of expected aggregate consumption expenditure (assumed to be an increasing function of N) and expected aggregate investment expenditure. It followed that employment, and therefore income, is determined by the equation φ(N) = f(N), that is to say the condition that aggregate supply equals aggregate demand, the former being constrained by the latter. The principal policy implication of this theory is that if an increase in employment and income is desired, it may be necessary to increase aggregate demand.

In his summary of his income determination theory, Keynes also stated that he would use wage units rather than prices as his measure of value, and that he would assume that 'money wage and other factor costs are constant per unit of labour employed' (Keynes, 1936, p.27), an assumption he made solely to simplify the exposition, which he was to drop later. An implication of these procedures is that an increase in aggregate demand will induce an increase in aggregate supply without any increase in the general price level being required; to put it briefly, in the macroeconomy, demand creates its own supply.

The *General Theory* does not contain any diagrams illustrating its income determination theory. Subsequent to its publication, apart from the IS-LM diagram (dealt with in Chapter 47), a number of substantially different attempts were made to represent Keynes's theory diagrammatically. As we shall see, each of these diagrams can be viewed as illustrating a combination of a function or functions representing a behavioural

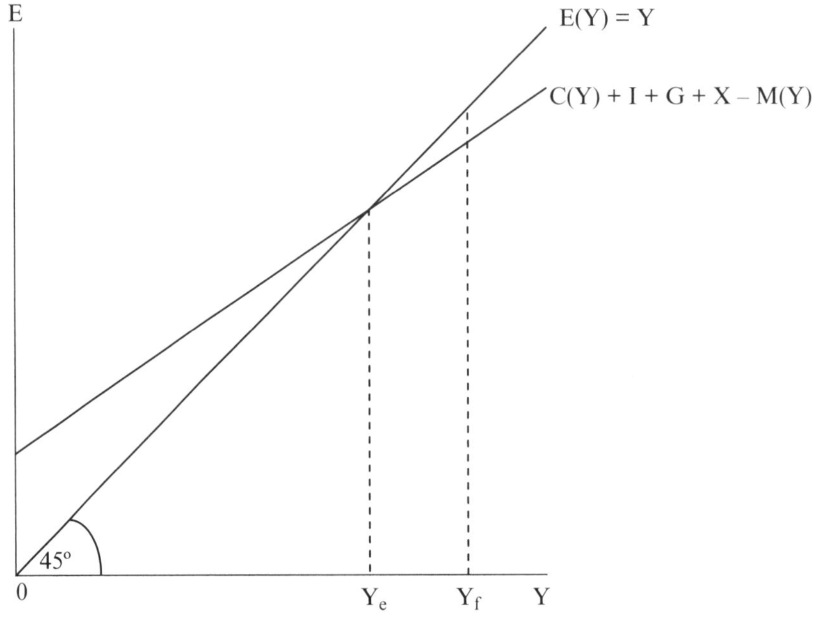

Figure 46.1 *45 degree or Keynesian cross diagram*

relationship or behavioural relationships and an equilibrium equation determining income.

In two of these attempts, Keynes's income determination theory is reduced to a single function and an equilibrium equation. One of these is illustrated in Figure 46.1, a four-sector version of what is alternatively known as the 45 degree or Keynesian cross diagram, drawn in income (Y)-expenditure (E) space. In this figure, the horizontal axis measures real income, of which the equilibrium level of income (Y_e) and the full employment level of income (Y_f) are two examples, and the vertical axis measures the after-taxation components of expected aggregate demand for output, namely consumption (C), investment (I), government expenditure (G) and exports (X) net of imports (M). Figure 46.1 includes only one schedule representing a function, namely the aggregate demand, or expenditure, schedule. This schedule is assumed to have a positive intercept on the vertical axis, and a slope determined by the marginal propensity to consume, to invest (a propensity often assumed to be zero), and to import, each out of income. The other component of Figure 46.1 is the 45 degree line, the locus of all positions where expected expenditure equals income (E (Y) = Y, the equilibrium equation that this figure illustrates), representing equilibrium in the commodity (or goods and services) market. In the *General Theory,* unlike in his *Treatise on Money*, Keynes defined income as equal to the value of output. Thus the aggregate demand schedule and 45 degree line intersection, where uniquely the value of output demanded equals the income generated by its production, determines the equilibrium level of income, which may or may not coincide with the full employment level of income (in Figure 46.1 it is drawn falling short). This diagram illustrates the Keynesian theory that income, or output, is constrained by demand, a theory that Keynes contrasted with Say's Law, namely that supply creates its own demand.

Remarkably, a 45 degree macroeconomic diagram pre-dates the publication of the *General Theory,* appearing in Jantzen (1935, p.79), though the focus of this diagram was on maximisation, rather than determination, of an open economy's national income. Unaware of the Jantzen diagram, in 1938 Samuelson prepared Keynesian cross diagrams on slides for use in lectures.[1] The 45 degree diagram was published initially in Samuelson (1939, p.790), in which Figure 1 illustrates the equilibrium level of income first, in the absence of investment, as that level where all income is consumed, and second, in a 'healthy society' where investment does occur, as that level where all income is either consumed or invested; in the second case, a constant level of investment is added to a consumption schedule with a declining slope, the latter reflecting Keynes's 'psychological law' that as income increases, the marginal propensity to consume decreases. Government expenditure and taxation were added in Hansen (1945, p.383), and exports and imports were added as well at least as early as Harcourt, Karmel and Wallace (1967, p.241).

The 1939 diagram reappeared in the first edition of Samuelson's *Economics: An Introductory Analysis* (1948, p.260); it was only subsequently that the curved aggregate demand schedule came to be replaced by a linear one. The effectiveness of the 45 degree diagram as a means of conveying Keynes's income determination theory resulted in its nigh-universal use in macroeconomics textbooks over the subsequent three to four decades. From the late 1970s, however, textbooks gave increasing prominence to the aggregate supply-aggregate demand diagram discussed last in this chapter.

The second diagram based on a single function version of the Keynesian income determination theory arises out of the fact that in the *General Theory*, in a two-sector economy, the aggregate demand that generates output consists of consumption and investment (I), and that part of income not consumed is defined as savings (S). Thus an equivalent to the 45 degree diagram is to be found in a diagram in which the vertical axis is used to measure not aggregate demand but savings and investment. A

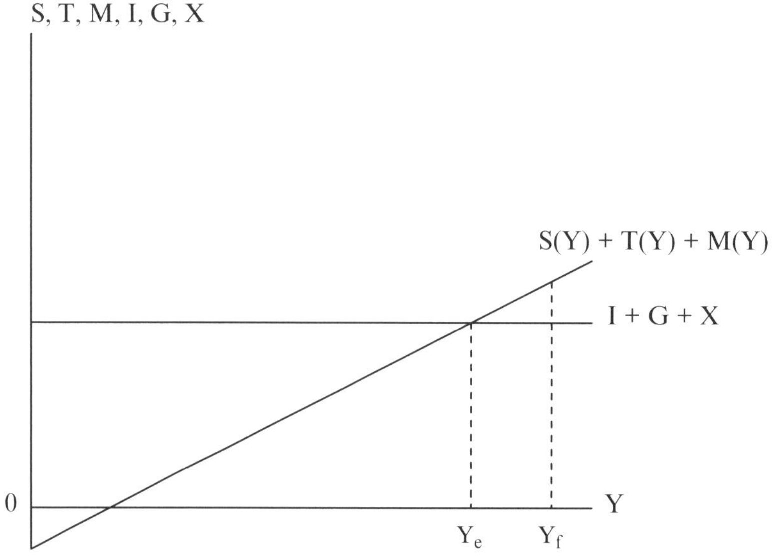

Figure 46.2 Injections–withdrawals or Keynesian cross diagram

four-sector version of this alternative Keynesian cross diagram is portrayed in Figure 46.2.

In Figure 46.2, the horizontal axis measures income, while government expenditure and exports are added to investment to make up injections, measured on the vertical axis, and taxation (T) and imports are added to saving to make up withdrawals, alternatively known as leakages, also measured on the vertical axis. The equilibrium level of income is determined by the intersection of the upward-sloping withdrawals schedule and the (horizontal) injections schedule, the single function in this case being W = W(Y), where W stands for withdrawals, which is equated with J, representing injections, to generate equilibrium. A variant of this diagram, which assumes that investment is a function of income, and therefore involves a second function J = J(Y), portrays an injections schedule which slopes upwards but less steeply than the withdrawals schedule.

The two-sector version of this diagram may have first appeared in Samuelson (1948, p.260), where it precedes the 45 degree diagram, and it was also reproduced on the cover of each of the first three editions of Samuelson's textbook, with the aim of drawing attention to the difference between the macroeconomic Keynesian cross and the microeconomic Marshallian cross; imports and exports were added at least as early as Kindleberger (1953, p.166). In later textbooks, the injections-withdrawals

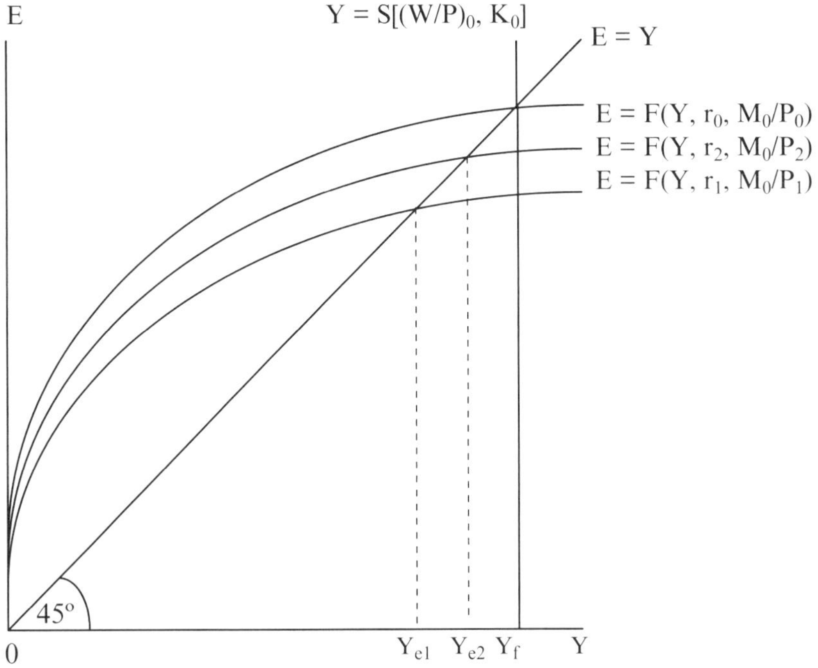

Source: Adapted from Patinkin (1956).

Figure 46.3 Patinkin diagram

diagram was commonly presented only as a complement to the 45 degree diagram.

Dissatisfied with the omission of any reference to aggregate supply in the Keynesian cross diagrams, Patinkin (1956, p.215), building on Patinkin (1949), added a vertical aggregate supply line $Y = S[(W/P)_0, K_0)]$ to the 45 degree diagram, its position being determined by $(W/P)_0$, representing the value of the real wage rate emerging from his flexible prices general equilibrium macroeconomic model, and by $(K)_0$, representing a capital stock taken as given. This diagram, with minor modifications to labels so as to highlight the dynamic movement to full employment, is reproduced in Figure 46.3, whose aggregate demand schedule illustrates the commodity market function in Patinkin's involuntary unemployment general equilibrium system, namely $E = F[Y, r_0, (M_0/P_0)]$, with r_0 and P_0 designating the equilibrium values of the interest rate and the price level respectively, and M_0 designating the money supply; the equation of this function with the supply function generates equilibrium in the commodity market.

According to the Pigou or Real Balance Effect, as the price level (say) falls, the value of an economy's net stock of wealth (or 'outside wealth') with a fixed money value increases and leads to an increase in consumption. Patinkin argued that according to this effect, an expenditure schedule that cut the 45 degree line to the left of the aggregate supply line would gradually shift up because of the consequent fall in the price level, eventually resulting in all three schedules intersecting at the same point (price level falls are assumed to be accompanied by equivalent money wage falls, keeping the aggregate supply schedule in the same position). In macroeconomic policy terms, however, Patinkin was a Keynesian, as he believed that demand deficiency might persist for a very long time, because of the relative ineffectiveness of price level falls and the possible adverse consequences for demand and hence income of their effect on price level expectations.

The assumption of a constant price level is also dropped in the remaining two Keynesian income determination diagrams to be considered. Of these, one is drawn in employment-revenue required or employment-revenue realised space. This is sometimes known as the aggregate supply-aggregate demand diagram, but to avoid confusion with the next and last Keynesian income determination diagram to be discussed in this chapter, I shall label it the Z/D-N diagram, after the space in which it is drawn. The Z/D-N diagram is portrayed in Figure 46.4.

In Figure 46.4, the horizontal axis measures employment and the vertical axis measures revenue (required, or realised). An origin-based Z curve with an increasing upward slope, reflecting diminishing returns to labour with a given capital stock, shows the revenue required by entrepreneurs to generate each level of employment; a D curve with a positive intercept on the vertical axis and a decreasing upward slope, reflecting a diminishing marginal propensity to consume, shows the revenue realised from the demand associated with each level of employment. The equilibrium level of employment, and therefore of income, is determined by the intersection of the Z and D curves; for this equilibrium to be stable, the only requirement is that the slope of the D curve eventually be less than that of the Z curve, which Weintraub (1957) showed to be highly probable given the impact on demand of likely changes in the distribution of income resulting from an increase in employment.

The Z/D-N diagram illustrates the 'two functions' version of the Keynesian income determination theory, to be found in Keynes's own summary of his theory, namely $Z = \varphi(N)$ and $D = f(N)$ (though in the diagram, output is measured not in wage units but in prices); the equating of these two functions generates the equilibrium level of employment, and therefore of income. As a representation of Keynesian income

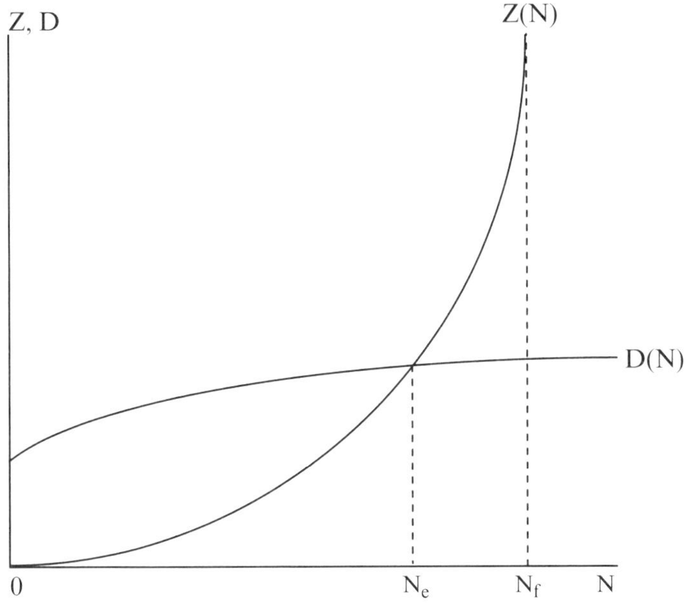

Figure 46.4 The Z/D-N diagram

determination theory, however, a disadvantage of the Z/D-N diagram, shared by the aggregate supply-aggregate demand diagram to be discussed next but not by the Keynesian cross and Patinkin diagrams, is that if its assumption of a constant money wage rate is overlooked, it can be interpreted as implying, wrongly, that an alternative Keynesian solution to unemployment is a lowering of the aggregate supply schedule by a reduction in the money wage rate.

Fusfeld (1985) claims to have been taught a version of the Z/D-N diagram in 1941 by Arthur E. Burns, who in turn claimed to have discussed it with Keynes during the latter's visit to Washington in that year, the second claim being disputed in Patinkin (1988). Be this as it may, the Z/D-N diagram probably first appeared in published form in Dillard (1948, p.30), though no explanation was provided there for the characteristics of the Z curve other than its upward slope. Dillard's preference seemed to be for the 45 degree diagram (see Dillard, 1948, p.34), which is the basis for most of his discussion of the Keynesian income determination theory. By contrast, after using both diagrams in publications dating from 1951, from 1956 Sidney Weintraub dropped the 45 degree diagram altogether in favour of the Z/D-N diagram.

During the 1950s and 1960s, the Z/D-N diagram was taught to a

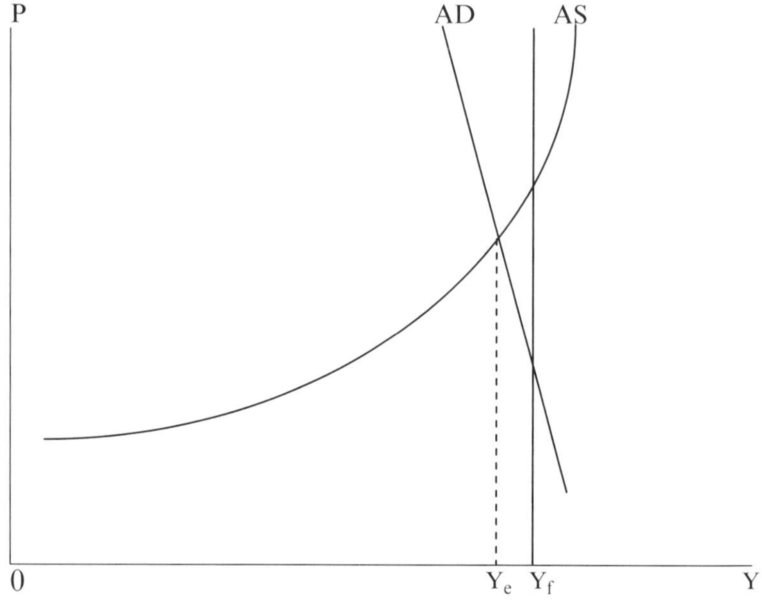

Figure 46.5 The AS-AD diagram

substantial proportion of macroeconomics students. Dillard's book was widely used, as was that by Stonier and Hague (1953), whose page 382 features a Z/D-N diagram based on Dillard's version, but adds a justification of the increasing slope of the Z curve in terms of increasing unit cost by assuming that to bring about a given change in employment, the same proportional change in revenue is required. A substantial though probably smaller proportion of macroeconomics students learnt of the Z/D-N diagram through their use of Davidson and Smolensky (1964), whose page 145 diagram is based on Weintraub's work.

The remaining Keynesian income determination diagram is drawn in real income–price level space. This diagram, commonly known as the aggregate supply-aggregate demand (henceforth AS-AD) or aggregate demand-aggregate supply diagram, is portrayed in Figure 46.5. In this figure, the horizontal axis measures real income and the vertical axis measures the general price level (P). An increase in the price level induces an increase in aggregate supply for one or more of the following reasons: in the short run some of the input prices faced by firms, such as wages, are constant; or the increase in the price level more than offsets the increases in costs faced by firms as the economy moves towards full employment;

or there is asymmetric money illusion; or there is a lag before price level expectations adjust. The aggregate supply schedule consequently slopes upwards to the right, reaching a maximum which in the short run can exceed the full employment level that is sustainable in the long run. While the aggregate demand schedule might be expected to be vertical, since any change in the price level by definition affects the value of output and the level of income equally, it is universally drawn sloping downwards to the right, the better treatments making reference to one or more of the following reasons: as the price level (say) falls, the Pigou or Real Balance Effect comes into operation; or the interest rate falls, stimulating investment (the Keynes Effect, a misnomer as Keynes did not believe it would be effective); or income is redistributed towards those with a relatively high propensity to consume; or, expecting the drop in the price level to be temporary, people switch from future to present consumption; or consumers are subject to money illusion; or net exports increase. While many textbooks imitate microeconomic diagrams by drawing the aggregate demand schedule not as a straight line but as a curve convex to the origin, I suspect that none has given a reason for doing so. Equating the two functions of the price level, namely the aggregate demand and aggregate supply functions [D(P) = Y and S(P) = Y], generates the equilibrium level of income.

The AS-AD diagram was probably first used, albeit with axes reversed compared with Figure 46.5, in lectures given by Jacob Marschak in 1948, published as Graph 19:II in Marschak (1951). Marschak justified the respective decreasing and increasing slopes of the aggregate supply and aggregate demand curves by assuming money illusion on the part of workers and consumers respectively, explicitly admitting that in the absence of this assumption, his aggregate supply curve would instead be a horizontal straight line and his aggregate demand curve would instead be a vertical straight line. Marschak drew the schedules as curves, as opposed to sloping straight lines, assuming the aggregate supply curve to be convex to the income axis due to diminishing returns to labour, and assuming the aggregate demand curve to be convex to the origin apparently on the ground that it was related to the rectangular hyperbola used to illustrate the quantity theory of money. A variant of this diagram draws the aggregate supply schedule with an initial horizontal section, followed by an upward-sloping section illustrating capacity constraints faced by individual firms, followed in turn by a vertical section illustrating the maximum output the economy is capable of producing. In this version of the diagram, which appeared for example in Bronfenbrenner and Holzman (1963, p.596), the horizontal section of the aggregate supply schedule is often described as 'Keynesian', because over this range, a rightward shift in the aggregate demand schedule will generate an increase in income without any rise in the price level.

The AS-AD diagram subsequently appeared in macroeconomics textbooks at least as early as McKenna (1955, p.210), which, following Brownlee (1948), derived the sloping aggregate demand schedule not from money illusion but from the Keynes Effect, and reappeared with increasing frequency in the late 1970s and in the 1980s, following the emergence of stagflation. Initially, it supplemented the 45 degree diagram, but in time it took precedence, the 45 degree diagram even being relegated to the penultimate chapter, for example, in Barro (1984, p. 494).

In textbooks, the AS-AD diagram is commonly derived from either the 45 degree diagram or the IS-LM diagram, but this procedure has been criticised by some as logically inconsistent (see Rao, 1998), perhaps most cogently in Colander (1995). So derived, the criticism runs, when the price level changes, the AD schedule incorporates the multiplier repercussions of a shift in the 45 degree diagram aggregate demand schedule, and therefore represents not demand but an equilibrium also incorporating supply; as a consequence, the AS-AD diagram contains two mutually incompatible aggregate supply schedules, an implicit (demand-constrained) one as well as an explicit one, and only an implicit aggregate demand schedule. Further, it can be argued that to describe an equilibrium schedule that 'shows the level of real GDP for which desired aggregate expenditure equals actual GDP' (Chapter 49, this volume) as an aggregate demand schedule may mislead some students and others into thinking that the AS-AD diagram has implications identical with those of a Marshallian supply and demand diagram, and consequently to the erroneous belief that any demand constraint on income will be automatically removed by a fall in the price level.

NOTE

1. Source: Samuelson, Paul (2008), Letter replying to author, 30 October.

REFERENCES

Barro, Robert (1984), *Macroeconomics*, New York: Wiley.

Bronfenbrenner, Martin and Franklyn D. Holzman (1963), 'Survey of Inflation Theory', *American Economic Review*, 53 (3), pp. 593–661.

Brownlee, O.H. (1948), 'Money, Price Level, and Employment', in Francis M. Boddy (ed.), *Applied Economic Analysis*, New York: Pitman.

Colander, David (1995), 'The Stories We Tell: A Reconsideration of AS/AD Analysis', *The Journal of Economic Perspectives*, 9 (3), pp. 169–88.
Davidson, Paul and Eugene Smolensky (1964), *Aggregate Supply and Demand Analysis*, New York: Harper and Row.
Dillard, Dudley (1948), *The Economics of J.M. Keynes*, New York: Prentice Hall.
Fusfeld, Daniel R. (1985), 'Keynes and the Keynesian Cross: A Note', *History of Political Economy*, 17 (3), pp. 385–9.
Hansen, Alvin (1945), 'Three Methods of Expansion Through Fiscal Policy', *American Economic Review*, 35 (3), pp. 382–7.
Harcourt, G.C., P.H. Karmel and R.H. Wallace (1967), *Economic Activity*, Cambridge: Cambridge University Press.
Jantzen, Ivar (1935), 'Lidt planøkonomisk Teori', *Nordisk Tidsskrift for Teknisk Økonomi*, I, pp. 72–116.
Keynes, J.M. (1936), *The General Theory of Employment Interest and Money*, London: Macmillan.
Kindleberger, Charles (1953), *International Economics*, Homewood, IL: R.D. Irwin.
Marschak, Jacob (1951), *Income, Employment and the Price Level: Notes on Lectures Given at the University of Chicago, Autumn 1948 and 1949*, New York: A.M. Kelley.
McKenna, Joseph P. (1955), *Aggregate Economic Analysis*, New York: Dryden Press.
Patinkin, Don (1949), 'Involuntary Unemployment and the Keynesian Supply Function', *Economic Journal*, 59 (234), pp. 360–83.
Patinkin, Don (1956), *Money, Interest, and Prices: An Integration of Monetary and Value Theory*, Evanston, IL: Row, Peterson.
Patinkin, Don (1988), 'Keynes and the Keynesian Cross: A Further Note, With a Reply by Daniel R. Fusfeld', *History of Political Economy*, 21 (3), pp. 537–47.
Rao, B. Bhaskara (1998), *Aggregate Demand and Supply: A Critique of Orthodox Macroeconomic Modelling*, New York: St. Martin's Press.
Samuelson, Paul (1939), 'A Synthesis of the Principle of Acceleration and the Multiplier', *Journal of Political Economy*, 47 (6), pp. 786–97.
Samuelson, Paul (1948), *Economics: An Introductory Analysis*, New York: McGraw-Hill.
Stonier, Alfred W. and Douglas C. Hague (1953), *A Textbook of Economic Theory*, London: Longmans, Green.
Weintraub, Sidney (1957), 'The Micro-foundations of Aggregate Demand and Supply', *Economic Journal*, 67, pp. 455–70.

47. The IS-LM diagram

Warren Young

Whether the IS-LM diagram has been praised as 'the core of modern macroeconomics', vilified as 'bastard Keynesianism', or utilized as a common analytical device for debate between 'fiscalists' and 'monetarists', it has been at the forefront of economic discourse from the late 1930s onwards. In this survey, I focus on the origin of the diagram in its CC-LL (Hicks, 1936) and IS-LL (Hicks, 1937) vintages. I then proceed to deal with the cardinal difference in derivation between Hicks's IS-LL (1937) and Hansen's IS-LM diagrams (1949). Finally, the impact of the diagram on interpretations and representations of Keynes's *General Theory* is assessed. Extensions to the diagram are also dealt with in the closed-economy context; the open-economy setting of the diagram will be dealt with in Chapter 48.

HICKS'S SEPTEMBER 1936 CONFERENCE DIAGRAM

Hicks's account of the genesis of his 1937 diagram is that it emanates directly from the use of his 'Value and Capital methods' of reducing a three equation system into two, and the concomitant diagrammatic representation of these resultant equations (Young, 1987, 98–102). While other ways of generating the diagram have been described elsewhere (Young, 1987, 94–97), for our purpose here, Hicks's account is taken at face value, as he only claimed 'responsibility' for the IS-LL diagram, and *not* the equations now considered to be 'IS-LM' (Young, 1987).

But there is a version of his diagram that predates the 1937 IS-LL diagram. This version – the CC-LL diagram – was presented by Hicks himself on the morning of 26 September 1936 at the 'symposium on Keynes', at which Harrod and Meade also presented their interpretations of Keynes's system. It should be recalled here that as Hicks himself wrote to Meade, in his own conference paper, he borrowed Harrod's equations and Meade's notation, and would have to produce his own paper 'out of

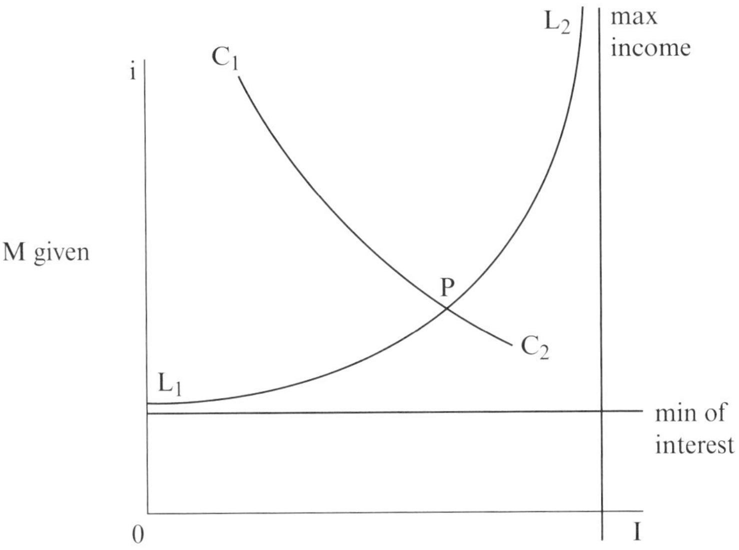

C_1, C_2 = marg eff of cap
The rele. importance of C_1, C_2 & L_1, L_2 in determining i & I depends where P is.

Source: Young (1987)

Figure 47.1 Hicks's CC-LL diagram (September 1936)

a hat' (Hicks to Meade, 6 September 1936, reproduced in Young, 1987, 35).

The diagram was copied 'off the blackboard' by Arthur Brown, then a D. Phil student at Oxford, and his copy is reproduced in Figure 47.1 (Young, 1987). In this diagram, Hicks specified both a minimum rate of interest (i) and a maximum level of (nominal) income (I). More important, however, is Hicks's specification of C_1C_2 as the 'marginal efficiency of capital' and the determination of i and I by the intersection of the C_1C_2 and L_1L_2 curves, rather than the IS and LL curves, as in the published version of his paper (Hicks, 1937).

HICKS'S 1937 DIAGRAMS

In his 1937 paper, Hicks presented three diagrams. The first (Figure 1, 1937, 153) was his IS-LL diagram. The second (Figure 2, 1937, 153) is usually cited as only illustrating the 'liquidity trap'. When placed in the context of the text of his 1937 paper, however, Hicks's Figure 2 shows continuity between his 1936 and 1937 diagrams regarding the 'minimum' interest rate and 'maximum' income level 'which can be financed with a given amount of money' (1937, 154). Indeed, he noted that 'Keynes does not stress' the latter, going on to say, regarding the LL curve (1937, 154) that 'we can think of the curve as approaching these limits asymptotically'.

However, it must also be remembered that in his 1937 paper, Hicks's diagrammatic approach only starts to appear in Section II, in Figures 1 and 2 on page 153, almost halfway through the paper. At this point, he presented his diagrams as a means not only of explaining the difference between Keynes and 'revised and qualified Marshallian theories', but also as a way to explain the difference between the implications of the three 'fundamental equations' (1937, 149) of 'the General Theory' as against those of 'orthodoxy' by 'recourse to a diagram', that is to say, his 'Figure 1', or IS-LL diagram (1937, 153).

In presenting his proposed equation system in verbal format, Hicks describes the demand for money (liquidity preference) as a function of nominal income and interest. He describes the 'demand for capital' (1937, 149) in terms of investment and marginal efficiency of capital as a function, first, of the interest rate (1937, 153) and then of nominal income and the interest rate (1937, 156). He then presents an additional equation relating the amount of investment to the level of saving and nominal income (1937, 153) and also interest rate (1937, 156).

Hicks recalled (as recounted in Young, 1987, 98) that he utilized his Value and Capital methods to reduce these three equations into two, so as to be able to draw his 'diagram', or as he also called it, his 'little apparatus' (1937, 156). And indeed, his IS-LL 'diagram' (Figure 1, 1937, 153) reflects the concatenation of the 'two equations' needed 'in order to determine' investment (1937, 149).

CC-LL AND IS-LL DIAGRAMS AND HICKS'S 'VALUE AND CAPITAL METHODS'

Hicks then went on to link 'the schedule of the marginal efficiency of capital' to his Figure 1 (1937, 154). The importance of this linkage follows directly from Hicks's 1936 CC-LL diagram, which in my view, was reconstructed into IS-LL in section IV of his 1937 paper via his Value and Capital methods (1937, 156–159, 1939; Young, 1987).

This can be seen as follows. In section IV of his 1937 paper, Hicks first talked about having 'invented a little apparatus', and went on to develop what he called 'The Generalized General Theory', which he 'set out' in

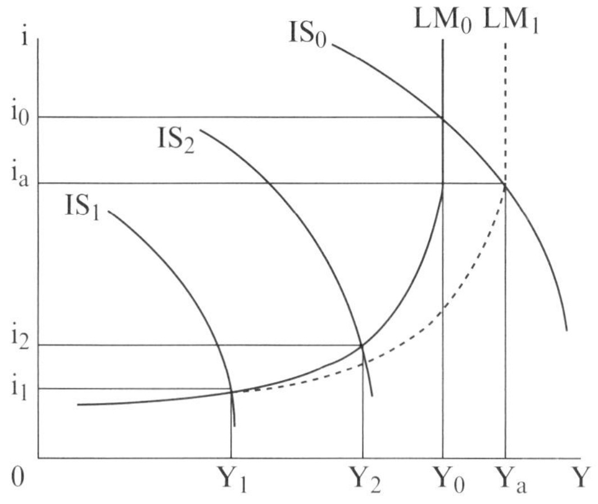

Source: Hansen (1949)

Figure 47.4

in both equational and diagrammatic form gained ground, and was even extended, from the static Keynes-Lange (Lange, 1938) and quasi-dynamic Lange-Timlin (Timlin, 1942) systems to dynamic systems by Samuelson (1941) and Modigliani (1944) (on this, see Young, 2008).

The diagrammatic approach was also later extended into multi-quadrant and multi-dimensional representations by Palander (1942), Scott (1951), Lindahl (1954), and Smith (1956), and was also further expanded by Hicks himself to trade cycle analysis in his 1950 volume, *A Contribution to the Theory of the Trade Cycle* (Hicks, 1950).

But one more element remains to be dealt with in the story of the IS-LM diagram, that is, Hansen's 1949 contribution, which linked his name to that of Hicks. Now, in contrast to Hicks's 1937 derivation of his IS-LL diagram, Hansen's 1949 IS-LM diagram emanated from a concatenation of equational-diagrammatic representations utilizing a consumption, rather than a savings function; he thereby also utilized the Keynesian cross diagram developed by Samuelson a decade earlier (Darity and Young, 1995), and the consumption function representation of Keynes's system that Samuelson first proposed as early as 1941 (1941, 114), and which he repeated in *Foundations of Economic Analysis* (1947). Hansen's popularization of the IS-LM diagram in both his 1949 book, *Monetary Theory and Fiscal Policy* (see Figure 47.4), and in his 1953 pedagogical volume, *A Guide to Keynes,* has linked his name to Hicks, even though his contribution was only expositional; this oversight was remedied by this author and others (Hansen, 1949, 1953; Young, 1987; Darity and Young, 1995).

INTERPRETING AND REPRESENTING KEYNES'S GENERAL THEORY

Whether or not the IS-LM diagram is a *valid* interpretation or representation of Keynes's *General Theory* and its central message has been the focus of debate between Keynesians of various schools and vintages. This is not the place for a detailed survey of the controversy between those Keynesians who attacked IS-LM and saw the diagram as the manifestation of 'Bastard' Keynesianism on the one hand (for example, Robinson, 1971), and those Keynesians who actively utilized the diagram in their theoretical and policy analysis. Moreover, *alternate diagrammatic representations* of Keynes's *General Theory* system were developed and applied in *Keynesian* economic analysis, such as the Z-D (Aggregate Demand-Aggregate Supply) diagram of Weintraub (1957, 1958), and Pasinetti's equational-diagrammatic system (1974).

The IS-LM approach and diagram, however, while influential in converting many economists in the US and elsewhere to Keynesianism from 1937 onwards (on this, see Young, 1987), has *evolved* beyond being 'a suggested interpretation' of Keynes's *General Theory* (Hicks, 1937).

Indeed, the *plasticity* of the approach and its *extension* into *augmented* forms has enabled the diagram to become the basis for more *sophisticated* diagrammatic approaches such as AS-AD, which even include endogenous (rational) expectations, thus making the approach more acceptable to those of non-Keynesian predilection. And it is this *metamorphosis* that has enabled the *ongoing* utilization of the IS-LM diagram and approach, in *both* economic analysis and pedagogy (on this, see the papers in Young and Zilberfarb, 2000).

REFERENCES

Darity, William and Warren Young (1995), 'IS-LM: an inquest', *History of Political Economy*, 27, 1–41.

Hansen, Alvin (1949), *Monetary Theory and Fiscal Policy*, New York: McGraw-Hill.

Hansen, Alvin (1953), *A Guide to Keynes*, New York: McGraw-Hill.

Hicks, John (1936), 'Mr. Keynes and the 'Classics': a suggested interpretation', paper presented at the 'symposium on Keynes' held at the *European Meeting of the Econometric Society*, New College, Oxford, 26 September 1936.

Hicks, John (1937), 'Mr. Keynes and the 'Classics': a suggested interpretation', *Econometrica*, 5, 147–159.
Hicks, John (1939), *Value and Capital*, Oxford: Clarendon Press.
Hicks, John (1950), *A Contribution to the Theory of the Trade Cycle*, Oxford: Oxford University Press.
Kaldor, Nicholas (1937), 'Prof. Pigou on money wages in relation to unemployment', *Economic Journal*, 47, 745–753.
Lange, Oskar (1938), 'The rate of interest and the optimum propensity to consume', *Economica*, 5, 12–32.
Lindahl, Eric (1954), 'On Keynes's economic system: part two', *The Economic Record*, 30, 159–171.
Lutfalla, George (1937), 'Compte rendu des travaux de la VI réunion européenne de la Société Internationale d'Econometrie (Oxford, 25–29 September 1936)', *Revue d'Economie Politique*, 51, 424–445.
Modigliani, Franco (1944), 'Liquidity preference and the theory of interest and money', *Econometrica*, 12, 45–88.
Palander, Tord (1942), 'Keynes's allmana teori', *Ekonomisk Tidskrift*, 44, 233–249 (translation by Finn Borg, provided by Don Patinkin).
Pasinetti, Luigi (1974), *Growth and Income Distribution*, Cambridge: Cambridge University Press.
Robinson, Joan (1971), *Economic Heresies*, London: Macmillan.
Samuelson, Paul (1941), 'The stability of equilibrium: comparative statics and dynamics', *Econometrica*, 9, 97–120.
Samuelson, Paul (1947), *Foundations of Economic Analysis*, Cambridge MA: Harvard University Press.
Scott, Ira (1951), 'An exposition of the Keynesian system', *Review of Economic Studies*, 19, 12–18.
Smith, Warren (1956), 'A graphical exposition of the complete Keynesian system', *Southern Economic Journal*, 23, 115–125.
Timlin, Mabel (1942), *Keynesian Economics*, Toronto: University of Toronto Press.
Weintraub, Sidney (1957), 'The microfoundations of aggregate demand and supply', *Economic Journal*, 67, 455–470.
Weintraub, Sidney (1958), *An Approach to the Theory of Income Distribution*, Philadelphia: Chilton.
Young, Warren (1987), *Interpreting Mr Keynes: the IS-LM Enigma*, Oxford: Polity-Blackwell.
Young, Warren (2008), 'Is IS-LM a static or dynamic 'Keynesian' model?' in Robert Leeson, ed. *The Keynesian Tradition*, Houndsmills, Basingstoke: Palgrave-Macmillan.
Young, Warren and Ben-Zion Zilberfarb, eds (2000), *IS-LM and Modern Macroeconomics*, Boston, MA and London: Kluwer-Springer.

48. The Fleming-Mundell diagram

Russell Boyer and Warren Young

MUNDELL-FLEMING AND MUNDELL'S DIAGRAMS

The open economy IS-LM-BP curve diagram has been one of the most widely used in macroeconomic textbooks. Although other diagrammatic representations of the open economy have been developed, such as the Salter-Swan-Corden-Meade dependent economy approach, IS-LM-BP has proved its value through its standard form, simplicity and versatility, since it first appeared in Mundell (1963) (where these curves are denoted by XX-LL-FF, notation that we utilize here). Although the diagram is usually cited as a key element in the 'Mundell-Fleming model', perhaps a better description of the construct is Mundell's diagrammatic representation of the 'Fleming [equational] model' (Cooper 1976). Indeed, Mundell (1963) provided a diagram which could be said to represent Fleming's (1962) equations, similar to the case of IS-LM, where Hicks (1937) provided a diagram representing the equations of Harrod and Meade (see Chapter 47, on IS-LM).

Mundell's construct is diagrammatic representation for the specific case of perfect capital mobility. The diagram (see Figure 48.1) contains two panels. The horizontal axis is common to the two panels, and measures real output. The upper panel has the interest rate measured on its vertical axis, and this is the panel that all textbooks which utilize the diagram reproduce in their presentations. The lower panel measures the value of the exchange rate on its vertical axis, but the information provided by it is not clear-cut. One needs the further direction which is supplied by the upper panel before it is possible to know how much to shift the loci in the lower panel. In the case of fixed exchange rates, the lower panel provides no new information at all. It is incumbent on the analyst to shift the curves in such a way that the value of the exchange rate does not change, but we knew that before we began. For the case of flexible exchange rates, the size of the movement in the value of the exchange rate is of interest. But this information is available from the upper panel, since precisely the

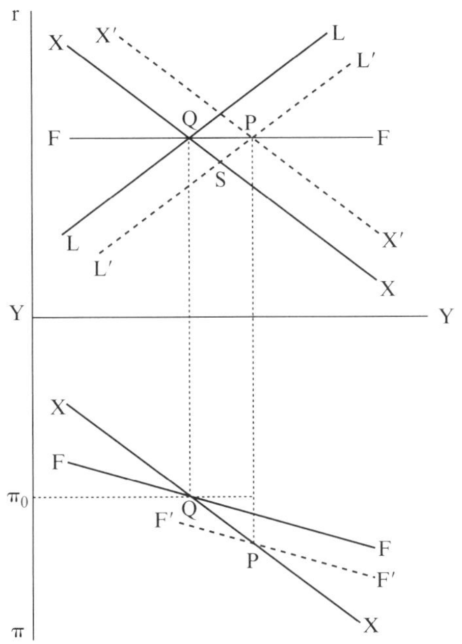

Source: Mundell (1963)

Figure 48.1 Mundell's diagram: monetary policy

same parameter values are relevant to the shifts there that appertain to the movements in the lower panel.

Two of the loci are from Hicks' (1937) IS-LM paper: XX represents equilibrium in the domestic goods market, and LL, equilibrium in the domestic assets market. The former has a negative slope, because some expenditure is sensitive to interest rate. With a higher value for the interest rate, such expenditures are reduced, and, *ceteris paribus*, the level of output must be lower. One of the variables held constant is the value of the exchange rate. Defining this as the domestic-currency price of a unit of foreign currency, a rise in the exchange rate raises the price of foreign goods relative to domestic goods. The resulting lower relative price for domestic goods increases demand for them and output responds accordingly, so that XX shifts to the right. The LL locus is positively sloped, for a given quantity of money and given values of domestic-currency prices. Everywhere along this locus, the quantity of money demanded is constant, consistent with its supply being given, so that for these points there is equilibrium in the domestic money market. The reason is that

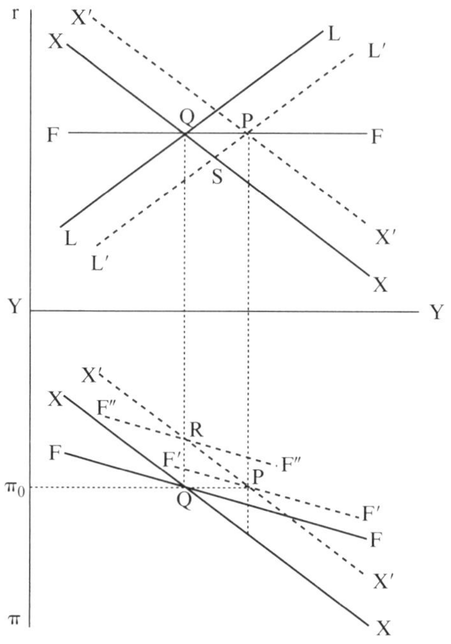

Source: Mundell (1963)

Figure 48.2 Mundell's diagram: fiscal policy

an increase in interest rates causes the quantity of money demanded to be lower, since bonds, an alternative form in which to hold funds, are providing a higher yield. If this is matched by an increase in output, then the resulting higher volume of transactions necessitates an increase in the quantity of money held. In the right proportions, these two influences on money demand exactly offset each other and demand is back at its original (equilibrium) value. An increase in the money supply causes a rightward shift in LL. The final curve, FF, was added by Mundell so as to represent equilibrium in the foreign exchange market. In the perfect capital mobility case shown, this locus is horizontal, a situation which has a very simple interpretation: if domestic bonds are perfect substitutes for foreign bonds, then their rates of return must be equal. No matter what the level of domestic output, the yield on domestic bonds must equal the yield available from holding foreign financial instruments. The economy is assumed to start in equilibrium at point Q, where there is market clearing (so that supply and demand are equated) of all the markets analyzed above.

Earlier Mundell diagrams (1960, 1961a) bear a resemblance to this definitive version, in that they have the interest rate measured along the vertical axis, and the curves in these diagrams represent internal and external balance. These earlier diagrams seem applicable to both the fixed- and the flexible-exchange-rate cases, just as is the later 1963 diagram. It was widely recognized that switching between these regimes amounted merely to an inversion, in terms of their endogeneity and exogeneity, of the roles of the money supply and the exchange rate. This point had been noted by Meade (1951, 190) and highlighted by Friedman and Schwartz (1963, 89).

All the earlier Mundell figures (1960, 1961a) are seemingly like the IS-LM diagram with a curve added to represent the effects of an economy's openness in its trading relationships with the rest of the world, and with the capacity to analyze either fixed or flexible exchange rate regimes within its confines. Such an interpretation, however, is misleading. In fact, the diagrams are quite different. Only the last Mundell contribution (1963) serves all these purposes, and that is why it has been so widely utilized.

For example, Mundell (1960) has the terms of trade (rather than income) along the horizontal axis. Furthermore the terms of trade by definition include in their calculation the value of the exchange rate. Thus a change in the exchange rate amounts to a movement along these curves, rather than a shift in either of them, which one finds in the later 1963 diagram. In addition, although this earlier diagram is meant to represent both the fixed- and the flexible-exchange-rate cases, the argument is that in terms of comparative statics, there is no distinction between the two in the determination of the values of real variables (the point that had been emphasized by Meade for the simplest benchmark case). Indeed, the switch of roles which this early Mundell paper envisages is entirely in the dynamics, since he fully accepts Meade's argument. In order to 'isolate most clearly the dynamical dissimilarities' of the two exchange rate regimes, it is assumed that money prices are flexible. It is the actions of the Central Bank which cause 'an inversion of the roles, in the dynamic adjustment process, of the terms of trade and the rate of interest' (Mundell 1960, 228). The reader may be surprised to find that, although the title of Mundell's 1960 article is 'The Monetary Dynamics of International Adjustment under Fixed and Flexible Exchange Rates', the money supply never makes an appearance as a separate variable, nor does the exchange rate play an important role. Moreover, this paper does not conduct any comparative static exercises, but faults Meade (Mundell 1960, 242) for referring to 'ease of adjustment', without distinguishing dynamic effects from static ones. What one finds is that Mundell's argument is phrased entirely in terms of differential equations, with an analysis of the conditions needed for stability, and for direct (rather than cyclical) approach.

A similar reading of Mundell (1961a) identifies differences from the later Mundell diagram, so that it is problematic to see it as the first appearance in print of the famous diagrammatic framework. On the horizontal axis is money income. While the reader is encouraged to think in terms of either a classical model (for which real income is given, and price is the adjusting variable) or a Keynesian model (for which real output is changing, and prices are fixed), the IS-LM diagram and the Mundell (1963) diagram are quite specific that only the Keynesian case is being considered. At the end of this paper, Mundell (1961a, 168) considers an economy which is in recession. But the diagram cannot persuasively be used to analyze this case, since the low level of money income could be due to a low price level, rather than to a depressed level of economic activity. In turn, the obvious remedy, expansionary financial policies, may have no effect on employment, because their impacts may be entirely on the price level rather than on production.

At this point, it should be noted that Mundell (1961b) and (1962) are derivatives of the Mundell (1961a) framework. In particular, Mundell (2002, 9) readily concedes that the 1962 paper is merely a dynamization of the argument in the earlier article.

In addition, Mundell's earlier 1961(a) diagram portrays the low capital mobility case in which the FF locus is steeper than the LL locus. While this may be considered a small point, it is nonetheless true that Mundell (1969, 263) faults Fleming for countenancing such a case, since this leads to an ambiguity as to the effect of expansionary fiscal policy on the state of the balance of payments. Furthermore it is quite the opposite case from the one that appears in Mundell's 1963 paper. Perfect capital mobility, of course, causes the FF locus to be horizontal, and therefore necessarily it is less steep than the LL locus.

It is interesting to note that Mundell (1963, 482) says that his purpose in writing his 1963 paper was to deal with defects that arose in the earlier (1960) paper for the perfect capital mobility case. But, in fact, in the original published version of the 1960 paper, the FF locus is horizontal in two of the nine figures in the paper. Although Mundell (1960, 237) says at first that the FF locus 'is flat if capital is perfectly mobile', he then goes on to assert that the horizontal curves shown in 'Figures IV and V are drawn on the assumption that capital is almost completely mobile'. It is curious that the condition is described in these terms, but the wording indicates that Mundell understood the conflict that arises between a Central Bank's setting the values of interest rates, and the pressures on those yields that are due to a high degree of capital mobility.

On the other hand, the discussion in Mundell (1961a) focuses on a single policy initiative (monetary policy), and a single exchange rate regime (fixed rates). This paper appears very much to be a formalization of the argument which one finds in Friedman's (1953, 171) celebrated essay 'The Case for Flexible Exchange Rates', but there is no acknowledgement of any debt to that source, but rather a nod towards Hume's famous mechanism for balance of payments adjustment.

Mundell's (1961a) paper considers a general degree of capital mobility. Had it dealt in that general setting with both fixed and flexible exchange rates, its diagram would have had priority over Mundell (1963). Instead, by focusing exclusively on fixed exchange rates, this portrayal fails to exploit the power which arises from the later 1963 diagram. In any case, by ignoring fiscal policy in this paper, Mundell failed to discover the key crowding-out result which is Fleming's (1962, 372, 378) celebrated achievement.

MUNDELL'S 1963 DIAGRAM AND FLEMING'S 1962 EQUATIONS

Mundell's (1963) paper deals with the perfect capital mobility case and does so without equations written out explicitly. Mundell's 'half' of the Mundell-Fleming model for the small-country case is not presented in a mathematical or equational form that distinguishes between markets for stocks and markets for flows. Mundell (1963, 479) says that monetary policy is ineffective under fixed exchange rates with perfect capital mobility, and this result is shown clearly in Figure 1 of the 1963 paper (see Figure 48.1). The question is whether ineffectiveness occurs if capital mobility is less than perfect. The answer is that in the time frame which Mundell (1963) considers, and within the confines of Fleming's equations, monetary policy has no impact on real output, no matter what the degree of capital mobility (see Mundell 1961a, 159). In contrast, with a proper specification of the asset markets, this result does indeed depend on the degree of substitutability between domestic and foreign assets (Marston 1985, 872).

Mundell (1963) says that fiscal policy is ineffective under flexible exchange rates with perfect capital mobility. The second figure of that paper demonstrates this result (see Figure 48.2). The same question arises in this case. Does this result hinge on the degree of capital mobility? Fleming (1962) notes in his text, and in his mathematical appendix, that in his equational framework, this result holds only with perfect capital mobility. In contrast, with a proper specification of the asset markets, this result does not depend on the degree of substitutability between domestic and foreign assets. On the contrary, it depends entirely on the assumption, which both Fleming (1962) and Mundell (1963) adopt, that asset market conditions are not directly dependent on the value of the exchange rate.

Finally, Mundell (1963) says numerous times that with perfect capital mobility, the level of real output and the nominal quantity of money are proportional in equilibrium positions. So under flexible exchange rates (for which the Central Bank can set and maintain any quantity of money which it chooses), an expansionary monetary policy causes output to increase by the same percentage amount as the money supply is augmented. This result is a valid deduction only of the Fleming model (1962, 374, 379). It is not a valid deduction of the (verbal) model which Mundell (1963) presents. No attempt is made to demonstrate this result in Mundell's (1963) Figure 1 (see Figure 48.1). This is not surprising, since it is not a valid deduction of his model. Indeed, the diagram as drawn is not consistent with this result, since the LL loci in it do not converge as one proceeds leftward along them.

LIMITATIONS OF MUNDELL'S 1963 DIAGRAM: THEORY AND PEDAGOGY

Most recent presentations of international economic theory have Mundell's 1963 diagram playing only a minor role. The reason is that in a two-dimensional diagram, for which there are only two separate axes available, the user does not want to obviate the function of one of them. But this is precisely what this diagram does. We know from the start that the value of the interest rate cannot change (unless it is changed exogenously, presumably due to changing financial-market conditions in the rest of the world). To measure the interest rate on the vertical axis amounts to wasting that axis. A far more informative presentation of these results can be made with the money supply or the exchange rate measured along one of the axes, replacing the unchanging value of the interest rate.

Indeed, Mundell's 1963 diagram is sufficiently complex that some authors and textbooks feel a step-by-step derivation is justified. One finds such derivations in articles by Michaely (1968) and Wrightsman (1970), and in textbooks such as Branson (1972), or Caves, Frankel and Jones (2002). In contrast, many textbooks feel that the mechanisms highlighted by Fleming (1962) and Mundell (1963) are no longer of interest (see, for example, Krugman and Obstfeld 2006). More common today are diagrams which capture the essence of the Dornbusch (1976) view rather than the Mundell-Fleming model (see, for example, Obstfeld and Rogoff 1996). As an example of the inconsistencies which one finds in identifying models in the open macroeconomy, Obstfeld and Rogoff (1996, 609) declare the mechanism which Dornbusch championed as being the essence of what they call 'the Mundell-Fleming-Dornbusch model'. They use the expression at least seven times in their graduate textbook. In contrast, the identical mechanism is central to the key framework employed in the undergraduate textbook by Krugman and Obstfeld (2006). In that book, this expression is not to be found. More precisely, in that textbook, Mundell's name is not attached to this macromodel, and Fleming's name does not make any appearance whatsoever.

REFERENCES

Branson, W. 1972. *Macroeconomic Theory and Policy*. New York: Harper and Row.

Caves, R., Frenkel, J. and Jones, R. 2002. *World Trade and Payments* 9th ed., Boston, MA: Addison-Wesley.

Cooper, R. 1976. 'Monetary Theory and Policy in an Open Economy'. *Scandinavian Journal of Economics* 78: 146–63.

Dornbusch, R. 1976. 'Expectations and Exchange Rate Dynamics'. *Journal of Political Economy* 84 December: 1161–76.

Fleming, J. 1962. 'Domestic Financial Policies under Fixed and under Floating Exchange Rates'. *IMF Staff Papers* 9: 369–79.

Friedman, M. 1953. 'The Case for Flexible Exchange Rates' in *Essays in Positive Economics*, 157–203. Chicago, IL: University of Chicago Press.

Friedman, M. and Schwartz, A. 1963. *A Monetary History of the United States 1867–1960*. Princeton, NJ: Princeton University Press.

Hicks, John 1937. 'Mr. Keynes and the "Classics": A Suggested Interpretation'. *Econometrica* 5: 147–159.

Krugman, P. and Obstfeld, M. 2006. *International Economics: Theory and Policy* 7th ed. Boston, MA: Addison-Wesley.

Marston, R. 1985. 'Stabilization policies in open economies', in R. Jones and P. Kenen (eds), *Handbook of International Economics*, volume 2, Amsterdam: North-Holland, chapter 17, 859–916.

Meade, J. 1951. *The Balance of Payments*. Oxford: Oxford University Press.

Michaely, M. 1968. 'The Impact of Alternative Government Policies under Varying Exchange Systems: Comment'. *Quarterly Journal of Economics* 82: 508–10.

Mundell, R. 1960. 'The Monetary Dynamics of International Adjustment under Fixed and Flexible Exchange Rates'. *Quarterly Journal of Economics* 74: 227–57.

Mundell, R. 1961a. 'The International Disequilibrium System'. *Kyklos* 14: 153–72.

Mundell, R. 1961b. 'Flexible Exchange Rates and Employment Policy'. *Canadian Journal of Economics and Political Science* 27: 509–17.

Mundell, R. 1962. 'The Appropriate Use of Monetary and Fiscal Policy for Internal and External Stability'. *IMF Staff Papers* 9: 70–7.

Mundell, R. 1963. 'Capital Mobility and Stabilization Policy under Fixed and Flexible Exchange Rates'. *Canadian Journal of Economics and Political Science* 29: 475–85.

Mundell, R. 1969. 'Contribution to "Summary of Discussion"', in R. Mundell and A. Swoboda (eds), *Monetary Problems of the International Economy*, Chicago, IL: University of Chicago Press, 257–65.

Mundell, R. 2002. 'Notes on the Development of the International Macroeconomic Model', in A. Arnon and W. Young (eds) *The Open Economy Macromodel: Past, Present and Future.* London and New York: Kluwer-Springer.

Obstfeld, M. and Rogoff, K. 1996. *Foundations of International Macroeconomics.* Cambridge, MA: MIT Press.

Wrightsman, D. 1970. 'IS, LM, and External Equilibrium: A Graphical Analysis'. *American Economic Review* 60.1: 203–8.

49. The aggregate demand aggregate supply diagram

Richard G. Lipsey

The aggregate demand and aggregate supply curves are designed to apply simple Keynesian income-flow models to situations in which the price level and national income are endogenous variables, affected by both supply-side and demand-side shocks.

THE DERIVATION OF THE AGGREGATE DEMAND CURVE

A simple Keynesian model can be laid out in five equations: (49.1) the division of real expenditure, E, into three parts, one that is positively related to real income, Y, one that is negatively related to the interest rate[1], R, and one that is autonomous, a; (49.2) an equilibrium condition of the goods market that desired expenditure should equal actual income;[2] (49.3) the real demand for money, M_d, which varies positively with real income and negatively with the interest rate, R; (49.4) the assumption that the central bank holds the nominal supply of money, M_s constant at some value M^*; (49.5) the equilibrium condition that the real demand for money equals the real supply M_s/P, where P is the price level.[3]

Stated in linear form, these relations are:

$$E = a + zY + bR \ (b<0<z<1) \tag{49.1}$$

$$E = Y \tag{49.2}$$

$$M_d = dY + eR \ (e<0<d) \tag{49.3}$$

$$M_s = M^* \tag{49.4}$$

$$M_d = M_s/P \tag{49.5}$$

If we plot (49.1) and (49.2) on an *E-Y* diagram with *R* treated as a constant, we obtain the famous diagonal cross diagram. If we substitute (49.1) into (49.2), and plot the resulting equation in a *Y-R* diagram, we obtain the famous *IS* curve, which in linear form is:

$$R = -\left(\frac{a}{b}\right) + \left(\frac{1 - z}{b}\right)Y \qquad (49.6).$$

If we substitute (49.3) and (49.4) into (49.5), treating *P* as a constant, and plot the resulting equation on a *Y-R* diagram, we obtain the famous *LM* curve, which in linear form is:

$$R = \frac{M^*}{eP} - \left(\frac{d}{e}\right)Y. \qquad (49.7)$$

Finally, if we substitute (49.6) into (49.7), eliminating *R* and treating *P* as a variable, we obtain the aggregate demand curve:

$$Y = \frac{a}{(1 - z) + bd/e} + \left(\frac{M^*}{\{d + e(1 - z)/b\}}\right)P^{-1} \qquad (49.8)$$

This equation gives the locus of all *P-Y* combinations that will simultaneously equate the goods market, $E=Y$ and the money market, $M_d = M_s/P$, when the nominal money supply is an exogenously determined constant, M^*. It does not imply anything about what supply is actually produced, only that for any *P-Y* combination on the AD curve, the money market and the goods markets would clear in the sense that people would be willing to hold the existing stock of money ($M_d = M_s$) and would be just willing to buy the indicated output ($E= Y$) *if* that output were produced. The denominator in the first term is the IS-LM multiplier, which determines the horizontal shift in the curve when autonomous expenditure, *a*, changes. The bracketed part of the second term determines the slope of the curve itself.

Examination of the signs of the parameters included in equation (49.8) shows three key characteristics of the AD curve. First, it is negatively sloped as shown in Figure 49.1.[4] Neither money illusion nor any other special assumptions are needed to obtain this negative sign of the slope, nor is it necessary to include wealth that varies with the price level in the expenditure function (although this would contribute to the negative slope). What is critical in this version is the assumption of a fixed money supply. Then, according to equations (49.1) – (49.5), an increase in *P* reduces the real money supply, drives up the interest rate, and reduces interest-sensitive expenditure, leading to a reduction in equilibrium real

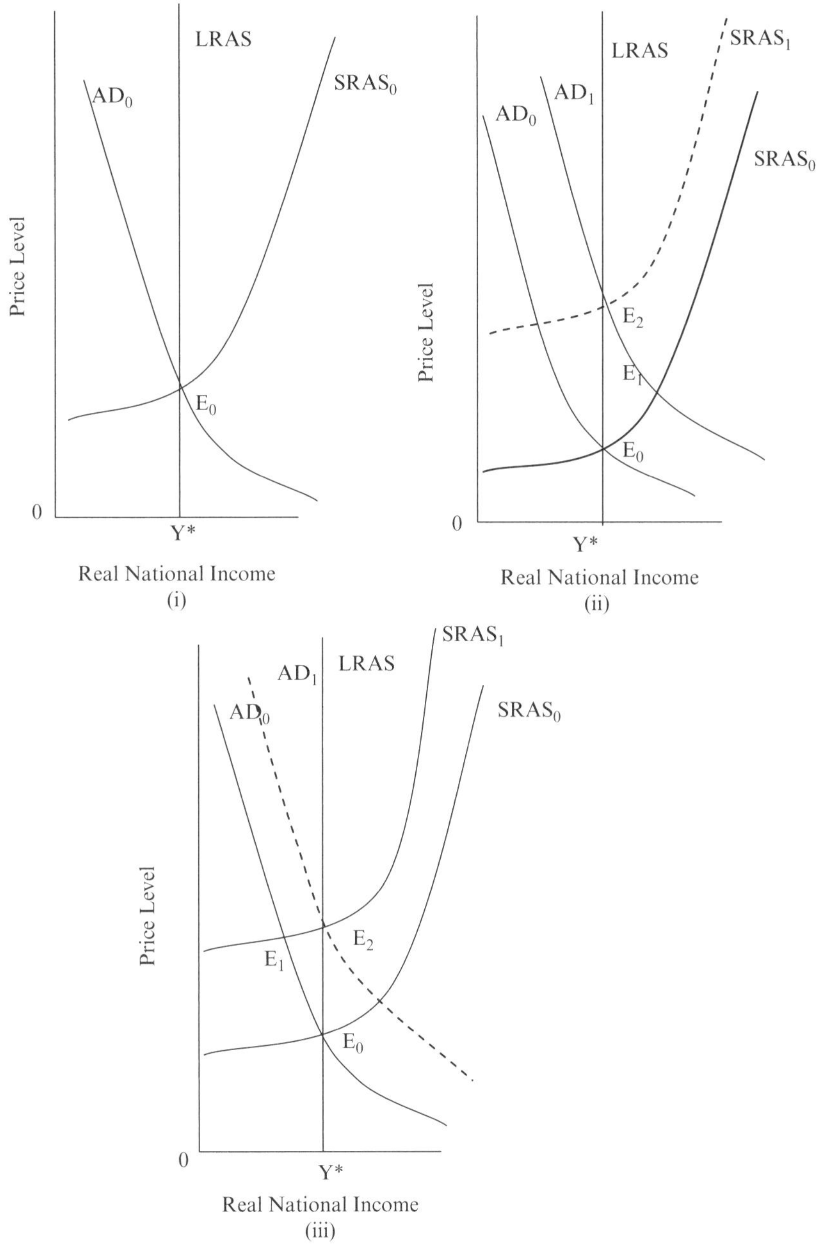

Figure 49.1 The comparative statics of the AD-AS model

income.[5] Second, although the behavioural relations (49.1) and (49.3) are linear in form, equation (49.8) introduces a non-linearity that makes the AD curve non-linear. Third, the precise slope of the curve at each point is determined by all four behavioural parameters, *b, d, e* and *z*.

THE DERIVATION OF THE AGGREGATE SUPPLY CURVES

The short-run aggregate supply curve (SRAS) relates total real national income positively to the price level. It is understood to be a short-term relation since its persistence in the long run would imply money illusion. In the most common textbook treatment, the rational for a positively sloped SRAS curve is that wages respond to any shock more slowly than output prices. The SRAS curve is then derived formally for firms in both perfect and imperfect competition by assuming that wage rates are fixed. An increase in output prices, *P*, then causes an increase in profitability and an increase in output, moving the economy upwards along a positively sloped SRAS curve, such as is shown in Figure 49.1. Similarly, if the price level falls while input prices are constant, firms will contract output.

If we assume that there is a unique non-accelerating-inflationary level of unemployment (NAIRU) and an associated level of income, *Y**, then for a given set of parameter values, there will be an equilibrium price level, *P**. This implies a vertical long-run aggregate supply curve (*LRAS*) and a vertical long-run Phillips curve at Y*. The *SRAS* curve through *P** will be positively sloped because of the different adjustment lags for prices of output and of factor inputs when *Y* diverges from *Y**.

THE EQUILIBRIUM AND COMPARATIVE STATICS OF THE AD-AS MODEL

Figure 49.1 (i) shows the long-run equilibrium of the *AD-AS* model at E_O with income *Y**. Both the goods market and the money market are in equilibrium in the sense that desired expenditure is equal to actual production and the demand for money is equal to its supply. At the point of long-run equilibrium, the *AD*, *SRAS* and *LRAS* curves all coincide.

Figure 49.1(ii) shows the effect of an aggregate demand shock, one that can be caused by an increase in autonomous expenditure, *a*, in the propensity to consume, *z*, in the amount of expenditure associated with each interest rate (as indicated by a decrease in the absolute value of *b*), in the nominal supply of money, *M**, or a decrease in its demand (shown by a decrease in the absolute values of d or e in equation (49.3)). The aggregate demand curve shifts from AD_0 to AD_1, taking the equilibrium from E_0 to E_1, indicating a rise in income and the price level.[6] The excess demand indicated by $Y > Y^*$ causes wages and other costs to rise, shifting the SRAS curve to the left until full equilibrium is restored at E_2, indicating the original level of income, Y^*, and a higher price level. A fall in aggregate demand when income is originally at Y^* has the reverse effects, first lowering income and the price level. Then, as excess supply ($Y < Y^*$) lowers costs,[7] the *SRAS* curve shifts to the right, finally returning income to Y^* at a lower price level. The division of the short-run effects between a change in Y and in P depends on the slope of the *SRAS*. This curve is usually drawn rather flat to the left of Y^*, indicating that the impact effects of a decline in aggregate demand are felt more in a fall in output and less (if any) in a fall in the price level.

Figure 49.1 (iii) shows the effect of an aggregate supply shock, which can be caused by cost increases that, from the point of view of the economy in question, result from exogenous causes for example, increases in the price of imported petroleum or food products or unit wage costs.[8] The aggregate supply curve shifts from $SRAS_0$ to $SRAS_1$, taking equilibrium from E_0 to E_1, indicating a rise in the price level combined with a fall in the level of income, a stagflation. If this is a once-for-all shift and nothing else is done, income will remain below Y^* until the excess supply, $Y < Y^*$, drives down unit wage costs sufficiently to shift the *SRAS* curve back to its original position at $SRAS_0$. If the shock is once-for-all and the monetary authority accommodates the rise in the price level by increasing the nominal money supply appropriately, the aggregate demand curve can be shifted to AD_1, restoring Y^* but at a higher price level than ruled before the supply side shock. If, however, the supply shock is repeated frequently, the effect of monetary validation may well be a continued stagflation as both the *AD* and *AS* curves shift upwards, with Y continuously less the Y^*.

After the first oil price shock of the early 1970s, most economists seemed baffled to explain the resulting stagflation. This is surprising because, as noted below, the tools of AD-AS were available to explain stagflation as a cost-induced upward shift in the *SRAS* curve. Instead, many influential economists declared the end of Keynesian economics and wondered if anything could be salvaged from the wreckage. But by the late 1970s, the Keynesian model (whose prototype is laid out in equations (49.1) – (49.5) above) had been amended by the addition of an expectations augmented Phillips curve. The model then explained the effects of single demand and supply side shocks as well as the accelerating inflationary effects of using monetary expansion to accommodate continued supply side shocks or in an attempt to maintain income indefinitely above Y^*.

THE ADJUSTMENT MECHANISM

When added to the AD-AS model, an expectations augmented Phillips curve determines how fast input prices adjust to a situation in which $Y \neq Y^*$ and hence how fast the *SRAS* curve shifts to restore long run equilibrium. If the short-run Phillips curve for any given expected rate of price inflation has the usually assumed curvature, the adjustment to excess demand, $Y > Y^*$, is faster than the adjustment to excess supply, $Y < Y^*$. (See Chapter 50 for a discussion of the Phillips curve.)

THE MODEL IN THE LITERATURE

The above exposition follows most standard textbook treatments of the subject. Michael Schneider discusses the early origins of AD-AS analysis in Chapter 46, *Keynesian Income Determination Diagrams*, and we do not need to repeat this discussion here.

The AD Curve

Because the curve is sometimes derived through a mixture of graphical and verbal analysis, there has been argument in the literature about the sign and magnitude of the curve's slope and its linearity or non-linearity. We have already observed, however, that the sign of the behavioural parameters *b, d, e* and *z* determine that the AD curve is negatively sloped; the precise value of these parameters determine the magnitude of the curve's slope at each point on the curve; and the curve is non-linear because of the non-linear relation between real national income and the price level.

In elementary textbooks, the curve is often derived from the Keynesian diagonal cross diagram before asset markets have been introduced. Using equations (49.1) and (49.2) above, the stock of wealth is added to the expenditure function and the interest rate is assumed to be constant. An exogenous rise in *P* then reduces wealth denominated in money terms, shifting the expenditure function downwards and leading to a fall in equilibrium income. Various alternate *P*s can then be plotted each against the resulting equilibrium level of *Y* to determine an AD curve.

In a frequently cited article, Colander (1995) states that the AD curve is typically defined in text books as a *ceteris paribus* demand curve similar to individual market demand curves. This may be so in some textbooks, although he does not cite any, but certainly not in all of them. For example, William Branson (1979: 69) calls it 'the economy's demand curve' and stresses that 'it does *not* reflect the ordinary substitution effect of a rising price reducing demand. Rather, the rising aggregate price level *P* reduces equilibrium output demanded, *y*, by tightening the money market, raising the interest rate, and thus reducing investment.' Also, Lipsey and Chrystal (2007, p. 635) state that it is 'a curve that plots all combinations of the price level and national income that yield equilibrium in the goods and asset markets – i.e. that yields *IS-LM* equilibrium'.

Colander goes on to argue, in a critique cited in this volume by Schneider (Chapter 46), that the AD curve is logically inconsistent because although it purports to be a *ceteris paribus* demand curve, it has an implicit supply reaction in it. Since equations (49.1) – (49.5) are valid equations, and the substitutions are algebraically correct, there can be nothing mathematically illogical in equation (49.8) itself, or in its derivation. Nor is there an implicit supply reaction in it. The AD curve merely shows combinations of *P* and *Y* for which total output (if it were produced) would be exactly demanded (desired expenditure equals actual income) and people would be willing to hold the total stocks of money and 'bonds' (when the interest rate is one of the model's endogenous variables).[9]

The SRAS Curve

The assumption that input prices adjust more slowly than output prices, being formalized in an *SRAS* curve drawn for *given* input prices and shifting as these prices change, has been the most common rationale since the *SRAS* curve was first introduced. See, for example, McKenna (1965: 149–50). Interestingly, Irving Fisher (1925) showed this relation empirically for an earlier period. His results were restated in a 1926 article, which was reprinted posthumously in the *Journal of Political Economy* under the title 'I discovered the Phillips Curve' (1973). It is a misconception that Fisher's empirical piece was an early study of the Phillips curve, as he is explicit that the causal sequence runs from the price level, *P*, to output, *Y*. In modern terms, this is an *SRAS* curve not a price-Phillips curve, where the relation runs from *Y* to $\dot{P}$.

I have stressed the most common explanation of the positive slope of the *SRAS* curve. In contrast, Friedman, Phelps, Lucas, Sargent and others argued that only relative prices mattered for behaviour. According to them, *P* and *Y* are positively associated in the short run only because agents are fooled by a general rise in the price level into thinking that the relative prices of the goods or services that they supply have risen. This created an errors-only *SRAS* curve. Keynesians countered that one of the main advantages of the price system was that it coordinated actions of agents who were responding to just a few readily available price signals. According to the standard theory of the firm, for example, profit-maximizing competitive firms only need to know the money prices of their own products and their own inputs.[10] Although this explanation of a misreading of price signals is no longer commonly held, the errors-only *SRAS* curve can be derived in some more plausible forms.

For example, in his version of the sticky wage derivation of the positive slope of the *SRAS* curve Mankiw (2007: 374–87) assumes that labour has a target real wage when it fixes its rates for one period in advance. Then, for example, an unexpected monetary expansion lowers interest rates and raises demand, causing firms to raise their prices and output, while labour gets an unexpected decrease in its real wage. According to this argument, if labour had foreseen the rise in prices, it would have increased the money wage rate to compensate and the economy would have jumped immediately to a new higher level of wages and prices with no change in output. So the *SRAS* curve is positively sloped only became labour fails to correctly foresee the next period's prices when it sets the wage for that period. Thus the *SRAS* curve takes the form:

$$(Y - Y^*) = \alpha(P - P^e) \tag{49.9}$$

Mankiw argues that the three most common explanations of the curve's positive slope all imply the relation in (49.9), which is an errors-only *SRAS* curve. He also argues that this formulation makes the *SRAS* and the Phillips curve just two ways of showing a single relation between prices and income, one static, the *SRAS* curve, and one dynamic, the Phillips curve. In his essay on the Phillips curve in this volume (see Chapter 50) Lipsey argues that this claim is valid for Mankiw's version of the underlying theories but not for others.

Here I only consider the implication that *SRAS* must be an errors-only curve. From the earliest days of the Keynesian revolution, economists stressed that impulses spread slowly though the economy, moving from market to market in real time. Friedman himself suggested that it took 18 months for a monetary shock to work itself through the economy. Thus, even if a forthcoming monetary shock was well publicized and fully understood, its first impacts would be in a small section of the economy and the effects would spread slowly, changing prices and outputs as they went. Say, for example, that the central bank begins to buy up treasury bills, thus lowering short-term interest rates and providing banks with more liquidity. Commercial banks will begin to lend and people influenced by the short-term rate will begin to borrow and spend. This will raise income and employment where the funds are spent, and at the same time, the impulse will spread through the whole interest rate structure, causing other agents to alter their borrowing and lending behaviour. It will take a long time, however, before the impulse reaches all corners of the economy. Similarly, the full effects of what initially are localized real shocks, such as an increased government spending on infrastructure, spread slowly through the economy. Furthermore, since technological change is constantly adding new products, altering production functions for existing ones and changing the nature of factor inputs, no one can know where the price and output structures will settle down, even if there are no further disturbances from the monetary, expenditure or technology sides of the economy. So in the cases of both real and monetary shocks, agents down the line have little option but to wait until changes in prices that are relevant to them are revealed as they happen.

One problem with the sticky wage version, whatever form it takes, is that it implies countercyclical variations in real wages. They fall during expansions and rising during contractions, whereas the balance of evidence shows a mild tendency for real wages to vary procyclically. This suggests that an explanation common among earlier Keynesians may be more appropriate. There is ample empirical evidence that firms have horizontal short-run marginal cost curves. This agrees with the predictions of theory as long as the fixed factor, K, is subject to an inequality constraint, such that its use can be varied up to the maximum amount available ($K \leq \bar{K}$). (For a discussion of the theory behind flat cost curves see Lipsey 1981, 274–278, where the empirical evidence is also reviewed.) Variations in demand are then first met by variations in output at more-or-less constant prices. Then, as wages and other input costs adjust, prices rise in response. This produces procyclical variations in real wages and a relatively flat *SRAS* curve up to full capacity output. (At Y^*, firms are assumed to be operating at somewhat less than full capacity in order to be able to meet demand fluctuations.)

The Adjustment Process

Colander (1995) also attacks what he regards as the typical textbook verbal statement of the adjustment that takes the model from its short-run to its long-run equilibrium. He does this by considering a leftward shift in the *AD* function applied to only a vertical long-run *AS* curve with no *SRAS* curve.[11] He then develops several arguments.

First, the last time the U.S. price level fell was in the 1930s, so the downward adjustment in the price level is unrealistic. This of course is not a criticism specifically of AD-AS analysis but of all theories that deal with long-term equilibrium in the face of negative shocks. Furthermore, in the case of AD-AS analysis, most textbooks point to the slowness with which the assumed adjustment works in the face of negative shocks. For example, Lipsey and Chrystal (p. 428) state: 'The SRAS curve shifts to the left fairly rapidly when GDP exceeds *Y**, but it shifts only slowly when GDP is less than Y*'. This implies: 'If the economy is to avoid a lengthy period of recession or stagnation, the force leading to recovery must usually be a rightward shift of the AD curve rather than a downward drift of the SRAS curve'.

Second, Colander argues that the Keynes and Pigou effects are too weak to do the adjusting. Two points are relevant here. First, the Keynes effect (the influence of a change in the interest rate on expenditure) and the Pigou effect (the influence of a ΔP-induced change in wealth on expenditure), in so far as they are modelled, influence the *slope* of the *AD* curve and have nothing to do with *shifts* in the *SRAS* curve. As Branson (1979, 69) puts it 'Changes in equilibrium variables on the demand side of the economy as a result of price changes are *movements along the demand curve*'. When a contractionary shock shifts the *AD* curve, as in Figure 49.1 (iii), the automatic adjustment in that model must come from the *SRAS* curve, which means that unit money costs must fall so that desired output rises until the vertical *LRAS* curve is reached through a shift of the *SRAS* curve and a movement along the *AD* curve. Second, weakening the Keynes effect, that is, lowering *e* in equations (49.3) and (49.8) has two opposing results. It lowers the IS-LM multiplier and hence reduces the leftward shift in the *AD* curve for any given real contractionary shock. *Ceteris paribus*, this reduces the amount of price level adjustment that is necessary to restore *Y**. It also steepens the *AD* curve and hence, *ceteris paribus*, increases the amount of price adjustment needed to restore *Y**. The net effect of these two opposing forces is unclear.

Third, Colander argues (1995, p. 177, italics in the original) that 'as all this indirect dynamic adjustment is taking place, *the participants in the goods market are assumed to be making no adjustments of their own*'. Instead they 'are sitting around, waiting for equilibrium to be brought about by the falling price level's effect on the money supply, even though firms cannot sell all their goods'. But Colander can say this only because he omits the *SRAS* curve from his analysis, describing only a shifted *AD* curve and a vertical *LRAS* curve. Most textbook treatments contain something like the following: 'The SRAS curve probably . . . is relatively flat for low levels of output . . . [which] implies that at low levels of GDP (well below potential) shifts in aggregate demand primarily affect output' (Lipsey and Chrystal, p. 416). Such a case is illustrated in part (iii) of Figure 49.1.

ACKNOWLEDGEMENTS

I am indebted to Kenneth Carlaw, Christopher Ragan, and William Scarth for comments and criticisms.

NOTES

1. In equilibrium with P constant, the real and nominal interest rates are equal. So as long as we are only doing formal comparative statics, one rate can be used in both the goods and money equations. However, out of equilibrium with P changing, the two rates are not equal and it is necessary to allow for the real rate in the expenditure equation and the nominal rate in the money demand equation. For a full analysis of the complexities that then arise see Scarth (1996, Chapter 4).
2. In the early years of Keynesian theorizing, there was confusion over equation (49.2), which was often interpreted as expressing the definitional identity of *realized* output and *realized* expenditure. Klappholz and Mishan (1962) criticized the mistaken belief that empirical propositions could be deduced from definitional identities. Lipsey (1972) surveyed the literature on national income theory and found numerous examples of such attempts and argued that E must be interpreted as *desired* expenditure and Y as actual output (or GDP). This makes (49.2) the non-definitional equilibrium condition that agents desire to purchase exactly the output that is being produced.
3. Following the classic article, Tobin (1958), equation (49.5) can be seen as a portfolio balance equation giving the conditions in which asset holders will not want to substitute between money and bonds.
4. Replacing the parameters with their signs, gives for the denominator of the constant term $\{(+)+(-)(+)\}/(-) = (+)$ and for the coefficient on P^{-1}: $\{(+)+(-)(+)/(-)\} = (+)$. Thus the AD curve has a positive intercept on the Y axis and the two variables are negatively related to each other.
5. Alternatively, the central bank can be assumed to fix the interest rate, in which case the money supply becomes an endogenous variable and the negative slope of the AD curve requires a Pigou effect in terms of nominally denominated 'outside wealth', that is, money that is regarded as an asset by the public but not as a liability by the central bank and/or nominally denominated local debt that is held abroad.
6. If the change is in autonomous expenditure, a, the horizontal shift in the AD curve is $\Delta Y = K\Delta a$, where K is the multiplier. Again, there is no implicit or actual supply reaction here. All this shift tells us is that, with this new level of a, income and output would have to increase by ΔY if the goods market and asset markets were to remain in equilibrium at an unchanged level of P.
7. If labour productivity is constant, a wage-driven fall in unit costs of production requires a fall in money wages, while if productivity is rising, a wage-driven fall in unit costs requires only that money wages rise more slowly than productivity.
8. This must be a shock that does not significantly shift the LRAS as well, as would a major technological advance. (Unlike the assumption of real business cycle theory, actual technological shocks are strongly biased towards increasing Y^* and hence shifting the *LRAS* curves in Figure 49.1 to the right.)
9. Colander gives his argument for an implicit supply reaction by considering the simplest textbook derivation from a goods market equilibrium only (no asset market), as described in the diagonal cross derivation in the above text. He then describes a debate between an imaginary student and his not-very-bright professor. Given space constraints, I content myself with showing that my standard derivation has none of the inconsistencies that Colander argues it has. The effect on Y of a rise in P in this simple no-asset model depends on how much the change in P shifts the E function. This is the ΔP-induced shift in expenditure magnified by the multiplier, which depends on the slope of the E function. The resulting new P-Y combination tells us only that at the new price level, the goods market would be in equilibrium if that new amount of Y was produced. There is no actual supply reaction, either explicit or implicit. The slope of the AD curve is determined solely, as has already been observed, by the parameters in the expenditure and money demand equations. Similarly, when asset markets are introduced, a movement from one point on the AD curve to another initiated by a change in P tells us what the level of production, Y, would have to be if both the goods market and the asset

markets were to clear. The AD curve is thus not a *ceteris paribus* curve but a locus of equilibrium points.

10. I have given my objection to this formulation in Lipsey (2000).
11. In his own words (1995, p. 176): 'To understand this problem, consider the situation where both wages and prices are perfectly flexible, so the AS curve is perfectly vertical'.

REFERENCES

Branson, William (1979), *Macroeconomic Theory and Policy*, Harper and Row: New York, 2nd edition of a text first published in 1972.

Colander, David (1995), 'The Stories We Tell: A Reconsideration of AS/AD Analysis', *The Journal of Economic Perspectives*, 9(3), 169–188.

Fisher, I. (1925), 'Our Unstable Dollar and the So-Called Business Cycle', *Journal of the American Statistical Association*, 20 (156), 179–202.

Fisher, I. (1973), 'I Discovered the Phillips Curve: "A Statistical Relation Between Unemployment and Price Changes"', *The Journal of Political Economy*, 81 (2 part II), 496–502.

Klappholz, K. and E. Mishan (1962), 'Identities in Economic Models: "Nothing Will Come of Nothing" – King Lear', *Economica*, 29 (114), 117–128.

Lipsey, Richard G. (1972), 'The Foundation of the Theory of National Income: An Analysis of Some Fundamental Errors', in B. A. Corry and M. H. Peston (eds), *Essays in Honour of Lord Robbins*, London: Weidenfeld and Nicolson, pp. 3–42.

Lipsey, Richard G. (1981), 'The Understanding and Control of Inflation and Unemployment: Is there a Crisis Macro Economics?', *Canadian Journal of Economics*, 14, 545–576.

Lipsey, Richard G. (2000), 'IS-LM, Keynesianism and the New Classicism', in Roger E. Blackhouse and Andrea Salanti (eds), *Macroeconomics and the Real World, Volume 2: Keynesian Economics, Unemployment, and Policy*, Oxford: Oxford University Press, pp. 57–82.

Lipsey, Richard G. and Alex Chrystal (2007), *Economics*, Oxford: Oxford University Press, 11th Edition.

Mankiw, N. Gregory (2007), *Macroeconomics*, New York: Worth Publishers, 6th edition.

McKenna, Joseph P. (1965), *Aggregate Economic Analysis*, New York: Holt Rinehart, 2nd edition of a text first published in 1955.

Scarth, William M. (1996), *Macroeconomics: An Introduction to Advanced Methods*, Toronto: Dryden Press, 2nd edition.

Tobin, James (1958), 'Liquidity Preference as Behavior Towards Risk', *Review of Economic Studies*, 25 (2), 65–86.

50. The Phillips curve

Richard G. Lipsey

Two distinct theories concerning the disequilibrium relation between the real variables of income and unemployment on the one hand and the money variables of wage rates and prices on the other hand have been around for a long time in the economics literature. In Theory 1, the causal relation runs from money to real variables: changes in the money price level and the money wage rate cause changes in income and unemployment. In Theory 2, the causal relation is reversed: changes in the real variables of income and unemployment cause changes in the money variables of prices and wage rates. The fact that these two theories have one implication in common, that there is a trade-off over some time period between unemployment and inflation, does not necessarily make them identical theories. In some versions, both relations are merely the dynamic and static versions of a single relation that links real and monetary variables. In other versions, however, the two are distinct relations, differing, for example, in the behaviour that underlies them and the policies that might shift them.

The textbook short-run aggregate supply curve (SRAS) that relates the price level, P, to national income, Y, concerns Theory 1 (see Chapter 49). Theory 2 was given its modern form when A. W. Phillips (1958) reported finding a stable relation between the percentage of the labour force unemployed, U, and the rate of change of money wages, $\dot{W}$, in the U.K. between 1861 and 1957; when Richard Lipsey (1960) formalised Phillips' interpretation that the state of demand in the labour market, as indicated by the percentage of the labour force unemployed, caused the observed changes in wages; and when Paul Samuelson and Robert Solow (1960) christened this relation 'The Phillips Curve'.

THE BASIC CURVE

Although many different specifications have been used, the simplest form of the Phillips curve is

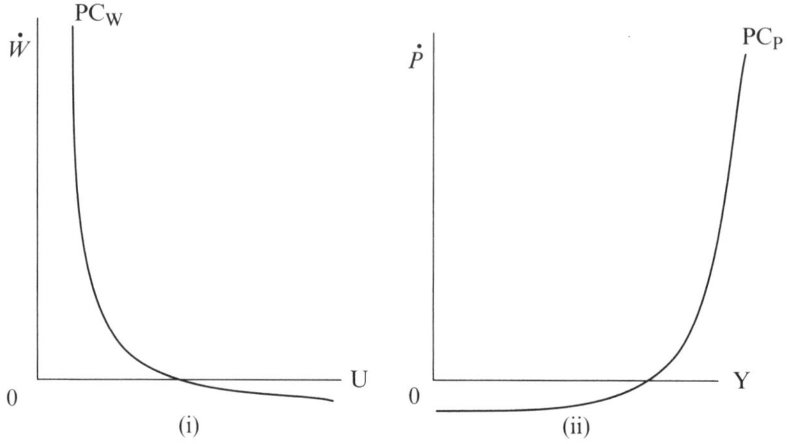

Figure 50.1 Wage- and price-Phillips curves

$$\dot{W} = aU^{-1} + b \tag{50.1}$$

where a is some positive constant, b is the asymptote, usually taken to be a small negative percentage, and dots over a variable indicate its proportionate rate of change. The curve is shown as PC_w in Figure 50.1(i). Its shape implies that wage inflation rises without limit as U approaches zero but falls by less than b as U rises towards 100 per cent.

Later, the influence of expected changes in the price level was added formally[1] and the curve became 'the expectations-augmented Phillips Curve', which in simplest form is

$$\dot{W} = aU^{-1} + b + c\dot{P}^e \tag{50.2}$$

where $\dot{P}^e$ is the expected rate of change of the price level. There is then a family of Philips curves, each one corresponding to a specific expected rate of price inflation as shown in Figure 49.2 (which is adapted from Lipsey 1977).

If the coefficient c is unity, the expected price changes are passed on fully as actual wage changes. Now let price changes be equal to wage changes in excess of productivity growth plus exogenous shocks, such as changes in import prices, multiplied by a 'pass-through' constant d:

$$\dot{P} = \dot{W} - \dot{g} + d\dot{X}. \tag{50.3}$$

Profit margins are assumed to be a constant percentage over costs and so are omitted from this equation. It was argued by early Keynesians that

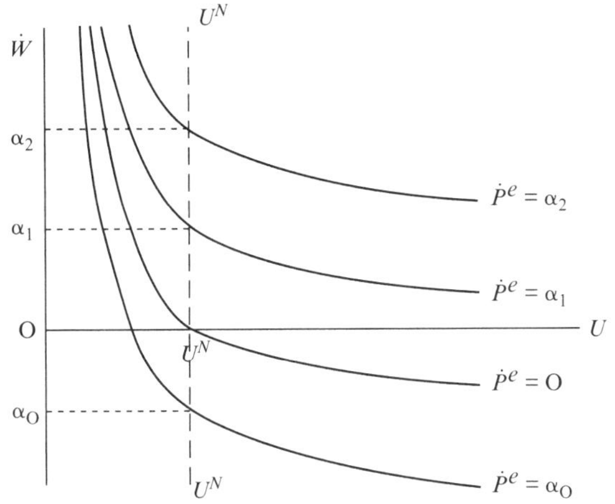

Source: Adapted from Lipsey (1977, p. 54)

Figure 50.2 Expectations-augmented Phillips curves for various expected inflation rates

this assumption was supported by ample empirical evidence and, even if margins did vary cyclically, such variations could not be responsible for any sustained inflation independent of the behaviour of costs.

In the steady state, expected inflation must equal actual inflation:

$$\dot{P}^e = \dot{P} \tag{50.4}$$

Substituting (50.4) and (50.3) into (50.2), yields:

$$U = a/(\dot{g} - b - d\dot{X}). \tag{50.5}$$

Thus, in this theory there is only one level of U compatible with the equality of actual and expected inflation, while that U is compatible with any $\dot{W}$ and $\dot{P}$. That level, which came to be called the 'non-accelerating-inflationary rate of unemployment' or NAIRU, is shown by the vertical dashed line at U^N in Figure 50.2.[2] (Its associated level of income is called Y^* hereinafter.) Inspection of (50.5) shows that the NAIRU is predicted to be higher, the higher are both a and b, increases in which shift the Phillips curve to the right, the lower is $\dot{g}$, the rate of productivity growth, and the higher are both $\dot{X}$, external shocks, and d, the pass through of those shocks to the price level.

When money wage changes are assumed to be independent of productivity growth, as in Phillips' original development, the natural rate varies negatively with such growth because the higher the productivity growth, the higher the wage change and the lower the unemployment rate that are compatible with stable prices. In early natural rate theorising, however, productivity growth was usually assumed to be associated with equal percentage increases in wage rates. When $\dot{g}$ is thus added positively to equation (50.2), it cancels out with the $\dot{g}$ in the price equation, so that the natural rate depends only on the position of the wage-Phillips curve and supply-side shocks.

THE PLACE OF THE CURVE IN MACRO MODELS

In early Keynesian macroeconomics, real income was determined for any given price level by the textbook IS-LM model or one of its many more elaborate versions. 'Closure' – the simultaneous determination of real income and the price level – was usually provided by an aggregate supply curve, relating the level of national income to the price level, that was perfectly elastic up to full employment income, Y^*, and perfectly inelastic at Y^*. This was the 'reverse-L', upward-ratcheting, kinked, aggregate supply curve. Below full-employment income, the price level was fixed so that fluctuations in desired expenditure caused fluctuations in income and employment. If desired expenditure exceeded the full-employment income constraint, prices would rise until the excess demand was eliminated. Because the price level was assumed to be rigid downwards, any further reduction in desired expenditure would lower income and employment at the new higher price level. When the IS-LM model was closed in this way, there was an automatic adjustment mechanism that would eliminate excess aggregate demand, but none that would eliminate deficient aggregate demand, since the economy could come to rest anywhere on the perfectly elastic portion of the *AS* curve.

In 1954 and 1957, Phillips published his two pathbreaking papers on stabilisation policy, showing that such policies could easily act perversely by destabilising the economy – and this long before Milton Friedman popularised the idea. He closed his models with a curve such as PC_P in Figure 50.1(ii)), relating the rate of change of the price level to the deviation of actual income from Y^*, a deviation that was later called the 'income gap':[3]

$$\dot{P} = p(Y - Y^*) \tag{50.6}$$

Then in his famous 1958 paper, he provided the empirical underpinning of (50.6) by relating the rate of change of money wage rates to level of unemployment as shown by the curve PC_W in Figure 50.1(i).

The 'wage-Phillips curve' (PC_W) and the 'price-Phillips curve' (PC_P) shown in Figure 50.1 are related by the assumption that unemployment is negatively associated with the income gap.[4] In Keynesian theory, the link between changes in aggregate demand, *AD*, and changes in the price level was provided by a transmission mechanism that went from changes in aggregate demand to changes in income and output, to changes in the demand for labour input, to changes in unemployment and in wage costs, and finally to changes in the price level. In symbols, starting from full-employment equilibrium: $\uparrow AD \rightarrow \uparrow Y \rightarrow \uparrow D_L \rightarrow (\downarrow U, \uparrow W) \rightarrow \uparrow P$. The justification for having price changes following rather than leading wage changes was provided by the theory of the flat marginal cost curve, as described later in this chapter. The job of the wage-Phillips curve was to determine the rate at which the wages costs and hence the prices of output would change because of excess aggregate demand or supply. Lipsey (1960) explained the link between $\dot{W}$ and labour market conditions by assuming that the excess demand for labour was linearly related to changes in the wage rate and non-linearly related to the level of unemployment. Subsequently many alternative interpretations of the Phillips curve were suggested, but the demand-driven interpretation eventually prevailed.

In the early 1960s, the Phillips curve, in either its PC_W or PC_P form, replaced the kinked aggregate supply curve as the preferred method of closure, at least in the UK. When used to close the IS-LM model, it took the form of the price curve shown in Figure 50.1(ii). Figure 50.3 is reproduced from Lipsey (1977:54) with the lettering on the axes changed to conform to the usage in the present essay. The figure shows the closure for the simple case of zero expected inflation and zero cost-push shocks. (More realistic analysis requires mathematics instead of graphics.) The original position is given by $(I\text{-}S)_1$ and $(L\text{-}M)_1$, with equilibrium at Y^*. A monetary expansion then shifts the *LM* curve to $(L\text{-}M)_2$ increasing income to Y_1 in both parts of the figure. According to the price-Phillips curve, inflation rises to $\dot{P}_1$. This shifts the *LM* curve to the left, with rising *R* and falling *Y*, until equilibrium is restored at Y^*.

The effect of closing the model with the Phillips curve was to remove the vertical portion of the reverse-L aggregate supply curve, making it perfectly elastic over its entire range. It was often said that the curve allowed the effect of a demand shock to be divided between a change in income and a change in the price level. This is not correct. The IS-LM demand part of the model fully determines real income. All that the Phillips curve does is to determine the rate of inflation or deflation when $Y \neq Y^*$ and hence the speed at which Y^* is restored by the monetary adjustment mechanism (a rise in *P* lowering the real money supply *M*/*P* and thus shifting the *LM* curve to the left). If the Phillips curve is very flat for $Y < Y^*$ (and $U >$

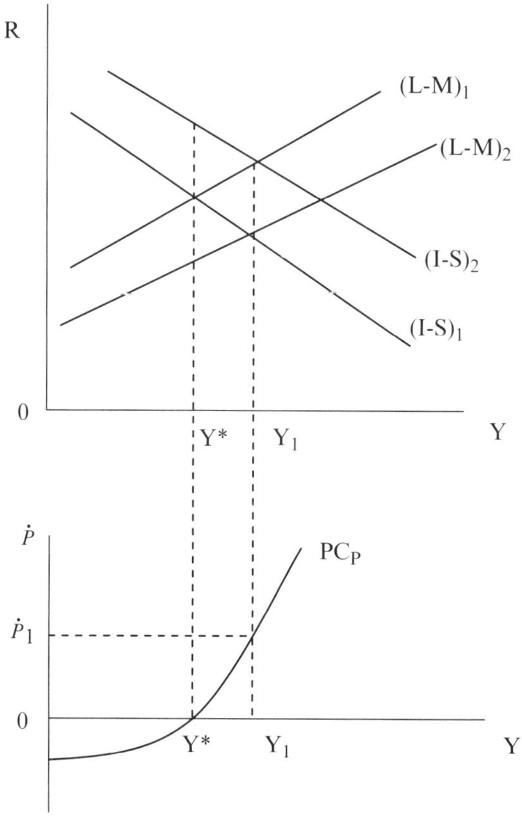

Figure 50.3 An IS-LM model closed by a price-Phillips curve

U^*), the automatic price adjustment mechanism works slowly, if at all, to remove recessionary gaps, and recovery from a recession must come, as it usually does, from the demand side (as declining inventories of durable consumers' and capital goods need replenishing and as new technological advances provide new opportunities for investment).

Later, stagflation made the AD-AS analysis popular (see Chapter 49). The IS-LM part of the model was compressed into an *AD* curve and the perfectly elastic aggregate supply curve implicit in the IS-LM model was replaced by a positively sloped short-run aggregate supply curve relating income positively to the price level in the short run. The graph of the model is shown Figure 50.4, with the AD-AS diagram stacked above a price-Phillips curve.[5] A demand-side shock, either from the expenditure or the monetary side, shifts the *AD* curve from AD_0 to AD_1, and the impact

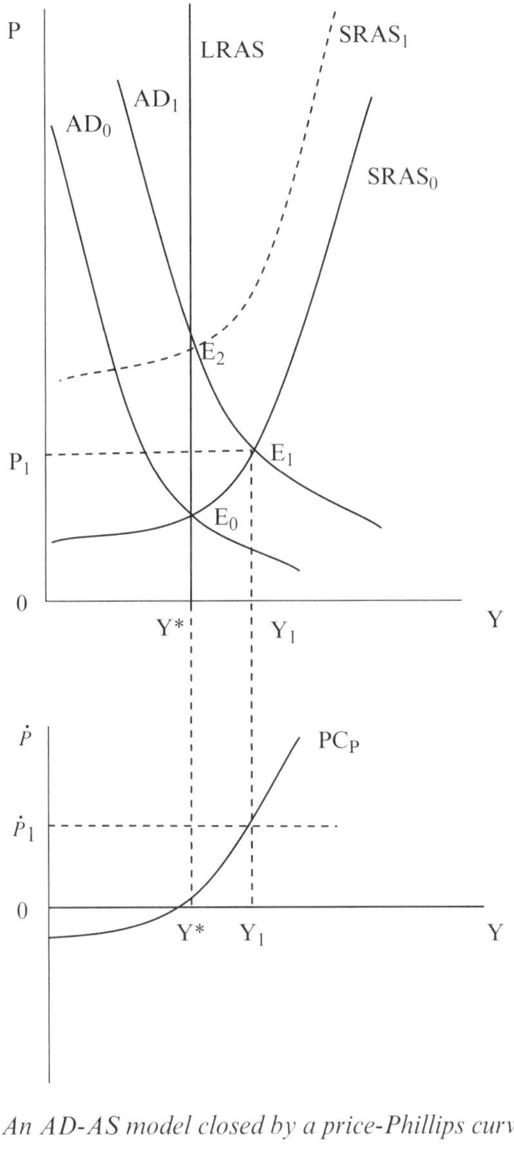

Figure 50.4 An AD-AS model closed by a price-Phillips curve

effect is to raise real income to Y_1 and the price level to P_1. Thus, unlike the Phillips curve, the shape of the SRAS curve does divide the impact effect of a demand shock between a rise in real income and a rise in the price level. The place of the Phillips curve is then to determine how fast wage costs adjust. In the figure, the rise of income to Y_1 causes the price level initially to rise at the rate $\dot{P}_1$, shifting the SRAS curve leftwards and so pushing Y back towards Y^* until equilibrium is restored at E_2.

THE CURVE IN THE PAST AND THE PRESENT

Early Developments

Humphrey (1985) identifies several economists as precursors of Phillips. But like so many others, Humphrey applies the term 'Phillips curve' both to Theories 1 and 2 (see the beginning of this chapter). Of those he mentions, John Law seems to fall into neither camp, David Hume, John Stuart Mill, Irving Fisher, Henry Thornton, and probably Thomas Attwood, deal with Theory 1 type relations. The first two of these took the position associated with modern new classicists that it is errors of perception that account for the positive association between P and Y, while the next two, and probably Attwood as well, appealed to lags between input costs and output prices for the explanation. In contrast, Jan Tinbergen, Klein and Goldberger, A. J. Brown and Paul Sultan dealt with the Theory 2, Phillips curve type of relation in which disequilibria in product and labour markets cause changes in P and W.

Santomero and Seater (1978) provide a superb review of the developments, both theoretical and empirical, from the time of Phillips's 1958 article until the late 1970s. The reader is referred to that article for details as I have only space to mention a few of the key developments. Early empirical work seemed to show a better defined curve for the UK than for the US. However, studies using quarterly data did much better than those using annual data for both the UK and the US. There was much discussion about the adequacy of the statistics, and various authors tried alternative specifications to model the state of the labour market, including unplaced applicants and unfilled vacancies. Various additional explanatory variables were tried and profits showed up significantly in some studies but not others.

The Curve as a Menu of Choice

In the *IS-LM* model closed by the Phillips curve of equation (50.1), money is neutral in its level since an increase in the money supply shifts the *LM* curve to the right and sets up the previously described monetary adjustment mechanism that returns income to Y^*. However, if the curve is assumed to apply over all time periods, this closure makes money non-neutral in its time derivatives. For example, let an expenditure shock shift the *IS* curve from $(I\text{-}S)_1$ to $(I\text{-}S)_2$ in Figure 50.3 and let the monetary authority validate the resulting inflation by increasing the money supply at the same rate as the price level is rising. This prevents the *LM* curve from shifting leftward from its position at $(L\text{-}M)_1$ so that the economy remains indefinitely at a level of income greater than Y^*, in this case Y_1, while inflation is steady at a constant rate, in this case $\dot{P}_1$.

There is debate about when the Phillips curves came to be regarded as providing policy makers with this long-run trade-off between $\dot{P}$ and U. Both Laidler (1997) and Leeson (1997) argue that this interpretation of the curve as a 'menu of choice' was not intended by Phillips but entered the literature well after his original publication. In any case, whatever its disputed origins, the belief in the existence of a Phillips curve 'menu' of choice came to be widely accepted by the early 1960s.

Empirical Problems

The Keynesian model closed by the Phillips curve ran into two distinct difficulties, starting in the mid-1960s. First, the Phillips curves seemed to be shifting upwards as each level of unemployment began to be associated with ever higher rates of wage inflation, and each income gap with ever higher rates of price inflation. Second, in the 1970s, the new phenomenon of stagflation mystified many contemporary observers. High and rising levels of unemployment were associated with high and rising levels of wage and price inflation.

The New Classical Critique and the Neo-keynesian Response

The new classical critique of Keynesian economics in general and the Phillips curves in particular made use of these two developments. One line of criticism concerned the upward drift in measured Phillips curves. This became an effective assault on those who saw the Phillips curve of equation (50.1) as providing a permanent menu of choice among various $\dot{P} - U$ combinations. Critics pointed out that if monetary expansion was used to hold Y significantly above Y^*, inflationary expectations would sooner or later cause the actual rate to accelerate. Edmund Phelps (1967) derived a negatively sloped Phillips curve for zero inflationary expectations, but when he added inflationary expectations to his model, the curve became vertical.

The second major line of new classical criticism related to stagflation. Lucas and Sargent (1978) asserted that the 1970s provided a 'decisive test' of Keynesian economics, a key element of which is the trade off between inflation and output (p. 56). The result of this 'test' was 'the spectacular failure of the Keynesian models' (p. 54), an 'econometric failure on a grand scale' (p. 57).

Two points are relevant here. First, the Phillips curve was never a part of the Keynesian core in Lakatos' sense of the term, its place being only to provide an explanation of the speed of price and cost adjustments when $Y \neq Y^*$ and $U \neq$ NAIRU. Second, although many economists were correctly castigated for accepting equation (50.1) as a menu for long-term choice, once equation (50.2) had replaced equation (50.1), the expectations-augmented Phillips curve was available to close income flow models that made no mystery of stagflation. An upward shifting *SRAS* curve, caused by rising prices of petroleum and its many by-products, could cause P to rise while Y fell. If the stagflation was validated by the monetary authorities, it could continue and, as expectations adjusted to it, the inflation could accelerate with Y remaining continuously below Y^*. Various versions of this model entered the textbooks in the latter part of the 1970s. Elementary textbooks used the crude form of the AD-AS model outlined here, while intermediate texts used a more elaborate difference equation version.

ARE THE AS AND THE PHILLIPS CURVES INDEPENDENT CONCEPTS?

The view that the AS and the Phillips curve represent two separate theories has been seriously challenged in some modern macro theorizing. For example, in his widely used intermediate macro textbook, Mankiw (2007), considers an errors-only *SRAS* curve in which output deviates from Y^* and U from U^* because people do not correctly anticipate the prices that will rule over the relevant time span:

$$(Y - Y^*) = \alpha(P - P^e), \tag{50.7}$$

which can also be written

$$P = P^e + \left(\frac{1}{\alpha}\right)(Y - Y^*). \tag{50.8}$$

Now subtract last year's price level to each side of equation (50.8) to obtain:

$$P - P_{-1} = P^e - P_{-1} + \left(\frac{1}{\alpha}\right)(Y - Y^*) \tag{50.9}$$

Using dots for the change from one year to the next this becomes:

$$\dot{P} = \dot{P}^e + \left(\frac{1}{\alpha}\right)(Y - Y^*) \tag{50.10}$$

This is an expectations augmented price-Philips curve. It can be turned into a wage-Phillips curve by substituting the relation between the income gap and the unemployment gap.

What Mankiw has shown is that in any theory in which the actual price level is equal to the expected price level plus a constant times the actual income gap (equation (50.8)), it follows that the rate of change of the actual price level will equal the rate of change of the expected price level plus a constant times the income gap. The *AS* curve and the Phillips curve are just a static and dynamic way of expressing a single relation between the income (or unemployment) gap and prices.

The critical part of Mankiw's argument is that equation (50.7) is implied by all the main explanations of a positively sloped *SRAS* curve, sticky wages, sticky prices and imperfect information. There is space to consider only one of these and I select the sticky wage explanation. Start by assuming a constant actual and expected price level with $Y = Y^*$. According to Mankiw's version of this theory, labour sets its money wage over the contracting period as a target real wage. Faced with a perfectly elastic supply curve of labour at the going wage rate and a negatively sloping short-run marginal product curve of labour, and its implied positively sloping short-run marginal cost curve of output, each firm has a unique desired employment (and hence output) for each product price that it sets. A rise in aggregate demand with wages constant over the contracting period leads each firm to raise its price and move up its short-run cost curve, increasing output and profits. (This assumes that firms set their own prices in imperfectly competitive markets. If markets are perfectly competitive, the same result occurs when firms raise output in response to a market-determined price rise, rather then raising their own prices directly.) In either case, there is a positively sloped, short-run relation between Y and P, which is the *SRAS* curve. Since the actual price level has now risen above what was expected, labour receives an unexpected fall in its real wage and will raise money wages in the next contracting period. This shifts the *AS* curve upwards.

One of the critical parts of this explanation is the existence of a functional relation between the price of a firm's product and the amount that it is willing to supply in the short run. In contrast, one important version of the Keynesian explanation of the *SRAS* curve refers to the strong evidence that many manufacturing and service firms have marginal and average variable cost curves that are flat over a wide range of output. The textbook U-shaped, short-run cost curve arises when a variable amount of one factor, say, labour, is applied to a fixed amount of a second factor, say, capital. Then only one quantity of labour leads to the least-cost ratio of the variable to the fixed factor. However, although the firm's plant and equipment is fixed in the short run, it is often possible to use less than this amount by such means as working shorter hours, shortening the work week, eliminating one shift, or temporarily closing one or more of a set of identical facilities. This maintains the least-cost ratio of the variable factor to the amount of the 'fixed' factor actually employed. So the difference between the flat and the textbook U-shaped short-run cost curves depends on the kind of constraint that the fixed factor exercises on production decisions. If we let the amount of the fixed factor be K^* and the amount actually employed be K, then in the case of the U-shaped cost curve, $K = K^*$, while in the case of constant cost up to capacity, $K \leq K^*$. Since many firms normally plan to produce at something like 90 per cent of full capacity output in order to hold some capacity in reserve to meet fluctuations in demand, it follows that when the use of the fixed factor can be varied up to its maximum fixed amount, the firms will encounter constant marginal and average variable costs over a range from far below to something like 10 per cent above normal output.

If firms only altered their profit margins infrequently, charging what looks in the short run like conventional mark-ups, and if sticky wages were the only cost, the short-run *AS* curve would be perfectly elastic over a range up to full capacity. However, some inputs are sold in competitive markets, where prices vary with current market conditions and some firms do raise the profit margins when demand and output rises. For these reasons, the *AS* curve may have some modest positive slope in spite of wages being slow to adjust.

This explanation of the positively sloping *SRAS* curve carries no implication for the Phillips curve. In the short run, wages might respond according to a normal Phillips curve, or they might be totally insensitive to demand, or they could depend on union power, or the impact on employment patterns of technical change, or any other variables. All that matters here is that once we depart from explanations that turn on some agents having incorrectly anticipated prices over the period over which their price or wage is fixed, the link that Mankiw establishes between the *SRAS* and the Phillips curve no longer holds.

The key aspect of these other explanations of the behaviour of wage costs is that they break the unique relation between the amount of labour supplied and the real wage rate shown by the positively sloped supply curve of labour found in most neoclassical models. The alternative Keynesian view is that wages are not determined on perfectly competitive auction markets but are set with longer run considerations in view. As Robert Hall (1980) put it, wages are determined by the economic climate not the economic weather. Thus when demand falls, firms lay off workers but do not try to lower the wages of those who are retained until all involuntary unemployment has been eliminated. Similarly, when demand recovers, firms take on workers but at the going wage rate. Labour unions may push harder on wages when there is a labour shortage and firms may do some competitive bidding for labour, thus putting upward pressure on wages as the expansion continues. But these pressures may vary over time according to such things as the strength of union power, the nature of technical change or the stance of government policy towards labour.

TWO LINES OF SUBSEQUENT DEVELOPMENT

In the last 30 or so years, both the Keynesian and new classical approaches have been elaborated and subjected to much empirical testing. (For an excellent critical description of these developments see Gordon 2008.) In the process, the clear analytical distinction between the short-run aggregate supply curve and the Phillips curve has become blurred. If one specifies specific lags to account for deviations of Y from Y^* and U from NAIRU over time, the explanations of why these deviations occur and of how fast they adjust become intermixed. Modelling the lags implies modelling how fast they would lead to adjustment from a single expenditure or monetary shock. (Pioneering work in this area has been done by Blanchard 1987 and Gordon 1990.)

The substantive issues are, however, still distinguishable. First, why do deviations from Y^* and the NAIRU occur? Is it because of errors, lags, flat cost curves or some other reason? This is the Theory 1 question. Second, is there some stable relation between the magnitude of the deviations and the speed of the adjustment process that pushes Y towards Y^* and U towards NAIRU and, if so, how fast does the system work to reduce the deviations? These are Phillips curve, Theory 2, questions. Any answer that relates, either explicitly or implicitly, the speed of adjustment to the extent of the deviations, no matter how they are measured and what are their causes, carries with it an implied Phillips curve.

A FINAL WORD[6]

The existence of a unique level of unemployment and real income (the NAIRU and its associated Y^*) at which inflation neither accelerates or decelerates, a level that is compatible with any non-accelerating rate of inflation or deflation, depends critically on one key assumption. This is that the labour market equilibrium exists on a 'razor's edge', with wage changes responding precisely to all deviations from the NAIRU, accelerating whenever U remains below the NAIRU and decelerating whenever U remains above the NAIRU. Similarly, $\dot{P}$ must accelerate as long as Y remains above Y^* and decelerate when the reverse holds. There is, however, no really hard evidence that either labour or goods markets react smoothly and continuously in this way. A unique equilibrium NAIRU and Y^* is an assumption that is inculcated in most of us by our theoretical training. For example, Friedman (1968) was relying on most economists' training when he referred to the Walrasian equations 'grinding out' a unique NAIRU and Y^*. However, this is a static view of the world. Instead, the real world is constantly changing as new technologies replace old ones. Anyone who compares the structure of any industrialised economy in 1970 with what it is today cannot but be impressed by the constant, sometimes revolutionary, changes that are generated by new technologies. So the belief in the unique NAIRU and Y^* is nothing but a maintained assumption for which there is little compelling evidence.

In response to these worries, some theories allow the NAIRU to vary. But for these to be meaningful theories, the NAIRU and Y^* must be explained in such a way that their existence can be tested empirically. As long as they are free to take on shifting values that best 'explain' the data, there is no real theory, only *ex post* data tracking.

Perhaps Keynesians were too hasty in following the new classical economists in accepting the view that follows from static models that stable rates of wage and price inflation are poised on the razor's edge of a unique NAIRU and its accompanying Y^*. The alternative does not require a long-term Phillips curve trade-off, nor does it deny the possibility of accelerating inflations of the kind that have bedevilled many third world countries. It is merely states that industrialised economies with low expected inflation rates may be less precisely responsive than current theory assumes because they are subject to many lags and inertias, and are operating in an ever-changing and uncertain world of endogenous technological change, which has no unique long-term static equilibrium. If so, the economy may not be similar to the smoothly functioning mechanical world of Newtonian mechanics but rather to the imperfectly evolving world of evolutionary biology. The Phillips relation then changes from being a precise curve to being a band within which various combinations of inflation and unemployment are possible but outside of which inflation tends to accelerate or decelerate. Perhaps then the great debates of the 1940s and early 1950s that assumed that there was a range within which the economy could be run with varying pressures of demand, and varying amounts of unemployment and inflation, were not as silly as they were made to seem when both Keynesian and new classical economists accepted the assumption of a perfectly inelastic, one-dimensional, long-run Phillips curve located at a unique Y^* and NAIRU.

ACKNOWLEDGEMENTS

I am indebted for comments and suggestions to Christopher Ragan, Robert Leeson and William Scarth.

NOTES

1. Phillips (1954) and Lipsey (1960) had both considered such an effect but had not added it formally to their theories.
2. For example, let $a = 9$, $\dot{g} = 3$, $b = -1$ and $\dot{X} = 0$. This yields a NAIRU of 2.25 per cent.
3. When I worked with Phillips on my 1960 article, he repeatedly referred to Bent Hansen (1951) as his source of this relation. Indeed, Hansen uses this relation many times in his theorising about inflation.
4. For a simple example, let the behavioural relation be $U = e/Y$. Substituting this relation into equation (50.2) in the text and then substituting (50.2) into (50.3) yields $\dot{P} = (a/e)Y + b - \dot{g} + d\dot{X} + cP^e$. The rate of price inflation is then related negatively to productivity growth and positively to national income, cost push shocks, the expected rate of inflation and the asymptote on the Phillips curve – an increase in which shifts that curve upwards. Note that since productivity changes do not enter the wage equations of (50.1) and (50.2), increases in $\dot{g}$ reduce price inflation. In contrast, if they do enter the wage equation with a positive sign, they cancel out the negative $\dot{g}$ in the price adjustment equation and productivity growth has no effect on inflation.
5. The operative force is the wage-Phillips curve but to show the stacking with P on the AD-AS diagram, we make use of the relations $\dot{P} = p(\dot{W}) = w(Y - Y^*)$.
6. For an elaboration of the views expressed in this section see Carlaw and Lipsey (2010).

REFERENCES

Blanchard, Olivier J. (1987), 'Aggregate and Individual Price Adjustment', *Brookings Papers on Economic Activity*, 18 (1), 57–109.

Carlaw, Kenneth I. and Richard G. Lipsey (2010), 'Darwinian versus Newtonian Views of the Economy: The Schumpeterian versus New Classical Theories', paper presented to the 13th International Schumpeter Society Conference in Aalborg, Denmark, 21–24 June 2010.

Friedman, Milton (1968), 'The Role of Monetary Policy', *American Economic Review*, 58, 1–17.

Gordon, Robert J. (1990), 'What is New-Keynesian Economics?' *Journal of Economic Literature*, 28 (3), 1115–71.

Gordon, Robert J. (2008), 'The History of the Phillips Curve: An American Perspective', Keynote Address at *Market, and models in the AWH Phillips*

Tradition, Australasian Meetings of the Econometric Society, Wellington, New Zealand, 9 July.

Hall, Robert E. (1980), 'Employment Fluctuations and Wage Rigidity', *Brookings Economic Papers*, 10th Anniversary Issue, 91–123.

Hansen, Bent (1951), *A Study in the Theory of Inflation*, London: Allen and Unwin.

Humphrey, T.M. (1985), 'The Early History of the Phillips Curve', *Federal Reserve Bank of Richmond Economic Review*, 71 (2), 17–24.

Laidler, David (1997), 'The Emergence of the Phillips Curve as a Policy Menu', in B. Curtis Eaton and Richard G. Harris (eds), *Trade, Technology and Economics: Essays in Honour of Richard G. Lipsey*, Cheltenham: Edward Elgar, pp. 88–106.

Leeson, Robert (1997), 'The Trade-Off Interpretation of Phillips's Dynamic Stabilization Exercise', *Economica*, 64 (253), 155–71.

Lipsey, Richard G. (1960), 'The Relation Between Unemployment and the Rate of Change of Money Wage Rates: A Further Analysis', *Economica*, 27 (105), 1–13.

Lipsey, Richard G. (1977), 'The Place of the Phillips Curve in Macroeconomic Models', in A.R. Bergstrom, A.J.L. Catt, M.H. Peston and B.D.J. Silverston (eds), *Stability and Inflation: A Volume of Essays to Honour the Memory of A.W.H. Phillips*, New York: John Wiley and Sons, pp. 49–75.

Lipsey, Richard G. (1981), 'The Understanding and Control of Inflation and Unemployment: Is there a Crisis in Macro Economics?', *Canadian Journal of Economics*, 14, 545–76.

Lucas, R.E. and Sargent, T. (1978), 'After Keynesian Macroeconomics, and Response to Friedman', in *After the Phillips Curve: Persistence of High Inflation and High Unemployment*, Boston: Federal Reserve Bank of Boston, pp. 49–83.

Mankiw, N. Gregory (2007), *Macroeconomics*, sixth edition, New York: Worth Publishers.

Phelps, Edmund (1967), 'Money Wage Dynamics and Labour-Market Equilibrium', *Journal of Political Economy*, 76 (4), 678–711.

Phillips, A.W. (1954), 'Stabilisation Policy in a Closed Economy', *Economic Journal*, 64 (254), 290–323.

Phillips, A.W. (1957), 'Stabilisation Policy and the Time-Forms of Lagged Responses', *Economic Journal*, 67 (266), 265–67.

Phillips, A.W. (1958), 'The Relation between Unemployment and the Rate of Change of Money Wages Rates in the United Kingdom, 1861–1957', *Economica*, 25 (100), 283–99.

Samuelson, Paul A. and Robert M. Solow (1960), 'Analytical Aspects of Anti-Inflation Policy', *American Economic Review Papers and Proceedings*, 50 (2), 177–94.

Santomero, A. and J. Seater (1978), 'The Inflation-Unemployment Trade-Off: A Critique of the Literature', *Journal of Economic Literature*, 16 (2), 499–544.

51. The UV or Beveridge curve

Peter Rodenburg

1. DOW AND DICKS-MIREAUX'S UV CURVE

The UV curve originates from the work of two British economists, Dow and Dicks-Mireaux (hereafter DDM). In their seminal 1958 paper they were interested in measuring excess demand in the goods market for the guidance of Keynesian fiscal policies. Since excess demand is unobservable, they suggested using data on vacancies and unemployment in the labour market as a proxy. The application of this simple idea was possible for Britain since the British Government had started collecting data on unfilled vacancies from notification at labour exchanges in 1946. DDM argue that, though the recording of vacancies at labour exchanges might be incomplete or faulty, the behaviour of vacancies relative to unemployment shows that vacancy statistics can be considered as rather reliable indicators. DDM presented the unemployment and vacancy data in an unemployment-vacancy (UV) space and connected successive observations (Figure 51.1).

An important feature that DDM assumed about the behaviour of unemployment is that unemployment below a certain level would be decreasingly sensitive to demand. That is, a further increase in demand should lead to a disproportionately small decline in unemployment rates (and vice versa for vacancies). Following this rationale and based on the observations of Figure 51.1, (particularly the years 1951–56), DDM derive an idealized UV curve as a rectangular hyperbola (Figure 51.2).

The idealized UV curve has the following features. Firstly, an inverse relation between vacancy and unemployment rates. When the economy is in recession (point 1), it experiences high unemployment rates and low vacancies rates; and vice versa in an upswing (point 3). Each point on the UV curve represents a different degree of aggregate demand, and, across the various stages of the business cycle, the economy moves along the idealized UV curve. Secondly, the hyperbolic and convex shape of the UV curve represents the feature that a further increase in demand leads to a disproportionately small decline in unemployment rates. This 'increasing

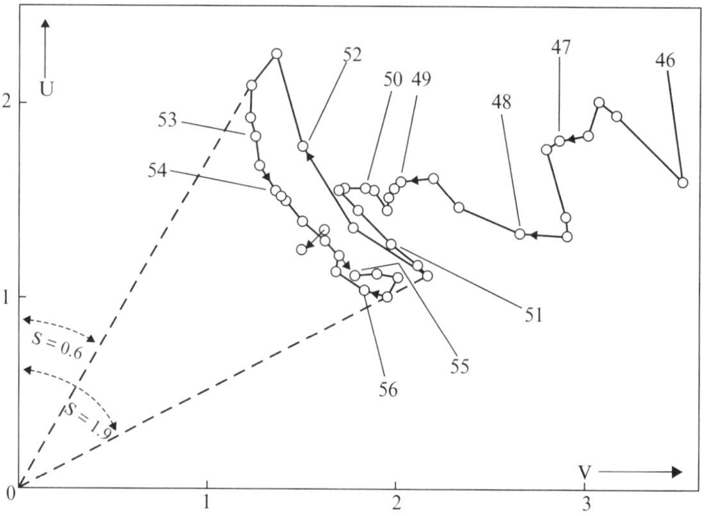

Source: DDM, 1958: 4

Figure 51.1 Relation between unemployment and vacancy rates in a UV space for Great Britain, 1946–1956

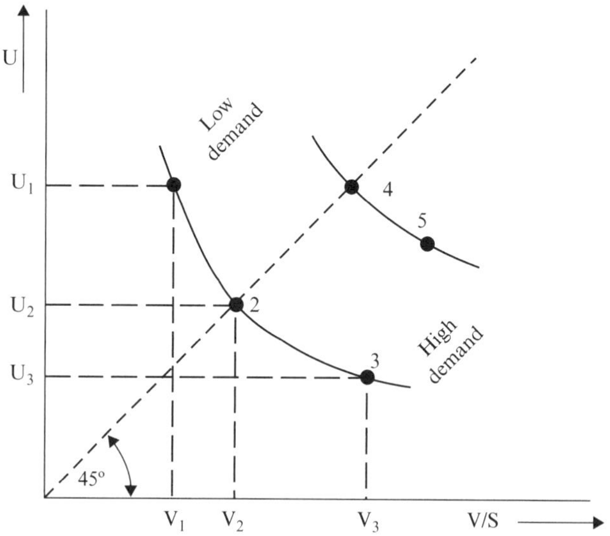

Source: DDM, 1958: 4

Figure 51.2 Idealized UV relations (with v/s = adjusted vacancy rate)

insensitivity of unemployment', as DDM called it, clearly resembles the neoclassical idea of decreasing returns to input factors as found in production and utility functions. Later empirical studies estimate this hyperbolic UV relation as $\log v = \beta_0 + \beta_1 \log(1/u) + \varepsilon$. Thirdly, different degrees of maladjustment (structural unemployment) correspond to different idealized UV curves, further or closer to the origin. And fourthly, a 45 degree auxiliary line can be constructed to represent zero excess demand.

2. THE UV CURVE STABILITY DEBATE

The work of DDM, as well as theoretical work by Holt and David (1966) and Gordon (1966), inspired a series of empirical studies in the late 1960s and throughout the 1970s, estimating the relation between unemployment and vacancies.[1] Cohen and Solow, in 1967, found a stable relationship between unemployment and vacancies, but almost immediately after publication, other empirical studies found supposed 'breakpoints' in the UV curve, suggesting shifts of the curve further or closer to the origin, corresponding to higher or lower levels of structural unemployment. This obviously raised questions about the stability of the UV relation and the usefulness of the UV curve as a structural relation for economic analysis and measurement, and resulted in a vast number of empirical studies since the 1970s with an abundance of specifications of the UV curves, all of which incorporate additional variables, dummy variables or lagged variables. Econometric analysis usually provided no or only very little evidence for the alternative hypotheses tested, and after three decades of testing and specifying the UV curve, economists remain agnostic as to the exact causes of the changes.

3. THE IMPACT OF THE UV CURVE ON ECONOMIC THEORY

The UV curve was put forward by DDM as a practical measurement device to guide economic policy. Its place in economic theory was therefore not immediately clear. The UV curve obviously had some attractive features, in the sense that it provides a macro-framework that shows that unemployment and vacancies coexist simultaneously in the absence of excess demand, or the novel insight that some unemployment will exist even at very high levels of demand, but its explanatory power was low. And more importantly, although the UV curve was empirically supported, there was no theoretical foundation for it.

The introduction of the UV curve had several effects on macroeconomics, the most important ones being the following. Firstly, it introduced a method, which later became known as UV analysis, for the decomposition of unemployment into different types: deficient-demand (or cyclical) unemployment and structural unemployment. This was clearly consistent with DDM's purpose of doing measurement for guiding Keynesian policies. Later, in the first half of the 1970s, economists of the National Institute of Economic and Social Research (NIESR) in London developed the UV analysis further so that they could decompose the non-deficient demand component of unemployment into a structural and a frictional component of unemployment, so that a classification arises that corresponds to the 'traditional' classification: a division of unemployment into frictional, structural and deficient demand unemployment (Brown, 1976). Secondly, both the UV curve and the Phillips-curve (see: Chapter 50) were used to clarify the post-war policy debate on 'full employment' that was instigated by Keynes' *General Theory* (1936) and Beveridge's *Full Employment in a Free Society* (1944), as both curves provided macroeconomic notions of equilibrium in markets, though these notions were inconsistent and conflicting (Rodenburg, 2011). The equilibrium implied by the UV curve is in terms of equilibrium between vacancies and unemployment rather than the neoclassical equilibrium notion in terms of equilibrium prices (wages), and is therefore more akin to Beveridge's definition of full employment, which he phrased as 'having always more vacant jobs than unemployed men, not slightly fewer jobs' (1944: 18). Most likely for this reason, the UV curve also became known in the 1980s as the Beveridge curve; other factors included the fact that the UV curve enabled economists to analyse many of the problems Beveridge addressed, such as the mismatch between unemployment and vacancies, both at aggregate and industry levels, trend versus cyclical changes and measurement problems of vacancies. Beveridge, however, never drew the curve and the exact origin of the term remains obscure.

Thirdly, the simultaneous coexistence of unemployment and vacancies was at odds with neoclassical notions of market clearing. It was, for example, unclear how the UV curve should be explained in a simple Marshallian supply and demand analysis (see: Chapter 1). The growing awareness that labour markets may perhaps not clear as instantaneously as other markets necessitated a theory of simultaneous coexistence of unemployment and vacancies in equilibrium. This was solved by, among others, Hansen (1970), who incorporated the UV curve in a Marshallian supply and demand framework by integrating elements of Gordon (1966) and Holt and David (1966). In this way, he provided a comprehensive, neoclassical theory of friction within a Marshallian supply and demand framework, and showed that unemployment and vacancies can coexist theoretically. Finally, in the 1980s, the UV curve gave a strong conceptual impetus and empirical support to new equilibrium theories of labour markets, such as search theory and matching models of unemployment, which currently dominate contemporary economic thought on unemployment. Important contributions were made at the London School of Economics by Pissarides, Layard, Nickell and Jackman, currently at the LSE Centre of Economic Performance, and Mortensen, Blanchard and Diamond in the USA. Whereas the contributions of NIESR were empirical and concerned with the decomposition of unemployment changes, especially at the regional level, the LSE contribution to search and matching theory was more theoretical. As a consequence of the shift to the search theory paradigm, studies using UV analysis became rare in the 1980s.

4. THE ROLE OF THE UV CURVE IN CONTEMPORARY ECONOMICS

The role of the UV curve in search theory is different from its role in 1960s and 1970s macroeconomic theories. The key idea of matching models is that the complicated and stochastic process of job search is captured in one single, well-behaved, aggregate mathematical function, called the matching function.[2] The idea of a labour market divided into frictionless submarkets is abandoned and replaced by one mathematical function accounting for flows in the labour market in equilibrium. Without explicit reference to the source of friction, the equilibrium outcome is defined in a small set of variables. In its most elementary form, the matching function is: $M = m\,(U, V)$. In a UV space, the matching function is stable and convex to the origin, and exhibits diminishing returns to input factors; that is, it corresponds with the empirically found UV curve. The matching function framework enables economists to analyse the effect of heterogeneous groups of workers with different characteristics in terms of probabilities of in- or outflow. Workers with a higher rate of job finding experience shorter periods of unemployment and lower rates of structural unemployment. Workers and job vacancies are no longer considered as homogeneous and both therefore have to spend time and resources in order to find a good match. Even in the absence of deficient demand for labour, unemployment and vacancies coexist as a consequence of this time-consuming search process. After unemployed workers and vacancies are brought together by this stochastic matching technology, matching models focus consequently on the division of the outcome of this productive match, often as a bargaining process, where the surplus is divided according to a surplus-sharing rule. Two equilibrium-generating mechanisms are usually explored: the effects of wage adjustments and the effects of labour market tightness adjustment. The equilibrium outcome, that is, when the values of the variables *U*, *V* and *W* (wage) are determined by equilibrium conditions, is at the intersection of the stable UV curve and the job creation curve, a straight line with slope θ, the labour market tightness (see, for example, Pissarides, 1999). The UV curve is thus nowadays used as an analytical device to derive the consequences of, for example, labour market tightness, or differences in skills or productivity of workers. The correlation between *U* and *V* data is thus still valid today, but economists are no longer seeking causal structure at the macro-level. In fact, the UV curve is nowadays used in a very similar way to production and utility functions. And, for the same reason as for production or utility functions, a Cobb-Douglas type of matching function is often assumed.[3]

The UV curve is currently, however, also treated in another, more empirical and applied way, namely as a diagnostic tool for the labour market. Soon after the introduction of search theory in the early 1980s, a debate broke loose in modern macroeconomics – particularly in the USA – on 'sectoral shifts' or 'reallocation shocks' versus 'aggregate disturbances' as unemployment rose rapidly at that time, both in Europe and the USA. The debate started with Lilien's sectoral shift hypothesis: the idea that intersectoral (and intrasectoral) labour reallocations affect unemployment at an aggregate level. Idiosyncratic shocks will cause flows of labour from declining sectors to booming sectors. In fact, the debate was, once again, about the nature of unemployment and was in some ways a renewed version of the structuralist versus deficient demand debate of the 1960s in the USA. The issue became how to identify the effects of aggregate demand changes from structural changes (at the level of sectors) and the UV curve soon acquired a dominant place in the analysis and empirical tests of the sectoral shift hypothesis. If a sectoral shock hits the economy and structural unemployment rises, the UV curve will shift outward, resulting in a positive *U-V* co-movement and a positive correlation between vacancies *V* and the variance of the reallocation shocks. Similarly, an aggregate shock will result in a movement along the UV curve: a negative co-movement of *U* and *V*, and a negative correlation between *V* and the variance of the reallocation shocks. In this way, contemporary applied labour economists take the UV curve as an important diagnostic device for the analysis of shocks, and more generally, as an indictor of the state, performance and efficiency of the labour market, even though the causes of shifts of the UV curve are not fully understood, and even though interpretations of shifts are hindered by changes in in- or outflows.

5. CONCLUSIONS

In retrospect, it can be concluded that the paradigmatic change in unemployment theory from Keynesianism to neoclassical search theory also shaped the role and use of the UV curve. It came into being at a time when economists had a strong belief in the effectiveness of Keynesian, aggregate demand management and the main concepts that UV analysis aimed to measure, such as excess demand and cyclical unemployment, are important Keynesian concepts. Their measurement, however, became more-or-less superfluous with the fall of Keynesianism. Shifts of the UV curve were not considered by advocates to be a serious threat to UV analysis mainly because of the optimistic belief in the 1970s and 1980s that the underlying cause or causes of the shift of the UV curve could be identified and could be accounted for in the specification of the UV curve. The inability to do so rendered the UV curve underdetermined. It became impossible to distinguish between different movements of the UV curve: movement along the UV curve necessary for measurement; deliberate attempts by economic policy to move the UV curve inwards in order to reduce structural unemployment; and unintended structural shocks of the UV curve for reasons yet unknown. Search theory circumvents the problems inherent to UV analysis by analysing flows and overcomes the identification problem by assuming Cobb-Douglas type of UV curves. In this way the apparently inductively established empirical UV curve changed into a deductively derived UV curve which is firmly rooted in and reinforces neoclassical economics. The paradigmatic change from Keynesianism to neoclassical search theory changed the role and interpretations of the UV curve from a measurement device of aggregate demand for Keynesians and an interpretation of full employment, to an equilibrium condition for neoclassical search theorists and an important diagnostic tool for the labour market.

Labour economic research of the last decades has given much emphasis to the Phillips curve and the UV curve as macroeconomic structural relations. Though the UV curve has played second fiddle for a long time due to the dominant place of the Phillips curve in economic analysis, the renewed interest in the UV curve is growing and it will undoubtedly serve an important function as one of our prime 'looking glasses' into the labour market for the time to come.

NOTES

1. See for reference, Rodenburg, 2011.
2. For a survey of the matching function see, for example, Petrongolo and Pissarides (2001).

3. Petrongolo and Pissarides (2001) show that the Cobb-Douglas specification of the matching function commands a fair amount of empirical support. There are however no compelling theoretical reasons why the matching function should be of the Cobb-Douglas form.

REFERENCES

Beveridge, W. (1944), *Full Employment in a Free Society*, London: George Allen and Unwin Ltd.

Brown, A.J. (1976), 'UV-analysis' in Worswick, G.D.N. (ed.), *The Concept and Measurement of Involuntary Unemployment*, London: George Allen and Unwin Ltd.

Cohen, M.S. and Solow, R.M. (1967), 'The Behaviour of the Help-Wanted Advertising', *Review of Economics and Statistics*, vol. 49, no. 1, 108–10.

Dow, J.C.R. and Dicks-Mireaux, L. (1958), 'The Excess Demand for Labour: A Study of Conditions in Great Britain, 1946–1956', *Oxford Economic Papers*, vol. 10, 1–33.

Gordon, A.R. (1966), *The Goal of Full Employment*, New York: John Wiley and Sons Inc.

Hansen, B. (1970), 'Excess Demand, Unemployment, Vacancies, and Wages', *Quarterly Journal of Economics*, vol. 84, no. 1, 1–23.

Holt, C.C and David, M.H. (1966), 'The Concept of Job Vacancies in a Dynamic Theory of the Labor Market', in: *The Measurement and Interpretation of Job Vacancies: A Conference Report of the National Bureau of Economic Research*, New York: NBER.

Keynes, J.M. (1936), *The General Theory of Employment Interest and Money*, London: Macmillan.

Petrongolo, B. and Pissarides C.A. (2001), 'Looking into the Black Box: A Survey of the Matching Function', *Journal of Economic Literature*, vol. 39, 390–431.

Pissarides, C.A. (1999), *Equilibrium Unemployment Theory*, Cambridge, MA: MIT Press.

Rodenburg, P. (2011), 'The Remarkable Transformation of the UV Curve', *European Journal of the History of Economic Thought*, vol. 18, no. 1, March.

52. The demand curve for money

David Laidler

It is nowadays uncontroversial that the demand equation for money determines the demand for a stock of the economy's means of exchange and some of its close substitutes as a function of some 'scale' variable (real wealth or national income, say), the opportunity cost of holding it (the difference between its own rate of interest and representative returns on other assets) and the general price level. This last relationship is one of strict proportionality, because rational agents make choices about real quantities that are independent of the units in which they are measured. Even so, an extensive literature – see Laidler (1993) – has debated such empirical matters as money's precise definition and this function's stability.

Under the gold standard, the classical explanation of the price level as depending upon the cost of production of the precious metals had always co-existed uneasily with the quantity theory of money, which stated that, if money's velocity of circulation and the level of real output were held constant, the price level would vary in strict proportion to the quantity of money in circulation, But by the late nineteenth century, the cost of production theory of value was being superseded by one based on the idea of marginal utility and sometimes articulated in terms of a supply and demand apparatus. Thus, though relative prices and the price level had once seemed explicable by a single theory, they now required separate and apparently unrelated approaches.

Alfred Marshall, a leading exponent of the new theory of value, sought to eliminate this awkwardness. His theoretical ideas about money, diagram and all, date from about 1871 (see Whitaker, 1975, Vol. 1, pp.165–177 and Vol. 2 p. 278). Marshall's demand curve related desired holdings of nominal money to its price in terms of goods, that is, the inverse of the general price level. Arguing that the typical agent, and agents in the aggregate too, would, *ceteris paribus*, find it convenient to hold a given fraction of real wealth as money, Marshall drew this curve (Md in figure 52.1) as a rectangular hyperbola. With the supply of money, Ms, which he thought of as consisting of gold coin and convertible paper currency, given at time

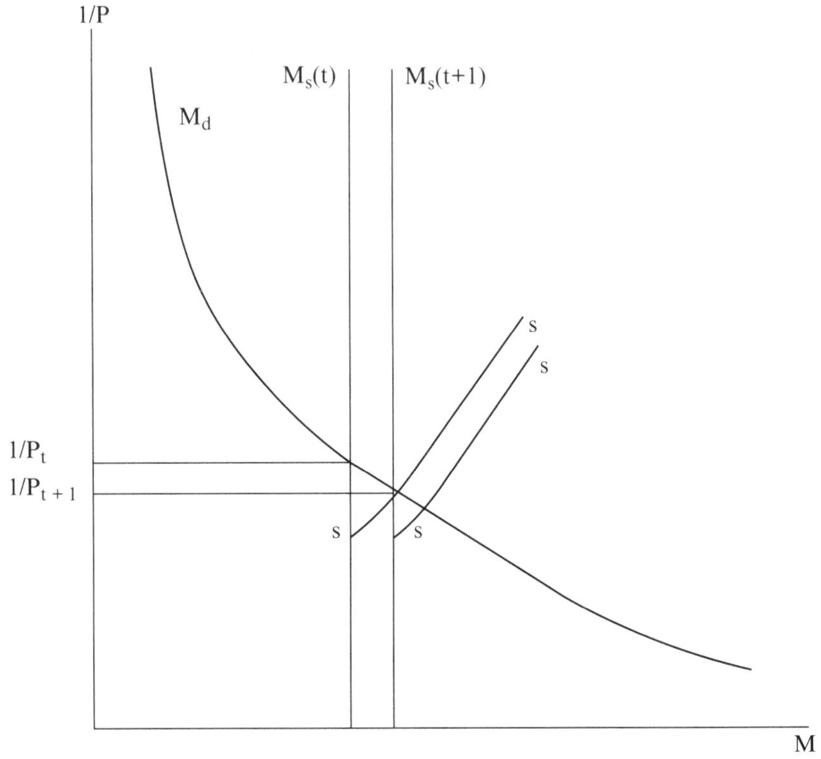

Figure 52.1 Marshall's demand and supply curve for money apparatus

t, the general price level P(t) was then determined. This analysis obviously has the price level varying in proportion to the supply of money, and is now routinely referred to as the quantity theory's 'Cambridge' or 'stock-supply-and-demand' version, but Marshall did not attach the quantity theory label to his own work.

Starting with the initial equilibrium depicted in Figure 52.1, Marshall noted that if the marginal cost curve of production of new gold, s-s, lay below Pt at the beginning of time t, then new production would increase the money stock to Ms(t+1) by its end, and raise the price level to P(t+1); and so on, period by period, until new production became unprofitable. Marshall nevertheless believed that the most important forces affecting the value of money at his time worked on the demand side – for example, economic growth or innovations in banking – and argued that the cost of production had therefore only a remote influence on the value of money. Such ideas tended to undermine claims that the gold standard provided a uniquely 'natural' basis for the determination of the price level and hence its political legitimacy too.

The monetary upheavals created by World War 1 and its aftermath would destroy the gold standard and accelerate monetary theory's shift, set in motion by Knut Wicksell (for example, 1898), towards studying the influence of the interest rate on saving and investment and the monetary system's capacity to disrupt the smooth workings of the economy. In the eventually dominant Keynesian variation on this theme, a substantial extension of Marshall's theory of the demand for money played a key part.

Specifically, Keynes (1936, Ch. 15) argued that the Cambridge version of the quantity theory was adequate to explain money held for 'transactions' and 'precautionary' motives, but had to be supplemented by a theory of the 'speculative' demand for money to arrive at a 'liquidity preference' function which he wrote (p. 199) as M = L1(Y) + L2 (r), with M nominal money, Y nominal income, and r the rate of interest. Mabel Timlin (1942, Chs 5 and 6) seems to have given the first diagrammatic exposition of this equation and its implications, but it was Franco Modigliani's (1944) that become better known.[1]

Keynes simplified the choice underlying L2, 'the demand for money to hold' as Modigliani called it, to one between perpetual bonds and money, and treated the former's coupon yield, r, as a proxy for the opportunity cost of holding the latter, because, over a finite time horizon, expected capital gains or losses on bonds arising from changes in r also contributed to their prospective yield. At some 'high' value of r, when only a rise in the price of bonds could reasonably be expected, the cost of holding money as a speculative asset would be so large that L2 would go to zero. On the other hand, at some 'low' but still positive level, a rise in r that would generate capital losses large enough to offset any interest receipts would be so likely that money would either be preferred to bonds or at least become their perfect substitute.

In Figure 52.2, the speculative demand curve for money thus originates on the vertical axis at the 'high' rate of interest r', and becomes horizontal at the 'low' rate r'' and can be used to demonstrate Keynes's view that interest rate variations may not always be available to bring a depressed economy back to full employment. For example, for a given quantity of nominal money, a decline in prices and therefore nominal income will lead to a release of money balances from L1, shown as a rightward shift of a vertical supply curve of speculative balances, S, in Figure 52.2. If nominal income falls when r is at a 'high' level, from Y4 to Y3 say, the interest rate too will fall, with expansionary consequences for aggregate demand; but if r is already low, as when income falls from Y2 to Y1, the money

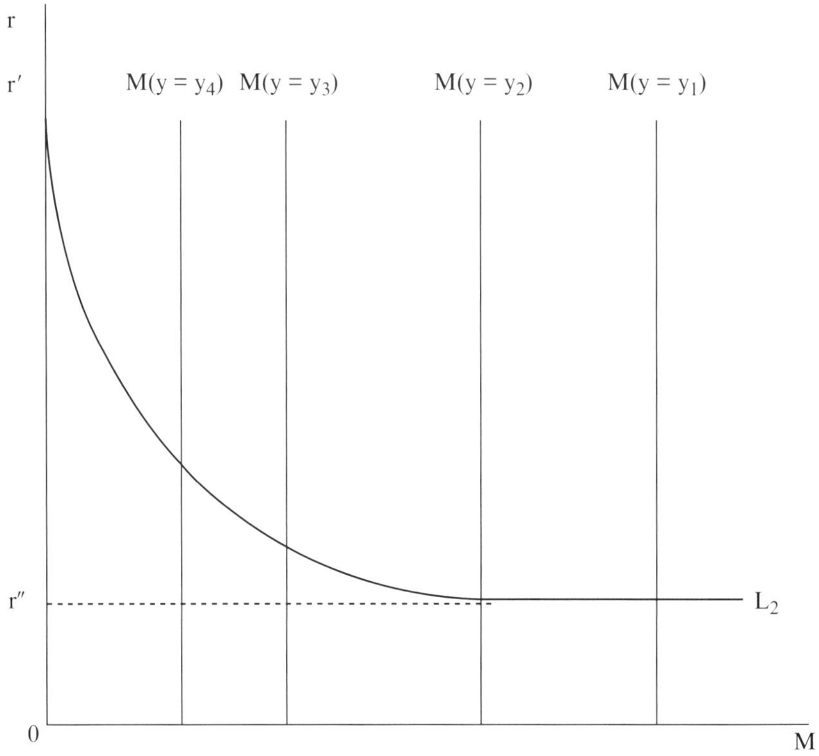

Figure 52.2 Modigliani's demand curve for 'money to hold'

that this releases will disappear into the 'liquidity trap' represented by the L2 demand curve's horizontal segment, the interest rate will remain unchanged, and so will aggregate demand.

The nowadays uncontroversial proposition that the demand for nominal money is strictly proportional to the price level provided the raison d'etre for the hyperbolic form of Marshall's demand curve, but was glossed over in Keynes's account of the demand for money, particularly with regard to his L2 function, and also by Timlin and Modigliani among others. The frequent confusion and occasional errors to which this led were not definitively straightened out until the (1956) appearance of Don Patinkin's *Money Interest and Prices*, where, hardly coincidentally, both of the diagrams discussed here, and several variations on them, were deployed in a comprehensive effort to integrate Keynesian macroeconomics with the general theory of relative prices whose early development had prompted Marshall's work on the demand for money.

NOTE

1. I am grateful to Robert Dimand for referring me to Timlin's unjustly neglected book, which Modigliani cited somewhat grudgingly.

REFERENCES

Keynes, J.M. (1936), *The General Theory of Employment Interest and Money*, London: Macmillan.

Laidler, D. (1993), *The Demand for Money: Theories, Evidence and Problems* (4th ed.), New York: Harper Collins.

Modigliani, F. (1944), 'Liquidity Preference and the Theory of Interest and Money', *Econometrica*, 12 (January), 45–88.

Patinkin, D. (1956), *Money Interest and Prices*, New York: Harper Bros.

Timlin, M. (1942), *Keynesian Economics*, Toronto: University of Toronto Press.

Whitaker, J. (ed.) (1975), *The Early Economic Writings of Alfred Marshall* (2 vols), London: Macmillan.

Wicksell, K. (1898/1936) *Interest and Prices* tr. R.F. Kahn for the Royal Economic Society, London: Macmillan.

53. Non-neutrality of money

He-Ling Shi

INTRODUCTION

In economics, Non-neutrality of money is the idea that a change in the stock of money affects not only nominal variables in the economy such as prices, but also has effects on real variables like employment, consumption and real GDP. It is an important departure from the classical dichotomy – which holds that money supply will only affect nominal variables. Non-neutrality of money implies that the monetary authority (for example, central bank) can affect the real economy (for example, the number of jobs, the size of the GDP, the amount of investment) by changing money supply. Non-neutrality also explains, contrary to the traditional neutrality thesis, why a financial crisis could happen.

The idea of Non-neutrality of money can be traced back to Keynes (1936), and its modern incarnation has been collectively called New Keynesian Economics (Mankiw and Romer, 1991), which strives to provide microeconomic foundations for Keynesian economics. A variety of market imperfection has been introduced to produce Keynesian macroeconomic effects. Central to this literature is the microfoundation of price stickiness and the assumption of monopolistic competition.

A commonly used explanation of why prices adjust slowly, along with the price stickiness approach, is 'menu costs' (Mankiw, 1985). This idea is that the reason firms do not change their prices immediately is the costs that they must incur in order to do so – for example, the cost of making a new catalog, price list and so on. Price stickiness is also present in the labor market in the form of nominal and real wage rigidity. In the prevalence of implicit and explicit labor contracts (Taylor, 1980) and labor union and wage bargaining (McDonald and Solow, 1981), firms are not able to change wages immediately in response to the change in price level. The efficiency wage model (Akerlof 1984, Yellen 1984) adds another rationale for wage rigidity.

Besides sticky prices, another market imperfection built into most New Keynesian models is the assumption of monopoly competition (Ng, 1977,

1980; Blanchard and Kiyotaki, 1987). Since Ng's 1980 *Economic Journal* paper is regarded by Marris (1991, p.215) as one 'which effectively started the modern movement' in providing an imperfect competition foundation for macroeconomics, and his 'representative firm' approach (a method supported by a fully general equilibrium analysis; see Ng 1986, App.3I) can be easily represented by diagrams familiar to university undergraduates, this entry focuses on Ng's works (including Ng 1998).

1. NON-NEUTRALITY OF MONEY IN MONOPOLY WITH NO FREE ENTRY

For a representative firm with non-perfect competition (compelled by either product differentiation or increasing returns), the firm faces a downward-sloping demand curve, as illustrated in Figure 53.1. The initial equilibrium is at A, where the MC curve cuts the MR curve. An increase

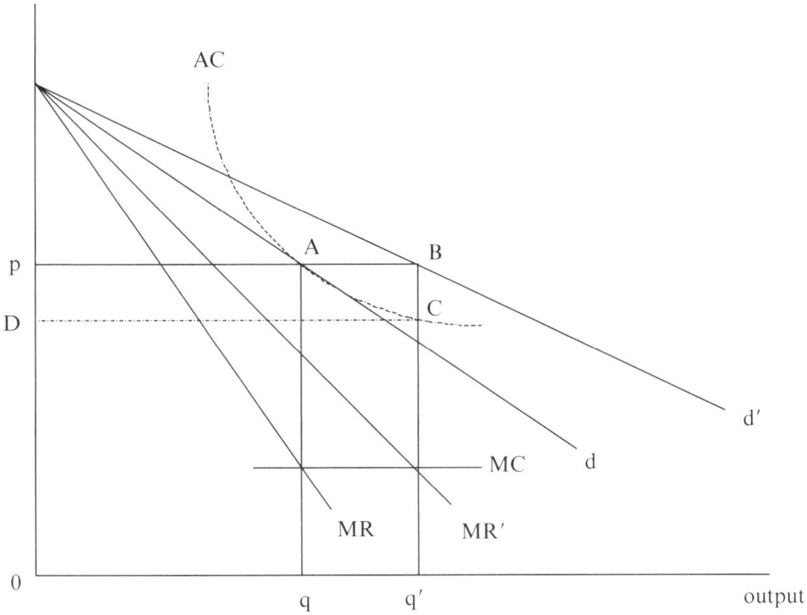

Source: See Ng (1986)

Figure 53.1 Nominal aggregate demand expansion with a constant marginal cost results in an increase in output and no change in price in the short run

in nominal aggregate demand may shift the demand curve to d' and hence the MR curve to MR′. (This is a proportional shift with no change in the price elasticity of demand at any given price, for example, elasticity at B is the same as that at A.) If the MC curve is horizontal over the relevant range and does not shift, as illustrated in Figure 53.1, the new equilibrium is at B, with an increase in output and no change in price. (The absence of a price change is important since a change in the price by the representative firm means a change in the general price level which will shift the demand curve, making B no longer the final equilibrium point.) Alternatively (not illustrated), if the upward shift in the MC curve as aggregate output expands is offset by the downward-sloping MC curve and/or the increase in the (absolute) demand elasticity (which lift MR at a given price), we may still have an increase in real output with no change in price. The representative firm approach implies that the outcome will happen in the whole economy.

It may be thought that it is unlikely for the slope of the MC curve, the shift in the MC curve, and the change in MR (through a change in demand elasticity) to be at such a precise combination that the profit maximizing price remains exactly unchanged. However, for our non-neutrality of money result to hold, we only need the resulting profit-maximizing price not to increase. If it remains unchanged, we have the case of a continuum of equilibrium as illustrated in Figure 53.1 for a specific case. If the profit-maximizing price decreases (due either to the MC curve being downward sloping or the demand curve become more elastic), the demand curve d′ and the MC curve (which are drawn given the price level being equal to p) will both shift. The MC curve will shift vertically downward and the demand curve will both shift vertically downward (with the lower price level) and proportionately rightward (with a higher real aggregate demand, as the price level falls relative to the nominal aggregate demand). The combined shifts are such as to lead to further output expansions and price falls. Thus, if the responses of costs and demand elasticities are to lead to a fall in the price level, we have a cumulative expansion as aggregate demand increases, a case even more radical than a continuum of equilibria. We may refer to both cases as non-traditional, which demonstrates the Non-neutrality of money.

It is true that, for the case where a change in nominal aggregate demand may increase real output without affecting the price level (with Figure 53.1 illustrating a specific sub-case of this case), we really have multiple or even a continuum of equilibria over the relevant range. However, this continuum of equilibria may be precisely the result of non-perfect competition in the following sense. With perfect competition, we must have a unique equilibrium under certain traditional assumptions such as no money illusion, no time lags and the absence of indeterminacy at the firm level. (Graphically, the marginal cost curve and the demand curve both move up or down by the same extent, leaving the intersection point of profit maximization unchanged). This is the microfoundation of the traditional result of neutrality of money, which is based on perfect competition.) Under the same traditional set of assumptions, the introduction of non-perfect competition alone (in the sense of not introducing menu costs or other transaction costs or distortions) may make a continuum of equilibria prevail. It is true that this possibility depends on certain appropriate conditions regarding how costs respond to output (both the output at the firm level, referring to whether MC is upward or downward sloping; and the aggregate output at the economy level, referring to how MC shifts, for example, through changes in wage rates, as aggregate output and employment change). However, the introduction of non-perfect competition also makes such conditions more likely to be fulfilled as horizontal or even downward-sloping MC curves and an increase in absolute demand elasticity become possible.

2. NON-NEUTRALITY OF MONEY IN THE LONG RUN WITH FREE ENTRY

The above demonstration of the possible continuum of equilibria and non-neutrality of money in a non-perfectly competitive economy is within a model with a given number of firms. It may thus be thought that if the long-run variation in the number of firms is taken into account, the possibility will no longer exist. However, allowing for free entry and exit of firms, it has been demonstrated (Ng 1986, Ch. 4) that the possibility of a continuum of equilibria and non-neutrality of money still exists without considering any friction. Certain (more complicated than above) appropriate conditions regarding costs and demand elasticity are sufficient. In fact, since the entry of new firms as aggregate demand increases makes the absolute demand elasticity higher by increasing the degree of competition, the appropriate conditions for a continuum of equilibria are easier to satisfy in this respect. This is illustrated in Figure 53.2. The representative firm is initially at equilibrium at A, where MR=MC and p=AC. An increase in aggregate demand shifts the demand curve to the right and makes it more elastic (competition effect), making it possible for the firm to reach a higher equilibrium point at B with no change in price, even if the cost curves shift upward as the aggregate output of the economy expands.

One policy implication of the non-neutrality of Money is that aggregate

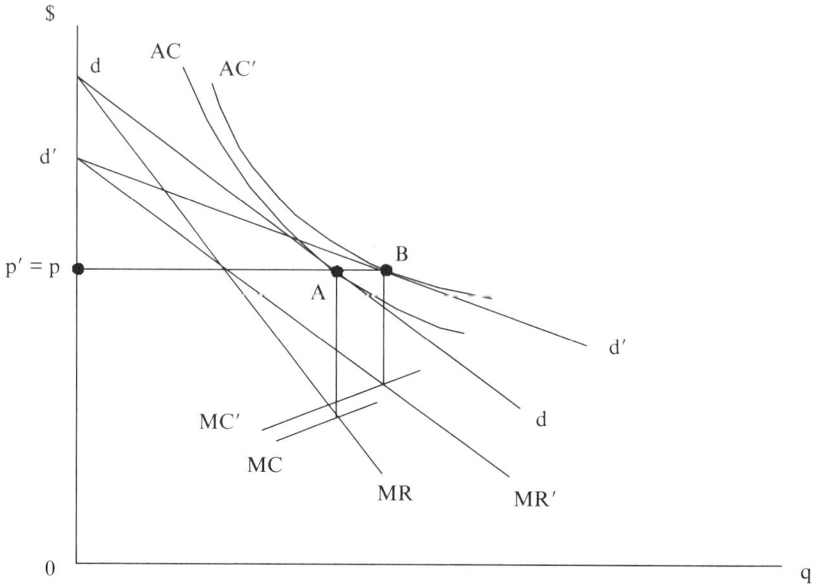

Source: See Ng (1986)

Figure 53.2 Nominal aggregate demand expansion with upward shifting marginal cost results in an increase in output and no change in price in the long run

demand management – including the change of money stock – could affect real economic variables, such as employment, consumption and real GDP. In the presence of 'menu costs' and imperfect competition – which is a compelling assumption in the modern real world – inadequate contractionary monetary policy could drag the economy into recession; while in the midst of financial crisis, expansionary monetary policy – including the increase in money supply and lowering of the in interest rate – could help the economy to recover.

REFERENCES

Akerlof, George (1984), 'Gift Exchange and Efficiency Wages: Four Views', *American Economic Review*, 74 (May), 78–83.

Blanchard, Olivier and Kiyotaki, Nobuhiro (1987), 'Monopolistic Competition and the Effects of Aggregate Demand', *American Economic Review*, 77 (4), 647–666.

Keynes, John Maynard (1936), *The General Theory of Employment, Interest and Money*, London: Macmillan.
Mankiw, N. Gregory (1985), 'Small Menu Costs and Large Business Cycles: A Macroeconomic Model of Monopoly', *Quarterly Journal of Economics*, 100, 529–539.
Mankiw, N. Gregory and Romer, David (eds) (1991), *New Keynesian Economics*, Vols 1 and 2, Cambridge, MA: MIT Press.
Marris, Robin (1991), *Reconstructing Keynesian Economics with Imperfect Competition*, Cheltenham: Edward Elgar in association with the United Nations University World Institute for Development Economics Research, Helsinki, Finland.
McDonald, Ian and Solow, Robert (1981), 'Wage Bargaining and Employment', *American Economic Review*, December, 71 (5), 896–908.
Ng, Yew-Kwang (1977), 'Aggregate Demand, Business Expectation, and Economic Recovery without Aggravating Inflation', *Australian Economic Papers*, 16, 130–140.
Ng, Yew-Kwang (1980), 'Macroeconomics with Non-Perfect Competition', *Economic Journal*, 90, 598–610.
Ng, Yew-Kwang (1986), *Mesoeconomics*, London: Wheatsheaf.
Ng, Yew-Kwang (1998), 'Non-Neutrality of Money under Non-Perfect Competition: Why do Economists Fail to See the Possibility?', in Arrow, K. J., Ng, Y.-K. and Yang, X. (eds), *Increasing Returns and Economic Analysis*, London: Macmillan, pp. 232–252.
Taylor, John B. (1980), 'Aggregate Dynamics and Staggered Contracts', *Journal of Political Economy*, 88 (1), 1–24.
Yellen, Janet (1984), 'Efficiency Wage Models of Unemployment', *American Economic Review*, May, 74 (May), 200–2008.

54. The Laffer curve

Roger Middleton

The Laffer curve represents graphically the principle that tax revenue (T) does not peak at the highest tax rate available to the fiscal authority but at t*, some way short of the maximum, this irrespective of whether it be an individual tax on a good, service or factor income, or a hypothetical aggregate tax system. In the case of an income tax, and most but not all Laffer curve applications have been such cases, revenue T is thus zero when t is zero and 100 per cent (at which point – rationally – all production in the money economy would cease), with t* the point of maximum revenue and the shaded area the 'prohibitive range' (Figure 54.1, which follows Laffer's unorthodox presentation of the dependent variable on the horizontal axis). This embodies the long-established 'proposition that increases in tax rates discourage market-sector production and may therefore, beyond a certain level, be counterproductive in raising tax revenue' (Laffer 1981, p. 1). In Laffer's (2004) retrospective formulation,[1] taxation has two effects on revenue: one purely arithmetic, whereby a change in tax rates alters the revenue per unit of tax base, and the other economic, allowing for the potential impact that tax rates have on incentives and thus the level of economic activity.

1. HISTORY AND SIGNIFICANCE

The proximate origins of this fiscal precept as the Laffer curve are somewhat shrouded in mystery, but are dated to 1974 and involve a Californian professor of business economics (Arthur Laffer), two presidential aides, a Washington restaurant and a cocktail napkin upon which was drawn a diagram which has since become immortalised as the Laffer curve. In fact, there is no novelty in the theoretical proposition that, given certain conditions (the so-called 'prohibitive range'), a reduction in tax rates could yield an increase in total revenue, with such arguments traceable to a range of pre-classical economists through to J.M. Keynes. Latterly, Laffer (2004) admitted such a provenance and claimed only to be a populariser.

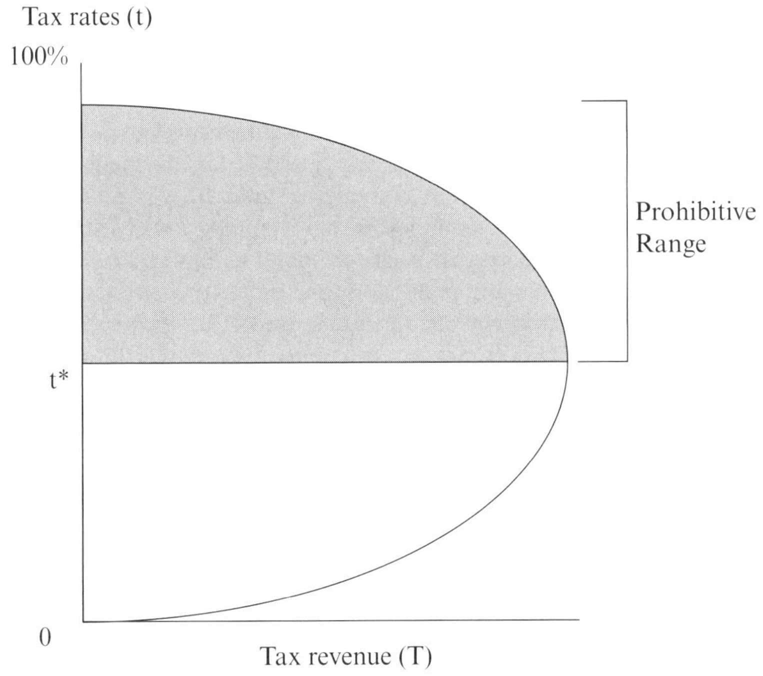

Source: Adapted from Laffer (2004)

Figure 54.1 The Laffer curve

The Laffer curve rose to prominence because of the particular economic and political conditions of mid-1970s America. Economically, critics of Keynesian economics used stagflation to undermine the case for big government, whilst politically a post-Watergate Republican Party fed off the crisis, transforming an incipient tax revolt into a full-scale campaign for tax cuts. This came to fruition with the Reagan presidency and the implementation of the Kemp-Roth inspired 1981 Economic Recovery Tax Act (which reduced the top marginal income tax rate from 70 to 50 per cent), with the Laffer curve serving as a major device in the rhetorical armoury deployed by the supply-siders to square the circle that tax cuts would lessen, not widen, the budget deficit.

With the particular circumstances of its genesis, the Laffer curve is of interest at many levels, only some of which are about scientific economics. First, there are questions about its diffusion, for it came to prominence because of the actions of a financial journalist, Jude Wanniski of the *Wall Street Journal*, with academic economists playing a later and less committed role. Indeed, many of those identified as leading supply-siders, such as Martin Feldstein (Reagan's first chairman of the Council of Economic Advisers), were unpersuaded by the evidence about the effects of the 1981 Act on revenue raising and thus deficit reduction (Feldstein 1995 was more positive about the 1986 Tax Reform Act).

Secondly, fundamental questions are raised about the diagram itself, with frequent observations that embodying as it does a mathematical truism about minimum revenue levels, it instantly provides the appealing prospect that there must be scope to increase T if t can be reduced, providing of course that the political opportunity (or better still empirical evidence) exists that current tax rates are in the prohibitive range. On this, Hal Varian (1989) captures the political potential for action and hyperbole: 'It has been said that the popularity of the Laffer curve is due to the fact that you can explain it to a Congressman in six minutes and he can talk about it for six months'. For Varian, the Laffer curve was of particular interest because it embodied elements of both good and bad economics: bad theory because of the inference that 'because the Laffer effect *can* occur it *does* occur' and good because the economist's basic demand-supply toolkit can be applied 'to determine what magnitudes the elasticity parameters have to be for the Laffer effect to occur'.

Thirdly, the Laffer curve provides a case study of policy transfer with relevance to comparative political economy and the emergence of the so-called Washington consensus of mainstream economics. An Anglo-American comparison is particularly instructive, for many of the structural conditions for tax reform and the reaction against big government were similar in the two countries: a mix of economic underperformance perceived as more structural than cyclical, an apparent crisis of the policy paradigm and an opposition party seeking a distinctive new programme which would secure at least the median voter. However, the Laffer curve hardly features in the British policy debate (this when the highest income tax rate was 98 per cent before reform commenced), for after initial promotion by a prominent supply-sider/monetarist economist of the early Thatcher years, it quickly languished and never acquired the political salience that it did in the US. The majority of the British economics establishment were quickly scathing in their criticism of Laffer, while even Geoffrey Howe, Margaret Thatcher's first Chancellor, explained: 'My Treasury team and I had never succumbed – never seriously anyway – to the mistaken interpretations of Lafferism, which have led some US policymakers so far astray' (quoted in Middleton 1997, p. 2). Moreover, when the time did arrive for the most spectacular reductions in British marginal and average income tax rates (the 1988 budget, which set the highest rate at 40 per cent), the then Chancellor did not see fit to mention Laffer in his rendition of Britain's supply-side driven economic renaissance under the Conservatives. Laffer features not in his memoirs, nor indeed in those of Thatcher. We conclude that Laffer serves a distinctively and peculiarly American need, something that becomes even clearer as we now turn to the more technical economics of the Laffer curve.

2. EMPIRICS OF THE LAFFER CURVE

Peacock (1989) evaluates the first decade of the Laffer curve, albeit from an avowedly 'libertarian disposition' (p. 39), with Fullerton (2008) the most recent survey of the empirical evidence. The latter provides a suitable starting point because Fullerton (1982) was the first substantive survey of the analytics and empirics of the Laffer curve, including calculating the labour supply elasticity necessary for a Laffer effect. His general equilibrium model yielded t^* at 79 per cent, suggestive that US tax rates were not then in the prohibitive range.

However, as Fullerton (2008) makes clear, this early model and its elaboration by others was problematic. First, there are certain conceptual difficulties relating to labour supply and the aggregation of tax systems, with heterogeneity endemic to both. Second, the progressive nature of tax systems (in the US and elsewhere, heavily dependent on income taxes) meant inevitably that it was difficult to distinguish a genuine Laffer effect (which requires high marginal tax rates *and* high labour supply elasticities) from a redistribution of tax revenue paid by different groups of taxpayers with different elasticities, which does not constitute a true Laffer effect. Most income tax structures in most countries are progressive and have multiple rates, whereas the Laffer curve has only a single (flat) rate. Thus tax cuts may apply only to some bands of taxpayers or may apply differentially across the tax bands. Moreover, even within an income band, some taxpayers will respond differently from others. Such aggregation problems make it difficult to determine empirically the effects of a 'tax cut'. Thirdly, because the Laffer curve itself is not well defined, it matters how the revenue is spent, with recent work on the dynamic Laffer curve utilizing endogenous growth models to find that it is not t^* that is the crucial variable but the tax rate adjusted for income transfers (more evident in OECD-Europe than the US). In short, if there is a Laffer curve, it is a 'shifty' curve (Becsi 2000). Fourthly, there are considerable doubts about whether the Laffer effect might be nothing more than, or at least explained in large part by, activity shifts between the measured and unmeasured (black) economy.

Initial work on labour and capital supply and their responsiveness to taxation soon revealed that the typical numeraire (hours worked for labour supply) failed to capture the whole range of taxpayer responses to shifting incentives. From this has emerged much empirical work to estimate e (the implied elasticity), defined by Fullerton (2008, p. 840) as the elasticity of taxable income with respect to a change in the marginal net-of-tax share (1−t), such that 'If the economy really had only a single tax rate t, then the revenue-maximizing tax rate $t^* = 1/(1+e)$'. Fullerton reports that these studies suggest an implied elasticity of about 1.5, giving a t* of around 40 per cent and not the original estimates of 70–80 per cent. Nonetheless, these studies are also problematic. First, and most importantly, in the English-speaking OECD, but less so in continental Europe, income inequality has grown significantly since the 1970s; thus top incomes were rising irrespective of tax changes. Secondly, there are a number of technical problems to do with definitions of taxable income and the permanence of responses to tax changes. Panel data and natural experiment testing by, amongst others, Goolsbee (1999), who modelled six tax changes between 1922 and 1975, suggest that the results for the 1980s are atypical. Thus:

> The notion that governments could raise more money by cutting rates is, indeed, a glorious idea. It would permit a Pareto improvement of the most enjoyable kind. Unfortunately, for all of us, the data from the historical record suggest that it is unlikely to be true at anything like today's marginal rates. It seems that, for now at least, we will just have to keep paying for our tax cuts the old-fashioned way' (p. 44).

Fullerton (2008, p. 841) concurs:

> In summary, if you choose to oversimplify the world by using a single elasticity and a single tax rate, and if you ignore other problems . . . with the whole concept of the Laffer curve, then the recent mid-point estimate of [the overall elasticity of taxation] $e = 0.4$ implies that tax revenue is maximized at $t^*=1/(1+e) = 71$ per cent.

In short, this is way above prevailing marginal let alone average rates in the greater part of the OECD.

3. CONCLUSIONS

As 'a testable hypothesis the Laffer curve has not fared well' (Goolsbee 1999, p. 2); indeed, a recent US Treasury Department (2006) report on the 1981 tax reforms, the *sine qua non* of the supply-siders' doctrine, calculates a revenue loss of 3 per cent of GDP. At the time and since, scientific economic analysis thus raises grave doubts about the Laffer curve. Subsequently, low taxation has become part of the Washington consensus, and in terms of ersatz economics, the Laffer curve reigns supreme. This itself is of interest, as is Varian's (1989) complaint about the 'sordid history of the use of the Laffer curve in public policy debates in the US'; however, primarily research interest in the Laffer curve lies more in the realm of the history of economic doctrines and political economy than scientific economics, although this is not to deny that it has acted as a spur to the revival of classical public finance theory and offshoots such as public choice theory, although interestingly in the *locus classicus* of that latter literature, there is no mention of Laffer nor his curve (Mueller 2003).

The Laffer curve clearly feeds off the enduring appeal of trade-offs and tipping points for policy entrepreneurs. If the Phillips curve (see Chapter 50) be accepted as the favoured diagram of the Keynesian era, then the Laffer curve has pride of place as the supply-siders' favoured schematic. Moreover, as with another famous diagram, the Kuznets curve on inequality and income per capita (see Chapter 58), the Laffer curve has proved capable of more general application. Thus, just as the former has evolved inter alia into the environmental Kuznets curve, the Laffer curve has been utilised in a number of areas: for example, early on by public choice theorists to analyse the behaviour of political agents and the stability conditions for political equilibrium; and more recently in a host of policy areas relating to crime, foreign aid and social policy.

Currently, there is evidence that the Laffer curve and the flat tax campaign have formed something of an alliance in the US and the UK. Given global turbulence since 2007 and the risks of a great depression, there is now every prospect that the Laffer curve will be rejuvenated by the potential, similar but not identical to the opportunities offered during the 1970s, to utilise the current crisis of policy and performance to cut taxes on a promise that it would be revenue raising.

NOTE

1. The broad elements first appeared in Wanniski (1978), with Laffer's (1981) first major formulation as the lead article in the inaugural issue of the *Cato Journal*, a neoconservative policy journal. The Canto *et al.* (1983) model is the most frequently cited initial academic formulation of the Laffer curve model.

REFERENCES

Becsi, Zsolt (2000), 'The shifty Laffer curve', *Federal Reserve Bank of Atlanta Economic Review*, Third Quarter, 53–64.

Canto, Victor A., Joines, Douglas H. and Laffer, Arthur B. (1983), 'Tax rates,

factor employment, market production and welfare', in Victor A. Canto, D.H. Joines and A.B. Laffer (eds) *Foundations of Supply-Side Economics: Theory and Evidence*, New York: Academic Press, 1–24.
Feldstein, Martin (1995), 'The effects of marginal tax rates on taxable income: a panel study of the 1986 Tax Reform Act', *Journal of Political Economy*, 103, 551–72.
Fullerton, Don (1982), 'On the possibility of an inverse relationship between tax rates and government revenues', *Journal of Public Economics*, 19, 3–22.
Fullerton, Don (2008), 'Laffer curve', in Stephen N. Durlauf and Lawrence E. Blume (eds) *The New Palgrave Dictionary of Economics*, 2nd edn, London: Palgrave, IV, 839–41.
Goolsbee, Austan (1999) 'Evidence on the high-income Laffer curve from six decades of tax reform', *Brookings Papers in Economic Activity*, no. 2, 1–64.
Laffer, Arthur B. (1981) 'Government exactions and revenue deficiencies', *Cato Journal*, 1, 1–21.
Laffer, Arthur B. (2004), 'The Laffer curve: past, present and future', *Backgrounder*, 1765 1 June http://www.heritage.org/research/taxes/upload/64214_1.pdf, accessed 9 January 2010.
Middleton, Roger (1997), 'Whatever happened to the Laffer curve', http://eis.bris.ac.uk/~hirm/paperdownloads.htm, accessed 9 January 2010.
Mueller, Dennis C. (2003), *Public Choice III*, Cambridge: Cambridge University Press.
Peacock, Alan T. (1989), 'The rise and fall of the Laffer curve', in Dieter Bös and Bernhard Felderer (eds) *The Political Economy of Progressive Taxation*, Berlin: Springer-Verlag, 25–40.
US Department of the Treasury (2006), *Revenue Effects of Major Tax Bills*, http://www.ustreas.gov/offices/tax-policy/library/ota81.pdf, accessed 9 January 2010.
Varian, Hal (1989), 'What use is economic theory', http://people.ischool.berkeley.edu/~hal/Papers/theory.pdf, accessed 9 January 2010.
Wanniski, Jude (1978), 'Taxes, revenues and the "Laffer curve"', *Public Interest*, 50, 3–16.

Growth, income distribution and other topics

55. Intertemporal utility maximization – the Fisher diagram

Thomas M. Humphrey

Francis Y. Edgeworth invented indifference curves in his 1881 *Mathematical Psychics*. Similarly, Vilfredo Pareto pioneered the use of transformation, or production possibility curves in his 1906 *Manual of Political Economy*. But Irving Fisher in his 1907 *The Rate of Interest* was the first to combine indifference curves and a production possibility curve together with a budget line in a single diagram and use it to illustrate an individual's optimum intertemporal consumption choice, or optimum investment decision, as well as his utility gains from borrowing and lending in the credit market. Fisher's demonstration, largely reproduced in his 1930 *The Theory of Interest*, is definitive: modern analysts have hardly improved upon it.

Fisher's two-period diagram first appears on page 409 of *The Rate of Interest* (see Figure 55.1). Two commodities, labeled present and future consumption, are measured on the horizontal and vertical axes respectively. The production possibility curve *ZPW* shows alternative combinations of the two goods that the individual can produce given his resources and investment technology. The curve depicts his opportunity, moving, say, from point *W* to point *P*, to transform units of present consumption into a larger number of units of future consumption by saving (that is, not consuming) today, and investing the proceeds into productive capital projects yielding positive net returns. The curve forms the efficient outer boundary or frontier of feasible investment possibilities. Inefficient ones are represented by the swarm of dots beneath the curve.

The curve's slope-minus-unity at any point measures investment's marginal rate of return over cost, or difference between investment's absolute yield in the form of extra future consumption and its cost in terms of sacrificed present consumption, this difference expressed as a fraction of the amount invested. The curve's slope-minus-one also measures the ratio of the marginal productivities of capital in one- and two-year investment projects respectively.

The curve's concave shape, and resulting flattening of its slope as

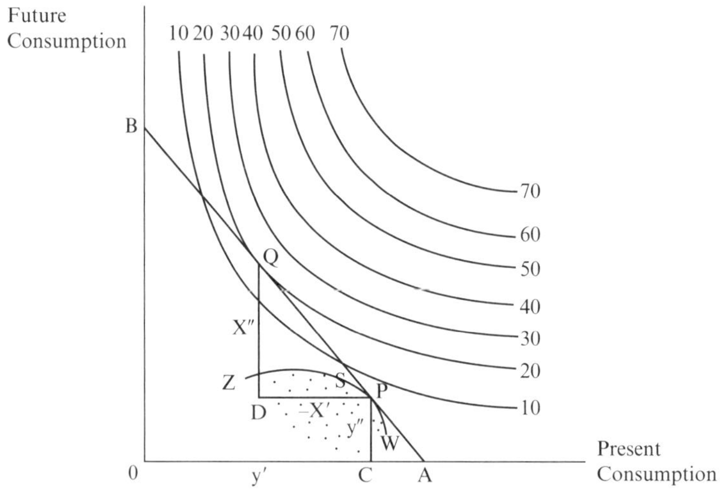

Source: Fisher (1907)

Figure 55.1 Fisher's 1907 diagram of intertemporal utility maximization

one moves up and to the left along it, represents diminishing marginal returns to investment as the sacrifice of successive units of consumption today yields progressively smaller increments of consumption tomorrow. (Actually, Fisher has the curve becoming flat-to-slightly-convex in its upper range, indicating zero or negative returns. Modern versions show the curve everywhere concave throughout its entire length, which extends to both axes.) The message is that one should invest in real capital projects as long as the curve has a steeper slope than a line representing the market interest rate on loans, because such projects yield higher returns than could be earned by lending in the loan market. Conversely, one should avoid investing along segments of the curve flatter than the interest rate line, because higher returns are available through lending.

The set of convex iso-desirability curves (as Fisher called them) labeled *10, 20, 30* and so on. constitute the individual's indifference map. Each curve shows alternative combinations of present and future consumption yielding equal amounts of utility, or satisfaction. Higher curves represent higher, and lower curves lower levels of utility. The convexity of the curves, and resulting steepening of their slopes as one moves up them, represents diminishing marginal rate of substitution of present for future consumption (or diminishing marginal utility of the latter in terms of the former) such that successive unit decreases in today's consumption require progressively larger increases in tomorrow's to keep the level of utility unchanged.

Finally, the budget line AB is the highest of a series of parallel straight lines, each of which has a slope equal to the gross rate of interest $(1 + r)$ prevailing in the loan market, and each of which corresponds to a particular discounted present value of future and current consumption, identical for any point or consumption bundle on a given line. Higher budget lines represent higher – and lower lines lower – present values. Line AB, the highest attainable on the production frontier and the one indicating maximum present value, becomes absolutely crucial when the individual has access to the loan market as well as to his production frontier.

Given the opportunity to lend and borrow at the interest rate depicted by the slope of AB, the individual does two things. First, he produces or invests at the point P of maximum present value on the production frontier where the latter is tangent to line AB. Then he moves along that line, trading PD $(= x')$ units of consumption now for DQ $(= x'')$ units of consumption tomorrow – the latter receivable as repaid principal plus accumulated interest on the loan – to reach his point of maximum constrained satisfaction at tangency point Q on his highest achievable indifference curve. At these double tangency points, the slopes of the three curves – production frontier, indifference curve and budget line – are the same, implying equality of marginal rate of return of investment, marginal rate of substitution in consumption, and real interest rate. In short, given the opportunity to trade at the prevailing interest rate, the individual produces the time stream of consumption having the highest present value and then trades it for a preferred stream lying beyond the production frontier. The utility or satisfaction yielded by the preferred stream compared to lower utility levels that would result were the individual constrained to consume on his production frontier constitute the gains from intertemporal trade.

Now Fisher realized the special condition under which line AB holds, and went to great lengths to emphasize it. He explained that the loan market, and associated interest rate line AB, effectively separates the individual's investment decision from his consumption preferences represented by his indifference map. With separation, the agent as producer first maximizes the present value of investment without regard to his consumption tastes and preferences. No indifference curves intervene to influence his investment decision. That decision, however, produces a time stream of consumption that he then alters by borrowing and lending in the loan market until he reaches the stream that maximizes his satisfaction. This outcome, Fisher noted, fails to hold in the absence of loan markets when the individual, deprived of the opportunity to consume beyond his production frontier, is constrained to consume upon it as well as produce upon it. In this case, the isolated individual chooses the common tangency point S of production frontier and highest attainable indifference curve (not drawn), with the slope of the tangent curves determining the interest rate. Here separation is impossible, and consumption preferences together with production opportunities jointly determine the investment decision.

Fisher's diagram shows the individual lender responding to a given rate of interest. But market equilibrium requires the interest rate to be such as to balance aggregate lending with aggregate borrowing. Fisher states that borrowers will come to the loan market equipped with diagrams similar to those of lenders. The only difference is that borrowers' *PDQ* trade triangles will lie southeast of their production points, rather than northwest as is the case of lenders. The interest rate must adjust, rolling budget lines around production frontiers, until the lengths of the legs of the borrowers' *PDQ* triangles are the same in sum but opposite in sign to those of the lenders. At this point of zero net balance, the loan market clears: aggregate desired borrowing matches aggregate desired lending. Moreover, since borrowing equals the excess of desired investment over saving, and lending the excess of desired saving over investment, it follows that the real interest rate equilibrates aggregate desired saving and investment too, just as classical investment theory requires.

Since Fisher's original presentation, analysts have put his diagram to two main uses. First, finance textbooks apply it to the modern business corporation, stressing the Fisher Separation Theorem. That theorem states that perfect capital markets and the resulting competitive interest rate line render the firm's investment decisions independent of the preferences of its owners. Management chooses the volume of investment that maximizes the present value of the firm regardless of the indifference maps of the stockholders, who nevertheless unanimously approve of a decision that maximizes their wealth and thus their consumption opportunities. Moreover, because stockholders in a perfect capital market can structure or configure their own asset portfolios to achieve maximum utility, separation also implies independence of investment and financing decisions. Management is free to fund the value-maximizing level of investment in any way it sees fit. As noted, Fisher already had recognized this theorem (albeit without naming it) for the individual agent.

Second, international trade textbooks extend Fisher's diagram to the small, open, price-taking economy to demonstrate its gains from trade. In this context, the diagram applies to the choices of a nation, not an individual, although the nation is treated as if it were an individual maximizing entity. The diagram is given a one-period interpretation: instead of present and future consumption, quantities of two currently tradable goods are now measured on the axes. The diagram then has the nation producing the goods bundle *P* that maximizes national product valued at world prices. With the slope of line *AB* now measuring not the interest rate, but rather the world relative price of the traded goods, the country exports *PD* of the good in which it has a comparative cost advantage in exchange for imports *DQ* of the good in which it has a comparative disadvantage. In so doing, it ends up consuming at its constrained maximum level of utility *Q*. The difference between this post-trade utility level and that holding at autarky point *S*, where the country would produce and consume in the absence of trade, constitutes the gain from trade. That the diagram just as readily depicts international as well as intertemporal trade testifies to its versatility. Fisher can claim to have invented what has been called 'the sacred diagram of the trade theorist'.

REFERENCES

Edgeworth, Francis Y. (1881), *Mathematical Psychics*. London: Kegan Paul.
Fisher, Irving (1907), *The Rate of Interest*. New York: Macmillan.
Fisher, Irving (1930), *The Theory of Interest*. New York: Macmillan.
Pareto, Vilfredo (1906), *Manual of Political Economy*, 1971 translation of 1927 edition. New York: Macmillan.

56. The diagrams of the Solow-Swan growth model

Barbara J. Spencer and Robert W. Dimand

INTRODUCTION

Robert M. Solow (1956) and Trevor W. Swan (1956, 2002) independently developed the neoclassical growth model. Swan (1956) was published ten months later than Solow (1956), but involved a more complete analysis of technical progress, which Solow treated separately in Solow (1957). The distinguishing feature of the neoclassical growth model is the assumption that inputs are substitutable in production. The earlier growth models of Harrod (1939) and Domar (1946) were interpreted by Solow (1956, p. 65) as assuming fixed-coefficient production technologies that gave their models 'knife-edge' equilibria, with the implausible implication that any deviation at all from equilibrium would cause the model to diverge further and further away from equilibrium. However, Swan (1956, p. 343) regretted that 'some of his [Harrod's] readers seem to have been misled into the belief that, in Harrod's model, equality between the warranted and the natural rates of growth can occur only "by a fluke"' and insisted that his own model only made explicit the implications of a mechanism that Harrod (1948) had 'stated very clearly'.[1] Swan went on to quote Harrod (1948, p. 96) on how a progressive decline in the interest rate (and hence of the marginal product of capital as capital accumulated) would equate the natural and warranted growth rates.

Although the models of Solow (1956) and Swan (1956) are fundamentally the same, there are some significant differences, including differences in the diagrams that illustrate the model. The Solow diagram highlights the substitutability of labour for capital by measuring the capital/labour ratio along the horizontal axis. The levels of output and investment per head are shown on the vertical axis. The Swan diagram relates the output/capital ratio along the horizontal axis to the rates of growth of output, capital and labour along the vertical axis. This focus on rates of growth is particularly useful for illustrating the effects of changes in the rate of technical progress (see Dixon, 2003). Swan (1956) also considers effects on growth arising from a fixed supply of a third factor, land, which creates diminishing returns. We present the Swan diagram in Section 1 because we believe it provides an easier introduction to the model. We then follow in Section 2 with the Solow diagram, explaining the more intricate effects of capital/labour substitutability. Section 3 contains a brief history of the development of the Solow-Swan model.

1. THE SWAN DIAGRAM

Figure 56.1 presents the basic Swan diagram. Output, denoted Y, is produced under constant returns to scale by labour, L, and capital, K. In the simplest version of the model, labour is assumed to grow at a constant (and exogenous) rate, $n \equiv (dL/dt)/L$, which is represent by a horizontal line in Figure 56.1. All labour is fully employed. Assuming that saving is a fixed proportion, s, of income, investment, dK/dt, is equal to saving, sY, and the rate of growth of capital is given by $(dK/dt)/K = sY/K$. Since Y/K varies along the x axis in Figure 56.1, the rate of growth of capital is simply a straight line through the origin with slope s. Assuming no technical progress, the rate of growth of output, denoted $y \equiv (dY/dt)/Y$, is intermediate between the rates of growth of labour and capital, as shown by the lower dotted arrows.[2] Equilibrium is at E, where the rates of growth of capital, labour and output all coincide. To the left of point E, output is

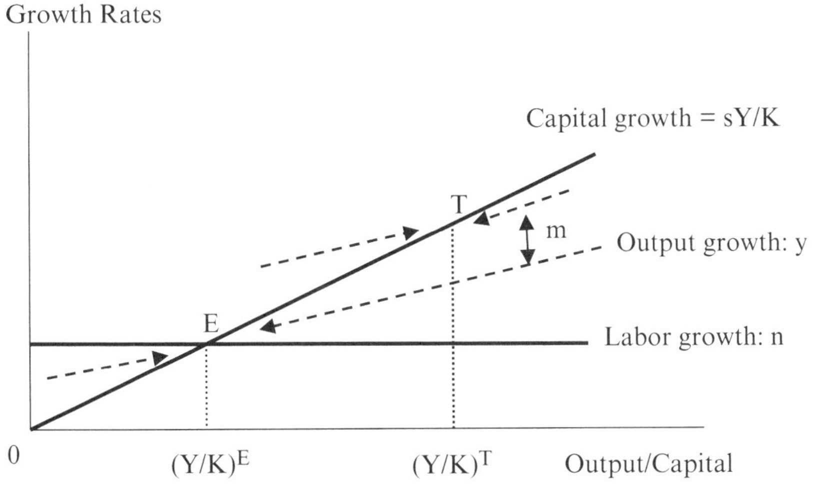

Figure 56.1 The Swan diagram

growing faster than capital, so Y/K rises towards $(Y/K)^E$. To the right of point E, output is growing more slowly than capital, so Y/K falls.

The model suggests the surprising result that an increase in capital formation through a rise in the willingness to save, s, is not a route to increased long-run growth. An increase in s would increase the slope of the capital growth line, causing both it and the growth line for output to swing upwards. Initially capital grows faster and there is a rise in the rate of growth of output per head (since y is above n), but in equilibrium, the growth rates for capital and output must return to their original level equal to the growth rate of labour, which is unchanged at n. However, equilibrium involves a higher output per head since the increase in investment raises the marginal productivity of labour. Correspondingly, the output/capital ratio is reduced below the original $(Y/K)^E$ in Figure 56.1 due to the lower marginal productivity of capital.

By contrast, an increase in the rate of technical progress raises long-run growth. As shown by the higher dotted arrows, an exogenous rate, m, of 'neutral' technical progress shifts up the growth rate of output by m.[3] The outcome is a new equilibrium at T with a higher output/capital ratio, $(Y/K)^T$. A useful insight is that once equilibrium is achieved, a steady rate of technical progress increases both Y and K at the same rate so as to maintain Y/K constant. As explained by Dixon (2003), a greater productivity of labour directly increases Y/L, but the higher output also induces more saving and capital formation so as to maintain a constant ratio of capital to labour measured in efficiency units.

2. THE SOLOW DIAGRAM

Figure 56.2 represents the basic Solow diagram. To examine the equilibrating role of the capital/labour ratio, Solow (1956) uses a general linearly homogeneous (constant returns to scale) production function to express the output/labour ratio or output per head as a function, $Y/L = F(k, 1)$ where $k \equiv K/L$. As shown by the dotted line, 0A, in Figure 56.2, an increase in k increases output per head at a decreasing rate. Investment per head, given by $(dK/dt)/L = sY/L$, is a fixed proportion, s, of output per head as shown by the solid line, 0B. The vertical distance between lines 0A and 0B represents consumption per head. With no technical progress, equilibrium requires that the rate of growth of capital equal the rate of growth of the labour supply: that is, $(dK/dt)/K = n$, which implies $(dK/dt)/L = nk$. As illustrated in Figure 56.2, nk is straight line from the origin with slope n. Hence the equilibrium is at point E, corresponding to a capital/labour ratio of k^E and an output/

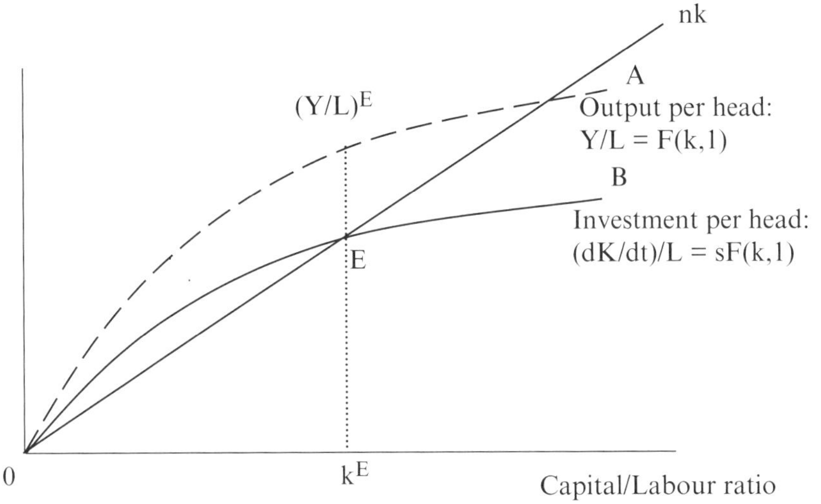

Figure 56.2 The Solow diagram

labour ratio of $(Y/L)^E$. If k is initially to the left of k^E, then capital is growing faster than labour, which leads k to rise. Similarly, if k is to the right of k^E, then k falls.[4]

In Figure 56.2, an increase in the propensity to save, s, increases the slope of the line 0B, causing the equilibrium capital/labour to rise above the original k^E. Output per head increases (from the movement to the right along 0A), but consumption per head, represented by the vertical distance between lines 0A and 0B, falls. Technical progress causes both an upward shift in 0A and a movement along 0A due to the rise in the capital to labour ratio. A constant rate of technical progress would cause 0A to continuously swing upwards. The seminal contribution of Solow (1957) was to address how technical progress represented by upwards shifts in 0A could be estimated separately from movements along 0A. Figure 56.2 can be adjusted to allow for neutral technical progress by defining the capital/labour ratio in efficiency units, but this obscures comparative static effects of changes in technical progress.

Solow (1956) points out the possibility of multiple equilibria. For example, if there is a region in which investment per head increases at an increasing rate with k, it is possible that the line 0B (representing investment per head) cuts the line nk in three places. There are then two stable equilibria, one at a low value of k and one at a high value of k, with an unstable equilibrium between the two stable equilibria.

3. HISTORY

Robert Solow's 1956 use of a variable capital/output ratio eliminated what he saw as an empirically implausible knife-edge equilibrium in the Harrod-Domar one-sector growth model. This followed from his earlier work generalising John von Neumann's fixed-coefficient, multi-sector growth model by introducing capital/labour substitution and variable coefficients (for example, Solow and Samuelson 1953). Trevor Swan first presented his growth model in July 1956 in an interdisciplinary seminar at Australian National University discussing W. Arthur Lewis's *Theory of Economic Growth* (1955). Swan had declined to talk about Lewis's chapter on capital but, when the economic historian Noel Butlin concluded his discussion of the chapter, presented his own model as a comment on Butlin's talk (Pitchford 2002, Dixon 2003). Swan used a general production function in his remarks in the seminar and in his post-seminar notes published posthumously as Swan (2002). But in Swan (1956), he followed suggestions by Conrad Leser and Geoffrey Sawer at the seminar to simplify the exposition by assuming a Cobb-Douglas production function and by putting the percentage rate of growth instead of units of output on the vertical axis of his diagrams. The cost of this change was a later misperception that Swan's analysis depended on the Cobb-Douglas functional form.

NOTES

1. Harrod's 'warranted' rate of growth arising from savings and investment behaviour is represented by the rate of growth of capital in the Solow (1956) and Swan (1956) models. In the absence of technical progress, Harrod's 'natural' rate of growth is the rate of growth of the labour supply.
2. If $Y = F(K,L)$ is linearly homogeneous, then $y = \alpha sY/K + \beta n$ where $\alpha \equiv F_K K/Y$, $\beta \equiv F_L L/Y$ and $\alpha + \beta = 1$. Swan (1956) assumed a Cobb-Douglas production function in which α and β are constants, but Swan's earlier model (Swan 2002), published posthumously, was more general (see Pitchford 2002).
3. For $Y = e^{mt}K^{\alpha}L^{\beta}$ with $\alpha + \beta = 1$, Swan (1956) obtains $y = \alpha sY/K + \beta n + m$. As shown by Swan (1964), Harrod-neutral (labour saving) technical change is required for the existence of steady state growth, but Hicks-neutral and Harrod-neutral coincide for a Cobb-Douglas production function.
4. From Solow (1956), $dk/dt = sF(k,1) - nk$.

REFERENCES

Dixon, Robert (2003), 'Trevor Swan on Equilibrium Growth with Technological Progress', *Economic Record* 79 (247), 489–492.

Domar, Evsey D. (1946), 'Capital Expansion, Rate of Growth, and Employment', *Econometrica* 14 (2), 137–147.
Harrod, Roy F. (1939), 'An Essay in Dynamic Theory', *Economic Journal* 49, 14–33.
Harrod, Roy F. (1948), *Towards a Dynamic Economics*, London: Macmillan.
Lewis, W. Arthur (1955), *The Theory of Economic Growth*, London: George Allen and Unwin.
Pitchford, John D. (2002), 'Trevor Swan's 1956 Economic Growth "Seminar" and Notes on Growth', *Economic Record* 78 (243), 381–387.
Solow, Robert M. (1956), 'A Contribution to the Theory of Economic Growth', *Quarterly Journal of Economics* 70 (1), 65–94.
Solow, Robert M. (1957), 'Technical Change and the Aggregate Production Function', *Review of Economics and Statistics* 39, 312–320.
Solow, Robert M. and Samuelson, Paul A. (1953), 'Balanced Growth under Constant Returns to Scale', *Econometrica* 21 (3), 412–424.
Swan, Trevor W. (1956), 'Economic Growth and Capital Accumulation', *Economic Record* 32 (63), 334–361.
Swan, Trevor W. (1964) 'Growth Models: Of Golden Ages and Production Functions'. In *Economic Development with Special Reference to South East Asia*, edited by K. Berrill. London: Macmillan for the International Economic Association, 3–16.
Swan, Trevor W. (2002) 'Economic Growth', *Economic Record* 78 (243), 375–380.

57. The Lorenz curve

Nanak Kakwani

INTRODUCTION

The Lorenz curve is widely used to represent and analyze the size distribution of income and wealth. Lorenz proposed this curve in 1905 in order to compare and analyze inequalities of income and wealth in a country during different epochs, or in different countries during the same epoch. When all income recipients are ranked in ascending order of income, the Lorenz curve is described by a function L(p), which is interpreted as the fraction of total income received by the lowest pth fraction of population. It satisfies the following conditions (Kakwani 1980):

(a) If $p = 0$, $L(p) = 0$

(b) If $p = 1$, $L(p) = 1$

(c) $L'(p) = \frac{x}{\mu} \geq 0$ and $L''(p) = \frac{1}{\mu f(x)} > 0$

(d) $L(p) \leq p$

where income x of a person is a random variable with probability density function $f(x)$ with mean income μ and $L'(p)$ and $L''(p)$ are the first and second derivatives of $L(p)$ with respect to p.

These conditions imply that the Lorenz curve is represented in a unit square. In Figure 57.1, the diagonal OB through the unit square is called the egalitarian line. The Lorenz curve lies below this line. If the curve coincides with the egalitarian line, it means that each person receives the same income, which is the case of perfect equality. In the case of perfect inequality of incomes, the Lorenz curve coincides with OA and AB, which implies that all the income is received by only one person in the society.

Because the Lorenz curve displays the deviation of each person's income from perfect equality, it captures, in a sense, the essence of inequality. The nearer the Lorenz curve is to the egalitarian line, the more equal will be

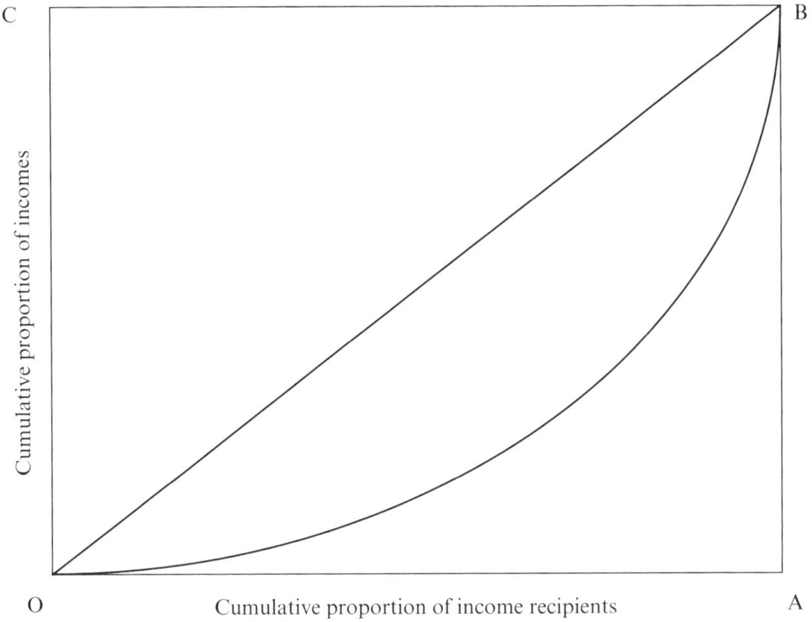

Figure 57.1 The Lorenz curve: L(p)

the distribution of income. Consequently, the Lorenz curve can be used as a criterion for ranking government policies or programs. Suppose there are two alternative government policies, which result in two different income distributions, X_1 and X_2. If the Lorenz curve of X_1 is above that of X_2 at all points, then, from an equity point of view, the first policy is preferred over the second. However, if the two Lorenz curves intersect, neither policy can be said to be more equitable than the other. Thus, the Lorenz curve provides only a partial ranking of distribution. Still it is a powerful tool and has been used widely as a convenient graphical device to describe distributions of income and many other variables that affect people's well-being.

RELATIVE AND ABSOLUTE INEQUALITY

Inequality may be measured in both relative and absolute terms. If inequality measures remain unchanged when the income of each person is altered by the same proportion, then such measures are called the relative measures of inequality. The Lorenz curve measures relative inequality because the curve remains unchanged when the incomes of all persons are increased or decreased by the same proportion. Alternatively, Kolm (1976) has proposed absolute measures of inequality which do not show any change in inequality when the income of everyone is increased or decreased by the same amount. According to Kolm, an equiproportional increase in all incomes must increase inequality because the richer persons will enjoy a higher incremental increase in the standard of living than those who are poorer.

Although inequality is commonly perceived as a relative concept, an absolute concept of inequality can also be attractive since government transfer policies are generally understood in terms of absolute benefits going to the poor. Suppose there are two persons with incomes \$100 and \$1000, a policy that gives \$15 to the poor and \$100 to the rich will not be readily accepted as pro-poor even if the poor benefits proportionally more than the non-poor. This policy has reduced the relative inequality but increased the absolute inequality. An absolute inequality curve can be written as

$$\phi(p) = \mu[p - L(p)].$$

This curve has the following properties:

(a) If $p = 0$, $\phi(p) = 0$

(b) If $p = 1$, $\phi(p) = 0$

(c) $\phi'(p) = (\mu - x)$

(d) $\phi''(p) = -\dfrac{1}{f(x)} < 0$

It can be proved that if the incomes of all persons are increased or decreased by the same amount, the curve does not change. In Figure 57.2, OA is the egalitarian line. If the curve coincides with the egalitarian line, this means that each person receives the same income, which is the case of perfect equality. The higher the absolute inequality curve, the greater will be the absolute inequality of income. The curve attains the maximum value at the point where $x = \mu$. A policy will be judged as absolutely pro-poor (anti-poor) if $\phi(p)$ shifts downward (upward).

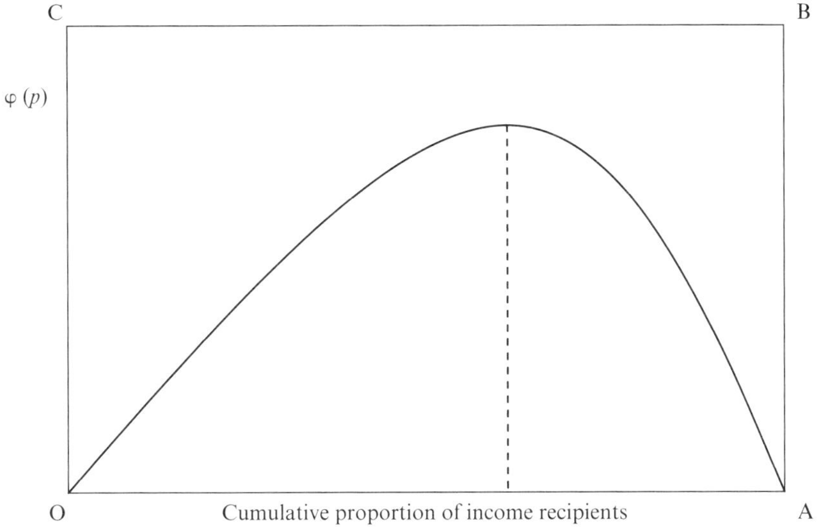

Figure 57.2 Absolute inequality curve: φ(p)

THE LORENZ CURVE AND SOCIAL WELFARE

Government policies should be judged on the basis of their impact on social welfare. According to this view, a policy X_1 should be judged as superior to another policy X_2 when the social welfare derived from X_1 is greater than that derived from X_2. Fortunately, under certain conditions, the ranking of distributions according to the Lorenz curve is identical to the ranking implied by the social welfare function. In 1970, A. B. Atkinson proved a theorem that showed that if social welfare is defined as the sum of individual utilities, and every individual has an identical utility function that is increasing in income and is concave, then the ranking of distributions according to the Lorenz curve criterion is identical to the ranking implied by the social welfare function – provided that the distributions have the same mean income and their Lorenz curves do not intersect. An important implication of this theorem is that one can evaluate alternative policies from the welfare point of view without knowing the form of the utility function except that it is increasing and concave, provided the Lorenz curves do not intersect. If the Lorenz curves do intersect, however, two utility functions that would rank the distributions differently can always be found.

Atkinson's theorem relies on the assumption that the social welfare function is equal to the sum of individual utilities and that every individual has the same utility function. These assumptions are rather restrictive. Fortunately, Dasgupta, Sen and Starrett (1973), as well as Rothschild and Stiglitz (1973), have demonstrated that the theorem is, in fact, more general and would hold for any symmetric welfare function that is quasi-concave.

The Lorenz curve makes the distributional judgments under the assumption that the two distributions have the same mean incomes. In practice, we can never have any two distributions with the same mean incomes. Working independently on extensions of the Lorenz partial orderings, Shorrocks (1983) and Kakwani (1984) arrived at a criterion that would rank any two distributions with different means. The new ranking criterion developed by them is given by $L(\mu, p)$, which is the product of the mean income μ and the Lorenz curve L(p):

$$L(\mu, p) = \mu L(p)$$

while the Lorenz ranking is based only on L(p). They proved a theorem which implies that if the generalized Lorenz curve of distribution X_1 is higher than the generalized Lorenz curve of distribution X_2 at all points, then we can say unambiguously that the social welfare implied by distribution X_1 will always be higher than the social welfare implied by distribution X_2. In other words, distribution X_1 is welfare superior to distribution X_2. This result holds for a wide range of social welfare functions. The only restriction on the social welfare function is that it should be symmetric and quasi-concave in individual incomes.

Figure 57.3 presents the generalized Lorenz curves for two distributions X_1 and X_2.

APPLICATIONS OF THE LORENZ CURVE

The Lorenz curve technique can be used to analyze relationships among the distributions of different economic variables. Based on the Lorenz curve, Kakwani (1977a) provided a number of theorems that have many applications in economics, particularly in the field of public finance, where the effect of taxation and public spending on income distribution is analyzed. Other areas in which these theorems can be applied are inflation as it affects income distribution, estimation of Engel elasticity, poverty and economic growth. The Kakwani (1977b) index developed in the context of measuring tax progressivity in 1977 is widely used to analyze equity in health.

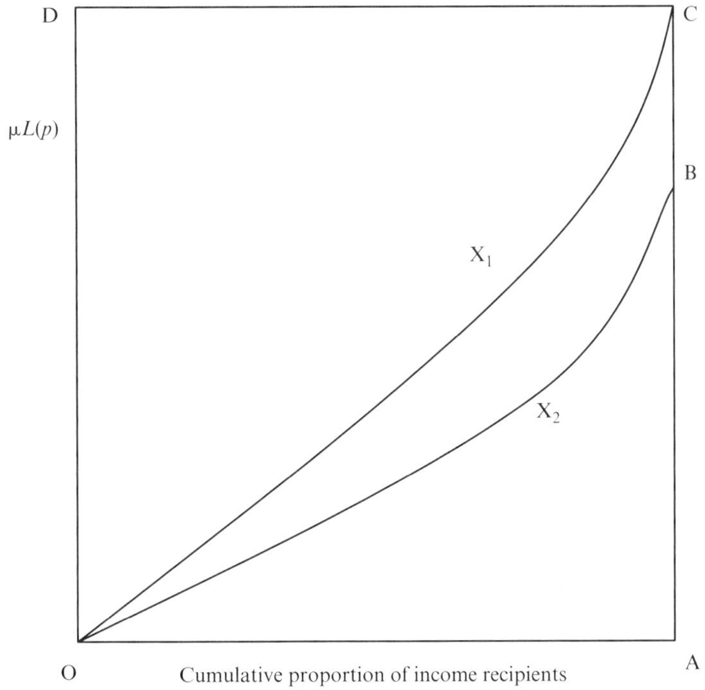

Figure 57.3 Generalized Lorenz curve: μL(p)

REFERENCES

Atkinson, A. B. (1970), 'On the Measurement of Inequality', *Journal of Economic Theory*, 2, 244–63.

Dasgupta, P., A. K. Sen and D. Starrett (1973), 'Notes on the Measurement of Inequality', *Journal of Economic Theory*, 6, 180–87.

Kakwani, N. (1977a), 'Applications of Lorenz Curves in Economic Analysis', *Econometrica*, 45, 719–27.

Kakwani, N. (1977b), 'Measurement of Tax Progressivity: An International Comparison', *Economic Journal*, 87, 71–80.

Kakwani, N. (1980), *Income Inequality and Poverty: Methods of Estimation and Policy Applications*, New York: Oxford University Press.

Kakwani, N. (1984), 'On the Measurement of Tax Progressivity and Redistributive Effect of Taxes with Applications to Horizontal and Vertical Equity', *Advances in Econometrics*, 3, 149–68.

Kolm, S. (1976), 'Unequal Inequalities', *Journal of Economic Theory*, 12, 82–111.

Lorenz, M. O. (1905), 'Methods of Measuring the Concentration of Wealth', *Journal of the American Statistical Association*, 9, 209–19.

Rothschild, M. and J. E. Stiglitz (1973). 'Some Further Results on the Measurement of Inequality', *Journal of Economic Theory*, 6, 188–204.

Shorrocks, A. (1983). 'Ranking Income Distributions', *Economica*, 50, 3–17.

58. Kuznets curve

Lisa Cameron, Lata Gangadharan and Sowmiya Ashok

In 1955, Simon Kuznets, the Nobel Prize winning economist, published an influential study on the historical relationship between income inequality and the level of per capita income. Kuznets (1955) argued that as countries develop, income inequality first increases, peaks, and then decreases. As shown in Figure 58.1, this creates an inverted U-shaped relationship, with income inequality (measured by the Gini coefficient) declining after a certain critical threshold level of income is reached. He documented this using both cross-country and time-series data. This empirical phenomenon is now known as the *Kuznets curve*. The work that Kuznets and his successors have undertaken has had a great influence on how the development process is viewed, even if subsequent studies have cast considerable doubt on the robustness of the relationship.

KUZNETS INVERTED-U CURVE

Interpretation of the Kuznets Curve

Kuznets (1955) not only was the first to uncover the statistical relationship described above but also put forth a theoretical explanation for this phenomenon. His theory was based on dual economy dynamics, which are generated by people moving from the agricultural to the industrial sector. The income distribution of the total population is a combination of the income distributions of the rural and urban populations. Kuznets observed that not only is the average per capita income of the rural population normally lower than that of the urban population; the rural population normally also has lower income inequality. In the early stages of economic development, the gap between the average incomes of rural and urban people widens as industrial productivity in urban areas increases. Rural–urban migration further increases inequality. Kuznets posits that eventually the income share of the lower groups within the

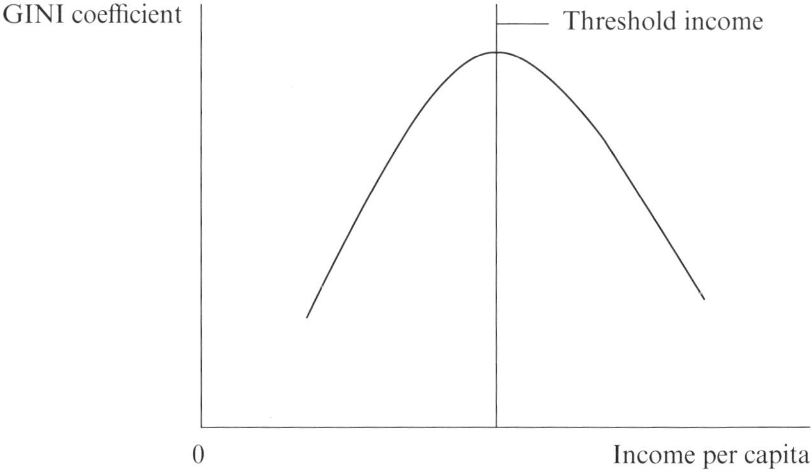

Figure 58.1 The Kuznets curve

non-agricultural sector of the population rises, as an increasing proportion of the urban population becomes 'native', that is, born into cities rather than having migrated from rural areas. Hence, these groups are more capable of securing greater income shares than was possible for the newly immigrant population coming from the countryside or from abroad, and this decreases inequality. Secondly, as a country becomes richer, the social policy adopted by governments such as increasing access to health services and education reduces the gap between the rich and the poor.

A Law or a Statistical Regularity?

A common interpretation of the Kuznets curve is that for nations to increase their per capita incomes, a necessary cost of progress over the longer haul is the short-term loss in equity that accompanies economic growth before the critical threshold level is reached. Thus, the Kuznets inverted U-hypothesis is interpreted as a law of economic growth and development. However, many argue that the relation Kuznets discovered between income and equity is, in fact, not a law but rather a statistical relation. For example, Cypher and Dietz (2004) argue that once nations pass the threshold level of income, government expenditures in the areas of health, education, social security, and other social and human capital areas tend to rise relative to total expenditures in the economy. Thus, although these improvements in equity and development are expected as governments are able to focus on broader development goals, the particular path which any nation follows in terms of the relation between its economic growth rate and development goals is at least partly a consequence of conscious public policy.

An alternative interpretation of the Kuznets curve draws on the political and institutional transformation of the West during the nineteenth century. Acemoglu and Robinson (2002) posit that a country's political economy is crucial to understanding patterns of inequality. In their view, the decline in inequality was not an unavoidable consequence of economic development, but an outcome of political changes forced on the system by the mobilization of the masses. Prior to the nineteenth century, there was only modest redistribution of income to the masses and political power was held by the elite in European countries. While the process of industrialization increased income inequality, it also mobilized the poorer segments of society by concentrating them in urban factories, thereby increasing the risk of political unrest. In response to this threat of revolution, the political elites were forced to undertake radical reforms ranging from income redistribution to fundamental political change (Acemoglu and Robinson, 2002). The authors acknowledge that this can explain the Kuznets curve in European countries, but that this pattern need not be a feature of all development processes.

Controversies with the Kuznets Curve

Even the empirical regularity of such a relationship has been the subject of some debate. List and Gallet (1999) argue that important intracountry or intercountry variations in the relationship are often ignored as studies typically use either cross-sectional data from several countries or time-series data from a single country. The evidence from more recent experiences of development is less supportive of Kuznets' hypothesis. While some countries like Brazil have experienced worsening equity along with economic growth even after the threshold level of income has been reached, others (Sri Lanka, for example) have been able to achieve equity and development well below the Kuznets' threshold income level (Cypher and Dietz, 2004). Further, Asian countries such as Japan, Taiwan and South Korea have experienced monotonically falling inequality (Acemoglu and Robinson, 2002). The Kuznets inverted U-relationship thus may only capture the average experience for a certain group of nations during a particular historical period.

The experience of the United States and several other developed countries (for example, Canada, Australia and the UK) did initially support Kuznets' conjecture. However since the 1980s, these countries have experienced increases in inequality. The shift away from a manufacturing base towards a service base in these countries is a possible explanation for the renewed positive relationship between income inequality and per capita income. List and Gallet (1999) identify a few studies that explain this phenomenon; Bishop *et al.* (1991) argue that the service sector is characterized by bimodal pay scales which result from a premium placed on education, and thus a shift towards a service base generates greater dispersion in income. This is further supported by Katz and Murphy (1992) and Bound and Johnson (1992), who find that US incomes have diverged since the early 1980s.

THE ENVIRONMENTAL KUZNETS CURVE (EKC)

The traditional Kuznets curve, has now become a vehicle for describing the relationship between measured levels of environmental quality and per capita income. The Environmental Kuznets Curve describes a relationship that has been found empirically between per capita income and certain indicators of environmental degradation (Nahman and Antrobus, 2005). This inverted U-shaped relationship between economic growth and measures of pollution indicators (environmental degradation) is shown in Figure 58.2 (Dinda, 2004).

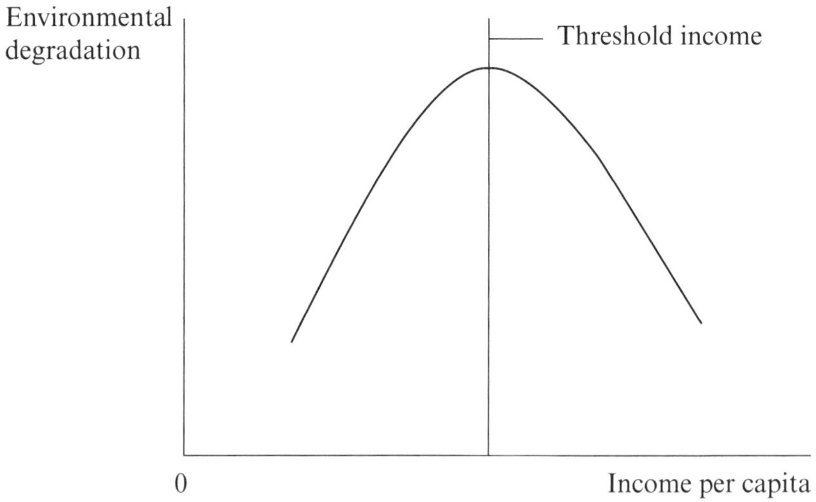

Figure 58.2 The environmental Kuznets curve

History of the EKC

The concept of an Environmental Kuznets curve emerged in 1991 with Grossman and Krueger's study of the environmental impacts of a North American Free Trade Agreement (Nahman and Antrobus, 2005). In their study, Grossman and Krueger (1991) expected to find that environmental quality deteriorates uniformly as the scale of economic activity increases. They examined the data on pollution levels and per capita income (as a measure of economic development) in a variety of countries and they observed startling results. They found that for both sulphur dioxide (SO_2) and dark matter (smoke), pollution levels were found to rise at low levels of per capita income, as expected, but to fall with per capita income at higher levels of income, giving rise to an inverted U-shaped relationship (Nahman and Antrobus, 2005).

This relationship came to be known as the Environmental Kuznets curve owing to the resemblance to the relationship observed by Simon Kuznets (1955) between economic growth and income inequality. Following this study, much empirical and theoretical work has been devoted to the relationship between economic growth and the environment. Nahman and Antrobus (2005) argue that writers in this field can be broadly classified either as optimists, who take the environmental Kuznets curve to imply that economic growth is ultimately good for the environment (for example, Beckerman 1992; Grossman and Krueger, 1995; Lomborg, 2001); or critics, who point to a number of methodological flaws evident in deriving the EKC or advocate caution in interpreting its causes and implications (such as Arrow *et al.*, 1995; Stern *et al.*, 1996; Stern, 2004).

Interpretation of the EKC

Optimists argue that the logic of the EKC is intuitively appealing.

> In the first stage of industrialization, pollution . . . grows rapidly because people are more interested in jobs and income than clean air and water, communities are too poor to pay for abatement, and environmental regulation is correspondingly weak. The balance shifts as income rises. Leading industrial sectors become cleaner, people value the environment more highly, and regulatory institutions become more effective. Along the curve, pollution levels off in the middle-income range and then falls towards pre-industrial levels in wealthy societies (Dasgupta *et al.*, 2002, p.147).

Arrow *et al.* (1995 cited in Dinda 2004) interprets the EKC as a natural transition from a clean agrarian economy to a polluting industrial economy, and, finally, to a clean service economy. At the take-off stage, economic development accelerates with the intensification of agriculture and other resource extraction, the rate of resource depletion begins to exceed the rate of resource regeneration, and waste generation increases in quantity and toxicity. Higher levels of development results in the gradual decline of environmental degradation as structural change towards services industries, coupled with increased environmental awareness and better technology come into play (Dinda, 2004).

Grossman and Krueger's own explanation (1991) for the observed improvement in environmental quality at higher levels of per capita income refers to a nation's ability to switch to cleaner technologies as there is a greater demand for improved environmental quality among its citizens which leads to more stringent environmental regulations. However, they also consider the possibility that the downward-sloping portion of the EKC might be explained by developed countries ceasing to produce pollution-intensive goods and instead importing them from countries with less stringent environmental regulations.

A similar claim is made by critics of the EKC. The observed decline in levels of certain pollutants at high levels of per capita income is attributed to the phenomenon called 'environmental dumping' whereby developed countries shift their heaviest polluting industries to less-developed countries. This threatens the belief that economic growth automatically leads to environmental improvements and may imply that the present-day developing countries may not follow the same development – environment path observed by developing countries in the past.

Controversies with the EKC

Conceptual critique

The failure of many empirical studies to discover an inverted U-shaped relationship for all types of pollutants has given rise to the widespread criticism that the EKC does not hold for all indicators of environmental degradation (Nahman and Antrobus, 2005). Environmental pollutants for which the EKC is most plausible include those having local impacts such as sulphur dioxide. However, evidence suggest that those pollutants (such as CO_2) that are most likely to impact human health on a massive scale and count from a global climate change perspective, continue to rise with per capita income levels (Dinda, 2004).

One of the most damaging criticisms of the environmental Kuznets curve hypothesis is based on the occurrence of international trade. The argument, as mentioned above, asserts that the downturn in emissions at higher levels of per capita income can be explained, at least to some extent, by the relocation of 'dirty' industries from developed to developing countries (Nahman and Antrobus, 2005). This does not, however, dispute the conventional interpretation of the EKC. Rather, the argument posits that the decline in environmental degradation is due to the international movements in pollution-intensive industries and changes in the patterns of international trade. These movements, if found to occur, 'would exaggerate any apparent decline in pollution intensity with rising income along the EKC' (Stern, 2003 cited in Nahman and Antrobus, 2005).

Methodological critique

Empirical studies have mostly used absolute measures of pollution like amount of emission (or pollution) rather than a relative measure (like emission per unit of output or per square kilometre). Use of a relative measure of pollution may reveal a U-shape or a monotonic relation with income rather than an inverted-U shape (Dinda, 2004).

Stern (1998 cited in Nahman and Antrobus, 2005) identifies a number of critiques regarding the EKC

> *(a)* the assumption of unidirectional causality from growth to environmental quality and the reversibility of environmental change; *(b)* the assumption that changes in trade relationships associated with development have no effect on environmental quality [*e.g.* Suri and Chapman, 1998; Arrow *et al.*, 1995; Stern *et al.*, 1996]; *(c)* econometric problems [*e.g.* Stern *et al.*, 1996; Ekins, 1997]; *(d)* ambient concentrations versus emissions; *(e)* asymptotic behaviour; *(f)* the mean–median income problem [*e.g.* Stern *et al.*, 1996; Ekins, 1997; Selden and Song, 1994]; and *(g)* the interpretation of particular EKCs in isolation from EKCs for other environmental problems [*e.g.* Arrow *et al.*, 1995; Suri and Chapman, 1998].

Hence there is little consensus about the robustness of this relationship and though it highlights the impact of income levels on environmental quality, it cannot be used to predict the experience of currently developing countries.

REFERENCES

Acemoglu, D. and Robinson, J.A. (2002), 'The political economy of the Kuznets curve', *Review of Development Economics*, 6(2), 183–203.

Arrow, K., Bolin, B., Costanza, R., Folke, C., Holing, C.S., Janson, B., Levin, S., Maker, K., Perrings, C. and Pimental, D. (1995), 'Economic growth, carrying capacity, and the environment', *Science*, 15, 91–95.

Beckerman, W. (1992), 'Economic growth and the environment: whose growth? Whose environment?', *World Development*, 20, 481–496.

Bishop, J., Formby, J. and Thistle, P. (1991), 'Changes in US earnings distribution in the 1980s', *Applied Economics*, 23, 425–434.

Bound, J. and Johnson, G. (1992), 'Changes in the structure of wages in the 1980s: an evaluation of alternative explanation', *American Economic Review*, 82, 371–392.

Cypher, James P. and Dietz, James L. (2004), *The Process of Economic Development*, New York US: Routledge.

Dasgupta, S., Laplante, B., Wang, H. and Wheeler, D (2002), 'Confronting the environmental Kuznets curve', *Journal of Economic Perspectives*, 16(1), 147–168.

Dinda, S. (2004), 'Environmental Kuznets curve hypothesis: a survey', *Ecological Economics*, 49, 431–455.

Grossman, G.M. and Krueger, A.B. (1991) *Environmental impacts of the North American Free Trade Agreement*, Working Paper 3914, Cambridge, MA: National Bureau of Economic Research.

Grossman, G. and Krueger, A.B. (1995), 'Economic growth and the environment', *Quarterly Journal of Economics*, 112, 353–377.

Katz, L. and Murphy, K. (1992), 'Changes in relative wages, 1963–87: supply and demand factors', *Quarterly Journal of Economics*, 107, 35–78.

Kuznets, S. (1955), 'Economic growth and income inequality', *The American Economic Review*, XLV, 1–28.

List, J.A. and Gallet, C.A. (1999), 'The Kuznets curve: what happens after the inverted-U?' *Review of Development Economics*, 3(2), 200–206.

Lomborg, B. (2001), *The Sceptical Environmentalist: Measuring the Real State of the World*, Cambridge: Cambridge University Press.

Nahman, A. and Antrobus, G. (2005), 'The environmental Kuznets curve: a literature survey', *South African Journal of Economics*, 73(1), 105–120.

Stern, D., Common, M.S. and Barbier, E.B. (1996), 'Economic growth and environmental degradation: a critique of the environmental Kuznets curve', *World Development*, 24, 1151–1160.

Stern, D.I. (2004), 'The rise and fall of the environmental Kuznets curve', *World Development*, 32(8), 1419–1439.

Index